Marginalised Populations in the Ancient Greek World

Intersectionality in Classical Antiquity
Series Editors: Mark Masterson, Victoria University of Wellington, Fiona McHardy, University of Roehampton and Nancy Sorkin Rabinowitz, Hamilton College

This series focuses on the intersection of gender and sexuality, in the Greco-Roman world, with a range of other factors including race, ethnicity, class, ability, masculinity, femininity, transgender and post-colonial gender studies. The books in the series will be theoretically informed and will sit at the forefront of the study of a variety of outsiders – those marginalised in relation to the 'classical ideal' – and how they were differently constructed in the ancient world. The series is also interested in the ways in which work in the field of classical reception contributes to that study.

Editorial Advisory Board
Patty Baker, Alastair Blanshard, Susan Deacy, Jacqueline Fabre-Serris, Cristiana Franco, Genevieve Liveley, Mark Masterson, Amy Richlin, Carisa R. Showden

Books available in the series
Exploring Gender Diversity in the Ancient World, edited by Allison Surtees and Jennifer Dyer
Women in the Law Courts of Classical Athens, Konstantinos Kapparis
Marginalised Populations in the Ancient Greek World: The Bioarchaeology of the Other, Carrie L. Sulosky Weaver

Visit the series web page at: edinburghuniversitypress.com/series-intersectionality-in-classical-antiquity

Marginalised Populations in the Ancient Greek World

The Bioarchaeology of the Other

Carrie L. Sulosky Weaver

EDINBURGH
University Press

Edinburgh University Press is one of the leading university presses in the UK. We publish academic books and journals in our selected subject areas across the humanities and social sciences, combining cutting-edge scholarship with high editorial and production values to produce academic works of lasting importance. For more information visit our website: edinburghuniversitypress.com

Grateful acknowledgment is made to the sources listed in the List of Illustrations for permission to reproduce material previously published elsewhere. Every effort has been made to trace the copyright holders, but if any have been inadvertently overlooked, the publisher will be pleased to make the necessary arrangements at the first opportunity.

Edinburgh University Press Ltd
The Tun – Holyrood Road
12(2f) Jackson's Entry
Edinburgh EH8 8PJ

First published in hardback by Edinburgh University Press 2022

Typeset in 11/13 Adobe Garamond by
IDSUK (DataConnection) Ltd, and
printed and bound by CPI Group (UK) Ltd,
Croydon, CR0 4YY

A CIP record for this book is available from the British Library

ISBN 978 1 4744 1525 5 (hardback)
ISBN 978 1 3995 2984 6 (paperback)
ISBN 978 1 4744 1526 2 (webready PDF)
ISBN 978 1 4744 1527 9 (epub)

The right of Carrie L. Sulosky Weaver to be identified as the author of this work has been asserted in accordance with the Copyright, Designs and Patents Act 1988, and the Copyright and Related Rights Regulations 2003 (SI No. 2498).

Contents

Figures

Acknowledgments

I owe my sincerest thanks to a number of people for their generous assistance and support throughout the challenging course of this project. First and foremost, I am grateful to the staff of Edinburgh University Press, particularly Senior Commissioning Editor Carol Macdonald, as well as Mark Masterson, Fiona McHardy and Nancy Sorkin Rabinowitz, the editors of the Intersectionality in Classical Antiquity series, and the reviewers of my book proposal and manuscript, all of whom have played crucial roles in the development of this book.

It is my distinct pleasure to acknowledge the assistance of scholars who contributed to the improvement of my manuscript. I owe a tremendous debt to Rebecca Futo Kennedy and Britney Kyle. Their fastidious scholarship provided a firm foundation for my understanding many of the issues addressed here, and their keen editorial eyes and sound advice shaped the final form of this book. I am thankful to Anagnostis Agelarakis, Alexandra Alexandridou, Geoff Bakewell, Anastasia Dakouri-Hild, Christopher Knüsel, Britney Kyle, Anna Lagia, Mandc Miles, Ian Morris, Christina Papageorgopoulou and Efrossini Vika for sending me digital offprints of their work and patiently answering any questions I posed to them. Special thanks are owed to Peter Papadakos, who translated skeletal reports from modern Greek to English, and Marcie Persyn, who tracked down and translated some ambiguous ancient Greek fragments. I am also grateful to Tyler Jo Smith and Renee M. Gondek for their constructive comments on various parts of the manuscript, and to Alana Dunn, who aided with the editing of the bibliography.

My work has benefited from the help of outstanding University of Pittsburgh undergraduate research assistants. Alexis Buncich, Meg Sanglikar and Ahona Raka Sarkar combed through skeletal reports to find patterns and evidence of social marginalisation, and Michael Russo carefully compiled a list of all the sites and regions mentioned in the manuscript so that they could be included on the maps that appear at the beginning of the book.

The illustrations that enliven this text were made possible through the generosity of many institutions, all of which are properly credited in the figure captions. I would like to especially thank Giovanni Di Stefano for permitting me to include photographs of skeletons from Kamarina (Sicily). Above all, however, I am indebted to the skill and expertise of Dan Weiss, whose masterful drawings can be found throughout this book.

Finally, I owe my deepest thanks to my parents, William and Patricia Sulosky, my brother, James, and my husband, David. They have endured my absences, encouraged my interests and bolstered my academic endeavours with patience and boundless love. If I have achieved anything, it is because of their unwavering support.

Abbreviations and Spellings

Journal title abbreviations follow the guidelines of the *American Journal of Archaeology*, the Deutsches Archäologisches Institut and the *Index Medicus*. Other abbreviations used in this volume are detailed below. Note that conventional Latin spellings are used for ancient authors and texts (e.g. Thucydides not Thoukudides), the names of mythical and historical figures (e.g. Hermaphroditus not Hermaphroditos), and places (e.g. Epidaurus not Epidauros). Also note that Latin, French, Italian and German terms are italicised while standard Greek ones (e.g. polis) generally are not.

FGrH	F. Jacoby (ed.), *Die Fragmente der griechischen Historiker* (Berlin 1923–59).
IG	*Inscriptiones Graecae* (Berlin 1825–)
IJO	*International Journal of Osteoarchaeology*
IJPP	*International Journal of Paleopathology*
LIMC	*Lexicon iconographicum mythologiae classicae* (Zurich 1981–2009).
ThesCRA	*Thesaurus cultus et rituum antiquorum* (Basel, Los Angeles 2004–2014).
West	M. L. West (ed.), *Iambi et elegi Graeci* (Oxford 1971).

For my husband, David:
οὐδ᾽ ἄμμε διακρινέει φιλότητος ἄλλο, πάρος θάνατόν γε μεμορμένον
ἀμφικαλύψαι (Apollonius Rhodius, *Argonautica* 3.1129–30).

Introduction: Hidden Lives

> The past lives of millions of ordinary people seem almost completely hidden from us now. Recent historical periods may be rich in surviving material culture and written sources, but even so many people still seem to be missing from our histories. They are concealed from us in historical and archaeological writing, just as they were concealed from (or by?) their contemporaries, whose narratives failed to represent them (Turner and Young 2007: 297).

We know a great deal about the ancient Greeks. We know what they ate, how they worshipped and how they fought. We know the types of houses they lived in and what they were furnished with. We know their politics, their philosophies and their arts. Despite all of this, our understanding of ancient Greek culture remains incomplete. With few exceptions, our knowledge is shaped by the narratives of the extraordinary members of society – men of high status, privilege and power. From the works of Herodotus, an aristocrat from Halicarnassus, to Xenophon, the Athenian son of a wealthy equestrian family, our libraries are filled with the writings of the elite. These men, though accomplished in their own right, experienced life in a markedly different way from the multitudes of ordinary people with whom they shared a society and a culture.

Likewise, the material culture of the people located at the centre of society – those whose histories have defined sociocultural normality – tends to be studied more often than that of others. Partially this is an issue of preservation; for example, grand houses of stone survive better in the archaeological record than modest dwellings of wattle and daub. Nevertheless, the resulting effect is that those who exist outside of societal norms, who occupy the periphery rather than the centre, become marginal in both a social and a material sense (Turner and Young 2007: 298).

When applied to individuals and groups, 'marginality' or 'social marginalisation' references the social, economic, political and legal spheres where people who are disadvantaged struggle to gain access to resources, which leads them to be ignored, excluded or neglected (Gurung and Kollmair 2005: 10).[1] Greek literary sources, for instance, suggest that marginalised individuals experienced social exclusion[2] (Herodotus 7.231–2; Aristotle, *Athenian Constitution* 22; Plutarch, *Aristeides* 73–4 on ostracism;[3] Bremmer 1983 on scapegoat rituals), legal discrimination (Demosthenes 57.3), criminalisation (Demosthenes 24.123; Forsdyke 2008), poverty (Lysias 24) and often premature death (Xenophon, *Hellenica* 1.7.35). Marginalised groups tend to be disenfranchised to varying degrees, which has the overall effect of reducing their historical impact, thus complicating attempts to glean details about their lives from literary and material records.

One archaeological sphere in which the marginalised can be identified more readily is the mortuary one. Burials provide a record of human experience because they contain multiple forms of evidence that allow us to reconstruct various aspects of life in the ancient world. The grave, its orientation and the position of the body within can be indicative of funerary rituals, and some aspects of identity, such as gender, profession, social status and ethnicity, are manifest in grave goods. Furthermore, analysis of human skeletal remains can reveal the deceased's age, biological sex and markers of physiological stress. When all of the components of a burial – material and biological – are interpreted together, marginalising factors, such as physical impairment, socioeconomic status and ethnicity, can be cautiously reconstructed. Some studies have already addressed the subject of marginality with funerary evidence (e.g. Papadopoulos 2000), but burial data generally remain underutilised. This lacuna has long been recognised, and as John Papadopoulos muses, 'perhaps the majority of social deviants and outcasts have always been, at least in the Greek world, right under our noses all the time, in formal burial grounds' (Papadopoulos 2000: 113).

In order to shed light on marginalised groups in the Late Archaic/Classical Greek world (ca. sixth to fifth/fourth centuries BCE), this book explores issues surrounding identity, including disability, poverty and ethnicity, from the perspective of bioarchaeology. This interdisciplinary study interprets burial assemblages within the context of contemporary literary and visual evidence in order to reconstruct the lived experiences of those who were relegated to the margins of Greek society (e.g. the physically impaired, the poor and non-Greeks). Ultimately, this book asserts that social marginalisation is more complex than ancient Greek literary sources lead us to believe, and that truly marginal individuals were intersectional, embodying not one, but multiple marginalising characteristics.

To lay the foundation for this bioarchaeological study of marginalised populations in the ancient Greek world, we begin with a discussion of the evidence, methods and theoretical frameworks that will be used. This Introduction opens with an overview of the burial evidence used to explore aspects of marginalisation.

In particular, the skeletal assemblages available for study, namely those that have been excavated and published, are listed. Also, the marginalising attributes that are discernible from mortuary contexts (i.e. physical impairment, socioeconomic status, and ancestry and ethnicity) are described, the reasons for omitting age and sex as discrete categories of analysis are explained, and the limitations of skeletal evidence are explored. The next section focuses on methods, detailing the bioarchaeological techniques that allow for the estimation of age at death, biological sex, stature, physiological stress and ancestry (the last with caveats) as well as the funerary archaeological methods that inform our understanding of burial practices and the ways in which identities are constructed through the use of material culture. The discussion then shifts to a description of the theoretical models of interpretation employed in this study. In particular, non-normative burial is used to identify the graves of potentially marginalised persons on a population level, while materiality is used to achieve the same goal on an individual level. The section that follows provides a brief introduction to the concept of intersectionality. Intersectionality is a constant thread that runs throughout the book, as the intersection of two or more marginalising characteristics impacts an individual's degree of social marginalisation. Finally, the Introduction's concluding section outlines the organisation of the rest of the book.

EVIDENCE

Although ancient Greek cemeteries have been the subjects of archaeological excavations since the nineteenth century, classical archaeologists have traditionally assigned primacy to material culture (e.g. grave goods, burial containers, grave markers) and little value to skeletal remains.[4] For example, human bones often were rudimentarily recorded and then discarded (Bourbou 2005: 177). Whenever skeletons were analysed, the reports were tucked away as appendices of excavation reports (e.g. Agelarakis 2002; Koukouli-Chrysanthaki 2002). Over the past three decades, shifting mentalities and methods have allowed for the publication of detailed cemetery monographs that consider all aspects of burial contexts, including analyses of the human skeletons and other forms of biological evidence (e.g. Carter 1998). Given their differing levels of exposure, information taken from these well-published sites tends to be cited in the scholarly literature more prevalently than that of appended skeletal reports. As a result, an investigation of all available skeletal data will undoubtedly reveal key details about ancient lifeways that have been previously overlooked.

This study of marginalised populations relies primarily upon the data-mining of published skeletal reports from cemeteries across the Late Archaic/ Classical Greek world (ca. sixth to fifth/fourth centuries BCE). Since the evidence from mainland Greece is well published and there is contextual consistency for the material, it comprises the bulk of the investigation. Although human remains from over 100 sites from the mainland and islands have been excavated and analysed (or are in the process of being analysed), the majority of these assemblages are prehistoric.[5] To date, only the following sites have yielded Late Archaic/Classical assemblages that have been analysed: Abdera, Agia Paraskevi, Agios Dimitrios, Akrefnio, Alos, Amphipolis, Argos, Athens, Corinth, Garitsa/Almyros, Karitsa/Kladeri, Kavousi, Laurion, Nea Philadelphia, Olympus tumuli, Olynthus, Pydna, Ramnous, Thasos, Thebes and Vergina (Fig. I.1; Lagia et al. 2014). The mortuary and biological records of the further reaches of the Greek world – the Black Sea, Sicily and southern Italy, North Africa – present certain challenges for comparative study, not least because they diverge in social structure and ethnic context from that of their mother cities (Dougherty and Kurke 2003). However, since biology and burial in these Greek communities overseas is a rich and fascinating topic, colonial material enters the investigation in a more piecemeal fashion, to complement the picture emerging from the central evidence and to cast it into high relief by way of contrast (Figs I.2 and I.3). The same is true regarding case studies from earlier and later periods of Greek history as they also sporadically enter the discussion to illustrate patterns of continuity and/ or change. Finally, visual and textual evidence from Greek art, material culture, inscriptions and literature is woven into the narrative to provide further insight into contemporary attitudes towards marginalised peoples. The reliability of these ancient sources is explored in Chapter 1 and in the individual chapters in which they appear.

There were a variety of factors that contributed to social marginalisation in ancient Greek society, but not all of these personal attributes can be identified from mortuary contexts. Groups that were marginalised in Greek society are readily identifiable in ancient literary sources (e.g. Demosthenes 22.55–64, 59.122; Aristotle, *Politics* 1326a18–22; Roberto and Tuci 2015), and it appears that an individual could be marginalised for at least one of the following reasons: (1) not belonging to the legal and religious communities of the state (e.g. foreigners, immigrants), (2) not belonging to the normative family (e.g. orphans, widows, illegitimate children), (3) practising undesirable professions and activities (e.g. potters, prostitutes), (4) participating in criminal activities (e.g. thieves, pirates), (5) not practising a settled and agrarian lifestyle and economy (e.g. migrant workers), (6) displaying behaviour deviant to existing norms (e.g. mental illness, cowardice), (7) low socioeconomic class (e.g. beggars), (8) disability or physical impairment (e.g. dwarfism). If several marginalising factors coincided, it could cause one's degree of marginalisation to increase (Grassl 2006). Likewise, the degree of marginalisation could also be compounded by issues relating to gender, as females, intersex individuals and feminine males frequently found themselves subordinated and lacking agency in sociopolitical arenas (e.g. Winkler 1990: 4–8; Brisson 2002: 2, 147–8).

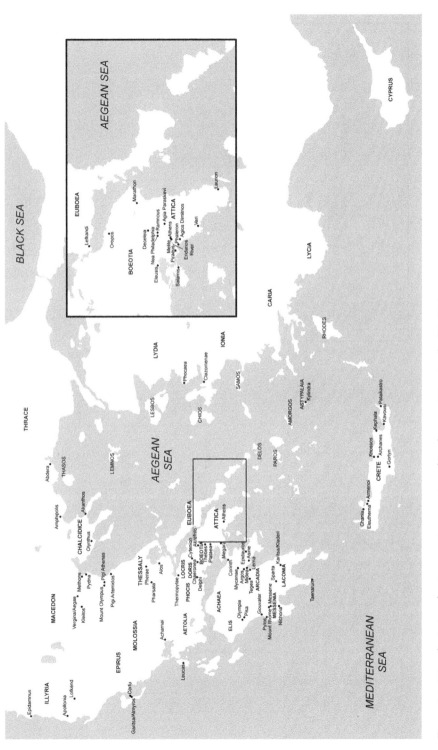

Figure I.1 Map depicting the Aegean sites mentioned in the text. Drawing by D. Weiss.

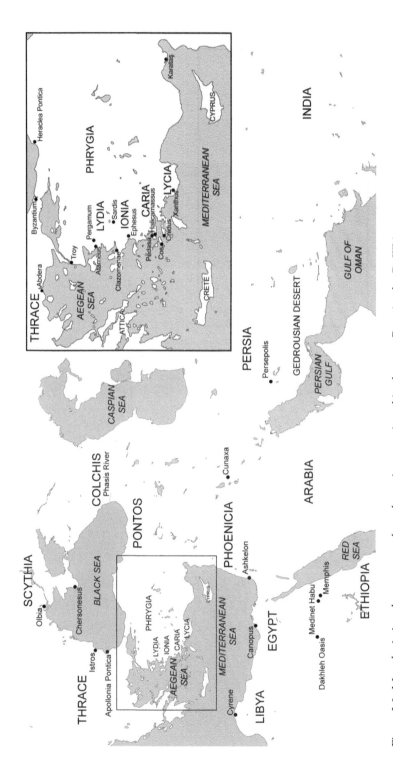

Figure I.2 Map depicting the eastern and southern sites mentioned in the text. Drawing by D. Weiss.

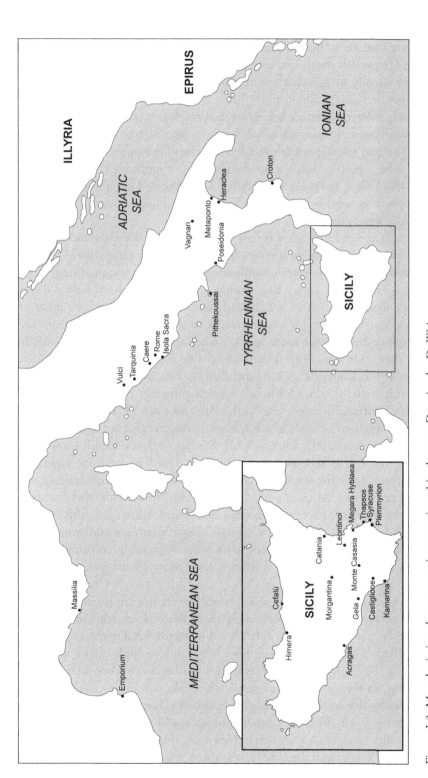

Figure I.3 Map depicting the western sites mentioned in the text. Drawing by D. Weiss.

Although we know that cowards (Herodotus 7.229–31; *Philogelos* 217) and prostitutes (especially those who were male citizens – Aeschines 1; Shapiro 2015: 292) were socially marginalised, there are no skeletal or material indicators in their graves that specifically identify them as such. Only physical impairments and ancestry (with caution; see below) are discernible from skeletal remains, while burial assemblages provide additional details concerning the identity, socioeconomic status and ethnicity of the deceased (see the following section on Methods for how these aspects of identity are discerned from mortuary contexts). In the chapters that follow, the skeletal and burial data presented in published archaeological reports are used to group and identify individuals who most likely came from marginalised groups.

Although age and biological sex are likewise identifiable from human skeletal remains, these attributes are not explored as discrete categories of analysis in this study, because they are subordinating, rather than marginalising, characteristics. That is not to say that women, children and the elderly did not experience discrimination in the ancient Greek world. From the moment of birth, females received prejudicial treatment, as the practice of infant exposure (see Chapters 2 and 3 for more on exposure) appears to have preferentially targeted them (Golden 1981; Harris 1982; Oldenziel 1987; Pomeroy 1983; Patterson 1985; Rousselle 2001; Scott 2001a; 2001b; Beaumont 2012: 91; Evans Grubbs 2013).[6] In adulthood, women generally experienced political and legal disenfranchisement (e.g. Lefkowitz and Fant 1992).[7] Furthermore, osteological analyses of skeletal assemblages have revealed sex-specific health disparities (e.g. Iezzi 2009; Liston 2012). Studies of dental health from Pylos (ca. 2000–1060 BCE; Schepartz et al. 2009b), Agia Paraskevi (ca. eighth to sixth centuries BCE; Triantaphyllou 2004), Almyros (ca. seventh century BCE to second century CE; Michael and Manolis 2014), Nea Philadelphia (ca. sixth to fifth centuries BCE; Papageorgopoulou 2004) and Athens (ca. fifth century BCE to third century CE; Lagia 2015a) have shown that men and women displayed differential dietary practices, with women possibly consuming diets richer in carbohydrates, which would have been relatively inexpensive and less nutritious than the more balanced diets of men. Moreover, in Classical Athens and elsewhere, children of both sexes generally were not considered to be full members of society until approximately three years of age (this understanding, however, has been found to vary according to time and space; Lagia 2007; Golden 2015: 141–53), which is most likely due to high infant mortality rates (Fox 2012).[8] Afterwards, the attributes ascribed to children were primarily negative, as they were seen as physically weak, morally incompetent and mentally incapable until they reached adulthood (Dasen 2008; 2011: 293–4; Golden 2015: 1–10). Finally, although old age could confer status and respect (e.g. eligibility to serve on the Spartan *Gerousia*), it was simultaneously viewed as woeful and tragic, and the elderly were often stereotyped as feeble, pathetic and lecherous (e.g. Gilleard 2007; Van Nortwick 2008: 122–53; Harokopos 2019). So, even though women, children and the elderly might have experienced discrimination at various points in their lives on account of their age or sex, each of these groups still served as active agents in vital societal roles and are not considered to be marginalised. Therefore, this study considers age and sex to be factors that impact, rather than cause, an individual's social marginalisation.

It is also important to note that any study of human skeletal remains is negatively impacted by various sources of bias. These include recovery bias (i.e. selective excavation and differential preservation of individuals), burial bias (e.g. the community had different ways of disposing of their dead, and the entire population was not interred in the same cemetery) and poor curation (resulting in the loss of excavated material; Roberts et al. 2005: 36–8). Furthermore, all skeletal samples are biased by the 'osteological paradox' (Wood et al. 1992). The osteological paradox is comprised of three issues which complicate attempts to make population inferences from archaeological samples. The first is demographic non-stationarity. A population has to be stationary (i.e. of constant size) for the age distribution of its dead to reflect actual mortality patterns. When it is non-stationary, as populations typically are, the age distribution reveals more about fertility than mortality. The second issue is selective mortality (i.e. mortality bias), namely that skeletal assemblages represent the weak and the sick, rather than the healthy living population. Hidden heterogeneity in risk is the third issue – individuals vary in terms of frailty, or susceptibility to illness, and the factors that contribute to this variation are not always self-evident (Wright and Yoder 2003). In general, scholars are divided on the problems raised by the osteological paradox, as some deny their significance and others attempt to find solutions (Milner et al. 2008: 567; Kyle et al. 2018).

METHODS

Bearing in mind the limitations of the evidence, archaeology nevertheless seeks to reconstruct past identities using material remains that survive into the present. In mortuary contexts, past identities are reconstructed through the use of multiple lines of evidence. Specifically, study of human skeletal remains can reveal information about the deceased's age, sex, stature, physiological stress and ancestry (though the last is complicated), while analysis of the various components of burials – especially burial type/container, spatial orientation, body position, amounts and types of grave goods – can divulge additional details about the deceased's identity and social status. The ways in which these details are gleaned from human remains and funerary assemblages are described below.

Bioarchaeological basics: Age, sex, stature and physiological stress

The basic information sought from the analysis of a human skeleton (Fig. I.4) is approximate age at death, sex, stature and markers of physiological stress. An individual's age is multifaceted, as it has chronological, biological and social components – all of which can be identified through careful skeletal analysis (Bass 2005: 12–19). The determination of chronological (or actual) age relies on the observation of physiological changes that are caused by either developmental or degenerative processes. It is much easier to determine age from developmental markers, such as bone and dental growth, because the relationship between chronological age and skeletal development is continuous and monotonic (i.e. an increase in age corresponds to an increase in any given measure of skeletal development). As a result, one can estimate the ages of immature individuals (called subadults) and younger adults (≤ 28 years) with a relatively high degree of success (Roberts 2009: 127). Age determination, however, becomes more difficult once an individual is skeletally mature, because the relationship between chronological age and skeletal degeneration (visible on the fibrous joints of the pelvis and sternal rib ends, as well as through dental wear) is influenced by multiple factors (Nawrocki 2010). Bone is a dynamic tissue capable of renewal, repair and remodelling in response to stressors and stimuli, such as genetics, disease, nutrition, behaviour, predisposition and environment. Any of these can affect the rates of skeletal degeneration, which can lead to discrepancies between the chronological and biological (or physiological) ages of adult individuals (Cox 2000: 64; Kemkes-Grottenthaler 2002). To correct for this bias, individuals are assigned to broad age categories, and multifactorial ageing methods are applied where possible (Cox 2000: 64–5).

The broad age categories assigned to skeletons also endeavour to encompass social age. The conceptualisation of age is an important component of social identity and is related more closely to culturally constructed attitudes and behaviours than the passage of time (Gowland 2006: 143).[9] For instance, initiation into some societies might occur at the onset of puberty (e.g. Samoa), while in others not until marriage (e.g. the Roman Empire).[10] Although this variation can complicate universal standardisation, the standard age categories used by bioarchaeologists, namely Infant (birth–3 years), Juvenile (3–12 years), Adolescent (12–20 years), Young Adult (20–35 years), Middle Adult (35–50 years) and Old Adult (50+ years), seek to incorporate all three age definitions. In theory, biological age is assessed and translated into a chronological age, which is often presumed to have a social age equivalent to modern Euro-American norms (Gowland 2006: 144).[11] However, for ancient populations, it is necessary to strip broad age categories of their connotations to social age and to turn instead to literary and archaeological evidence to theorise culturally appropriate age identities (Gowland 2006: 144; Sofaer 2011). In the ancient Greek world,

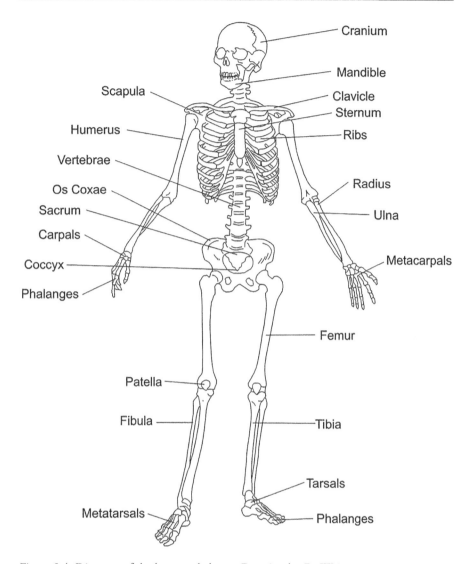

Figure I.4 Diagram of the human skeleton. Drawing by D. Weiss.

for example, the social age structure was dependent upon gender. Girls transitioned to adulthood at the time of marriage, when they were approximately
14 to 18 years of age (i.e. upon sexual maturation), while boys became 'adults'
when they acquired citizenship and military status, between 16 and 20 years of
age (i.e. upon sociopolitical maturation; Sourvinou-Inwood 1988: 78; Beaumont 2000: 45–7; Dillon 2002: 211–35; Oakley 2003: 163; Lawton 2007: 55;
Beaumont 2012: 15–24).[12] Thus, when analysing the mortuary context of, for

instance, a female Adolescent skeleton from an ancient Greek cemetery, one must be mindful that the grave might belong to an individual who is socially considered to be an adult rather than an adolescent, and adjust the archaeological interpretations accordingly.

Another aim of skeletal analysis is sex estimation. Sex, which is biological, is distinguished from gender, which is socially constructed (Hollimon 2011; Wesp 2017; also see Chapter 2 for a discussion of non-binary sex and gender). In most archaeological cases, biological sex (derived from skeletal analysis and/or genetic testing) and gender (discerned from grave goods or gender-specific burial practices) align, but there are always exceptions (e.g. the Anglo-Saxon so-called 'transvestite' burials: Lucy 2000: 89 and non-binary concepts of gender and gender roles: Stratton 2016). Nevertheless, sex estimation in adults relies primarily on the assessment of the morphological characters of the pelvis and skull, which are the two areas of the human skeleton that display the highest degree of sexual dimorphism (Bass 2005: 19–21). The pelvis is the most reliable indicator of sex, with an accuracy rate that ranges between 83 and 96 per cent. In general, female pelves are shaped wide and low for purposes of childbearing, while male pelves are typically high and narrow (Mays and Cox 2000: 118–19). The skull is the second-best indicator of sex, with female skulls tending to be light and gracile, whereas male skulls are heavier and more robust. Assessment of the cranium alone yields an accuracy rate of approximately 80 per cent, but that rate jumps to around 90 per cent when the mandible is included (Mays and Cox 2000: 119–20).

Sex is ideally estimated through the evaluation of sexually dimorphic characters of *both* the pelvis and skull, because human variation allows for the existence of robust females and gracile males (Acsádi and Nemeskéri 1970), and populations under extreme climatic stress typically display a reduction in sexual dimorphism (Waxenbaum and Feiler 2020). There are also instances when the sex estimation of the skull differs from that of the pelvis, and in this case, the sex derived from the pelvis is given primacy over that of the skull (e.g. Cummings and Rega 2008: 432). For this reason, sex should not be assigned definitively on the basis of the skull alone when pelves are absent or incomplete (Roberts 2009: 126). Furthermore, measurements of other sexually dimorphic bones (humerus, femur, metacarpals, metatarsals, ulna and calcaneus) can be taken to estimate sex when the skull and/or pelvis are absent, but this method can only be employed when the bones to be measured are complete and not fragmented (Bass 2005: 19–21).

Osteological sex estimation in subadults under 18 years of age is problematic and generally not recommended. Scholars have attempted to establish sex diagnostic criteria for younger individuals, but none of the current methods are reliable (Mays and Cox 2000: 121–5; Scheuer and Black 2000: 15–16; Lewis 2007: 47–55). The subfield of biomolecular archaeology, however, provides a solution, as the analysis of nuclear DNA (nDNA) can successfully determine the sex of subadults (as well as adults; Stone 2008: 463). Although there are drawbacks to genetic analysis of sex, which include high costs and the occasional failure to extract DNA due to sample degradation, nDNA analysis is still the most accurate method for the estimation of subadult sex (Brown 2000; Brown and Brown 2011: 160–2).

The stature, or height, of an individual is influenced not only by genetic potential, but also by environmental factors that are present during periods of bone growth, such as health, nutrition and exposure to sunlight. As a result, stature information can provide insight into a population's state of health.[13] Height is directly correlated to long bone length, so stature is estimated in adult skeletons based on the measurements of complete (or even fragmented) long bones (Steele 1970; Trotter 1970; Feldesman et al. 1990). Long bone measurements are used in conjunction with sex- and ancestry-specific regression formulae in order to produce an approximation of living stature.[14] These formulae produce the most accurate results when they are used with skeletons from the same population as the reference sample used to create the method, although exceptions do exist. For example, in the case of ancient Central and South Italian burials, researchers measured skeletons *in situ* (a luxury afforded to few osteologists since specialists are typically invited to study material after excavation) in order to produce an approximation of actual height and a guideline for selecting the most appropriate regression formula. They found that the most reliable estimates of stature were determined using Trotter's formula for African Americans (Trotter 1970; Formicola 1993; Becker 1999a; Giannecchini and Moggi-Cecchi 2008; Lazer 2009: 180). Another method of stature estimation, called 'Fully's method' or the 'anatomical method', measures the total heights of skeletal elements that extend from the top of the head to the bottom of the heel. Thus, the height of the skull, the maximum heights of vertebral bodies (including S1), the bicondylar length of the femur, the physiological length of the tibia, and the height of the articulated talus and calcaneus are all added together with a 'soft tissue correction' to estimate the living stature of an individual. This method, however, can only be used on complete skeletons and is therefore not applicable to most archaeological burials, where the human remains are frequently fragmented or incomplete (Fully 1956).

Physiological stress – defined as 'a physiological change caused by strain on an organism from environmental, nutritional, and other pressures' (Reitsema and McIlvaine 2014) – can be used as a proxy for health in past populations. To assess physiological stress, one generally begins with visual observation and description of abnormal changes to skeletal remains (Metcalfe 2007: 281). Pathological changes to the bone are called skeletal lesions. Skeletal lesions represent chronicity, which means that the individual survived the acute phase of a disease, its body adapted and reacted to the problem by forming new bone or destroying old bone, and the disease either was successfully treated or progressed into a chronic stage. Following this pattern, there are essentially three types of lesions: active, healing and healed. Active lesions are composed of woven bone (coarse and porous bone), healed lesions consist of lamellar bone (bone that is smooth and remodelled), and healing lesions display a mixture of woven and lamellar bone (Mays 2010: 181).

Skeletal lesions indicate instances of trauma, infection and childhood stress, as well as joint, infectious, metabolic, congenital and neoplastic diseases, dental caries, dental abscess, periodontal disease, calculus and other abnormalities (Ortner 2003; Aufderheide and Rodríguez-Martín 2005). Lesions, however, can only provide limited evidence. First, they reveal an individual's physiological stress at the time of death and are not accurate indicators of the individual's entire medical history. They also serve as a record of a disease's perimortem presence or absence, not its severity or duration. Furthermore, diseases that kill swiftly (e.g. plague epidemics) do not allow for the formation of lesions, and many diseases create similar skeletal lesions (e.g. leprosy, treponemal disease, tuberculosis, non-specific infection and scurvy can cause similar patterns of new bone to form on the tibia and fibula). To adjust for these limitations, the distribution patterns of the lesions must be recorded together with bone abnormalities in order to discern which disease is present through differential diagnosis (i.e. the gradual process of elimination that is based on known patterning of modern instances of the disease). Yet, without the presence of soft tissue or biomolecular evidence (e.g. virus DNA), a definitive diagnosis cannot be made, and only reasonable possibilities can be suggested (Roberts and Manchester 2007: 7–9).[15] Furthermore, since many archaeological skeletons are often fragmented, incomplete and poorly preserved, it is not always possible to identify all lesions that might have been initially present, resulting in the under-representation of pathologies.

When information regarding physiological stress is considered together with demographic attributes, such as age and sex, inferences can be drawn about these individuals and the populations in which they lived. For example, it is possible that the high prevalence rate of anaemia observed in the Black Sea region in the fifth to third centuries BCE, indicated by cribra orbitalia and porotic hyperostosis in skeletal remains, could have been caused by widespread sickle-cell anaemia resulting from endemic malaria (Keenleyside and Panayotova 2006).[16] Also, health disparities are often detected between males and females. For instance, an examination of Late Bronze Age (ca. 1300–1200 BCE) skeletons from Pylos revealed that many females were anaemic and consistently exhibited poorer dental health than males, which could be attributed to sex-based dietary differences or the biological demands of pregnancy, among other causes (Schepartz et al. 2009b). Thus, palaeopathological research draws on the aforementioned facets of bioarchaeological enquiry (i.e. age, sex and stature) in order to make statements about the health of individuals and populations and track the changes in disease rates and patterns over time.

Estimating ancestry: A complicated issue with a shameful past

Considerable attention was paid to human morphology during the late nineteenth and early twentieth centuries for the purposes of constructing hierarchical and typological racial classifications that assigned primacy to men of European descent. These early attempts by physical anthropologists and anatomists to understand human variation were both limited and flawed, and this approach was founded on the dual mistaken beliefs that (1) there are a finite number of 'pure' human races and (2) humans can be categorised according to race (see Armelagos and Goodman 1998). We now know that race is not biologically predetermined; it is instead a cultural invention constructed in the context of specific historical, social and political circumstances (discussed further in Chapter 1).

While there is a connection between human biodiversity and geography, neither factor has any connection to race, as Agustín Fuentes explains:

> There is, however, a general validity to the explanation that the widespread geographic distribution in humans has led to the broad range of human biodiversity. That is, human bodies are, in part, so variable because of our species' very wide distribution across the planet, with its diverse ecologies and landscapes. Different pressures shaped different bodies over time. This is evolution . . . We know that skin color, hair type, facial features, and body shape vary quite a bit across our species but not in any pattern that clusters into continental groups . . . Dark skin, for example, occurs in distinct populations in Africa, South Asia, Southeast Asia, Micronesia, and South America. Skin color is not a characteristic that pinpoints a person to a specific geographic place of origin. (2021: 150)

Thus, there is no evidence, genetic or otherwise, to support the claim that race has a biological basis, and it is clear that the physiognomic differences among humans fall within the range of normal biological variation (Tattersall and DeSalle 2011; Wagner et al. 2017; Fuentes et al. 2019).[17]

Although no respectable anthropologist would attempt racial classification today, race science persisted into the twenty-first century in the guise of ancestry estimation. Ancestry estimation is frequently utilised in forensic and physical anthropology and rooted in the understanding that biological environmental adaptations that occur over time cause people from different parts of the world to vary in appearance. As a result, certain skeletal characteristics should differ in frequency among broad geographical populations, and ancestry estimation seeks to use these morphological traits to group individuals into one of three categories: European,

East Asian and sub-Saharan African (Gill and Rhine 1990; Burns 1999). The diagnostic traits are concentrated primarily in the skull (Gill 1998), but additional adaptations are purportedly found in the postcranial skeleton (Klepinger 2006: 75–6) and dentition (Edgar 2005; Lease and Sciulli 2005).[18] Ancestry estimation methods recognise that no trait in itself is a definitive marker of geographical origin, so many characteristics are considered together before an individual is assigned to an ancestral group. Furthermore, it is acknowledged that ancestral group designation does not presume that an individual was born in a specific locale, but rather reveals which population predominately contributed to that person's ancestral background (Klepinger 2006: 66).

This approach to human ancestry is problematic for a variety of reasons. First and foremost, ancestry estimation perpetuates the myth of biological racial classification. The potential accuracy of ancestry estimation is also questionable because it is unclear whether all of the diagnostic traits are heritable. Of the seventeen cranial morphological traits used in ancestry estimation, only five have been proven to be heritable (DiGangi and Bethard 2021). This is equally true of postcranial traits. For example, it has been demonstrated that one commonly used trait – femoral subtrochanteric shape – is dictated by biomechanical, rather than genetic, adaptations (McIlvaine and Schepartz 2015). Moreover, the aetiology of the diagnostic traits can be ambiguous, as morphological characteristics attributed to sexual dimorphism (e.g. shape of the eye orbits) and age-related changes (e.g. metopic suture) tend to overlap with those used for ancestry estimation (St. Hoyme and İşcan 1989; Klepinger 2006: 66). Since the accuracy of ancestry estimation is dubious and its use (albeit unintentionally) supports biological racial classification, there has been considerable movement towards abolishing the use of ancestry estimation (Armelagos and Van Gerven 2003; DiGangi and Bethard 2021).

Advances in evolutionary theory and population genetics, as well as the development of new computational and statistical methods, have led to a better understanding of biological affinity (or 'relatedness') that seeks to divorce them from the racial biases of past scholarship (Stojanowski and Buikstra 2004). As a result, we have devised more responsible methods for measuring and interpreting human morphological variation on intra- and inter-population levels (Pietrusewsky 2014; DiGangi and Bethard 2021: 5). These methods, which include metric, non-metric and genetic analyses, will be discussed in detail in Chapter 4. Furthermore, it should be noted that investigations of biological affinity must always derive from a well-defined research question – in other words, it is inappropriate to identify biological affinity for its own sake. Responsible identification of biological affinity (especially in the context of Greek colonisation) allows us to explore hypotheses concerning past human behaviour, such as differential levels of physiological stress and variable access to resources among individuals and population groups.

Funerary archaeology basics: Interpreting burial practices and grave goods

In addition to the scientific details that can be gleaned from human remains, burial contexts themselves are rich sources of information regarding funerary customs and identity. The burial of an individual is accompanied by culturally appropriate displays of prescribed ritual actions that are performed to restore balance to a community that is experiencing temporary upset and disharmony due to the loss of a member (Parker Pearson 2005: 27, 194).[19] Funerary preferences and rituals can differ among cultures, settlements and even family groups, yet each component of a burial – from the treatment of the corpse to the gifting of grave goods – is intentional and symbolic (Metcalf and Huntington 2005: 24).

Funerary rituals involve the performance of both ephemeral and tangible acts. Ephemeral acts include powerful emotional displays (e.g. mourners crying, wailing, tearing at their hair and lacerating their cheeks) and appeals to the supernatural (e.g. prayer), whereas ceremonial performances (e.g. libation-pouring) and actions meant to sever the ties between the living and the newly deceased (e.g. ritual destruction of grave goods) often have material components (Parker Pearson 2005: 195). However, burial, or the interment of the body, is one of the final ceremonial acts performed by mourners, and it is accompanied by the most tangible series of actions associated with funerary ritual (Morris 2001: 1).

The various components of a burial (i.e. grave type, burial container, grave orientation, body position, head position and grave goods) are carefully constructed and imbued with symbolic meaning (Duday 2009: 24–5). The type of grave in which the body is interred can reveal socioeconomic status and/ or affiliation. For instance, a lavish built tomb (e.g. the so-called 'Treasury of Atreus' at Mycenae, a Mycenaean tholos tomb ca. 1250 BCE) most likely contained individuals of higher social status than those buried in nearby contemporary simple trench graves (Parker Pearson 2005: 139–41). Furthermore, in Greek Sicily, chamber tombs were often associated with local indigenous peoples (e.g. Sikels), whereas Greek Sicilians were typically interred in trench (*a fossa*) graves, *enchytrismoi* (pot burials), sarcophagi and tile-built (*a cappuccina*) graves (Shepherd 2005; Sulosky Weaver 2015: 63–71). The same pattern holds true for burial containers – marble sarcophagi cost more to commission than simple wooden coffins, and at Olbia in the Black Sea region, indigenous peoples were buried in painted wooden sarcophagi while Greek inhabitants frequently opted for pit burials, *enchytrismoi*, sarcophagi and niche tombs (Damyanov 2005). Grave orientation is also significant. For example, Late Minoan (ca. 1450–1190 BCE) tombs from Armenoi, Crete were constructed to face either the rising of the sun or moon (Papathanassiou et al. 1992: S43–55), and early Christian graves were oriented east–west so that the dead could witness the miraculous Second Coming of Christ when he appears in the east (Matthew 24.27; Constas 2006: 135).

The dead can be laid to rest in a number of different positions. One person can be placed in their own grave, or more than one body can be interred in a single grave (multiple inhumation). Skeletons are found lying on their backs (supine), on their stomachs (prone), on their sides with their legs flexed (interchangeably called flexed, contracted or hocker), and sometimes even sitting or standing (Parker Pearson 2005: 6). Burial choices such as these typically depended upon geographical location and cultural preferences (Kurtz and Boardman 1971: 188, 192–3). In Greek Sicily, for example, instances of multiple inhumation and flexed burial positions are generally associated with native non-Greek identity (Shepherd 2005; Sulosky Weaver 2015: 225–6). Finally, like grave orientation, the position of the deceased's head is often significant. For instance, in Anatolia (i.e. Phrygia, Lydia, Lycia) and Cyprus (ca. eighth to fourth centuries BCE in both locations) the dead were often positioned with their heads towards the entrance of their tomb (Baughan 2008: 58).

Grave goods are items that are buried with the deceased. Placement preferences are culture-specific, and grave goods have been found within, under, beside or on top of the burial container, or in the grave fill (Sprague 1968: 483). Objects left above ground at the grave site (e.g. ribbons, flowers, figurines etc.) can also be considered grave goods, but their lack of burial inhibits their preservation, so many of these deliberately placed objects – especially perishable items like flowers, food or textiles – disappear from the archaeological record.[20] Nevertheless, any given grave good assemblage might include some of the deceased's possessions, gifts from mourners, equipment for the afterlife (e.g. a coin for Charon or an oil lamp to light the way to the Underworld), and apotropaic talismans (e.g. magical amulets) designed to keep the dead safe, or alternatively, confined to their graves (Parker Pearson 2005: 7–11). Thus, grave good assemblages theoretically contain information about the deceased's socio-religious beliefs (e.g. items related to funerary ritual, such as oil-bearing vessels), family (e.g. statements of wealth, prestige or affiliation can be made through the inclusion of rare or sumptuous grave goods), community (e.g. artefacts which denote ethnic or political alignment) and personal identity (e.g. objects related to gender or occupation; Fahlander and Oestigaard 2008b: 7–9).

The interpretation of grave goods, however, is a challenging and precarious endeavour because each object is potentially imbued with multiple layers of significance (Robb et al. 2001; Parker Pearson 2005: 7–11, 21–44). An assemblage can be themed to reflect the deceased's character, social status, identity or accomplishments. Grave good assemblages can also be connected to ritual or to the intentional display of wealth. Displays of wealth, however, can be misleading and misrepresentative. Rather than reflect actual socioeconomic status, they may be born instead of a desire either to make one appear 'greater' in death (e.g. wealthier, more important etc.) than they were in life or to bolster the public image of the deceased's survivors (or both). This type of self-aggrandisement, for instance, is commonly attested in the burials of Roman freedmen (e.g. M. Roller 2006; Sulosky Weaver 2019a). Furthermore, grave goods can act as items of separation and transition – the Iban of Borneo place a knife in the grave to represent the severance of the ties between the living and the dead (Parker Pearson 2005: 11), and in many cultures, objects are ritually broken before they are placed in the tomb, in accordance with the belief that inanimate items must be 'killed' so that they can accompany the deceased to the afterlife (Bendann 1930: 115–20, 248–50; Grinsell 1961; Alexandridou 2013).

Various interpretive frameworks have been applied to burial assemblages.[21] Two of the most influential have been the processual and postprocessual approaches. The processual approach assumes that a society's burial complexities are directly related to its social organisation. In other words, the grave of an individual from a sedentary agricultural community should be more complex than that of a person from a hunter-gatherer tribe, as graves from agricultural communities are expected to contain more formal organisation and material culture than those of hunter-gatherers. Furthermore, details about the deceased's social persona (essentially the combination of 'identities' – for example, rich, mother, baker, soldier etc. – that an individual chooses to use when interacting with others; see Salamone 1982) are communicated through specific treatments of the body, such as grave type or grave orientation, and the inclusion of particular grave goods (Binford 1971: 17). Postprocessualists, on the other hand, believe that funerary rituals are an indirect reflection of society (Hodder 1980; 1982; Härke 1997: 21). Adherents of this theoretical framework tend to take two separate approaches to the origins of funerary practices, which they view as being rooted either in symbolism or in social structure. Symbolic, or contextual, interpretation is based on the understanding that human action is expressed in symbols. Even though actions are ephemeral, their symbolic patterns are preserved as material culture in the archaeological record. Thus, material culture is like language or text in that it is composed of signs (signifiers) and their meanings (the signified), which can be deciphered when placed in the proper context (Tilley 1989: 186; Härke 1997: 21). The sociological approach relies heavily on structuration theory (Giddens 1979), which maintains that 'society is not a given framework in which individuals play pre-ordained roles, but an interplay of rules (structuring principles) and actions (social practices), with ideology providing the legitimation for the former . . . [therefore] burial ritual is not a mere passive reflection of society, but the result of actions which contribute to shaping society itself' (Härke 1997: 21). As a result, postprocessualists understand that grave goods are not a reflection of wealth or social status, but rather a material manifestation of the survivors' claims regarding the deceased's property and position in society (Parker Pearson 1982: 101; Samson 1987; Härke 1997: 21).

Thus, the study of an archaeological funerary context with particular focus placed on mode of burial, spatial orientation, body position, amounts

and types of grave goods, and the ways in which these factors deviate from
established cemetery norms can reveal striking details about the deceased's
identity and social status (Robb 2007). When this information is coupled
with that derived from bioarchaeological analysis, a more complete portrait of the individual begins to emerge, and evidence indicative of physical
impairments, socioeconomic status, and non-Greek ancestry and ethnicity
can become clear. Although the previous discussions of bio- and funerary
archaeological methods have summarised and highlighted some of the ways
in which these marginalising personal attributes can be identified, detailed
descriptions of their methods of discernment can be found respectively in
Chapters 2 (disability), 3 (socioeconomic status) and 4 (non-Greek ancestry
and ethnicity).

THEORY

The general theoretical premise of this study is that burial assemblages are capable of revealing demographic, sociocultural, palaeopathological and identity-
related information about the lives of the deceased. When burial assemblages
are further analysed through the lenses of two specific theoretical frameworks,
non-normative burial and materiality, this allows for the identification and
interpretation of social marginalisation in mortuary contexts. The first, non-
normative burial, functions on the population level and requires an understanding of societal funerary practices.[22] A burial is classified as 'non-normative'
when it deviates in some manner from established cemetery norms. Social
marginalisation, diseases with social stigma, physical impairments, mental and
behavioural abnormalities, heresy, social transgression, superstition and violent
death, among other causes, have all been cited as reasons why an individual
might be buried in an atypical fashion (Tsaliki 2008: 3). Specific motivations
aside, Talia Shay's study of ethnographic burial data found that non-normative
burials share three commonalities: (1) the impetus for non-normative burial
varies cross-culturally; (2) non-normative burial might not reflect the status
of the deceased in life, but rather reflect circumstances surrounding death;
and (3) in so-called simple social systems, the differences between volitional
(e.g. crime) and non-volitional (e.g. illness) forms of social deviancy are not
recognised, which results in both groups being buried in a non-normative
manner (1985).[23]

    It can be difficult to discern non-normative burials in the archaeological
record because their identifying characteristics are period- and culture-specific.[24]
In order to recognise a burial as non-normative, excavators must have a firm
grasp of the range of what is considered 'normal' in the cemetery and be alert
for burials that deviate from established customs. Common patterns, nevertheless, have been observed across time and geographical locations, and Anastasia

Tsaliki has identified five basic archaeological criteria that can be used to identify non-normative burials:

> [1] Primary and secondary burials in unusual places and/or positions
> when compared to the ordinary burial customs of the cultural group or
> of the time period (e.g. skeletal remains in wells, pits or kilns, skeletons
> laid in a prone position), [2] Mass burials (inhumations and cremations),
> especially those without evidence or historical documentation for a cri-
> sis (e.g. epidemic, war, civil unrest) or those unique in the given burial
> ground, [3] Inhumations or cremations, in cemeteries or isolated, associ-
> ated with indicators of unusual ritual activity (e.g. cut marks, unusual
> artefacts of possible symbolic or ritual use), [4] Cremations found in
> an inhumation site and vice-versa, [5] Skeletons with evidence that may
> be indicative of crime, torture or special mortuary ritual (e.g. victims of
> infanticide, senicide, human sacrifice, cannibalism). (2008: 2)

Once a non-normative burial is identified, the next challenge is its interpretation (Weiss-Krejci 2013). There are many reasons why an individual might be
afforded an atypical burial, and it is often not possible to determine from archaeological contexts whether the deceased was, for instance, mentally ill, 'cursed' or
a heretic. Yet, in many cases we can assume that the deceased was socially marginalised because the majority of reasons that prompted non-normative burial (aside
from those associated with circumstances and manner of death) were the same
as those that fuelled social marginalisation. As a result, individuals who were
socially marginalised received parallel treatment in death – in other words, their
non-normative burial separated them from the rest of the community, reflecting
the separation they would have experienced during life (Shay 1985; Little and
Papadopoulos 1998; Papadopoulos 2000; Murphy 2008; Tsaliki 2008; Saracino
et al. 2017). Indeed, some scholars have suggested that '[social] marginalization
was the prime mover in deviant interments' (Perego et al. 2015: 150).

   Archaeological and literary evidence indicates that marginalised individuals
were buried non-normatively in ancient Greek societies. For instance, at various points throughout the history of Athens, individuals of low socioeconomic
status were excluded from formal burial (Morris 1987). Athenian criminals who
committed particularly heinous crimes were thrown into the sea (e.g. Diodorus
Siculus 16.35.6; Aeschines 2.142; Isocrates 5.115; Demosthenes 25.166), while
the others were cast into the 'Deadman's Pit' (Aristophanes, *Knights* 1362,
Wealth 431; Plato, *Gorgias* 516d; Xenophon, *Hellenica* 1.7.20), a manmade
feature most likely located outside of the city, below the promontory of the
Pnyx, between the Town Hall and Long Wall (Lindenlauf 2001: 88–9).[25] The
Spartans similarly disposed of criminals, and their equivalent of the Deadman's
Pit, the Keadas, was a natural depression presumably located either near the

village Parori in the district of Mistra or near Mt Taygetos near the village Tripi (Themelis 1982; Lindenlauf 2001: 89). Like criminals, political traitors and religious transgressors were also buried in a non-normative manner. At Phaleron, a recently excavated mass grave dating to the seventh century BCE contained shackled individuals that have been tentatively interpreted as the supporters of the failed Cylonian coup (Ingvarsson and Bäckström 2019; Prevedorou and Buikstra 2019). On the island of Delos, two Middle Adult females (ca. second to first centuries BCE) interred in a cistern appear to have been executed by *apotympanismos* (or *apotympanizomenos*) – an Athenian method of capital punishment that entailed nailing a person to a board or post and abandoning them to a die a slow and torturous death. The bodies of these women were discarded in the cistern of a house that contained atypical religious iconography, suggesting that they were executed for deviant religious practices and their bodies concealed on account of the law forbidding death and burial on the sacred island (Charlier 2008). Finally, individuals who experienced mental or physical impairments were purposely buried in wells. Archaeological evidence for this practice derives from Early Iron Age (ca. 900–850 BCE) and Hellenistic (second quarter of the second century BCE) wells at Athens and is attested for Bronze Age contexts at Corinth (Early Helladic), Eleusis (Middle Helladic), Argos and Mycenae (Late Helladic; Little and Papadopoulos 1998; Papadopoulos 2000; 2017: 602–6; Liston and Rotroff 2013; Liston et al. 2018: 25–52).

Even within cemeteries themselves, special quarters were often set aside for infant and child burials, the indigent, the enslaved, foreigners and socially deviant people (Shay 1985; Houby-Nielsen 1995; Triantaphyllou and Bessios 2005; Arrington 2010; Bourbou 2013).[26] Of these groups, the largest corpus of archaeological evidence exists for infant and child burials. Infants and children are typically under-represented in Greek cemeteries (Dasen 2013: 33; Shepherd 2018), which implies that they were, in many cases, excluded from formal burial alongside adults (e.g. Mycenaean Achaea, ca. 1800–1065 BCE: Jones 2018). Instead, they could be buried in age-specific clusters within a cemetery (e.g. Borgo necropolis at Gela, seventh to fifth centuries BCE: Orsi 1906), interred in domestic contexts (e.g. Oropos in Attica, ca. late eighth to early seventh centuries BCE: Vlachou 2007), placed in independent cemeteries (e.g. Kylindra on Astypalaia, ca. 600–400 BCE: Hillson 2009) or deposited in wells (e.g. Athens, ca. second quarter of the second century BCE: Liston and Rotroff 2013; Liston et al. 2018).[27]

Although non-normative burial frequently reflects social marginalisation, there are exceptions. In some cases, individuals who died violent, gruesome deaths are buried non-normatively (e.g. Tsaliki 2008: 10–11). For instance, an Adolescent male dating to the Middle Helladic period from Kouphovouno in Sparta (KE0213) was severed in half across the thighs (at the distal femora) from a violent perimortem trauma or injury. The upper portion of this individual was buried in an extended supine position, a rarity in the Kouphovouno, and the lower portion was placed parallel and upside down in relation to the torso (i.e. the toes of the lower limbs were facing the skull). DNA samples taken from the upper and lower portions of the body revealed that both segments belonged to the same individual. Yet, aside from the individual's violent death, there are no other indicators of why this person was buried non-normatively (Lagia and Cavanagh 2010: 342–4).

Additional examples can be found at Phaleron (ca. eighth to fourth centuries BCE), where a number of individuals suffered violent deaths. These persons were buried with their arms bound behind their backs (with either iron shackles or a perishable material like rope) in the prone position. Many had a stone slab marking their graves, and some had their feet removed (Ingvarsson and Bäck-ström 2019: 11). All of these abnormalities – binding the limbs of individuals who died violently, burying them face-down, removing their feet and conspicu-ously marking their graves – are suggestive of necrophobic practices. Necro-phobia, or the fear of the dead, is a widespread concept that has been present in Greek culture from the Neolithic period (ca. 6850–3300 BCE) to the present (Tsaliki 2008: 3). At the heart of this phobia is the belief that the dead are able to reanimate and exist in a state that is neither living nor dead, but rather 'undead'. Scholars refer to these beings as 'revenants' after the Latin word for 'returning' (*revenans*), and they are feared because it is believed that they leave their graves at night for the explicit purpose of harming the living. To prevent this, revenants must be sufficiently 'killed', which is usually achieved by incin-eration or dismemberment, or they can be trapped in their graves by being tied, staked, flipped onto their stomachs, buried exceptionally deep, or pinned with rocks or other heavy objects (Tsaliki 2008: 3). Tertullian (*On the Soul* 56) tells us that the ancient Greeks believed that there were 'special' dead who were angry with the living and capable of causing them harm. One category of the special dead, the *biaiothanatoi*, was composed of individuals who met violent deaths in various ways (Felton 2010: 96). It is possible that fear of the *biaiothanatoi* was the driving force behind their non-normative burial treatment at Phaleron.

There are also cases of extraordinary and heroised individuals who are buried non-normatively. These non-normative burials are different from those previ-ously described in that they are often monumental and serve as focal points of cultic veneration. Legendary figures (e.g. Pelops at Olympia), the war dead (e.g. Athenians and Plataeans at Marathon), the recently heroised (e.g. Aleximachos on Amorgos) and oikists (e.g. Battos, the founder of Cyrene) are numbered among those who would receive burials of this sort (Malkin 1987: 213–16; Whitley 1994; Ekroth 2015; Alexandridou 2017). One example of such a burial was discovered inside the city walls of Amphipolis. The cist grave contained a cremation burial interred in a silver larnax with a golden wreath. Based on the fragmentary vases found within the grave, the burial has been dated from the third quarter of the fifth century to the second quarter of the fourth century BCE. The deceased was a Middle Adult male, suggesting that the grave belonged to Brasidas, the Spartan general killed at the Battle of Amphipolis (ca. 422 BCE) and buried in the agora with honours commensurate to his newly conferred status as hero and honorary founder of the city (Thucydides 5.11.1; Agelarakis 2002; Koukouli-Chrysanthaki 2002: 67–72).

A further consideration that complicates the study of non-normative burials is that there are cases in which the deceased was a prime candidate for non-normative burial but did not receive one (e.g. Reusch 2020). For example, an Old Adult male buried in a limestone cist grave from Hellenistic Thasos (ca. fourth to first centuries BCE) has been identified as an execution victim. The individual was interred among clusters of family graves, and his burial treatment was unremarkable and within the norms of the cemetery. Osteological analysis, however, revealed that the man's sternum had been pierced by a *styrax* – the spike at the lower end of a spear shaft. The blow to the sternum was perpendicular rather than overhand, suggesting that the man was executed and not a casualty of war. Since his burial was normative, it was been posited that his execution was the result of political or military turmoil rather than criminal activity (Agelarakis 2019).

Even though there are always exceptions, the identification of non-normative burials in ancient Greek cemeteries allows for the creation of a pool of likely candidates of social marginalisation. Each component of a non-normative burial assemblage must then be carefully analysed in order to construct reasonable explanations for the burial's deviancy, since these could range widely, as the aforementioned examples demonstrate. However, it is also understood that there are many cases in which the motivation behind an individual's non-normative burial might never be discerned, especially in cases dealing with soft tissue pathologies (e.g. mental illness, blindness).

It is expected, however, that some individuals who experienced social marginalisation were buried normatively, which complicates their detection in the archaeological record. Presumably, the decision to bury a marginal figure in a normal fashion would be made by family and loved ones (Boutin and Porter 2014; Boutin 2016). People with physical impairments, for instance, might fall under this category, and would not be identified until analysis of the contents and components of their graves revealed tangible evidence of their condition (e.g. skeletal pathologies, mobility aids like canes, prosthetics). Yet, the candidates for this category (i.e. socially marginalised, but buried normatively) must be identified with care, otherwise cases such as the execution victim from Thasos might be lumped together with them.

The second theoretical framework, materiality, remedies situations like these, as it focuses on the components of individual graves and facilitates the identification of the socially marginalised in normative burials. Materiality is concerned with the ways in which people of the past created meanings and identities through the active use of material culture (e.g. DeMarrais et al. 2004; Meskell 2005; Miller 2005; Ingold 2007; Van Dommelen and Knapp 2010). Material culture can embody and reflect relationships – it is through the use of objects that people are able to express, reinforce, reinvent and renegotiate social relationships because the acts of making, using, transforming and depositing objects have social consequences (Hurcombe 2007: 103). As a result, the distinctions between natural and culturally modified objects are not always clear, as there are materialities associated with artefacts, landscapes, architecture, plants, animals and weather events, such as snow, ice and rain (Fahlander and Oestigaard 2008b: 4).

Of all natural objects, the materiality of the human body is perhaps the most influential in terms of social interaction. For instance, variables such as weight, hair and skin colour, age, sex and posture affect an individual's chance of success in numerous ways and also influence how they are perceived by others (Fahlander and Oestigaard 2008b: 4). After death, the deceased's identity and social relationships become codified and fixed in the archaeological record through formal burial. Burial reflects complex social processes and constitutes its own form of materiality, called the 'materiality of death', which is a nexus of many categories of interactions, including the materialities of identity (i.e. age, sex, gender, ethnicity), interments (i.e. grave goods), social change (i.e. hierarchies), the body (i.e. the corpse) and practice (i.e. rituals; Fahlander and Oestigaard 2008b).

The first category of interaction, the 'materiality of identity', can be difficult to discern. Although it is possible for the deceased to have made preparations for burial prior to death, in most cases the dead are buried by their survivors, whose opinions of their departed loved ones might not be entirely grounded in reality. For example, by investing in an expensive burial container, lavish adornments for the body, exquisite grave goods and an impressive funerary monument, the deceased can be elevated to a status far greater in death than what they experienced in life (e.g. Sourvinou-Inwood 1995; Sulosky Weaver 2019a). Accordingly, the skeletal material of the deceased are the only material remains that undoubtedly belonged to the deceased and were not manipulated by survivors. While it is possible to determine a person's biological sex, age, height and physiological stress from skeletal remains, issues of social status, profession and gender are not quite as clear, as these facets of identity are primarily conveyed through material culture (Fahlander and Oestigaard 2008b: 11).

Many different types of objects are used during funerary rituals. Some are taken away with the mourners upon the completion of the mortuary rituals, while others, such as oil-bearing vessels, could be buried with the deceased. As previously discussed, objects buried with the deceased are called grave goods and can include the clothing and jewellery which adorned the deceased (e.g. favourite adornments, family heirlooms or new items acquired for the funeral), a selection of the deceased's personal items (e.g. weapons, toiletry boxes, prosthetics) or gifts furnished by survivors (e.g. oil lamps to illuminate the trip to the Underworld) that might symbolically reflect relationships that once existed between the now-deceased and the living. Since all grave goods are deposited at the direction of either the deceased or the survivors, the 'materiality of the interments' typically signifies the deceased's social persona (Fahlander and Oestigaard 2008b: 8–9). One's social persona is the combination of 'identities' (e.g. rich, mother, baker) that an individual chooses to use when interacting with others (Salamone 1982). Personal agency is involved in the creation of a social persona, as one selects what identities to tout, but there are also cases in which the agency of the survivors manipulates the social persona of the dead (e.g. the aforementioned example of crafting a persona that is 'greater in death'; Dornan 2002). Yet, regardless of who is responsible for the final decisions, objects interred with the deceased are purposefully placed and are capable of revealing relationships not only between the living and the dead, but also those that are shared among the living.

Although one cannot necessarily ascertain an individual's socioeconomic status from burial assemblages, it is possible to determine which materials were considered prestige items. During the Archaic period in Syracuse, for example, the dearth and apparent clustering (i.e. possibly for 'family plots') of mono-lithic limestone sarcophagi suggest that they were high-status burial containers (Frederiksen 1999; Shepherd 2005: 118). In this manner, there are social and hierarchical relationships that can be discerned from the material culture of graves. A political and social vacuum follows the death of an individual, and that void must first be filled in order to restore balance to the community. The restoration process typically takes place at the funeral, where the social status and identity of the deceased are affirmed and accumulated wealth is reallocated. Thus, by studying the material remnants of these processes, the 'materiality of hierarchies and heritage' conveys information about past social structure and the way in which it was transferred, restructured, reallocated and challenged (Fahlander and Oestigaard 2008b: 10).

Death directly affects the 'materiality of the body' as it transforms the deceased individual from that of a vibrant, communicating, living being into a corpse – an inanimate object. Although a corpse is without life, it is still physical and material, and holds the potential to positively or negatively impact the living. In the minds of the living, corpses are imbued with symbolic and cosmological significance, so they require special treatment in order to mediate their transition from the realm of the living to the realm of the dead and to render benign their potential threat. Therefore, the materiality of the body considers the active ways in which the living interact with the corpse through its preparation (i.e. purification) and ultimate disposal (Fahlander and Oestigaard 2008b: 5–6). Associated with the materiality of the body is the 'materiality of practice', or rituals, which can be difficult to reconstruct in the archaeological record given its intangible nature. Although many ephemeral aspects of ritual defy reconstruction, material traces persist (e.g. pouring vessels for libations, oil-bearing vessels for anointing) and can provide insight into their relationships with the transient performance (Insoll 2004: 67–71; Fahlander and Oestigaard 2008b: 6–7).

The materialities outlined above appear to fit neatly into categories, but over-lap exists. For example, aspects of the body, grave goods and funerary monu-ment work together to project a cohesive social persona. These interrelationships, revealed by the analyses of human remains, grave goods and ritual practices, are interpreted cohesively through the lens of materiality theory, which makes it pos-sible to reach conclusions about the lives and customs of ancient peoples. Thus, materiality theory makes it possible to discern marginalising characteristics asso-ciated with identity, such as non-Greek ancestry/ethnicity and socioeconomic status, as well as physical conditions, such as mobility impairments, from norma-tive burial assemblages.

INTERSECTIONALITY

In addition to identifying instances of physical impairments, socioeconomic status and non-Greek ancestry/ethnicity in ancient Greek burials, this book is also concerned with individuals who embody the intersection of two or more of these categories. Intersectionality is defined by Avtar Brah and Ann Phoe-nix as 'the complex, irreducible, varied, and variable effects which ensue when multiple axes of differentiation – economic, political, cultural, psychic, sub-jective and experiential – intersect in historically specific contexts', and the coalescence of these axes 'emphasizes that different dimensions of social life cannot be separated out into discrete and pure strands' (2004: 76; also quoted in Joyce 2017: 4). Intersectionality theory developed as a legal concept in the 1980s, when Kimberlé Crenshaw established that race, class and gender were three systems of oppression and privilege that interacted together and could not be studied in isolation from one another (Crenshaw 2017). One cannot, for instance, explore issues related to gender without acknowledging that the experience of gender varies dramatically between White women and women of colour, as well as between women of higher socioeconomic status and those of lower socioeconomic status. One-dimensional studies that focus simply on gender, class or race assume a priori that experiences of sexism, classism or rac-ism are the same regardless of one's position in society. As a result, this mode of thought fails to capture the nuances and complexities of the actual situa-tion – namely that an American who is both Black and female is subject to discrimination on the basis of race, gender *and* some combination of the two. Furthermore, other systems of inequality, oppression and privilege have been identified since the 1980s (e.g. sexuality, ableism, ethnicity, citizenship, age), and analysing the intersection of these systems has led to a greater understanding of both social structures and systems of power (Romero 2017: 8–9).

The inherent challenge in applying intersectionality to archaeological assemblages is that it is difficult, if not impossible, to perceive all of the different sociopolitical systems that could have impacted the lives of past individuals (e.g. Fahlander 2012; Mant et al. 2021). Sexuality and citizenship, for instance, typically are not manifest in funerary contexts. On the other hand, the three marginalising characteristics upon which this book is focused – physical disability, low socioeconomic status and non-Greek ancestry/ethnicity – are identifiable in the archaeological record, but only if these aspects of identity are embodied in a physical (i.e. skeletal indicators, body position) and/or material (i.e. burial container, grave goods) manner. Where possible, individuals at the intersection of multiple marginalising characteristics will be identified and discussed at the end of each chapter. Furthermore, since gender is a crucial component of intersectionality, and biological sex and gender are often discernible from archaeological contexts (as previously discussed), this is one area of the study that will pay close attention to issues related to gender and its impact on an individual's degree of social marginalisation.

SCOPE AND ORGANISATION

As previously discussed, this study stands apart from the rest as it is the first comprehensive treatment of the biological and funerary evidence for marginality in the ancient Greek world. The book is organised into four chapters. Chapter 1 presents background information and serves two distinct functions. First, it addresses terminology, providing definitions for key concepts such as poverty, class, race, ancestry and ethnicity. Second, it surveys ancient attitudes towards marginalised individuals gleaned from contemporary visual and literary sources. This survey is not exhaustive, and focuses specifically on the reception of marginalising characteristics under investigation in this book, namely physical disability, low socioeconomic status, and non-Greek ancestry and ethnicity.

Chapter 2 is concerned with individuals whose skeletal remains display signs of physical disability. The chapter begins with a description of theoretical models of disability employed within the field of disability studies and how they can be applied to archaeological investigations of physical impairment. The section that follows considers evidence for the practice of infant exposure, while the remaining portions of the chapter focus on physical differences that are detectable on human skeletal remains, namely differences of limb (e.g. 'club foot'), stature (e.g. dwarfism), the cranium (e.g. craniosynostosis) and non-binary sex and gender (e.g. intersex). The bioarchaeological evidence of these conditions is surveyed and discussed in the context of contemporary literary and visual sources.

Chapter 3 is devoted to individuals of lower socioeconomic status. These individuals will be identified primarily by their burial assemblages (e.g. burial receptacles and grave goods), but this is a precarious endeavour. For example, sumptuous burials do not necessarily reflect the social status of the deceased. Mourners of higher socioeconomic status could choose to bury their loved one with a paucity of grave goods and display their wealth during other phases of the funerary ritual, such as the *prothesis* (the lying-in-state) or the *perideipnon* (the funerary banquet following the burial). Conversely, mourners of lower socio-economic status might elect to spend their resources on lavish grave goods as a way of honouring the deceased. Expensive gifts that are perishable, such as textiles, represent another complicating factor, as they leave behind no traces in the archaeological record. Nevertheless, it is clear that certain objects are intrin-sically more valuable than others, and burials which contain them represent displays of wealth that are relative to the culture and settlement from which they derive (Parker Pearson 2005: 78–9). Thus, an understanding of cultural context is essential, and Chapter 3 begins with a consideration of the methods and pitfalls associated with discerning social status from burial assemblages. This discussion sets the stage for the subsequent survey of the limited bioarchaeologi-cal evidence of the individuals who occupied the lowest positions of the Greek socioeconomic hierarchy.

Non-Greek ancestry and ethnicity are discussed in Chapter 4. Ancestry and biological affinity can be approximated from skeletal remains (with caution; see the discussion of this in Chapter 4) through the use of metric, non-metric and genetic traits (Pietrusewsky 2014; DiGangi and Bethard 2021: 5). Ethnicity, on the other hand, while difficult to identify and interpret, can be expressed through burial practices (e.g. tomb type, body position) and grave goods (e.g. non-Greek items vs. Greek items; Jones 1997; Shepherd 1999). Thus, the chap-ter begins with an explanation of the archaeology of ethnicity and ancestry, which details the ways in which migration, ethnicity and ancestry can be iden-tified in burials. After this methodological description, the bioarchaeological evidence of ancestry and ethnicity is presented.

Details of the four preceding chapters are synthesised in the Conclusion, allowing for the formulation of reasonable inferences regarding societal atti-tudes, interpersonal treatment and levels of inclusion of marginalised people within the ancient Greek world. Most notably, this study reveals a fundamental discrepancy between literary and archaeological evidence. Even though Greek literary sources provide us with myriad factors that purportedly prompted social marginalisation, Greek burials tell a different story. Instead, they reveal that marginality was closely connected to intersectionality, because the individu-als who displayed clear evidence of social marginalisation were also those who embodied more than one marginalising characteristic. As a result, this compre-hensive analysis provides us with a better understanding of those who found themselves outside the realm of Greek normative practices and the reasons why they were relegated to the fringes of society.

NOTES

1. Marginality theory has its origins in the early decades of the twentieth century. The concept of 'the Other' was introduced by Georg Simmel, a German sociologist, via the notion of 'the stranger' (1908: 685ff.). Essentially, strangers are members of the groups in which they live and participate, yet they remain distant and socially isolated. In other words, 'they are in the group but not of it' (Wood 1934: 45). Heavily influenced by Simmel's work, marginality theory subsequently derived from the discourse of the Chicago School of sociology in the 1920s. The theory was first articulated by Robert Park, a founding member of the school, in his seminal essay 'Human migration and the marginal man' (1928), and further developed by his pupil, Everett Stonequist (1937). As marginality theory evolved over the course of the twentieth century, it was often criticised for its lack of precision and differential usage, and scholarly consensus has historically varied in regards to terminology and appropriate case studies (e.g. Weisberger 1992; Mehretu et al. 2000; Billson 2005). For instance, the terms 'social marginality' and 'cultural marginality' are used inconsistently in the literature – in some cases they are viewed as discrete typologies (e.g. Gist 1967), and in others they are used interchangeably (e.g. Billson 2005). Nevertheless, marginality theory continues to play an important role in sociological enquiry today, and the scholarship of recent decades has made a considerable effort to redefine marginality and redress past imprecisions (Billson 2005).

2. Since the marginalised are often systematically excluded from participation in various sociopolitical spheres, they are also the subject of 'social exclusion' rhetoric. The concept of social exclusion originated in the 1920s with Max Weber, a German sociologist who identified exclusion as a form of social closure – the process whereby a group monopolises scarce resources for its own use (1978 [1921]; Burchardt et al. 2002: 1). Modern usage of the term, however, can be traced to the 1970s. René Lenoir, who served as secrétaire d'État à l'action sociale of France, decried that a tenth of the French population constituted 'the excluded', a group that was disconnected from mainstream society and composed primarily of the destitute and disabled (1974; Sen 2000: 1; Allman 2013: 7). The concepts of marginality and social exclusion are closely connected – indeed, some scholars consider 'social exclusion' and 'social marginality' to be synonymous (e.g. Klanfer 1965). There is, however, a slight difference between the two; in particular, social exclusion is an outcome of marginalisation as marginalised individuals and groups can be denied access to societal resources and opportunities. Accordingly, social exclusion is a contested and problematic term, primarily because it, like marginality, has been loosely defined and imprecisely applied in the literature (Sen 2000: 2; Burchardt et al. 2002: 1). Although the definitions of social exclusion are numerous and competing, they seem to share a common understanding that 'social

exclusion is not only about material poverty and lack of material resources, but also about the processes by which some individuals and groups become marginalised in society. They are excluded not only from the goods and standards of living available to the majority, but also from their opportunities, choices and life chances' (Millar 2007: 2).

3. In Athens, ostracism was an institutionalised form of social exclusion primarily levied against elite males for political purposes (Forsdyke 2000; 2005; 2008: 42; Allman 2013: 3–4). Although it was practised frequently in the predemocratic polis, Forsdyke argues that ostracism in the democratic polis was relatively moderate. Ostracism became a symbolic tool in this context: 'the annual proposal to hold an ostracism (often without actually holding an ostracism) [was] to remind the aristocrats of the power of the demos to determine the political shape of the community' (Forsdyke 2000: 233).

4. For the history of the study of human remains in Greece, see Kardulias 1994; Agelarakis 1995; Bourbou 2005; Roberts et al. 2005; Buikstra and Lagia 2009; Harvati et al. 2009; Eliopoulos et al. 2011; Nowak-Kemp and Galanakis 2012; Galanakis and Nowak-Kemp 2013; Lagia et al. 2014. Also note that pertinent bibliography can be found in MacKinnon 2007; Alexandridou 2015; Alexandridou and Kaklamani 2018.

5. Note that this number denotes the small number of sites that have been analysed, and it does not reflect the much larger number of assemblages that have been excavated, collected and stored, but *not* analysed (Lagia et al. 2014: 113).

6. Note, however, that the Athenian Agora Bone Well (second quarter of the second century BCE) did not yield evidence to support the preferential exposure of females (Liston et al. 2018: 52). For more on this assemblage, see Chapter 3.

7. Attitudes towards women differed among philosophers. On one end of the spectrum we find Aristotle, who deemed women to be inherently inferior to men (*Politics* 1254b12–15), and Plato on the opposite end, who argued that men and women could think and reason on the same level (*Republic* 454de, 455d, 456a; Demand 1998: 70–2).

8. During the Roman period, Pliny the Elder (ca. 23/24–79 CE) remarks that young children were not considered to be fully human until their first teeth had broken through (*Natural History* 7.15.72). Also, see Zuchtriegel 2018: 97–104 for more on the dichotomy between the marginality of living children and centrality of lavish burials for children who have died.

9. See Neils and Oakley 2003; Neils 2012 for discussions of age and ageing in the Classical period. Also note that Ginn and Arber (1995: 2) argue that discrepancies between chronological/biological age and social age should be seen as parallel to those that exist between biological sex and gender.

10. For a cross-cultural study of initiation at puberty, see Norbeck et al. 1962. Female initiation at marriage in the Roman Empire is discussed by Laurence 2000; Harlow and Laurence 2002.

11. Age categories used are those defined in Buikstra and Ubelaker (1994: 9).

12. Boundaries between the different stages of adulthood are not clear (see Chapter 2 for further discussion of the transition to old age), but further distinctions have

been identified for younger age groups: infancy (birth to 2 years), pre-pubertal childhood (subdivided into a younger group of 3 to 7/8 years and an older group of 7/8 years to 13/14 years) and pubertal childhood (13/14 years to adulthood; Beaumont 1994; 2000: 40). These categories are based on iconographic evidence from Athens (Beaumont 1994; 2012: 24–42) and are confirmed by the Athenian mortuary record, even though divisions based on burials differ slightly. For instance, in her study of the Kerameikos, Houby-Nielsen separates the age groups as follows: infant (birth to 1 year), small child (1 to 3/4 years), older child (3/4 to 8/10 years) and adolescent (8/10 years to adulthood) (1995; 2000).

13. Studies of the correlation between stature and health in more recent populations include Fogel et al. 1983; Kunitz 1987; Riley 1994; Gunnel et al. 2001; Haines et al. 2003.

14. All long bones can be used to determine stature, but the measurements of the femur produce the most accurate estimation of height, followed by the tibia, fibula, humerus, ulna and radius. Methods that attempt to estimate stature from the clavicle, metacarpals and metatarsals exist, but are less accurate (see Bass 2005: 29–30 for a summary).

15. Note that some bacterial, viral and parasitic diseases leave biomolecular signatures on the skeleton that can be detected through aDNA analysis (Gernaey and Minnikin 2000; Brown and Brown 2011: 242–65; Mays 2012b: 289).

16. Although Keenleyside and Panayotova (2006) discuss this hypothesis, their research indicates that the lesions present in their study sample were likely caused by other health stressors as well.

17. See St. Hoyme and İşcan 1989; Smedley and Smedley 2005; Sauer and Wankmiller 2009 for a history of thought and scholarship concerning the identification of 'race' in human remains. For a history of thought and scholarship on 'race' in archaeology, see Challis 2013.

18. Not all of the postcranial adaptations are accurate indicators of ancestry. McIlvaine and Schepartz's (2015) study of femoral subtrochanteric shape in skeletons from Albania has demonstrated that proximal femoral morphology is dictated by biomechanical, rather than genetic, adaptations.

19. Laneri describes the reasons why funeral rituals are fundamental to the interpretation of society: '. . . funerary rituals are necessary to separate the world of the living from the realm of the dead, while reinforcing the memory of the departed individuals as a fundamental part of the social relations of the living . . . [they] allow social, cultural and religious identities to be constructed, negotiated and contested through symbols and metaphors that are part of the materiality of the performance of the ceremonies associated with burial practices . . . [and they] are a fundamental moment in which the entire community strengthens its social structure and/or dominant ideologies through the manifestation of common beliefs' (2007: 5).

20. Careful excavation of a grave can reveal the previous existence of perishable grave goods. Fine mesh sieving and floatation of the soil from the grave can retrieve minute seeds, pollens and faunal remains. Also, the presence of partially empty spaces or areas of soil discoloration within the grave can indicate the former presence of organic materials (Nilsson 1998: esp. 7).

21. This is not an exhaustive review of archaeological theory as it relates to mortuary practice. Instead, it highlights the most prominent modes of interpretation that have been used by Anglo-American archaeologists since the 1970s and the inception of New Archaeology. For example, see Lull 2000 on the Marxist approach and Fahlander and Oestigaard 2008a on materiality.

22. Burials that deviate from established cemetery norms are often referred to as 'deviant', but the recent trend in scholarship has been to eschew this term because of its inappropriate negative connotations and opt for more neutral terms such as 'non-normative', 'atypical' or 'differential' (e.g. Aspöck 2008; Quercia and Cazzulo 2016: 28; Scott et al. 2020).

23. 'Social deviancy' is another concept that is tied to marginality. Introduced by Emile Durkheim (1895) at the end of the nineteenth century, social deviancy can be broadly defined as encompassing any behaviour that violates cultural norms (Forsyth and Copes 2014: xxv). Since acceptable norms naturally vary across cultures, Howard Becker reminds us that, 'in addition to recognizing that deviance is created by the responses of people to particular kinds of behavior, by the labeling of that behavior as deviant, we must also keep in mind that the rules created and maintained by such labeling are not universally agreed to. Instead, they are the object of conflict and disagreement, part of the political process of society' (1973: 18). Thus arises a situation in which those identified as socially deviant can become marginalised.

24. Although cemetery norms are period- and culture-specific and vary from cemetery to cemetery, see Kurtz and Boardman 1971; *ThesCRA* VIII, add. IV (2012) 1.e. Death and Burial in the Greek World, 363–84 (V. Vlachou) for general overviews of Greek burial practices.

25. At Phaleron, see Pelekidis 1916; Ingvarsson and Bäckström 2019: 11 for seventh-century BCE mass burial of around eighteen individuals who were identified as prisoners. They were tied with iron bonds to a wooden plank (a so-called *tympanon*), indicating that they had been subjected to a form of capital punishment called *apotympanismos*. Once affixed to the *tympanon*, death was administered via cudgelling, exposure (similar to the Roman practice of crucifixion) or the progressive tightening of a neck collar (Aristophanes, *Thesmophoria* 2.930ff.; Fine 1983: 420; Kucharski 2015: 24–7). For fourth-century BCE burials of convicts from Akanthos in Chalcidice, see Trakosopoulou-Selekidou 1993.

26. See Parlama and Stampolidis 2001: 272–3; Baziotopoulou-Valavani 2002; Littman 2009 for collective burials in Athens (ca. fifth century BCE) associated with the Athenian plague, or alternatively, some other mass casualty event during the Peloponnesian War.

27. There are other cases of intramural infant burial – for instance, infant cremations (ca. fourth to third centuries BCE) have been discovered in the south-west corner of the Athenian Agora (between the Areopagus and the Hill of the Nymphs). It has been suggested that these were the remains of infants who died prematurely or were exposed by their parents (Garland 2001: 82), although the latter explanation seems unlikely. An increase in intramural infant burial has been attested for this

time period (i.e. Late Classical/Early Hellenistic), which presumably reflects a widespread social/cultural shift (Lagia 2007: 305). Furthermore, children receiving differential burial treatment is a widespread phenomenon. For more on the bioarchaeology of children, see Lewis 2007; Halcrow and Tayles 2011; Thompson et al. 2014; Beauchesne and Agarwal 2018.

CHAPTER 1

Definitions and Reception of the Marginalised in Art and Literature

To properly contextualise the bioarchaeological evidence presented in the chapters that follow, this chapter addresses pertinent issues of terminology and reception. Beginning with a consideration of terminology, key terms that are commonly used in discussions of ancient identity, such as 'disability', 'deformity', 'poverty', 'class', 'status', 'ethnicity', 'ancestry' and 'race', are defined and situated in their original cultural contexts. The focus then shifts to the Greek reception of marginalised persons by surveying the literary and visual evidence for Greek attitudes towards disabled people, non-elite individuals of low socio-economic status and non-Greeks.

DEFINITIONS

Many of the terms and concepts explored in this book are far from self-evident. It is tempting to think that the concept of disability would have an ancient meaning similar to our modern understanding, but they simply do not equate. Indeed, scholars question whether the Greeks even recognised disabled people as a distinct group or class. To address issues of terminology, the sections that follow present definitions for key terms that will be used throughout this study of social marginalisation, namely disability, deformity, poverty, class, status, ethnicity, ancestry and race. Each concept is discussed in detail and situated within its original Greek cultural context.

Defining disability in the ancient Greek world

Today, 'disability' is generally defined as 'any condition of the body or mind (impairment) that makes it more difficult for the person with the condition to do certain activities (activity limitation) and interact with the world around them (participation restrictions)'.[1] However, scholars are divided on the question of whether there was a word for 'disability' in the ancient Greek world and cannot agree on the corollary issue of whether the disabled were recognised as a distinct minor group.[2] Some maintain that *adunatos*, which is often translated as 'unable', is the closest Greek equivalent to 'disabled'. Walter Penrose supports this position through the assertion that those considered to be *adunatoi* were exempt from military service and given financial assistance in Athens (Lysias 24; Aristotle, *Athenian Constitution* 49.2; Penrose 2015). Others, like Martha Rose (2003; 2017), argue that there are crucial differences between *adunatos* and our modern word 'disabled', as the meaning of the ancient term is broad and used in situations when something cannot be accomplished: 'Herodotus, for example, uses the same term, "unable" (*adunatoi*), in the context of a group of people who are unable to persuade another group of people (3.138) and to describe ships that had been disabled (6.16)' (2003: 14).

Setting that debate aside, what is clear is that the Greeks did have a series of words that were applied to physical deformities. *Pêros*, 'maimed' or 'deformed', and its variations (e.g. *anapêros*, 'much-maimed') generally refer to any physical appearance that deviates from the norm.[3] Other words that describe physical differences include *aischos*, 'disgrace or ugliness'; *astheneia*, 'weakness'; *ateleia*, 'incompleteness or imperfection'; *kolobos*, 'mutilated'; and *chôlos*, 'mobility impaired' (Rose 2003: 12–13). What these descriptors have in common is that they reflect the conspicuous nature of physical differences, which were extraordinary and 'fell short of bodily or aesthetic ideals' (Kelley 2007: 34). Today, words like 'deformity', 'malformation', 'defect' and their derivatives have ableist connotations when used in reference to persons with disabilities. Throughout this book, these terms are generally avoided, but they do appear in discussions of skeletal material where they are conventional anatomical descriptors.

Defining poverty and socioeconomic status in the ancient Greek world

The concept of poverty is slightly more complex than simply the economic condition of having little or no money or living barely above subsistence level.[4] As Clair Taylor explains, poverty:

> is better conceptualized as (i) a socially constructed category, which has (ii) both a material and a non-material element – that is, it is a social relationship as well as an economic condition – and (iii) it is created and maintained by structural inequalities (for example, status, gender, class) reinforced thorough (iv) a socially embedded discourse which often seeks to exclude, marginalize, or otherwise portray the poor as different from other members of society. Poverty, then, is the outcome of a process that is shaped by social relationship and therefore manifests itself differently in different time and places. Conceptualizing poverty as being the absence of wealth or lack of income simply will not do. (2017: 16–17)

Taylor further distinguishes between two types of poverty: absolute and rela-tive. She defines absolute poverty as 'the lack of sufficient resources to provide basic needs' (2017: 17). Relative poverty is comparative, as it measures poverty levels as relative to the rest of society. In Classical Athens, for instance, it is pre-sumed that the standard of living was relatively high and few individuals lived in absolute poverty. This assertion is supported by stable isotopic studies of diet (δ^{13}C and δ^{15}N, discussed in Chapter 3) from human remains in three cem-eteries from Attica and Athens: the Kerameikos, Plateia Kotzia and Laurion (Thorikos). From these analyses, it appears that the Classical Athenian diet was a nutritious one consisting of high levels of animal protein (meat and/or dairy) supplemented by vegetables, fruits and marine resources. Furthermore, average heights did not appear to be stunted, and there were no incidences of severe malnutrition in the samples, which suggests that basic needs were generally met and most individuals had access to nutritious food throughout the course of their lives (Lagia 2015a; 2015b). One important caveat, however, must be kept in mind when interpreting the results of this study. Although it is argued that the samples in the study represent a cross-section of the Attic population – Anna Lagia (2015a: 122) characterises the samples respectively as the 'upper social strata' (Kerameikos), 'ordinary people from demes of the urban center' (Plateia Kotzia) and 'slaves who worked in the numerous silver and lead mines of the locality' (Laurion) – it is still possible that the poorest individuals in the community were excluded in the sample because they were buried non-normatively. Nevertheless, patterns observed in Athens seem consistent with those of other Classical polities, so it is assumed that most people's basic needs were being met across the ancient Greek world (Taylor 2017: 17–18). For this reason, usage of the word 'poverty' and its variations in this study will refer to relative poverty.

The concept of 'status' is more difficult to define, as it is often conflated with 'class' and 'order'. Following Karl Marx, Geoffrey de Ste. Croix defines class as 'the collective social expression of the fact of exploitation, the way in which exploitation is embodied in a social structure' and a particular class is 'a group of persons in a community identified by their position in the whole system of social production, defined above all according to their relationship (primarily in terms of the degree of ownership or control) to the conditions of production (that is to say, the means and labour of production) and to other classes' (1981: 43). It is class, de Ste. Croix maintains, that underlies social dif-ferentiation in the ancient Greek world (1981: 42–69). Following Max Weber, Moses Finley objects to the use of 'class' because he maintains that there is no consensus on how to define it and a Marxist definition is not appropriate for an ancient society. A common example given for its inapplicability is that under the Marxist definition of class, the enslaved and free labourers should belong to the same social class – even though other factors make it plain that they do not – because neither owns the means of production (1973: 48–51). Finley prefers instead the term 'status', which he claims is 'an admirably vague word with a considerable psychological element' (1973: 51). Both Finley (1973: 45) and de Ste. Croix (1981: 42) agree, however, that 'order' is a useful term to describe the different types of juridically defined groups within ancient populations that possess 'formalized privileges and disabilities in one or more fields of activity, governmental, military, legal, economic, religious, marital, and *standing in a hierarchical relation to the other orders*' (Finley 1973: 45, original emphasis). For Classical Athens and other Greek city states, most scholars agree that there are three orders: citizens (privileged), metics (underprivileged) and the enslaved (unprivileged; Hansen 1991: 86). Some scholars have chosen to refer to these orders as 'status groups' and to use 'status' to denote the 'standing of each group within the resultant social hierarchy, together with its attendant privileges and disabilities, honour or lack thereof' (Hunter 2000: 1–2). It is this definition of status, which incorporates legal rights as well as social standing (Kamen 2013: 14), that will be used throughout this book unless it is qualified (e.g. socioeconomic status, social status). 'Class', however, will also appear in this book, but its use will be colloquial and general to refer to the tripartite division of economic status groups (i.e. upper class, middle class and lower class) that existed in Archaic and Classical Greek polities.

In order to discern a status group's standing in Greek social hierarchy, one must first understand the structure of the social hierarchy, which was predicated on political organisation. Across mainland Greece, political organisation varied over time and among poleis and ethne (see the last section of this chapter for more on ethne), but one perpetual common denominator was social stratification.[5] Beginning in the Early Iron Age (ca. 1100–800 BCE), settlements existed in two forms (Murray 1993: 55–68; Snodgrass 2001; Bintliff 2010: 16–18). The first, the scattered village type, consisted primarily of one-room dwellings. Villages were typically fortified, either in part or in their entirety, and many featured a chieftain's greathouse/communal hall (e.g. Lefkandi on Euboea, Nichora in Messenia and Emborio on Chios). The overall layout of the villages was unplanned and lacking formal organisation. With the exception of chieftains' houses/communal halls, where internal space was separated into rooms for feasting and other communal activities, the majority of the dwellings were small one-room structures. Presumably, the peasants who comprised the social majority did not require differentiated domestic spaces for social or economic purposes, and most daily activities must have taken place outside. The second settlement type was town-like. A town was a fortified collection of the villages previously described, closely clustered, and each village retained its own necropolis and chief (*basileus*), so the town itself was most likely run by a competitive oligarchy (e.g. Athens, Argos and Corinth). Regardless of settlement type, Early Iron Age social organisation was uniform, where 'a small warrior elite with a retinue of independent "yeoman farmers" controll[ed] a large body of dependent peasantry' and only the elite and middle-class farmers (and merchants) received 'the privilege of formal burial' (Bintliff 2010: 17).

Between 800 and 500 BCE, the city state (polis) form of government predominated across the Aegean mainland and islands. The typical polis was rather small, supporting 2,000–4,000 citizens, and consisted of dependent villages and farmsteads clustered around an urban centre which supported approximately 70–80 per cent of the population. Some poleis, such as Athens, Thebes and Sparta, were territorial states (i.e. *megalopoleis*) that often encompassed other towns in their regions or empires and could support upwards of 40,000 people. Sparta, however, was unlike any of its peers, as it never developed a regularly planned urban centre, retaining instead the close, scattered village arrangement of the Early Iron Age town-like settlement plan (Thucydides 1.10; Hansen and Nielsen 2004; Hansen 2006; Bintliff 2010: 18).

Major social changes accompanied the rise of the city state. The power and influence of the elite gradually and consistently eroded, and was replaced by increasing legal and political rights for free male citizens, including those in the middle and lower classes.[6] In many city states, it is likely that greater rights were extended to peasants because their labour was partially replaced by that of enslaved individuals, who were owned by virtually all free families with the exception of the poorest. By the Classical period (ca. 480–323 BCE), approximately half of the city states in the Aegean region had adopted a 'moderate democracy' where power was consolidated in the entirety of the free citizenry that was created by merging upper-, middle- and lower-class citizens into a single governing body.[7] The other half remained under the control of the aristocracy (in the form of tyranny or oligarchy), kings (especially in the far north of the mainland) or an Early Iron Age model where a large free middle-upper class dominated an equally large unfree serf population (e.g. Thessaly and Sparta; Archibald 2000; Bintliff 2010: 19–20). These systems remained more or less in place until the Macedonian conquests of Philip II and Alexander the Great in the fourth century BCE led to establishment of the Hellenistic kingdoms, signalling the end of the autonomous city state and its concomitant concept of citizen equality (Bintliff 2010: 26).

Defining ethnicity, ancestry and race in the ancient Greek world

Today, we use the term 'ethnicity' or 'ethnic group' to refer to clusters of people who identify with one another and share cultural traits that differentiate them from other groups. Common cultural traits typically include shared language, geographical locale or place of origin, religion, sense of history, traditions, values, beliefs and foodways, among others (Smedley and Smedley 2005). Often, ethnic groups are further bound by kinship and notions of shared descent, which are not necessarily predicated on biological relatedness and are often more important than actual biological affinity (MacSweeney 2009; Gruen 2013). Although there can be a biological component to ethnicity, ethnic boundaries are not delineated by biology. Instead, they are forged through social interaction. These boundaries are constantly negotiated, and group belonging is not fixed, but contingent upon the conscious choices of individuals (Barth 1969; McInerney 2001). It follows that ethnicity is situational and often political, meaning that ethnicity can become relevant or active (or the opposite) based on the context of specific social situations (Barth 1969; Cohen 1978; Hakenbeck 2007). In responding to social pressures and conflicts, ethnic identity subsequently 'creates group cohesion by clarifying inclusion and exclusion' (McInerney 2001: 59). As a result, ethnicity is dynamic, and ethnic groups are flexible, mutable and usually self-defined (Smedley and Smedley 2005: 17).

Ethnos, the root of our English cognate 'ethnicity', is a Greek term whose meaning evolved over time.[8] In Homeric Greek, ethnos refers to any type of homogeneous group, such as a herd or a flock (e.g. *Iliad* 7.115; *Odyssey* 10.526). By the mid- to late fifth century (e.g. Thucydides 1.18), ethnos means 'tribe', 'nation' or 'people', and specifically denotes an old-fashioned tribal political system that was often viewed as backward or marginal (discussed in detail later). In Xenophon we see a shift in the usage of ethnos, as it becomes an imprecise word equivalent to 'people': 'Of the ethne known to us in Asia, the Persians rule, while Syrians, Phrygians, and Lydians are ruled. On the other hand, in Europe, the Scythians are rulers but the Maeotae are ruled' (Xenophon, *Memorabilia* 2.1.10 as translated in McInerney 2001: 56). It is this understanding of ethnos, meaning 'people' or 'community', that becomes predominant in later sources (e.g. Stephanus Byzantinus, *Ethnica*; McInerney 2001).

Greek ethnicity is best described as 'nested'. Ancient Greeks had at least three distinct ethnic identities: they identified as Greeks, as members of a lineage group (e.g. Ionian) and as citizens of a polis (e.g. Athenian) or residents of an ethnos (e.g. Boeotian; Hall 1997).[9] Greek city states, which existed as autonomous units, developed a Panhellenic ethnic identity by the Classical period that separated them from the 'barbarians' who could not speak or reason in Greek (Hall 1989; Konstan 2001; McInerney 2001).[10] This Panhellenic identity – referred to as 'Greekness' or 'Hellenism' – is defined by Herodotus (8.144.2) as shared language, culture, religion and blood (i.e. hereditary descent).[11] These common denominators should be viewed as general, rather than specific, as regional variations caused Greeks to differ in terms of spoken dialect, cultural customs, religious practices (e.g. regional cults, regional religious syncretism, polis-specific religious festivals) and phenotypic expression (Cartledge 2002). Though still under the umbrella of 'Greekness', these variable traits were seen as signifiers of intrahellenic identities related to lineage groups and/or polis affiliation (Hall 1997).

The two major intrahellenic identities were Dorian and Ionian.[12] This divide was rooted in dialect (Dorian vs. Ionian), religious practices (e.g. the

Karneia was a Dorian sacred month: Thucydides 5.54; the Apaturia was a shared Ionian festival: Herodotus 1.146) and origins (juniority vs. seniority). In terms of origins, Greek tradition states that the Ionians were long established in the Aegean (in some cases, born of the earth they inhabited, like the autochthonous Athenians) before the arrival of Dorian invaders (see the discussion in Chapter 4 about the lack of supporting archaeological evidence for the so-called 'Dorian invasion'). Both groups continually redefined themselves over time (e.g. Crielaard 2009), and Dorian/Ionian distinctions multiplied through the course of the fifth century in response to the Peloponnesian Wars and escalating tensions between the leading Dorian state (Sparta) and the leading Ionian state (Athens). Ionian rhetorical constructs portrayed Dorians as upstart newcomers, while Dorians saw themselves as vigorous and strong in contrast to Ionians, who were weak, effeminate, fond of luxury and too closely tied to Asia Minor (Connor 1993; Zacharia 2008b).

Although Dorians and Ionians were the largest subgroups, there were other groups as well.[13] Among these are the Aeolians, who also had their own dialect. Beyond dialectal categorisations, Greeks were further subdivided based on their localised political community, which typically equated to residency in either an ethnos or a polis. In this context, an ethnos was a regional territory comprised of a people without an urban centre, central government or formal political union. The Achaeans and Aetolians, for example, were organised as ethne (e.g. Morgan 2000; Rzepka 2013). This social system predated, and persisted beyond, the development of the polis, and its people were linked by regional religious practices and kinship. A polis, or 'city state', is a self-governing political unit comprised of an urban centre and its hinterland, and notable examples of poleis include Athens, Corinth and Megara (Just 1989; McInerney 2001; Morgan 1991; 2001; Zacharia 2008b; Beck and Smith 2018). Although the distinctions between ethnos and polis appear relatively straightforward, there were some ethne that contained city states, such as Arcadia, Phocis and Boeotia.[14] In cases such as these, one would not swap an ethnos-based identity for a polis-centric one; rather one's intrahellenic identities would continue to compound.[15] For example, a person from the polis of Tegea in Arcadia would identify as both Tegean and Arcadian, just as Athenians would also simultaneously identify as residents of their respective demes and towns (Morgan 1999; Nielsen 1999; Pretzler 1999; Scheer 2011; Kellogg 2013).[16]

Greek ethnicities were not only nested, but also situational, as shifting sociopolitical circumstances could prompt an individual to assert one ethnic identity over all others. For instance, when regional or inter-polis conflicts arose, city particularism burgeoned, and polis identity superseded all other intrahellenic identities (Osborne 2012; Fowler 2018: 56). However, there was not a clear hierarchy, and city allegiance did not always come first. Thucydides (4.61) provides us with an illustration of how a regional identity became paramount in his account of the Sicilian Expedition. Around 424 BCE, a Syracusan named Hermocrates urged representatives of the Sicilian Greek city states to prioritise their common interests as Sikeliotai (Sicilian Greeks) above their civic (e.g. Syracusan, Kamarinean) and ethnic (e.g. Dorian, Ionian) identities so that they might repel the invading Athenians (Tartaron 2014).

The complexity of Greek ethnicity is a rich and fascinating topic, but only one facet – Panhellenism – is explored in this book. It is recognised that certain intrahellenic identities could prompt social marginalisation at various times and places across the ancient Greek world. For example, the priestess of Athena Polias sought to bar the Spartan king Cleomenes from the Athenian Acropolis because he was a Dorian (Herodotus 5.72.3), and Paros banned Dorians from the sanctuary of Kore in the mid-fifth century BCE (*IG* 7[5] 225; Hall 2003: 32). However, the interest here is to focus solely on the different cultural identities expressed by Greek and non-Greek peoples for the purpose of determining whether non-Greeks experienced social marginalisation during the Late Archaic/Classical period. The primary reason for this selection is because literary and visual sources suggest that there was widespread marginalisation of non-Greeks, and the same cannot be said for the various intrahellenic identities.

By comparison, non-Greek ethnicity is much more nebulous. Definition is lacking from the beginning, as the names of non-Greek groups and the boundaries of their territories are fluid. Although ancient literary sources provide us with the names of non-Greek groups, we do not know if they actually referred to themselves by those names or if they considered themselves to be monolithic groups.[17] We are also acutely aware that the meanings of names can change over time to refer to either different groups or different stages in the history of a single group. As a result, ancient and modern authors tend to use non-Greek names arbitrarily (Bonfante 2011: 9–10). In antiquity, for example, the blanket moniker 'Scythians' was used to describe a variety of different northern nomadic horse-riding tribes (Herodotus 1.215–16; Hippocratic Corpus, *On Airs, Waters, Places* 12–24). It was also used to specifically reference Iranian-speaking nomadic people who, from the seventh century BCE onwards, inhabited the steppes of the Black Sea region and buried their dead in elaborate tombs (Herodotus 4.2–3, 4.5–12, 4.17–27, 4.46, 4.59–76, 4.78–80, 4.93–6, 4.102–7). When we discuss Scythians today, we can offer more details, but our definition is equally enigmatic. Archaeologists define Scythians as:

[A] union of Indo-European nomadic horse-riding tribes that spoke a language derived from the northeastern branch of the Iranian linguistic family and occupied the steppes from the Black Sea to southern Siberia and into Central Asia ... Despite the wide geographic distribution of Scythian tribes, their culture revealed astounding consistency. The main archaeological feature of this culture is the so-called 'Scythian triad', which comprises a typical weapon, such as the gorytus (quiver) or the akinakes (short sword); specific horse harness; and a unique style of animal art. (Movsesian and Bakholdina 2017: 589)

The problems inherent in the ancient definitions are unresolved in this scholarly one – we still do not know if this collective group existed or what it called itself. In other words, it is unclear whether the disparate tribes we artificially unite under the banner of 'Scythian' would have even recognised or expressed a 'Scythian' identity. Despite their common cultural bonds, they might have asserted an independent, rather than collective, identity, choosing to be divided by difference rather than united by similarity.[18] Since we do not have enough extant information to carefully and precisely define non-Greek groups, their conventional names (e.g. Illyrian, Scythian, Thracian, Carian etc.) will be used throughout this book to denote a group of people with similar cultural markers living at a specific time (e.g. the Late Archaic/Classical period; Bonfante 2011: 9).

Ancestry is often more remote than ethnicity. Loosely defined, ancestry refers to an individual's family descent or origins, but ancestry can have both biological and social dimensions that do not necessarily correlate to one another. On the one hand, components of the biological dimension of ancestry are cautiously gleaned through analysis of biological phenotypes (e.g. biodistance analysis of non-metric skeletal variation) and genotypes (e.g. DNA analysis: mitochondrial DNA to reconstruct maternal lineages and Y-chromosome DNA to reconstruct paternal lineages). The social dimension of ancestry, on the other hand, is centred on narratives of kinship and descent. It is in this dimension that ancestry and ethnicity overlap, as membership in ethnic groups is frequently founded on, and reinforced through, notions of shared descent. Kinship does not always align with genetics because kinship structures are culturally prescribed social practices that have varied across time and geographical space (Brück 2021). As a result, an individual or ethnic group can have an understanding of their origins that is not reflected in their genetic profiles. María Cecilia Lozada provides a poignant example of this dissonance in her discussion of the reaction of the Mapuche Indians in the southern Andes to the results of their participation in the Human Genome Diversity Project:

> The project was designed to collect human tissue samples from a diverse range of modern humans in an effort to analyze and catalog the extent and patterning of genetic diversity. Using ancient mitochondrial DNA (aDNA), the Mapuche Indians were shown to cluster genetically with Amazonian groups, a finding that was at odds with their oral traditions regarding their collective past. In their view, they originated from a more local group with whom they had close cultural affinity. Many Mapuche

were not only surprised by the genetic findings but also quite upset, and they refused further participation in the Human Genome Diversity Project since initial results discounted their historical narrative. (2011: 137)

As the Mapuche example demonstrates, the construction of ancestral origins can be non-genetic, unquantifiable and strongly rooted in oral and cultural tradition (Lozada 2011).

Narratives of shared ancestry and kinship bonds were of particular importance to the collective identities of ancient Greek peoples (Hall 1997: 20–6; Malkin 1998: 134; Patterson 2010). Increased interest in genealogy is perceptible in the mid-sixth century BCE, and entire social communities used genealogy to situate themselves in space and time, tracing their lineage back to heroic, and often eponymous, ancestors (Hall 1997: 41). According to Hesiod's *Catalogue of Women*, all Greeks, or Hellenes, are descended from a single male ancestor named Hellen, and each of the major dialectal subgroups likewise descend directly from Hellen. Dorus, ancestor of the Dorians, and Aeolus, ancestor of the Aeolians, are sons of Hellen, while Ion, the forebear of the Ionians, is Hellen's grandson. Perceived ties of kinship could also cement political alliances and valorise requests for aid and assistance. This practice, termed kinship diplomacy, was frequently invoked between Greek colonies and their mother cities, but we also see cases in which broad pleas were broadcast to brethren poleis. An inscription from Xanthus in Lycia (ca. 205 BCE) provides a record of such a request made by an embassy from Cytenion in Doris. Appealing to their shared Dorian ancestry, the embassy asks Xanthus for financial aid to support the reconstruction of their defensive walls that had been compromised by earthquakes (Jones 1999).

In this book, evidence concerning both the social and biological dimensions of ancient Greek ancestry are considered together wherever possible. Primacy is admittedly assigned to biological evidence, as genotypic and phenotypic data are able to uniquely inform us about patterns of migration, gene flow and biological affinity. But the biological evidence is then interpreted through a cultural and contextual lens in order to paint a more accurate picture of human behaviour as well as population relatedness and identity (Lozada 2011).

Although ancestry and ethnicity are often conflated with 'race', these associations are erroneous. Race is not biologically predetermined; it is instead a cultural invention constructed in the context of specific historical, social and political circumstances. The confusion surrounding our modern understanding of 'race' is rooted in the way in which the word has been historically applied. Across the past three centuries, 'race' has had multiple meanings. It has been used variably to denote distinctions among groups (e.g. nationality, religion, ancestry, socioeconomic status, regional identification) as well as biological subcategories within a species (Atkin 2017). Over time, especially in the fields of anthropology and biological sciences, the result was that 'race' became synonymous with 'subspecies', and its use presumed that humans could be subdivided into discrete groups. We now know that there is no evidence, genetic or otherwise, to support this claim, and the physiognomic differences among humans fall within the range of normal biological variation (Tattersall and DeSalle 2011; Wagner et al. 2017; Fuentes et al. 2019).[19] Nevertheless, this particular understanding of race – the myth of race as biology – persists in the wider culture (Mukhopadhyay et al. 2014: 1–2).

If human biological variation is not indicative of race, then how do we explain differences among groups – especially differences that have been traditionally associated with race? Human biological variation can occur on three levels: species, population and individual. On the species level, humans are genetically homogeneous, especially in comparison to non-human species, because human macroevolution (major genetic changes) occurred approximately 300,000 years ago, and we have been one species with a single gene pool since then. However, microevolution (smaller genetic changes) is a continuous process and the source of biological variations that occur on the population and individual levels. There are four basic forces that influence macro- or microevolution: mutation (alteration in DNA base pairs at a particular location or locus that can be inherited – the only source of new human genetic material), gene flow (exchange of genes between populations through intermating), genetic drift (change in relative frequencies of genotypes in a population caused by random factors, such as group movement in or out of the population) and natural selection (selection for genetic traits that contribute to survival and reproductive success). Natural selection is responsible for the most conspicuous of human biological variation, because it is a mechanism that ensures that genetic forms better adapted to a particular environment prevail over other forms that are less adaptive. For instance, skin colour, which is a complex trait controlled by several genes, derives from the amount of melanin in one's skin. Skin acts as a form of natural sunscreen to shield our exposure to ultraviolet (UV) radiation. UV radiation is necessary for the production of melanin, but too much UV exposure is deadly to skin cells. Skin colour, therefore, is an evolutionary response to varying levels of UV radiation in the different microclimates. People closest to the equator who receive the most UV radiation have the most melanin and the darkest skin colour, while the people farthest from the equator have the least melanin and the lightest skin colour. These adaptions took place long ago, and the process was a gradual one – it is estimated that it would have taken thousands of years for the necessary mutations to accumulate through natural selection. Thus, natural selection and the environment work together to influence the genetic structure of human populations, and many of the adaptive phenotypic traits that have developed in response to environmental stimuli have been historically used as markers of race. Those that are not determined through natural selection enter populations through the processes of gene flow and genetic drift. Finally, although it is not considered one of the four basic evolutionary forces, culture also impacts evolutionary forces. For example, cultural inventions, such as agriculture and urbanism, alter the environment and impact population genetics, and some cultural conventions restrict mating across groups, such as socioeconomic groups (Mukhopadhyay et al. 2014: 47–68; Relethford 2017; Dunsworth 2021: 185–8).

Even though it lacks a biological basis, race still exists. Race is a culturally constructed classification system that dictates how humans are categorised and treated. Although we tend to view racial categories as fixed and immutable, they are culture-specific and fluctuate over time in response to power disparities and sociopolitical stimuli. Any form of classification reduces complexity and allows for the formulation of generalisations, which can lead to stereotyping (prejudicial or otherwise) and hierarchical arrangements. Race is no exception. It is typically a product of stratified societies and used ideologically to reinforce the legitimacy of the dominant group. There are no universal rules for the construction of racial categories: for instance, not all stratified societies have racial systems; some racial classifications are based on visible differences, like skin colour, while other cultures construct their classifications on the basis of other criteria, such as ethnicity, religion or language; in cultures where racial categories exist, races are not always ranked; and racial criteria and rankings can change over time (Mukhopadhyay et al. 2014: 89–91, 157–72; Gracia 2017). Nevertheless, racial designations can have deleterious effects on an individual's health and well-being. Ranked racial systems often promote the disenfranchisement of some racial categories, which leads to health disparities, such as higher incidence of morbidity and comorbidity and lower age at death. In this context alone, race and biology intersect as 'systemic racism becomes embodied in the biology of racialized groups and individuals, and embodied inequalities reinforce a racialized understanding of human biology' (Gravlee 2009: 54).

Race, therefore, becomes a cultural and structural mechanism for disenfranchisement. The American racial system illustrates not only this, but also how racial categories can change over time. The original system was binary and based on skin colour; one was either White or Black, and these categories were mutually exclusive (a child of a White parent and a Black parent was considered to be monoracial – Black). This changed in the late nineteenth century when Mulatto appeared as a census option for individuals of biracial descent. In the 1890 census, the Black racial options proliferated to include Quadroon (1/4 Black ancestry) and Octoroon (1/8 or less Black ancestry), and other categories were created as well, such as (American) Indian, Chinese and Japanese. Over time, new categories were added and old categories disappeared, but what stayed the same was the racial paradigm. Namely, that there were Whites and Non-Whites, and individuals of racially mixed descent were always placed in the racial category of the lower racial status parent (e.g. a child of an Indian father and a White mother would be labelled Indian). Race was considered to be fixed and permanent. People who fell under Non-White categories were historically seen as inferior to Whites, and they were kept segregated and disenfranchised through the enactment of laws and other coercive means (Mukhopadhyay et al. 2014: 165–6; Gracia 2017). As a result of widespread systemic disenfranchisement, racial inequality led (and continues to lead) to health disparities, such as higher incidence of cardiovascular disease, diabetes, stroke, certain cancers, low birth weight and preterm delivery (Gravlee 2009: 47).

As one might expect, race was not a straightforward concept for the ancient Greeks. The first complication is a matter of translation. Genos, the Greek word that is most often translated as 'race', is frequently used to reference birth or descent and thus is not actually suitable to be translated as race. Furthermore, genos is sometimes conflated with ethnos and phyle, which can also be used to signify people of shared kinship. As Rebecca Futo Kennedy explains, 'An *ethnos* is usually a group of people who share a government – among Greeks, the *polis* of one's origin is frequently an *ethnos*, while Hellene is sometimes a *genos*, sometimes an *ethnos*, and Ionian can be a *genos*, an *ethnos*, or *phulē*' (Kennedy 2016: 10–11). So it seems that the Greeks did not have a single term to denote the modern concept of race.

The fact that Greeks did not have a word for race does not mean that racial systems were absent in antiquity. Numerous scholars see evidence of racial (and racist) ideology in the ancient Greek world. Benjamin Isaac draws attention to racialised (2009) – or at the very least proto-racialised (2004; 2006) – attitudes that were present in Greek societies, as does Claude Calame (e.g. 2005: 135–56), Shelley Haley (e.g. 2009), Tristan Samuels (e.g. 2015) and Denise McCoskey (e.g. 2019). Most of these scholars point to the Greek/non-Greek dichotomy as the source of racial structuration; however, this approach ignores other nuanced distinctions that could lead to disenfranchisement, such as differences among Greek ethnicities, forms of government (e.g. polis vs. ethnos), gender and citizenship status.

Susan Lape (2003; 2010) and Rebecca Futo Kennedy (2014; 2019) have identified one clearly oppressive construct that rises to the level of racial categorisation in the ancient Greek world: the Athenian metic system. In Athens, race was formulated on the basis of democratic citizen status. Metics, which translates to 'resident foreigners' or 'immigrants', were a group of free non-citizens that included immigrants (non-Athenian Greeks and non-Greeks alike) and their descendants as well as freedmen and their descendants. In addition to having no vote or voice in matters of state, metics were required to pay a special tax and were governed by exclusionary laws that defined and regulated their status (e.g. they were not allowed to own land or a home without special exemption). One of the most poignant laws affecting metics was the Citizenship Law dating to ca. 451 BCE, purportedly introduced by Pericles.

This double-descent law declared individuals were only eligible for Athenian citizenship if both of their parents were native freeborn Athenians who were legitimately married. No child, for instance, of a female metic and a male citizen could become a citizen, even though this had been permissible prior to the law. The law was instated to preserve the purity of Athenian autochthonous descent, and just as language associated with purity is applied to descriptions of Athenian citizenship, language associated with disease and infection was used in reference to metics. As Rebecca Futo Kennedy notes: 'this language of infection and purity was used to segregate all non-Athenians into this category of "metic" that embodied institutional oppressions, dehumanization, and systemic abuses based on the supposed supremacy of Athens over all others – Greek or non-Greeks' (2019).

Even though race intersects with ancestry and ethnicity, it is, as previously stated, a cultural and structural mechanism for disenfranchisement that is closely tied to systems of power. Furthermore, Greek racial classifications were equally discriminatory towards non-Greeks and non-Athenian Greeks. As a result, the exploration of Greek racial ideology (i.e. the Athenian metic system) and its impact on individuals will be discussed later in this chapter and in Chapter 3, which focuses on issues related to socioeconomic status, but not Chapter 4, which is concerned with the dynamics between Greeks and non-Greeks and avoids discussion of inequalities among intrahellenic ethnicities.

RECEPTION OF THE MARGINALISED IN ART AND LITERATURE

In order to reconstruct attitudes towards the marginalised in the ancient Greek world, we must first turn to visual and textual sources. However, both lines of evidence can be misleading. Artistic representations, for instance, cannot be interpreted as documentary evidence of actual events, practices or attitudes. Instead, they are constructs composed of conventional types and motifs that are intended to convey messages or values chosen by artists in consultation with their patrons. These messages are culture- and context-specific and multivalent, which complicates their interpretation by the temporally and culturally removed modern scholar. For this reason, careful attention should be paid to all aspects of an artwork, for each detail holds the potential to reveal its meaning(s) (Isler-Kerényi 2015: 562–3). Moreover, Greeks rarely made 'art for art's sake', and even 'their most profound and aesthetically pleasing examples served a utilitarian purpose' (Smith and Plantzos 2012: 5). That utilitarian purpose imbued the art with agency. As James Whitley explains, since Greek works of art were 'created and used for a purpose, they are always entangled within a social and historical web of largely human relations, and they can never be divorced from practical human interests . . . [What matters about the objects is] how they "work" on (or through) someone looking, using, or touching them' (2012: 582). Understandably, the reconstruction of an ancient artwork's agency further complicates its interpretation.

Literary sources also must be read and interpreted with a critical eye. Ancient Greek authors can be biased by a variety of circumstances such as their socioeconomic status (e.g. the Old Oligarch), political affiliation (e.g. Xenophon), political agenda (e.g. writers of legal speeches) or gender (the majority of Greek authors were male). Moreover, marginalised figures might appear in various works as literary or dramatic devices. For instance, the physically impaired are objects of pity in Attic tragedy (e.g. Sophocles, *Oedipus Rex* 372, 412, 1033, 1035, 1178; *Philoctetes* 169–85, 225–8, 501, 507) and light-hearted devices of comic relief in comedy (e.g. Aristophanes, *Wealth* 266). The writings of the historians are also problematic. Consider Herodotus, the so-called 'Father of History'. Since antiquity, the reliability of Herodotus' ethnographic digressions has been questioned. Thucydides was one of his first critics. Although he does not mention Herodotus by name, Thucydides (1.21) assures his readers that he does not rely on hearsay or resort to storytelling, and this remark has been interpreted as a critique of Herodotus (Nippel 1996: 127). Also, some modern scholars see a wellspring of ethnocentrism beneath the unbiased veneer of Herodotus' ethnographic accounts. Detlev Fehling (1989) accuses Herodotus of fabricating his informants because he doubts that a non-Greek could provide such Hellenocentric accounts. François Hartog (2009 [1988]), on the other hand, argues that Herodotus' narrative is one of bipolar opposition, and that descriptions of non-Greeks served as a mirror through which Greeks were able to view themselves. The Otherness of non-Greeks was constructed in relation to Greek norms, with the practices of Scythians, Egyptians and Amazons in particular representing the inversion of Greek customs.[20] From this perspective, Herodotus' purportedly ethnographic accounts are structured according to Greek assumptions and categories to the point where his cultural relativism becomes ethnocentricity (Redfield 1985; Gray 1995; Romm 1996; Harrison 1998). But not all scholars share Hartog's view – for example, Rosalind Thomas (2002) calls for the study of Herodotus' writings within the context of fifth-century medical and scientific literature. From this vantage point, Herodotus does not appear to be ethnocentric, but rather one of many Greeks attempting to rationalise human differences. Thomas' position is supported by recent archaeological research. Askold Ivantchik (2011) carefully compared Herodotus' description of the funeral of a Scythian king (4.71–2) to archaeological data derived from excavations of Scythian burial mounds and concluded that Herodotus' description is reliable (see also Kim 2010). Ivantchik rejects Hartog's 'mirror' theory and speculates that Herodotus' source for this passage was most likely a Hellenised Scythian, or at least someone who had a detailed knowledge of Scythian burial customs and Iranian ideology.

Despite the limitations of visual and textual evidence, critical analysis of these sources can help us reconstruct ancient Greek attitudes towards the various groups under discussion in this book. The sections that follow discuss ancient Greek visual and textual evidence of the contemporary reception of disabled people, non-elites of low socioeconomic class and non-Greeks. The material presented here will inform and contextualise the bioarchaeological evidence in Chapters 2–4.

Reception of disabled people in the ancient Greek world

Literary references to disabled people abound. However, as previously discussed, these sources must be consulted with caution (Bredberg 1999; Roberts 1999: 81). Literary texts are often complicit in the 'ideology of the physical', as they 'embody the prejudices and debilitating attitudes of their own historical moments of production', and thus literature is both 'a utilitarian tool of transformation and a medium for further stigmatizing disability in the imaginations of its audience' (Mitchell and Snyder 1997: 13). For example, disabled characters in Athenian tragedies are viewed with a mixture of pity and contempt, while they are light-hearted devices of comic relief in Athenian comedies (Pütz 2007; Garland 2017).[21] Furthermore, although literary texts in general convey stereotypes and/or popular attitudes towards disabled people, they can be contradictory. If we consider disabled veterans, for instance, they might be praised for their bravery and virtue (Herodotus 6.115; Edwards 2012), but their physical appearance could cause them to be shunned, abandoned by their loved ones, and prohibited from performing religious rites (Sophocles, *Philoctetes*; Quintus Curtius 5.5.5–24; Miles 2003; Edwards 2012).[22] As Christian Laes explains, '[i]n a society where beautiful bodies were very much in favour as a sign of righteous and moral excellence, a conflict could arise between the veteran's deformed appearance and his inner virtue' (2011a: 936).

Like literary evidence, art is also a biased source of information (Weiler 2012; Dasen 2017). Greek representations of disabled people primarily date to the Hellenistic period and respond to artists' increasing interest in imperfect bodies – a rejection of the idealised bodies and forms of the Classical period (Pollitt 1986: 1–16; Stewart 2014; Jenkins 2015). Rather than providing reflections of contemporary realities, the Hellenistic iconography of physical difference was symbolic, and depictions of disabled people were used as apotropaic devices, lucky talismans and introspective stimuli (Trentin 2015: 92–3).

Interpretations of these literary and artistic sources vary widely, and scholars disagree on the issue of whether disabled people were socially integrated or socially marginalised in the ancient Greek world. One position maintains that ancient Greek cities, to a much greater degree than modern ones, were populated by people with a wide array of physical impairments (Rose 2003; 2017; Garland 2010: 178–9), and that 'people with even the most severe disabilities were integrated into communities that accommodated all ranges of ability'

(Rose 2003: 99).[23] Consequently, disabled people were not marginalised as long as they could participate to some extent in the socioeconomic life of their polis (Edwards 1997a: 35). The opposing view asserts that there was a marked distinction between those who were physically impaired and those who were not that often (but not exclusively) resulted in the marginalisation of the impaired (Vlahogiannis 1998: 18; Stiker 1999: ix, 24, 39–42; Penrose 2015: 502).[24] This position is typically supported by ancient Greek religion (Vlahogiannis 1998: 28–33; Dillon 2017: 169–70; Wilgaux 2018), as 'beauty and wholeness were regarded as a mark of divine favour, whereas ugliness and deformity were interpreted as a sign of the opposite' (Garland 2010: 2).[25] Plato reinforces these beliefs in his utopian *Laws* (6.759c), where he states that priests and priestesses should be physically perfect and legitimately born.

To further complicate the issue of social integration, attitudes towards disabled people most likely varied from polis to polis. For instance, the Athenians exempted those with physical impairments from military service and provided them with financial support (Dillon 1995: 30; 2017: 171). Literary evidence suggests that Sparta, on the other hand, did not always recognise physical impairments as an impediment to military service. Herodotus' account of Aristodemus illustrates this (7.229–31, 9.71). At Thermopylae, he contracted ophthalmia, a severe inflammation of the eye. Even though Leonidas acknowledged that Aristodemus was compromised and ordered him away from the battlefield, at home he was branded a coward and was socially marginalised until he was killed while attempting to redeem himself at the Battle of Plataea. Likewise, it seems that Agesilaus, despite his mobility impairment (Xenophon, *Hellenica* 3.3.3; Plutarch, *Agesilaus* 2.3), received the standard military training as a youth and later became king of Sparta over some of his compatriots' ableist objections (Plutarch, *Agesilaus* 3.7, 30; Penrose 2015; Boëldieu-Trevet 2018). Thus, since literary and artistic sources cannot provide definitive answers to the debate of social integration vs. marginalisation, we turn to bioarchaeological evidence in Chapter 2 to shed additional light on the matter.

Reception of the non-elite in the ancient Greek world

Wealth was unevenly distributed in city states of the ancient Greek world, so the poor were an ever-present component of society (Ober 1989: 192). In Thucydides' account of Pericles' funerary oration, it is made clear that there is no shame in being poor (2.37), but those who take no steps to avoid it have much to be ashamed of (2.40; Morris 2001: 125–6). Poverty was shameful and undesirable for many reasons, but primarily because it caused men to do undignified things and made them candidates for exploitation (Morris 2000: 116). Furthermore, the elite perspective linked wealth with virtue, so the absence of wealth was viewed as moral inferiority. The poor thus become equated with the 'bad' or the 'base' (Plato, *Gorgias* 478a; Isocrates 7.45; Demosthenes 57.36; Taylor 2017: 32–3). Nevertheless, impoverished individuals in most Greek polities were distributed among the three major status groups: citizens, metics and the enslaved.[26]

Beginning with citizens, it is estimated that 7.5–9% of citizens owned 30–5% of the land in Attica, 70–5% of citizens owned the remaining 60–5% of the land, and approximately 20% of citizens owned little or no land (Osborne 1991: 128–36; 1992; Foxhall 1992; Ober 2018: 20–1).[27] Based on those percentages, it is reasonable to assume that the bottom 20% of the Athenian citizenry was impoverished, especially since land was considered to be superior over all other forms of wealth (Burford 1972: 29). Many of these individuals would have been peasant farmers, who tilled the land of others outside of the urban centre, in the hinterland. Their location, and by extension socioeconomic status, ensured their marginalisation as it excluded them from regular participation in the political, athletic and social activities that were among the privileges of citizenship (Zuchtriegel 2018: 194). The people of the countryside were likewise marginalised in literary and artistic representations. In tragedies, they function as messengers and other minor characters (e.g. Sophocles, *Oedipus Rex*), and in comedy, they serve as the objects of jokes and ridicule (e.g. Menander, *Disagreeable Man*). Furthermore, artistic renditions of the countryside primarily consist of idyllic, bucolic scenes that typically omit labour and those who would have performed it (Osborne 1987: 18–21). A notable exception to this general trend is scenes of grape- and olive-gathering on Athenian vases.[28] Although these scenes show figures working, iconographic conventions indicate that the labourers are individuals of low social status. For instance, on an Attic black-figure amphora by the Antimenes Painter (ca. 520 BCE), four male figures harvest olives (Fig. 1.1). Three of the figures are dressed in loincloths, but the centrally placed figure who is crouching behind the tree is nude. His nudity in this context is an indicator of his low social status (Hurwit 2007), which is also conveyed through the distinctive cap that he and two additional figures (the figure to the right of the nude figure and the figure atop the tree) wear. Rustic caps such as these are often placed on the heads of labourers and servile figures to signify their status (Pipili 2000; Lee 2015: 49).

Other citizens in the bottom 20 per cent would have been employed as manual labourers or craftsmen.[29] Although there is some evidence that members of the aristocracy were engaged in craft production – for example, it has been asserted that the Kleophrades Painter, who began his career briefly before 500 BCE, was a man named Megacles, a member of the Alcmaeonid family (Kreuzer 2009) – the majority of craftsmen would have been significantly lower on the socioeconomic scale. Prejudice against individuals in these

Figure 1.1 Attic black-figure amphora (ca. 520 BCE) by the Antimenes Painter from Athens, Greece depicting a scene of olive-gathering (London, British Museum). Photo © The Trustees of the British Museum/Art Resource, NY.

professions, who were referred to as *banausoi*, was deeply rooted (Ober 1989: 272–7). Xenophon tells us that 'banausic activities are held in complete distain in the Greek cities . . . they spoil the bodies of the workmen and the overseers, because the nature of the work compels them to sit indoors, and in some cases to spend the day by the fire. Softening of the body leads to softening of the mind' (*Domestic Manager* 4.2–3 as translated in Burford 1972: 12). In some polities, the *banausoi* were denied full citizen rights, and Xenophon again provides us with a possible explanation of the logic behind this:

> Banausic occupations leave no spare time for friendship or the affairs of the city: the practitioners of such occupations are . . . bad friends and bad defenders of the city . . . If during an invasion the farmers and the craftsmen were separated out, and each group was asked whether it would vote for the defence of the country or for withdrawal to the fortresses, the farmers would vote for fighting, whereas the craftsmen would elect to sit still and risk nothing . . . The farmers therefore make the best and most loyal citizens. (*Domestic Manager* 4.2–3 as translated in Burford 1972: 29)

The low social status of *banausoi* is visually conveyed through art. For example, an Attic red-figure kylix (ca. 490–480 BCE) by the Foundry Painter depicts a scene from a bronze foundry (Fig. 1.2). Foundry workers are shown at the oven, resting, and assembling a statue of an athlete (presumably a high-jumper). The

Figure 1.2 Attic red-figure kylix (ca. 490–480 BCE) by the Foundry Painter from Vulci, Italy depicting craftsmen in a bronze foundry (Berlin, Staatliche Museum Inv. F 2294). Photo © bpk Bildagentur/Staatliche Museum/Johannes Laurentius/Art Resource, NY.

status of these individuals is signified in the same way as that of the aforementioned olive-gatherers; namely, they are engaged in labour, clothed in simple loincloths or nude, and one individual (heating a metal rod in the oven) dons a rustic cap (Lee 2015: 49).[30]

Aside from citizens, other social groups also lived in Greek polities. Aristotle notes that 'it is necessarily the case that city-states contain a large number of slaves, metics, and foreigners' (Aristotle, *Politics* 7.1326a as translated in Garland 2014: 152), and this was most likely true not only for grand and prosperous city states, but also small, agriculturally oriented ones (Garland 2014: 152). The latter two groups mentioned by Aristotle, metics and foreigners, are distinguished by their residency status. Free non-resident foreigners, called *xenoi*, lived in a polity for only a short period of time. In Athens, *xenoi* were required to have sponsors (*proxenoi*) who were responsible for protecting them and attesting to their status if it were ever called into question. Since *xenoi* were essentially visitors, they were not permitted to participate in government or own land and they were not required to serve in the military or pay taxes, with the exception of *xenika telê*, which was a market tax that was assessed if an individual wanted to conduct commercial transactions in the Agora (Demetriou 2012: 204–5). The lack of requisite military service and tax assessment, as well as their length of stay, differentiated *xenoi* from metics.

Metics, which translates to 'resident foreigners' or 'immigrants', were a group of free non-citizens comprised of both Greeks and non-Greeks alike.[31] Metics existed in at least seventy Greek city states (Burford 1972: 35), and their ranks consisted of immigrants (see Chapter 4 and below for more on migration) and their descendants as well as freedmen and their descendants. No Greek polity had anything that resembled an official immigration policy or quota. Immigration was, in fact, generally welcomed, especially in Athens, where immigrants were deemed to be economically beneficial, primarily because of the special taxes they were required to pay, but also due to the money generated by their participation in the economy (Bakewell 1999a; Ober 2010; Garland 2014: 152, 156).

Metics were politically and socially disenfranchised – they had no voice or vote in matters of state, and their actions were governed by exclusionary laws (discussed below). Although it might seem counterintuitive, there were numerous reasons that might compel an individual to leave their ancestral homeland for a place where their rights were severely restricted. These reasons were both positive (relating to the destination, a 'pull') and negative (relating to the homeland, a 'push') and were not mutually exclusive. Positive reasons to migrate might be economic, such as involvement in shipping or the prospect of better trade opportunities, while negative reasons could include sociopolitical instability or land shortage (Taylor 2011: 119–20). Immigrants came from all social ranks – upper, middle and lower classes. However, it was the middle class, primarily composed of merchants and craftsmen, who most likely had the greatest opportunities to improve their economic situations (Garland 2014: 153–4). Lower-class individuals, especially those who were manual labourers, would not have had the same economic potential, as wages were not particularly high. In fact, accounts from the construction of the Erechtheion state that enslaved and free received the same pay for the same kind of work (Burford 1972: 59).

We know the most about Athenian metics (Whitehead 1977). According to Plutarch (*Solon* 24.2), Solon was the first to permit skilled foreign workers to settle in Attica, in the sixth century BCE, with the provision that they brought their families with them. It is not clear, however, whether Solon's agenda was pro- or anti-immigration, because he also purportedly observed that Athens was 'filled with people who were constantly flooding into Attica from elsewhere in order to find security' (Plutarch, *Solon* 22.1 as translated in Garland 2014: 155). Epigraphic and literary evidence suggests that the reforms of Cleisthenes (ca. 508 BCE) were the first to grant official recognition to immigrants (Aristotle, *Politics* 1275b34–9; Baba 1984; Cecchet 2017), but the word used to refer to them, *metoikos*, does not occur in literature until ca. 472 BCE (Aeschylus, *Persians* 319).[32] Nevertheless, we know that after a statutory period of time (possibly a month, although the exact length of time is unclear), any foreigner seeking metic status was required to register for the right to reside in Attica, and failure to do so could result in immediate expulsion or enslavement. After an individual attained metic status, they were free to reside permanently in Athens, but they had to procure a citizen sponsor to act as their *prostatês* (guardian or patron). The sponsor most likely served as their legal representative and supervisor. Presumably, the sponsor reinforced civic and criminal accountability, because sponsors whose metics could not obey the law would reflect poorly on the reputation of their sponsor. This system was in place until the middle of the fourth century BCE, when the responsibilities of the sponsor were transferred to the courts (Garland 2014: 154–6, 159).

Athenian metics were required to bear certain civic responsibilities and were governed by exclusionary laws that defined and regulated their status. They paid a series of special taxes: the *metoikion*, a regular (possibly monthly) poll tax (one drachma for an adult male and half a drachma for a single female) and the *xenika telê*, a market tax for permission to trade in the Agora.[33] Metics were also required to perform military service (as hoplites or rowers) and participate in the religious life of the city (e.g. the Panathenaea). Although metics could freely take part in economic pursuits – conduct business, make contracts and lend money – they were not allowed to own land or property until the 350s BCE, when it became legal for the exceptional metic to receive land rights (*gês enktêsis*; Garland 2014: 156–8). They also could not vote in the Assembly or serve as a judge/juror (*dikastês*) or a magistrate (Watson 2010: 259).

One restrictive statute that significantly impacted the Athenian metic population was the Citizenship Law dating to ca. 451/450 BCE, purportedly introduced by Pericles (Patterson 1981; Boegehold 1994).[34] Before the passage of the law, Athenian metics could be granted the right of *epigamia*, or the legal recognition of the citizenship of children born of a marriage between a metic and a citizen (Burford 1972: 36). After the Citizenship Law was enacted, individuals were only eligible for Athenian citizenship if both of their parents were native freeborn Athenians who were legitimately married. No child, for instance, of a female metic and a citizen man could become a citizen. The law was instated to limit access to the resources of the polis and preserve the purity of Athenian autochthonous descent (discussed below; Lape 2003; 2010). A dichotomy was created between the two groups – as noted above, language associated with purity was applied to descriptions of Athenian citizenship, while language associated with disease and infection was used in reference to metics (Kennedy 2019).[35] Twenty years after the passage of the law, high casualty rates associated with the Peloponnesian War necessitated its amendment ca. 430/429 BCE to allow fathers whose legitimate Athenian offspring had died to adopt their children born to metic mothers so that these children might inherit property and preserve the family name. Pericles ironically found himself in this situation, and it was his advocacy that brought about the amendment (Carawan 2008). Later, in the fourth century BCE, restrictions tightened and intermarriage between citizens and metics was strictly forbidden, most likely because the offspring of mixed-status marriages were a perpetual source of anxiety and a threat to the integrity of the Athenian citizenry (Demosthenes 59.16; Bakewell 2008/9).

Although the law was generally not on their side, Athenian metics were still afforded a modicum of legal protection. If a metic was murdered, regardless of the circumstances, the act was treated as an unintentional homicide, which carried the maximum penalty of exile (Lape 2010: 48–9). Even though this seems an unfair and discriminatory law, especially since intentional homicide was punishable by execution, the law most likely represented an improvement in the legal status of metics from no protection to partial protection (Garland 2014: 158). Moreover, by rendering special services to the state, metics could earn additional rights, such as that of *isoteleia*, which meant they could pay the same taxes as a citizen (Garland 2014: 156).[36] Also, around 401/400 BCE, Athens granted citizen rights (not equivalent to citizenship) to the metics and their descendants who helped free the city state from the rule of the Thirty Tyrants (*IG* 2² 10; Bakewell 1999b; Garland 2014: 160).[37] On rare occasions, metics were naturalised. Even Sparta, the most xenophobic of city states (Thucydides 1.144.2, 2.39.1; Plutarch, *Moralia* 238e), granted citizenship to at least two foreigners – one was a highly valued seer, and the other was his brother (Herodotus 9.35.1). Likewise, Megara naturalised only two foreigners (Plutarch, *Moralia* 826c; Garland 2014: 152). In Athens, naturalisation was more common in the sixth century BCE (Aristotle, *Politics* 1275b36–7; Plutarch, *Solon* 24.4) than in the fifth or fourth century, but even then naturalisation was uncommon and happened only in extraordinary circumstances. For example, citizenship could be granted in cases of distinguished services rendered to the Athenian people (e.g. extraordinary financial or military aid), such as that of the freedman Pasion who was naturalised in the early fourth century, around 380 BCE. A successful banker, Pasion's generous benefactions to the Athenians earned the right of citizenship for himself and his descendants (Demosthenes 59.2; Carey 1991: 89; Lape 2010: 240–74; Deene 2011).[38]

Part of the impetus behind the strict separation of citizens and metics was the Athenian belief in their autochthonous origins (Loraux 2000).[39] Athenians understood that most other Greeks were of mixed descent (an Athenian and a foreigner, e.g. Euripides' *Ion*), whereas they themselves had originated from the soil of Attica and were pure, indigenous inhabitants of their native land (e.g. Plato, *Critias* 109d; Kennedy 2016: 15).[40] Autochthony was hereditary – the earliest Athenian kings, Cecrops and Erechtheus, were believed to have been born from the earth, and all Athenians were descended from these two men. Although the figures of Cecrops and Erechtheus were well established in Athenian legend and cult in the Archaic period, their artistic representations are not explicitly tied to the ideology of autochthony until around 490 BCE (Shapiro 1998; Cohen 2001: 241). After that point, depictions of the birth of Erechtheus, which took place on the Acropolis in the heart of Athens, became the visual illustrations of the concept of autochthony (Shapiro 1998). An example of the birth of Erechtheus that features both Cecrops and Erechtheus can be seen on a red-figure kylix cup (ca. 440–430 BCE) from Tarquinia (Italy) by the Codrus Painter (Fig. 1.3).

The myth of Athenian autochthony validated and supported Athenian exceptionalism. Autochthony was embedded in public discourse (Loraux 1986: 148–50; Pelling 2009; Kennedy 2016: 15) and provided as an explanation for Athens' rapid rise to power after the Persian Wars. Moreover, autochthonous descent was preserved through the aforementioned Citizenship Law of ca. 451/450 BCE (Clements 2016: 316). In order to perpetuate their autochthony, the Athenian citizenry needed to be 'pure'. To be otherwise was to be 'mixed' and inferior, so interactions between autochthonous Athenians and others needed to be carefully regulated (Kennedy 2016: 13–17).

Athenian autochthony underpinned their superior racial identity and justified their marginalisation of metics (Lape 2003; 2010; Kennedy 2014). As previously discussed, race is a cultural and structural mechanism for disenfranchisement that is used to reinforce the legitimacy and supremacy of the dominant group. Racial categories are culture-specific and fluctuate over time in response to power disparities and sociopolitical stimuli (Mukhopadhyay et al. 2014: 89–91, 157–72; Gracia 2017). In the case of the Athenians, their autochthony united them and served not only as the basis for political equality among citizens, but also for their inherent superiority. As Alan Shapiro notes,

Figure 1.3 Attic red-figure kylix (ca. 440–430 BCE) by the Codrus Painter from Tarquinia, Italy depicting the birth of Erechtheus (Berlin, Staatliche Museum Inv. F 2537). In the centre of the composition, Gaea emerges from the earth and hands the young Erechtheus to Athena as Cecrops (left), Hephaestus and Herse (right) look on. Photo © bpk Bildagentur/Staatliche Museum/Johannes Laurentius/Art Resource, NY.

autochthony implies 'that the Athenians are an older, purer, and nobler race than other Greeks, and hence natural born leaders of an alliance. They are the chosen people, as it were, favored and protected in their enterprise by the whole host of Olympian gods' (1998: 131). Autochthony, or lack thereof, also provided a rationalisation for the denial of political equality to metics (Lape 2010).

It is undisputed that metics were socially and politically disenfranchised, but there is some scholarly disagreement concerning the Athenian reception of metics. One position is that attitudes towards metics were generally favourable as long as metics abided by the laws, maintained their civic loyalty and stayed out of trouble (e.g. Euripides, *Suppliant Women* 891–900). The orator Lysias, for example, describes the behaviour of model metics: 'Neither my father nor my brothers nor myself ever appeared as prosecutors or defendants in any lawsuit. On the contrary, we conducted ourselves under the democracy in such a way as neither to cause nor to receive offence' (12.4 as translated in Garland 2014: 163). The opposing position, however, maintains that Athenian citizens exhibited perpetual anxiety towards metics (e.g. Wallace 2010; Bakewell 2013). Even though the Athenian racial system was founded on the supposition that there were natural differences between citizens and metics, Demetra Kasimis (2018) maintains that works by Euripides (*Ion*), Plato (*Republic*) and Demosthenes (57, *Against Euboulides*) demonstrate how metics could masquerade as citizens with relative ease. Far from innocent, any case of mistaken (or fabricated) identity bore the potential to muddy the purity of the Athenian citizenship. As a result, it was crucial that the citizen body define, regulate and supervise the metic population (Kasimis 2018: xv).

Moreover, attitudes towards metics shifted in response to sociopolitical stimuli. In times of war, latent tensions and hostilities towards metics could manifest. Sometimes these would result in persecution, as was the case in Syracuse in south-eastern Sicily ca. 396 BCE when the tyrant, Dionysius I, declared war on Carthage and his subjects responded by expelling many wealthy resident Carthaginians from Sicilian Greek territories. Diodorus Siculus paints a frightening picture of this event, as the Sicilian Greeks terrorised the Carthaginians 'not only by plundering their property, but also by seizing them and subjecting their bodies to all manner of torture and insult' (14.46.3 as translated in Garland 2014: 153). This extreme and pre-emptive reaction also might have been rooted in the understanding that metic loyalties become suspect during times of war. During the Sicilian Expedition, for example, Nicias reported to Athens that their fleet strength was declining because metics were deserting their posts and returning to their cities of origin (Thucydides 7.13.2, 7.63.3). Metic flight must have been a common occurrence, as Aeneas Tacticus (10.8) notes that the movements of citizens and foreigners were typically limited during times of war, and the orator Hyperides (3.29, 33) references an Athenian law (of uncertain date) that forbids metics from leaving Athens during wartime (Garland 2014: 163–4).

The degree and extent of prejudice directed towards the average metic would have been predicated on individual status and identity. Non-Greek metics presumably faced more casual prejudice than Greek ones (Whitehead 1977: 109–14). Xenophon (*Ways and Means* 2.3), for instance, was uncomfortable with the numbers of non-Greeks claiming metic status and thought it inappropriate that citizens were required to serve in the army alongside them (Garland 2014: 162). The servile origins of freedman metics, and even their descendants, could likewise be a source of prejudice, as courtroom speeches reveal that freedmen experienced considerable bias because they were considered to be 'irredeemably steeped in servile blood' (Lysias 13.18, 64; Demosthenes 22.61; Isaeus 6.49; Whitehead 1977: 114–16). Furthermore, poor metics – especially those engaged in professions requiring manual labour – might have encountered more discrimination than their wealthier counterparts (Whitehead 1977: 116–21). Metics, in general, were closely associated with money because what was known about them centred on financial issues. For example, they left their homes for better economic opportunities, and the majority were middle-class merchants and craftsmen (not farmers). Also, metics could not invest their money in the same manner as Athenian citizens (i.e. in property), so their assets were portable, less visible, and cause for speculation concerning the extent of their wealth (Bakewell 1999b: 10–11). Since metics had a reputation for being wealthy, poor metics were most likely deemed to be flawed in some serious manner. Metics who served as manual labourers or craftsmen almost certainly experienced additional discrimination on account of their occupation, as Greeks held great disdain for banausic employment and those engaged in it (Burford 1972: 12, 29).

The enslaved were another group that routinely engaged in banausic activities.[41] In the ancient world, slavery originated in the Near East long before the period of state formation in chieftaincies and nomadic groups, and the earliest enslaved people were most likely prisoners of war (Snell 2011: 6–7). From the Near East, the practice (with regional variations) spread to Egypt, the Aegean and the rest of the Mediterranean (Lewis 2018a: 93–266). The first documented evidence of enslaved individuals in the Aegean comes from Mycenaean Linear B tablets from Knossos and Pylos dating to the fourteenth and thirteenth centuries BCE (Andreau and Descat 2011: 17–19). Mentions of slavery are later pervasive from the works of Homer (e.g. *Iliad* 6.455; *Odyssey* 17.323) onward (Andreau and Descat 2011: 19–30). Although slavery was widespread throughout most of recorded Greek history, there were some notable exceptions.[42] In Greek mythistorical tradition, the earliest inhabitants of Greece, the Pelasgians, were not enslavers (Herodotus 6.137.3), and slavery was not a regular practice in the regions of Locris and Phocis until the middle of the fourth century BCE (Andreau and Descat 2011: 8).

With the exception of Locris and Phocis, slavery was ubiquitous in the Classical Greek world (Harrison 2019). Even the poorest households had enslaved individuals, and essentially anyone could be enslaved – men, women or children, Greeks or non-Greeks – though most of the enslaved were non-Greek. The non-Greek enslaved were procured through military conflict, trade, piracy and coercion, then purchased rather inexpensively – in late fifth-century BCE Athens a slave could be bought for as little as 150 and as much as 1,000 drachmas (Xenophon, *Memorabilia* 2.5; Coleman 1997: 180). The enslaved primarily derived from the regions surrounding Greek territory, ranging from the Balkans to Asia Minor and the Black Sea (Thompson 2003: 3; Braund 2011: 126; Lewis 2015). Most non-Greek enslaved seem to have come from Thrace, Phrygia and the Black Sea region, but almost every ethnic group known to the Greeks was most likely represented in the slave pool (Wiedemann 1988; Coleman 1997: 180–1; Lewis 2011).

Slavery is the most extreme form of disenfranchisement. It represents a relationship of near-total domination, with power entirely vested in the slaveholder. There are three facets of power that a slaveholder wields over the enslaved:

control through the use or threat of violence, control through psychological or influential means, and cultural authority, which has been described as 'the means of transforming force into right, and obedience into duty' (Patterson 1982: 2). At its basest level, slavery is a substitute for death, be it death in war or death as punishment for some criminal offence. However, the prospect of death is commuted, rather than erased, by slavery, and the commutation holds only as long as the enslaved acquiesces to powerlessness. If, for example, enslaved individuals choose to flee or rebel, death is the likely consequence. As a result, the enslaved ceases to exist independent of the slaveholder and becomes a social non-person. To be a social non-person, without personal agency or family ties, is to be socially dead. In this way, the enslaved forgoes a physical death for a social one (Patterson 1982: 1–5).[43]

Social death manifests physically and psychologically. Physically, social death occurs when the enslaved are stripped of their identities, which can be achieved through the changing of their names, physical branding or castration. In order to be identified as enslaved on sight, the enslaved are often required to dress in a prescribed, visually distinct manner, which might include special clothing, headgear, items of adornment (e.g. identifying tags) or hairstyles, including shorn heads. Their physical transformation serves as a constant reminder of the loss of freedom and independence, which has been replaced by utter dependence upon the slaveholder. Psychologically, social death is instituted when the enslaved's social bonds are dissolved. The enslaved are removed from their natal societies and become isolated as they lose their own cultural, religious and genealogical heritage and are unable to pass any of it along to their descendants. Natal social bonds are replaced by those constructed and legitimised by the slaveholder, and often there are structural mechanisms in place that prevent individuals from forming new bonds and social structures in their enslaved environs (Patterson 1982: 54–76).

The two enslaved populations of which we know the most are those of Athens and Sparta. Classical Athens was densely populated, more so than other Greek poleis, and its imperial territory was vast, extending throughout the Aegean islands to the shores of Asia Minor. Therefore, the Athenian form of slavery was probably unique and not representative of other city states, which were mostly smaller and less cosmopolitan. In this imperial centre, the enslaved comprised a substantial portion of the population, but we are uncertain of their exact numbers. Ancient literary sources provide us with estimates of the numbers of enslaved individuals living in Athens, but these sources are mostly Roman, and their tallies are suspect. Modern estimates are also unhelpful because they range widely, proposing that the enslaved could consist of anywhere from 15 to 40 per cent of the population (Rihll 2011: 49–50).

The Athenian enslaved were chattel slaves, meaning that they were bought and sold on market exchanges. Their commodification was underscored by their subhuman categorisation – Athenian enslaved individuals were referred to as *andrapoda*, or 'human-footed things' (e.g. Xenophon, *Anabasis* 4.5.4; Wrenhaven 2012: 13–15). The enslaved could be owned publically (e.g. temple slaves, Scythian policemen) or privately (e.g. in households, on farming estates). When privately owned enslaved individuals were introduced to the household, their former identities were obliterated as they were given new names and welcomed with rituals similar to those performed for new brides (Morris 2000: 150).

As previously discussed, most enslaved individuals were non-Greek, which resulted in an enslaved population that was primarily composed of outsiders who were heterogeneous and polyglot (Cartledge 2011: 79). Each slaveholder most likely preferred to acquire a heterogeneous lot of enslaved people, because, as Plato tell us, it was easier to manage enslaved individuals if they came from different cultures and spoke different languages (*Laws* 777d; Rihll 2011: 71). This, of course, prevented them from organising against their slaveholder, which could also be the reason why the enslaved could not form legally recognised families (Golden 2011: 143).[44]

The Athenian enslaved worked in a variety of contexts. As Dimitris Kyrtatas explains, 'slaves were employed by all wealthy and even many poor owners of cultivable land; they worked in mines and quarries, industries and shops, brothels and temples, the stock-breeding mountains and the ships that traversed the seas, in private households and in the public sector' (2011: 95). Many tasks relegated to the enslaved were ones that were deemed to be distasteful, such as domestic chores, manual labour and handcrafts. Interestingly, public slaves were often placed in roles of responsibility (e.g. public executioner, keeping records of state debtors, measuring grain allowances) since they were believed to be less corruptible than free individuals or private slaves because their only personal ties were to the state. Skilled private slaves, however, were also given a remarkable amount of responsibility. It was recognised that these enslaved individuals, especially those that exercised sound judgement, responded to reward better than punishment. They were sometimes permitted to live independently in the urban centre or the Piraeus and were allowed to earn a living. A portion of their wages would be remitted to the slaveholder, and the enslaved individual was permitted to keep the remainder (Rihll 2011: 52, 60–1, 64–5).

The enslaved were afforded little protection under the law. Corporeal punishment was entirely acceptable, as slaveholders (and people who were wronged by enslaved individuals) were entitled to beat and whip their enslaved (Plato, *Laws* 777a–d). The enslaved were permitted to testify in legal proceedings, but their testimony was only admissible if it had been provided under physical torture (Demosthenes 30.37). However, there was a statute that prohibited homicide, and this included the killing of enslaved people (Antiphon 5.48). There was also a *hubris* law, passed by Solon in the late sixth century BCE, which protected citizens and enslaved alike from aggressive, abusive arrogance, especially in public (Rihll 2011: 51–2, 54; Wrenhaven 2012: 65–71). This law offered the enslaved a modicum of protection, but at the same time, they were not permitted to bring suits against their slaveholders (Aeschines 1.17; Morris 2000: 150).

It seems that third parties could intercede on behalf of abused enslaved individuals. In a letter on a lead tablet found near a well in the Athenian Agora, an enslaved person named Lesis desperately entreats his mother and a man named Xenocles to come to his aid (Jordan 2000; Harris 2004). The letter reads:

> Lesis is sending (a letter) to Xenocles and his mother (asking) that they by no means overlook that he is perishing in the foundry but that they come to his masters and that they have something better found for him. For I have been handed over to a thoroughly wicked man; I am perishing from being whipped; I am tied up; I am treated like dirt – more and more! (as translated in Harris 2004: 157)

In his interpretation of the letter, Edward Harris (2004) maintains that Lesis must have been loaned or rented by his slaveholders to a foundry foreman who is mistreating him. Harris also asserts that Lesis' appeal to his mother suggests that she has some freedom of movement and is most likely a metic, whereas Xenocles could be her paramour or *prostatês*.

If an enslaved person like Lesis was being treated harshly, they were free to seek asylum at the Sanctuary of Theseus near the Agora in Athens. Theseus was deemed to be an appropriate patron of the desperate enslaved, because the legendary founder of Athens was purportedly sympathetic to exiles and fugitives (Plutarch, *Theseus* 36.2).[45] Occasionally, enslaved individuals would be granted permanent asylum inside of a sanctuary, such as at the Sanctuary of Heracles at Canopus in Egypt, where the enslaved seeking refuge were branded with sacred markings to indicate that they were under the protection of the god (Herodotus 2.113.2). But, for most of the enslaved seeking refuge, the objective was to request a change in ownership. By providing the enslaved with recourse to improve their situation, Athenian slaveholders sacrificed a portion of the absolute control they held over their enslaved people. This sacrifice, however, was presumably a conscious compromise made to reduce the numbers of runaways and discourage uprisings (Garland 2014: 146–8).

Despite the opportunity for redress that was offered to the enslaved, attempts to flee were common in the Classical period (e.g. Demosthenes 53.6). Approximately 20,000 Athenian enslaved individuals fled during the Peloponnesian War (Thucydides 6.91.6, 7.27.5; Coleman 1997: 180). There were professional slave hunters who would find enslaved persons for a fee, which typically consisted of either a bounty or ownership of the captured individual. Upon their return, runaway enslaved individuals would be taken to the Anakeion, a detention centre for the enslaved, which stood next to the Sanctuary of Theseus. As part of the intake process, they were most likely branded with a symbol that would mark them as former fugitives. For instance, an enslaved person named Theocritus bore the imprint of a stag that signified his propensity for flight (Athenaeus 612c). Marks such as these would be placed on the shoulder or head of the enslaved individual. The length of an enslaved person's stay at the Anakeion is uncertain, presumably as long as it took for their slaveholder to either retrieve or sell them (Andreau and Descat 2011: 138–41).

For the enslaved, the only guaranteed path to freedom was manumission, and this was apparently common in Classical Athens.[46] Enslaved individuals who were paid could put aside a portion of their earnings to buy their freedom, but manumission was primarily an act of benevolence on the part of the slaveholder. After death, slaveholders often freed their enslaved in their wills, but enslaved individuals were also freed during the life of the slaveholder for extraordinary acts of faithfulness or loyalty. Once the decision was made, manumission was remarkably simple – the only requirement being a public announcement made by the slaveholder (Aeschines 3.41, 44; Rihll 2011: 56–7).[47]

Upon manumission, freedmen could become metics. Demosthenes (36, *For Phormion*) asserts that a person's previous status should not be mentioned upon manumission, and that 'freedom included liberation from a humiliating past' (Rihll 2011: 56). Presumably, this allowed freedmen a fresh start and an opportunity to relocate. Manumission records indicate that most Athenian freedmen worked in the urban centre or the Piraeus, but others clustered together according to their industry. Wool-workers tended to congregate in Melite and Kydathenaion (demes within the urban centre of Athens), farmers were spread throughout Attica, and those engaged in mining lived in southern Attica (Taylor 2011: 130–1). Metic status, however, was not the boon it purported to be, but rather an institutionalised way for slaveholders to perpetuate their dominance over the formerly enslaved (Zelnick-Abramovitz 2005: 333). As previously discussed, metics were not entirely free, as they were politically and socially disenfranchised. They were also required to retain a *prostatês*, and in the case of freedmen, the *prostatês* must be the former slaveholder.[48] There were, nevertheless, some freedmen metics who were able to become naturalised citizens, such as the wealthy banker Pasion and his own former enslaved person Phormion (Demosthenes 36, *For Phormion*; Rihll 2011: 60).

Shifting our attention to Sparta, Helots were radically different from the Athenian enslaved in terms of their origins and opportunities. In the Classical period, Sparta was by far the largest Greek polis, as its territory encompassed two regions, Laconia and Messenia (ca. 8,400 sq. km), and was roughly three times larger than the more densely populated polis of Athens. Sparta was also densely populated with enslaved individuals – at the time of the Battle of Plataea, the ratio of the enslaved to Spartans was at least 7:1 (Herodotus 9.10). Some of these were chattel slaves of the same sort as one would see in Athens (Plato, *Alcibiades* 1.122d), but the vast majority were serf-like Helots. Helots were Greeks who were enslaved as a result of the conquest of their land, and the Spartan Helotry was composed of people originating from Laconia and Messenia (Cartledge 2011: 74–7).[49] Helots were public slaves and described as serf-like for numerous reasons: they were originally conquered rather than purchased; their status was ascribed at birth; and even though a small percentage served in the military or in households, Helots were primarily engaged in agricultural labour on land owned by Spartan citizens. Helots also differed from chattel slaves in that they were permitted limited freedoms, such as the ability to enjoy family lives (which was encouraged because it produced more Helots) in their own village communities and retain their own cultural and religious traditions (Luraghi 2008: 138–9; Kyrtatas 2011: 92).

Although Helots enjoyed limited freedoms, they also endured extreme measures of cruelty. Helots were assigned shameful and degrading tasks, and they were visually set apart by their dehumanising wardrobe, which consisted of a dog-skin cap and animal skins. Each year, they received a stipulated number of beatings, regardless of their behaviour, and any spark of rebellious spirit was cause for execution (Myron, *FGrH* 106 fr. 2). Helots deemed to be particularly dangerous would be summarily rounded up and executed in mass culling events (Herodotus 4.146; Thucydides 4.80; Cartledge 2011: 87). In addition to corporal and capital punishment, public humiliation was another perpetual component of their lived experience. Spartans would require Helots to sing vulgar songs and perform grotesque dances. Helots would also be given undiluted wine, and once they were drunk, they were paraded in front of young men in military messes (Smith 2010: 137). The purpose of this exercise was to discourage overindulgence by presenting Spartan youths with a distasteful demonstration of drunkenness and to reinforce the proper manner in which Spartans should behave (Plutarch, *Lycurgus* 28). However, none of these indignities compare to the brutality of the Crypteia, which is described by Plutarch:

> The officials [the Ephors] from time to time sent out into the country those who appeared the most resourceful of the youth [18- and 19-year-olds], equipped only with daggers and minimum provisions. In the daytime they dispersed into obscure places, where they hid and lay low. By night they came down into the highways and despatched any Helot they caught. Often too they went into the fields and did away with the sturdiest and most powerful of Helots. (*Lycurgus* 28 as translated in Cartledge 2011: 85)

The Crypteia was an annual ritual that occurred when the incoming board of Ephors declared war on the Helots so that they could be legally and legitimately killed without incurring religious pollution (Cartledge 2011: 84–6).

Helots were institutionally oppressed in order to discourage open revolt. In actuality, this policy had the opposite effect, as it fuelled the Helots' hatred of the Spartans and fanned the flames of rebellion. As Paul Cartledge (2011: 87) notes, the Helots had myriad reasons to rebel: (1) they were culturally homogeneous and understood themselves to be politically and socially disenfranchised members of a solitary group, (2) they had a sense of what an independent and empowered future might look like, (3) in Messenia, they were physically separated from the Spartan centre by a mountain chain, (4) they enjoyed 'strength in numbers' over the less numerous Spartans, and (5) the effects of the Peloponnesian War, a massive earthquake ca. 464 BCE and splits within the Spartan ruling class prompted a period of sociopolitical instability in Sparta. These motives served as a catalyst for at least one major Helot uprising in the fifth century BCE (Thucydides 1.101.2) and two failed coups instigated by the treacherous Spartans in the fifth (Thucydides 1.32.4) and fourth centuries BCE (Xenophon, *Hellenica* 3.3).

Since Helots were publically owned, only the Spartan citizen body could manumit them. Helots were routinely manumitted during the Peloponnesian War, presumably 'to divide and so more easily rule an ethnically homogeneous and potentially rebellious group or groups, and in order to provide a new kind of garrison troops drawn specifically from these Neodamodeis ("New Damos-types")' (Cartledge 2011: 81). Over time, all of the Helots were eventually liberated. The Messenian Helots, and most of Messenia, were emancipated from Sparta with the help of Thebes ca. 370/369 BCE. The Laconian Helots, however, were not fully emancipated until the Roman conquest in either 146 BCE (after the Battle of Corinth, when Macedonia became a Roman province) or 27 BCE (when Augustus reorganised Greece as the province Achaea; Cartledge 2011: 88).

It was clear to the ancient Greeks that not all slave systems were equal. For instance, the Helots of Sparta were very different from the enslaved of Athens. In particular, Helots were prone to revolt, while the Athenian enslaved were not, and for Plato, this was grounds for declaring the Spartan system of Helotage to be quite controversial (*Laws* 776c–778a; Kyrtatas 2011: 91–2). The Thebans clearly agreed with Plato, as they took a strong abolitionist stand by liberating Messenia and its Helot inhabitants from Sparta – most likely because the Messenian Helots were fellow Greeks. However, it seems that contemporary fourth-century views were divided. Aristotle considered slavery to be the 'natural' state of a non-Greek (*Politics* 1254b19–1255b; *Nicomachean Ethics* 1161b6), and he maintained that the institution of slavery was necessary in order to free citizens for intellectual and political tasks. This ideology holds that slavery was good for the enslaved, who derived benefit from being dependent on their slaveholders. The dependency of the enslaved was rooted in their inherent inferiority. The enslaved were deemed to be less than human, as they lacked rationality, and their bodies were best used as tools. Although he himself was an apologist for the institution, Aristotle acknowledges that there were some critics who disagreed with him and found slavery to be repugnant and contrary to nature (*Politics* 1253b–1255b; Goodey 1999; DuBois 2009: 58–63; Hunt 2011: 40–1; Monoson 2011; Wrenhaven 2012: 139–49).

In literature the enslaved are typically represented from an elite perspective.[50] In Old Comedy, enslaved characters are primarily negative, as they are gluttonous, scheming and untrustworthy (e.g. Aristophanes, *Knights*; Lee 2015: 49), but the trope of the clever, useful slave was also employed for comedic aims (e.g. Aristophanes, *Wealth*; Akrigg and Tordoff 2013). Enslaved characters in tragedy are slightly more dimensional, and there is sometimes an inversion of roles where the enslaved act like free persons and free persons act like the enslaved. An example of this can be found in Sophocles' *Women of Trachis* (52–63), where an enslaved woman steps beyond conventional boundaries to provide her mistress with advice that furthers the plot. It is possible that these dramatic character dynamics mimic the close confidential relationships that some slaveholders were known to share with their enslaved individuals, as revealed to us by law court speeches (e.g. Lysias 1.19–38; Wrenhaven 2012: 112–21).

In art, as in literature, the enslaved are also primarily depicted from the vantage point of the elite. In Late Archaic/Classical Athenian vase-painting, the enslaved are most often represented on sympotic vessels, lekythoi and loutrophoroi (Wrenhaven 2012: 76–7). When they can be identified, the enslaved often represent the opposite of the elite ideal. For example, the enslaved engage in labour/servitude, are of shorter stature than their slaveholders (i.e. hierarchy of scale), are physically distinct (e.g. cropped hair, pointed beards, tattooed, non-Greek physiognomy, large penises, ignoble postures) and wear rustic (rough woollen tunics, goatskin jackets, dog-skin caps, laced boots or sandals, headcloths) or non-Greek dress (Morris 2011: 192; Wrenhaven 2011; 2012: 78–86; Lee 2015: 49).[51] The enslaved continue to embody the antithesis of the elite ideal through the Hellenistic period, when it becomes difficult to differentiate between representations of the enslaved and other members of the lower classes. The depictions are caricatures meant to portray old impoverished figures (possibly enslaved, possibly free) using standard visual tropes such as 'drunken old woman', 'tired peasant' and 'flabby fisherman' (Pollitt 1986: figs 154, 156; Morris 2011: 191).[52]

There are also many instances in earlier vase-painting and sculpture in which the enslaved are difficult to visually distinguish from free figures. This observation applies to representations of enslaved and free craftsmen in workshop settings, but it is particularly evident in Classical funerary art (Oakley 2000; Wrenhaven 2012: 102–7). Johannes Bergemann notes that metics and the enslaved are commemorated on sculpted grave stelae in the same iconographic manner as elites (1997: 146–50). Take, for example, the representation of the enslaved woman on the Stele of Hegeso (Fig. 1.4). The inscription on the stele reveals the name of the deceased, Hegeso, and her patronymic. The sculpted figural scene depicts an elite matron who is presumably Hegeso, seated to the right in a high-backed chair (*klismos*) with a footstool. Hegeso chooses something from a box (possibly a necklace) held out to her by an enslaved female standing to the left with her head downcast. The enslaved woman's status is subtly delineated by gesture (i.e. downcast head), dress and size, and these distinguishing features are only apparent after careful visual analysis. Compared to Hegeso's elaborate tripartite attire consisting of a long, short-sleeved chiton, himation (mantle) and veil, the enslaved woman is dressed simply – her hair is bound in a headcloth and she wears a long, long-sleeved, diaphanous chiton (the *cheiridôtos chitôn*). Even though Hegeso is seated, she is proportionally larger than the enslaved woman (DuBois 2008: 73–6). One might question why representations of enslaved individuals are included on commemorative monuments for the elite.[53] Although many hypotheses have been proffered (e.g. emotional attachment to the enslaved person), the most likely scenario is that it represents a form of conspicuous consumption. The enslaved woman is a signifier of Hegeso's wealth in the same manner as her fine clothes, furniture and jewellery (Wrenhaven 2012: 107).

Athenians expressed considerable anxiety over not being able to identity an enslaved person on sight. Even though the three social groups discussed – poor citizens, metics and the enslaved – were mutually exclusive, a 'blurring of identities'

Figure 1.4 Stele of Hegeso (ca. 400 BCE) from Athens, Greece. Photo © Nimatallah/ Art Resource, NY.

could occur on these lower rungs of the socioeconomic ladder (Vlassopoulos 2009: 347). The Old Oligarch, writing in the late fifth century BCE, laments that enslaved were virtually indistinguishable from free in Athens on the basis of clothing, general appearance and demeanour (*Constitution of the Athenians* 1.10). The issue, according to Kostas Vlassopoulos (2009), lies in the unique democratic opportunities of Athens, which extended citizenship to peasants, artisans and shopkeepers (as opposed to city states like Corinth, which denied citizenship to craftsmen). These lower-class occupations were also shared by enslaved people, and the inevitable overlap made it difficult to distinguish enslaved from free. Indeed, the social groups routinely mixed in professional contexts, as T. E. Rihll notes: 'on the Acropolis of Athens and elsewhere, citizens, metics, and slaves worked side by side, receiving the same pay for completion of the same task' (2011: 65). As a result, the only way a free Athenian could broadcast his status was by participating in activities that enslaved persons were barred from, such as participating in civic (e.g. assemblies, courts, religious festivals) and social (e.g. gymnasia, bath houses) aspects of life (Rihll 2011: 50). Acting the part of the citizen, however, was not always the perfect solution. From Attic oratory we know that the enslaved, foreigners, the children of the enslaved and others successfully masqueraded as citizens for periods of time (Lysias 30.2, 5, 27; Aeschines 2.76; Demosthenes 21.149; 59; Lape 2010: 186–92; Deene 2011: 168). There were also cases in which citizens and freedmen were accused of being enslaved (Lysias 30; Demosthenes 29; Scafuro 1994; Vlassopoulos 2009). This blurring of identities, which occurred freely during the lives of the non-elite, did not end with their deaths. It was paralleled in the burial record, as we will see in Chapter 3.

Reception of non-Greeks in the ancient Greek world

In an attempt to understand natural phenomena, Greeks developed multiple rationalising theories regarding the origins of humans and human differences. Hesiod (*Works and Days* 109–81; cf. Van Noorden 2015) asserts that the gods created five 'races' of humans, and he numbered himself among the fifth. For Hesiod and later Greeks (Plato, most notably), these 'races' were sequential generations of people who were born and then destroyed – they did *not* represent the ancestors of diverse human populations (Kennedy et al. 2013: xiii). The Golden race was the first mortal generation created during the reign of Cronus. These people lived among the gods in harmony and without toil. They eventually died peaceful deaths, but live on as 'guardian' spirits. The Silver race, created during the rule of Zeus, was next, and Zeus eventually destroyed them for their impiety because they refused to worship the gods. Upon their deaths, they became the 'blessed spirits' of the Underworld. The Bronze race followed, but they were violent and bellicose by nature, and eventually destroyed one another. They left no named spirits, but eternally dwell in the Underworld. The fourth race was the race of Heroes. The people of this race fought at Thebes and Troy and now spend their afterlife on the paradisiacal Islands of the Blessed. The fifth and current one is the Iron race, and theirs is an existence of toil and misery.

According to another mythological tradition, most humans derived from a single source. The first people were shaped from clay by Prometheus (Pausanias 10.4.4), but humanity was ultimately destroyed by a flood.[54] Deucalion, the son of Prometheus, repopulated the world with his wife, Pyrrha. They each threw stones over their shoulders, and Deucalion's stones produced men, while Pyrrha's stones yielded women (Pindar, *Olympian* 9.40–6; Apollodorus, *Library* 1.7.2). There were some Greeks, like the Athenians, who removed themselves from this shared lineage entirely and claimed to be autochthonous – born from the earth itself. But for those who traced their origins to the postdiluvian world, it was clear that humans eventually diverged into separate groups and developed unique physical characteristics, languages and customs. What was unclear to them was how these differences developed (Kennedy et al. 2013: xiii–xiv).

Competing, often contradictory, theories were advanced in an attempt to explain human differences. Early theories of foreignness portrayed people who lived beyond the known Greek world (*oikoumenê*) as either monstrous or marvellous, such as the monstrous Cyclopes (*Odyssey* 9.105–39, 9.171–298) and the wise Egyptians described by Homer (*Odyssey* 4.219–32; Kennedy et al. 2013: 3), and this theory persisted through the Roman period. Focusing on the monstrous, or physiologically abnormal, Robert Garland (2016) refers to this phenomenon as 'ethnic deformity', which he defines as the understanding that some subdivisions of humans radically differ from the dominant group (i.e. Greeks). The extreme reaches of the known world were those that exhibited the highest incidence of ethnic deformities. These include Libya and Ethiopia in the south, India in the east and Scythia in the north. By no means are the boundaries of these territories set – Libya and Ethiopia are often confused with one another, as are Ethiopia and India, and what is considered to be India in antiquity actually lies within the borders of modern Pakistan. The physiologically abnormal can be separated into two groups: hybrids (e.g. centaurs, satyrs, sirens and the dog-headed Cynocephali; Herodotus 4.191; Aeschines, fr. 431; Karttunen 1984) and humans with a striking anatomical abnormality (e.g. the Astomi from India, who lack mouths, or the Blemmyes from Africa, who are headless and have faces on their chests; Strabo 2.1.9; Pliny, *Natural History* 5.43–6, 7.25–6). Various hypotheses have been proffered to explain Greek beliefs in these extraordinary peoples. Hybrid creatures, for instance, were probably credible because their iconography was firmly entrenched in the art of Egypt and the ancient Near East. Furthermore, observations of congenital conditions might have served as a mythical genesis of these peoples – for instance, someone born with the fatal condition of anencephaly might have supported the existence of the Blemmyes (the aforementioned people without heads). Perhaps most convincing, however, is the argument that encounters with people who deviated from the norm provided tangible proof that others with outlandish features could live in faraway lands. For example, persons with dwarfism lent credence to the existence of pygmies (see Chapter 2). In the Roman period, Pliny the Elder (*Natural History* 7.1.6) uses this argument himself to justify belief in ethnic deformity. Pointing to the Ethiopians, he maintains that their dark skin is incredible to those who have never seen it (Lenfant 1999; Garland 2016).

The burgeoning fields of science and Hippocratic medicine led to the development of new rationalising theories of human difference and the reconfiguration of old ones (Kennedy and Jones-Lewis 2016: 1–2). An apt illustration of this is the merging of ethnic deformity with the novel environmental theory. Since ethnic deformities are found at the edges of the known world, physiognomic abnormalities were believed to be evolutionary responses to environmental stimuli. Though nameless in antiquity, today this theory is termed 'environmental determinism' and is formally defined as 'the notion that a people's appearance, habits, customs, and health all stem from the land in which that people originates' (Kennedy and Jones-Lewis 2016: 2). In the Hippocratic treatise *On Airs, Waters, Places* (12–24), much attention is paid to the ways in which environment shapes physique and behaviour. For instance:

> . . . the physique of a man and his habits are formed by the nature of the land. Where the land is rich, soft, and well watered, and the waters are near the surface so that they become hot in the summer and cold in the winter, and where the climates are nice, there the men are flabby, jointless, bloated, lazy, and mostly cowards. Lack of eagerness and sleepiness are evident among them and they are stupid and witless. But where the land is barren, dry, harsh, and harried by storms in the winter or scorched by the sun in the summers, there one would find strong, lean, well-defined, muscular, and hairy men. By nature they are hard-working, wakeful, stubborn, and independent. They are fierce rather than gentle, more skilled, intelligent, and warlike than others. The things that grow in a land also conform to the climate. These are the most diverse natures and physiques among men. You will not go wrong if you use these rules as a starting point for further observations. (*On Airs, Waters, Places* 24 as translated in Kennedy et al. 2013: 42)

The two remaining rationalising models – genetic and cultural theories of human difference – are closely tied to one another. Genetic theories are rooted in the understanding that physical characteristics are heritable.[55] An example of this is the belief in autochthony, namely that a people can be born from the earth and that they, and their descendants, are more 'pure' than other human groups (discussed in the previous section). Cultural theories, on the other hand, maintain that culture and customs (e.g. religious practices, social and political institutions, language) are linked to ethnic identity. In practice, genetic and cultural theories are explicitly connected because moral qualities were believed to be heritable (i.e. genetic), and would result in the structuring of political and social systems (i.e. culture). For example, in the case of the autochthonous Athenians, their customs and culture are derived from their autochtony (Plato, *Menexenus* 237b–238b, 238e–239a). Furthermore, genetic and cultural theories also overlap with environmental ones, especially in the case of the Macrocephali, a people with elongated heads who inhabited the edge of the world in the Black Sea region (i.e. environmental). They originally achieved their unusual head shape through artificial cranial deformation (arguably cultural), but over time the need for human intervention was no longer necessary as cranial elongation had become a heritable trait (i.e. genetic; Hippocratic Corpus, *On Airs, Waters, Places* 14; Kennedy et al. 2013: 53, 65).

Some scholars view *On Airs, Waters, Places*, together with Herodotus' *Histories* and Hecataeus' *Periegesis*, to be the first examples of ethnographic discourse.[56] Greek ethnography, which can be defined as 'thinking about culture from the point of view of an outsider' (Skinner 2012: 16), was a branch of rational enquiry into human nature and difference that was informed by the aforementioned rationalising models of human difference (Nippel 1996: 129; Lo Presti 2012). Demand for knowledge of foreign lands and cultures increased in response to colonisation and prompted a burgeoning of ethnographic texts beginning in the sixth century BCE and proliferating throughout the fifth century (Nippel 1996).[57] We learn the most about non-Greeks from Herodotus, who spends almost half of his *Histories* describing their histories, cultures and practices (e.g. McCall 1999; Hartog 2002; Flower 2006; Munson 2006; Rood 2006; Figueira and Soares 2020). To compile his detailed account, he availed himself of the oral histories of numerous non-Greek peoples and written sources from the Near East (Murray 1996). Even though the organising theme of his narrative is the antithetical relationship between Greeks and barbarians, Herodotus' descriptions are often sympathetic and free from negative stereotypes to such a degree that Plutarch accuses him of being a *philobarbaros*, or 'barbarian-lover' (*Moralia* 857a; Coleman 1997: 196).[58] Herodotus' cosmopolitan perspective was most likely shaped by his own experience as a native of Halicarnassus in Caria. Caria was a region of ethnic admixture, and it is likely that Herodotus himself was part Carian (Georges 1994: 139). His multicultural upbringing allowed him to promote cultural relativism and convey to his audience that differing cultural practices and diverse languages are both comparable and translatable (Munson 2005).

It is perhaps best to conceptualise Herodotus' ethnographic digressions as the products of intercultural communication, and one could convincingly argue that Greek history is one of cross-cultural contact and exchange (Boardman 1994; 1999; Hodos 2006: 4–9; D. Roller 2006; Tartaron 2014; Malkin 2016).

Indeed, as Walter Burkert (1992), Martin West (1997), Martin Bernal (1987; 1991; 2001; 2006) and others (e.g. Morris 1992; Osborne 2009; Coleman and Walz 1997) have demonstrated, what we view as 'Greek' culture was heavily influenced by contact with ancient Near Eastern and Egyptian cultures, especially from the mid-eighth to mid-seventh centuries BCE. However, as the Greeks increasingly dispersed across the wider Mediterranean region, their intercultural interactions increased in frequency, duration and meaning.

Although the Greeks had previously interacted with a plethora of groups through trade and commerce, the dynamics of these interactions undoubtedly changed in the wake of colonisation (J. Hall 2002: 92; Hodos 2009; Vlassopoulos 2013a). The Greek colonial movement has been powerfully described as 'one of the most important cultural encounters in world history' (De Angelis 2016: 101).[59] Beginning in the eighth century BCE, more than 500 Greek colonies were founded along the coasts of the Black Sea, western Anatolia, the Adriatic Sea, Sicily, northern Africa, southern France and Spain (Fig. 1.5; Graham 1983; Hansen and Nielsen 2004).[60] Colonisation left a resounding impact on the population history of the ancient Mediterranean, and its effects were as widespread as they were monumental, ranging from the establishment of Mediterranean-wide trade networks to urbanisation to the spread of the alphabet (Malkin 1994; 2005; Boardman 2014; Rathmann et al. 2019).[61]

By the fifth century BCE, cultural contact and exchange had already been taking place in the Mediterranean for centuries. Intercultural contact was a reality for hundreds of thousands of people on account of long-established 'networks that moved goods, people, ideas and technologies, together with the consequences of Mediterranean-wide colonization and the effects of living under and working for great empires of the East (Assyria, Babylonia, Egypt, Lydia, Persia)' (Vlassopoulos 2013b: 50). There are many tangible examples of intercultural communication, including the setting of Greek myths (especially those involving the adventures of Heracles) in non-Greek lands (Georges 1994: 1–12), the use of Greek myth by non-Greeks (Erskine 2005), bilingual stelae in Memphis (Egypt), epitaphs of foreigners in Athens (Vlassopoulos 2013b) and Etruscan consumer preferences driving the sixth/fifth-century BCE Athenian pottery industry (Bundrick 2019). Indeed, Herodotus' ethnographic accounts, and most likely his informants, came from zones of cross-cultural contact where individuals and groups exchanged stories, negotiated identities and competed for prestige (Vlassopoulos 2013b). These cross-cultural zones, often termed the 'middle ground', are densely concentrated in areas impacted by Greek colonisation.[62]

Interactions in the middle ground varied in character. Sometimes, the encounters were antagonistic. Historical accounts describe Greeks driving locals from their lands to found Syracuse, Leontinoi and Catania in Sicily and Ephesus in Anatolia, and there is evidence to suggest that locals who occupied the territories surrounding Sybaris and Taris in southern Italy fled the Greek

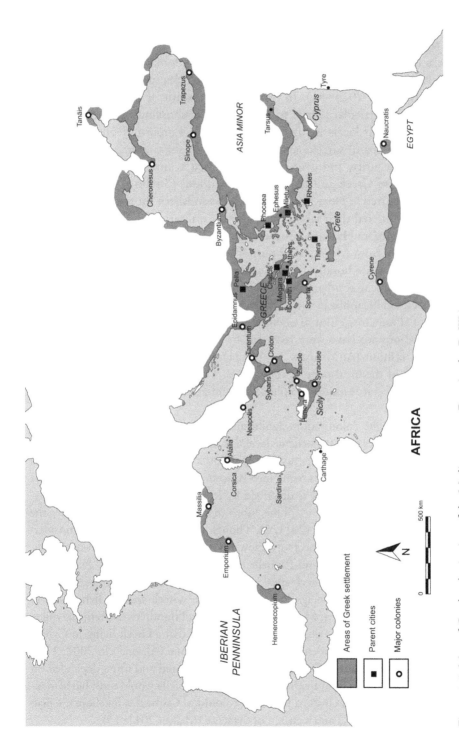

Figure 1.5 Map of Greek colonisation of the Mediterranean. Drawing by D. Weiss.

newcomers (Thucydides 6.3.2–3; Diodorus Siculus 11.76.3; Strabo 14.1.21). There are also tales of exploitation: the Greek aristocracy of Syracuse, called the *gamaroi*, enslaved locals to work their lands (Herodotus 7.155.2), and Greeks themselves were enslaved by locals in Poseidonia in southern Italy and by Scythians, Lydians and Persians in the Black Sea and western Anatolian regions (Garland 2014: 51). In other places, a spirit of cooperation existed. Phocaeans in particular appear to have made the conscious decision to peacefully coexist with locals in their settlements. At Emporium on the coast of north-eastern Spain, Greeks and locals chose to share a circuit wall for the purposes of security, and over time they created a unified state that boasts a combination of Greek and non-Greek institutions (Strabo 3.4.8).[63] A similar situation occurred at Heraclea Pontica, on the southern shore of the Black Sea, where locals offered their labour in return for military protection (Plato, *Laws* 6.776c–d). Megara Hyblaea, on the other hand, was founded in Sicily by settlers originally from Megara who purportedly were granted land by Hyblon, a local king in whose honour they named their new city (Thucydides 6.4.1–2). Finally, local Oscan residents were granted citizenship and were allowed to hold magistracies in Neapolis in southern Italy (Garland 2014: 49–51, 54). The true nature of these cross-cultural encounters, however, is difficult to reconstruct, as the versions we have were recorded by Greek and Roman historians in a one-sided fashion (Antonaccio 2001: 121), and none were penned from the perspective of the local peoples themselves. The direct evidence we do have is archaeological – it is material, epigraphic and architectural (Antonaccio 2003; Hodos 2006).

Unsurprisingly, colonisation significantly impacted Greek attitudes towards non-Greek peoples on a Panhellenic level.[64] It has been argued that the 'consciousness of a common Greek identity' (Nippel 2002: 279) began during the period of colonisation when Greeks came into contact with diverse new cultures.[65] The emergence of Greek identity is described by Irad Malkin as 'a process of convergence through divergence ... [T]he more the Greeks dispersed, somehow the more "Greek" they become' (2011: 5). Though they were separated by considerable distances, network connectivity allowed Greeks to share common narratives, ethnic genealogy, language and Panhellenic cults (Malkin 2011: 5).[66] It was these connections that made 'a Greek speaking resident in Cyrene in Libya similar not to his immediate Libyan neighbor, but to another Greek speaker living, say, in Massilia (Massilia, modern Marseille), at a distance of hundreds of maritime miles' (Malkin 2016: 286). This does not, however, mean that a Greek living in Cyrene would forsake a regional identity for a Panhellenic one (Antonaccio 2001: 114). As previously discussed, Greek ethnic identity was nested and often depended on context. For example, an individual from Syracuse in Sicily would most likely identify simultaneously as a Greek, a Dorian, a colonist of Corinth, a Sikeliote (Sicilian Greek regional identity) and a citizen of Syracuse (Malkin 2011: 19).

Presumably, conflicts with non-Greek peoples strengthened feelings of kinship among Greeks, which coalesced to form a dichotomous worldview in which all individuals fell into the categories of either 'Greek' or 'non-Greek' (Nippel 2002: 279–93). The precise moment when the Greek/non-Greek dichotomy codified is a matter of debate. Irad Malkin (1998: 268) argues for a ninth-century origin, considering the Greek/non-Greek divide to be a consequence of the Ionian colonisation of Asia Minor. Jonathan Hall (1997; 2002), on the other hand, maintains that it was developed a century later in the Archaic period as a result of the rise to prominence of Panhellenic sanctuaries at Olympia and Delphi and the strengthening of Panhellenic elite interactions through intermarriage and participation in the Olympic Games. Hyun Kim (2013) pushes the date several centuries to the late sixth/early fifth century as a product of the Ionian Revolt, while Benjamin Isaac (2004), an outlier, sees it as a creation of fourth-century philosophers and rhetoricians. Nevertheless, the view held by the majority is that it was crystallised by the Athenians in the aftermath of the Persian Wars (post-480 BCE) as a tool of Delian League propaganda (e.g. E. Hall 1989; J. Hall 1997; 2003).[67]

Large enclaves of non-Greeks did not exist in the Greek mainland during the Late Archaic/Classical period. Small groups of non-Greeks worked and resided in cosmopolitan cities, but this was not a widespread phenomenon. Some of these groups were mercenaries, as Athens employed a Scythian police force, and both Athens and Sparta hired Thracians to serve as light armed auxiliaries in their armies (Xenophon, *Hellenica* 2.4.12; Wiedemann 1988: 155; Bäbler 1998; Osborne 2000: 34–8). Also, there are accounts of Phoenicians and other non-Greeks (especially Carians, Egyptians and Thracians) in the Piraeus (e.g. Bakewell 1997: 226; Demetriou 2012: 188–229), and Xenophon claims that non-Greeks, including Lydians, Phrygians and Syrians, immigrated to Athens in the first half of the fourth century BCE (*Ways and Means* 2.3). In general, Athens was open to immigrants, who were called metics, or 'resident foreigners'. In Plutarch's biography of Solon, the Athenian lawgiver remarks 'that Athens was filled with people who were constantly streaming into Attica from elsewhere to find security' (*Solon* 22.1 as translated in Garland 2014: 5). The majority of these immigrants were other Greeks who sought to take advantage of the economic opportunities that could be found in Athens. There must, however, have been an influx of non-Greek immigrants as well. For example, Athenian vase potters and painters of the sixth and early fifth centuries BCE sometimes have foreign names, such as Amasis (a Hellenised version of an Egyptian name), Lydos (the Lydian), Thrax (of Thrace), Kolchos (of Colchis) and Skythes (of Scythia; Boardman 1991: 12). Also, the Old Oligarch, writing in the late fifth century BCE, notes that the Athenians set themselves apart from other Greeks by embracing non-Greek customs (*Constitution of the Athenians* 2.7–8). Margaret Miller (1997) finds support for this statement, as she maintains that the Athenians embraced, adapted and appropriated various aspects of Persian material culture after the Persian Wars. Nevertheless, this admixture of different peoples and cultures – Greek and non-Greek – is unlikely to have occurred in every Greek city state, because Athens' open-door policy was not shared by poleis like Sparta and Megara, which were notoriously restrictive (Thucydides 1.144.2, 2.39.1; Plutarch, *Moralia* 238e, 826c; Garland 2014: 152, 161).

Non-Greeks were referred to as 'barbarians', an onomatopoeic term referring to people who speak unintelligible gibberish – literally 'bar-bar' (Strabo 14.2.28; Coleman 1997: 178). In itself, barbarian (*barbaros*) is a comparatively old term. It has a Sanskrit cognate (*barbara*, which means 'stammering'), and a version of it appears in Linear B tablets from Pylos (ca. 1200 BCE), where it roughly translates to foreigner, specifically 'someone not from Pylos'.[68] At this early phase, the barbarian label is not pejorative, but descriptive, and the same is true when a derivative of it appears in Homeric Greek. *Barbarophonos*, or 'of incomprehensible speech', is used in the *Iliad* (2.867) to describe the Carians fighting for Troy, who either spoke Greek badly (García Alonso 2017) or were deemed especially outlandish and foreign (Ross 2005).[69] However, the meaning of the word shifted dramatically in direct response to the existential threat posed by the Persians at the beginning of the fifth century. After that point, the word commonly appears in Athenian drama as either an ethnic designation or pejorative (García Alonso 2017). Furthermore, dramatic representations of barbarians portray them in a negative light as unsophisticated or unintelligent; lawless, savage and unjust; despotic as well as servile; and effeminate, luxurious, highly emotional and cowardly (Hall 1989: 121–33; Goldhill 2002; Saïd 2002).

While Greeks were united by shared language, culture and religion, non-Greek 'barbarians' were bound simply by what they were not.[70] Collectively, they were the antithesis of Greeks (Shaw 1982/3; Hall 1997: 47; Cohen 2000b; Huang 2010). Whereas Greeks valued moderation, they perceived non-Greeks as lacking control, stereotyping them as over-indulgent, especially with violence, food, drink and sex (Briant 2002; Zacharia 2008b). In comparison, Greeks believed themselves to be superior in terms of strength, virtue, intelligence (Browning 2002: 257–61) and sophistication of language (*Homeric Hymn to Apollo* 162f; Aeschylus, *Seven Against Thebes* 463; Herodotus 4.183; Sophocles, *Women of Trachis* 1006; Eubulus 108 KA; Tuplin 1999: 49–50). These negative connotations are particularly evident in art. For example, in fifth-century Athens, Amazons were frequently used to represent the antithesis of proper Athenian women – wild, unrestrained and morally inferior (Hardwick 1990; DuBois 1991; Stewart 1995).

The conceptualisation of the non-Greek as the unrestrained inferior 'Other' provided justification for military conquest and slavery. The Athenian orator, Isocrates, exhorts Athens, Sparta, and even Philip II, to conquer barbarian Asia in order to prevent its prosperity and liberate the Greeks living there (e.g. 5.132; Mitchell 2007: 12; Huang 2010: 563).[71] His younger contemporary,

Aristotle, considered slavery to be the 'natural' state of a barbarian (Aristotle, *Politics* 1254b19–1255b; *Nicomachean Ethics* 1161b6; Lape 2010: 46–50).[72] In the Classical Greek world, the enslaved were ubiquitous.[73] Even the poorest households had enslaved individuals, and the vast majority were foreign.[74] Foreign enslaved persons were procured through military conflict, trade, piracy and coercion, then purchased inexpensively (Xenophon, *Memorabilia* 2.5; Coleman 1997: 180; Lewis 2019). As discussed in the previous section, the enslaved primarily derived from the regions surrounding Greek territory, ranging from the Balkans to Asia Minor and the Black Sea (Braund 2011: 126; Thompson 2003: 3).[75] Most foreign enslaved individuals seem to have come from Thrace, Phrygia and the Black Sea region, but almost every ethnic group known to the Greeks was most likely represented in the slave pool, even sub-Saharan Africans (Wiedemann 1988; Coleman 1997: 180–1; Lewis 2011). Commonly called 'Ethiopians', sub-Saharan African enslaved persons were coveted on account of their general rarity and exotic features (e.g. the Man of Petty Ambition in Theophrastus, *Characters* 21; Snowden 1970: 19, 184–6; Goldenberg 2009; Braund 2011: 126).[76] Nevertheless, the foreign origins of the enslaved were closely linked to their servile status, which most likely served to reinforce Greek notions of superiority. Furthermore, Rebecca Futo Kennedy (2014: 107) notes that ethnic prejudices in Athens must have increased in response to non-Greek freedmen becoming metics and adopting professions of ill repute.

Although it seems counterintuitive, some Greeks claimed descent from non-Greeks. In fact, Plato provocatively suggests that everyone's ancestry might include barbarians (*Theaetetus* 175a), and the mythistory of the Pelasgians supports this (Tuplin 1999: 61). The Greeks believed that the prehistoric Pelasgians were a pervasive non-Greek aboriginal people who lived throughout the wider Aegean region and as far west as Italy, and there was an understanding that isolated groups of them, and their descendants, still existed in the Classical period (e.g. Homer, *Iliad* 2.681–6, 2.819–22, 16.233–6, 17.288–91; *Odyssey* 19.175; Aeschylus, *Suppliant Women* 250–3, 605–24; Herodotus 1.56–7, 2.50, 2.52.1, 6.137–40; Thucydides 1.3, 1.57, 4.109; Strabo 5.2.4. 13.3.3; Diodorus Siculus 5.80.1).[77] The Pelasgians were autochthonous (Aeschylus, *Suppliant Women* 250–3), and Herodotus (1.57.2–3, 58) implies that the Dorians, and later the Athenians, were Hellenised Pelasgian ethne. However, the Pelasgians' relationship with the Athenians was particularly complicated and contradictory. Even though the Pelasgians supposedly instructed the Athenians in matters of architecture, agriculture and religion (Hecataeus, *FGrH* I fr. 127), the Athenians eventually expelled them from Attica (Herodotus 6.137–40). Despite their relative obscurity, the mythical Pelasgians played an important role in Greek culture, as they represented the archetypal non-Greek group. They often served as a foil to the Greeks, and Pelasgian stories usually end with their eviction and disenfranchisement (Laird 1933; Fowler 2003; Sourvinou-Inwood 2003; McInerney 2014).

Beyond Attica, Greek individuals, cities and regions traced their mythical lineages to foreign ancestors who brought Eastern wisdom and knowledge to Greece.[78] For instance, Spartan kings believed they were descended from either Syrians or Egyptians (Herodotus 6.53, 55). Also, major cultural achievements were ascribed to the immigrant heroes who ruled Argos, Thebes and Pisa. Danaus (former king of Egypt, founder of Argos) and Cadmus (Phoenician, founder and king of Thebes) are variably attributed with the introduction of the alphabet (Herodotus 5.58; Ephorus, *FGrH* II 70 fr. 105; Hecataeus, *FGrH* I 1 fr. 20), Danaus purportedly brought agriculture, the rites of Demeter, ship-building and navigation to Argos (Hesiod, fr. 128 West; Herodotus 2.171.3; Apollodorus, *Library* 2.1.4), while Pelops (Phrygian or Lydian, king of Pisa) was the legendary founder of the Olympic Games (Pausanias 5.8.20; Edwards 1979; Miller 2005; Malkin 2015). However, Margaret Miller describes the adoption of immigrant ancestors as a double-edged sword: 'On the one hand, one could enhance one's prestige; on the other, one risked losing caste in a different ideological context, by having one's ancestors characterised as foreigners and barbarians' (2005: 68). Indeed, Plato capitalises on the negative connotations of foreign pedigree, as he proclaims that the Athenians, who were autochthonous, were Greek by nature, while the Peloponnesians and Thebans, who were descended from non-Greeks like Cadmus, Aegyptus and Danaus, were only nominally Greek (*Menexenus* 245c–d; McInerney 2014: 47). Moreover, in Athens the claim that citizens had foreign or servile ancestors was a common tactic used in Attic courts of law and Old Comedy to discredit and malign political opponents and enemies. As previously discussed, those two attributes – foreign and servile – could be interpreted as essentially the same since most of the enslaved in Athens had foreign origins (Lape 2010: 64–71).

There are other indicators that the Greek/barbarian polarity might not have been as rigid a construct as scholars have traditionally assumed. There seems to have been an understanding that positive character traits could be manifest by anyone, and some non-Greeks were admired for their skill and moral character. An Attic funerary inscription dating to the third quarter of the fifth century praises the skills of a Phrygian woodcutter who most likely died fighting for the Athenians during the Peloponnesian Wars: 'This is the beautiful tomb of Manes, son of Orymaios, the best of the Phrygians there ever were in wide Athens. And by Zeus, I never saw any woodcutter better than me. He died in war' (*IG* 1³ 1361 as translated in Vlassopoulos 2007b: 15). Furthermore, literary sources suggest that moral character and ethnicity were not inextricably linked: for example, 'whoever is well set up by nature is well born, even if he's [an Ethiopian]' (Stobaeus, *Anthology* 86.493, attributed to Epicharmus, as translated in Tuplin 1999: 59) and 'if a man is of good character it doesn't matter if he's an Ethiopian, and it is absurd to abuse someone for being a Scythian' (Menander, fr. 612 as translated in Tuplin 1999: 59).[79] Non-Greeks could distinguish themselves in other ways as well. For instance, Herodotus (1.603) recounts barbarian displays of remarkable intellect, and Plato concedes that conditions favourable to the emergence of philosopher kings might exist in remote barbarian locales (*Republic* 499c). Also, in some extraordinary cases, exceptional barbarians, such as Cyrus the Great, were held out as paradigms worthy of emulation (e.g. Xenophon, *Cyropaedia*; Plato, *Laws* 3.694a; Hirsch 1985).

To further complicate the matter, it was not always clear who the barbarians were. Panhellenic identity could be relatively flexible, and the Macedonians and Epirotes provide two cogent examples of this. Both groups lived on the northern edge of the Greek world, and whether or not they were considered to be Greek fluctuated according to sociopolitical circumstances (Mitchell 2007: 204–6). The earliest mention of the Macedonians is in Hesiod's *Catalogue of Women* (fr. 7 West) where they are called the cousins of the Greeks. Herodotus (5.22; 8.137.1; 9.45.2) and Isocrates (5.32–4, 76–7) note that the Macedonians are descended from the Argives, and therefore Greek, while Thucydides (2.80.5–6, 2.99.3, 4.124.1, 4.126.3) maintains that only the Macedonian kings are Greek, and their subjects are not. However, in an impassioned speech decrying Macedonian expansion, Demosthenes (9.31) denies that the Macedonians are even remotely related to the Greeks. Although the question of Macedonian Greekness was debated throughout Philip II's rule, it was Alexander's conquest of Asia that 'tacitly settled the issue' (Mitchell 2007: 205; cf. Hornblower 2008: 55–8). Similarly, the Greekness of the people of Epirus was also questioned. In some historic traditions, the area around Dodona is identified as the original homeland of the Greeks (Aristotle, *Meteorology* 352a33–b3), and Dodona itself was an important Greek oracular centre (Herodotus 1.46.2–3) whose status was eventually eclipsed by Delphi. Also, as early as the seventh century BCE, Molossia was thought to be the kingdom of Peleus, father of Achilles (Pindar, *Nemean* 4.51–3, 7.38–40), and the Molossian royal family was believed to be descended from the son of Achilles, Neoptolemus, and the Trojan princess Andromache (Euripides, *Andromache* 1243–6). The Greekness of the Molossian royal family might have been generally accepted in the Classical period, but the status of their subjects was uncertain – in some cases they are considered to be Greek (e.g. Herodotus 2.56.1), in other cases they are unequivocally non-Greek (Thucydides 1.47.3, 1.50.3, 2.68.9, 2.80.5, 2.81–2, 2.99.2, 2.99.6; Malkin 2001b; Mitchell 2007: 205–6).

Even on an individual level, non-Greeks could be difficult to identify. An interesting example of this is conveyed to us by Xenophon (*Anabasis* 3.1.26–31). After Cunaxa, Xenophon argued that the Ten Thousand should return to Greece. All officers agreed with him save for one, a speaker of the Boeotian dialect named Apollonides. In his dissent, Apollonides emphasised that their position was a precarious one and that their only hope was to appeal to the Persian king for safe passage. Given the Persian king's recent deceit, which led to the slaughter of the Greek generals, Apollonides' argument was met with incredulity. Xenophon retorted, 'This man is a disgrace to his homeland and indeed to the whole of Greece, because he is Greek yet of such a kind as this' (3.1.30 as translated in Harman 2013: 83). At this point, one of the officers denounced Apollonides' Greekness: 'But this man belongs neither to Boeotia nor to any other part of Greece, for I have seen that he has both ears pierced like a Lydian' (3.1.31 as translated in Harman 2013: 83). With no further proof necessary, a man who had heretofore been considered Greek was branded non-Greek and ejected from the group. Xenophon provides no further commentary as to whether or not Apollonides actually was a Lydian. Rather, 'The sight of his ears speaks for itself, declaring his non-Greekness, and outweighs dialect as evidence of identity . . . [T]he conflict between the message conveyed by his accent and that communicated by his ears is not explained, leaving the reader with the suspicion that he has been conveniently scapegoated' (Harman 2013: 83). Effectively, the Greeks could continue their journey home, content in the knowledge that they had removed the barbarian, and his treasonous ideas, from their midst.

By the end of the fifth century, Greek intellectuals were questioning whether 'barbarian' was a useful human taxonomy. Plato argues that the Greek/barbarian dichotomy is a false one, but it does not prevent him from using non-Greek stereotypes on occasion. For example, he contrasts Egyptians and Phoenicians, who are said to love money, with Greeks, who love knowledge (*Republic* 435e–436a), and observes that Greeks and barbarians are enemies by nature (*Republic* 470c). However, Plato also maintains that 'barbarian' is an unnatural category encompassing large numbers of diverse and mutually incomprehensible peoples (*Politics* 262c–263a; Tuplin 1999: 57; Kamtekar 2002; García Alonso 2017: 17–18). Another late fifth-century writer, Antiphon, recognised that barbarians and Greeks, despite their cultural differences, shared common human traits: 'For in nature all of us are equally in all respects created to be either barbarian or Greek . . . For we all breathe through the mouth and nostrils . . . and we weep in pain; and we receive sounds with our hearing; and we see by eye with our vision; and we work with our hands; and we walk with our feet . . .' (Antiphon 87b44a as translated in Tuplin 1999: 59). Yet, these unique examples are the exceptions, and general rejections of a stark distinction between Greeks and barbarians are scarce in ancient literature (Tuplin 1999: 59). On the contrary, stereotypes continued to perpetuate, and there was no movement towards accepting non-Greeks as equals (Coleman 1997: 197).[80]

Greek superiority over non-Greeks was reinforced through visual culture (Lissarrague 2002). After the conclusion of the Persian Wars, battle imagery symbolising conflict and defeat of a foreign foe (e.g. Trojans, Persians, Amazon, giants and centaurs) became standard in Greek art, and the theme was explored in all media (Cohen 2012: 475). Most representations of non-Greeks, however, are found on vases, and the majority of the iconographic evidence dates to the fifth century BCE.[81] In vase-painting, ethnic identity is not constructed consistently, but there are cultural markers that set non-Greeks apart from Greeks, namely lack of self-control, body modification, dress (including adornment and coiffures) and physiognomy (Lee 2015: 49–51). Self-control, or *sôphrosynê*, was a Greek ideal that is characteristically lacking in representations of non-Greeks. A tattooed Thracian woman on a red-figure column krater by the Pan Painter (ca. 470 BCE) illustrates this.[82] Holding a sword and scabbard, she runs wildly to the right, her hair disarrayed and her breasts and legs visible through her garment – respectable Greek women were never displayed so chaotically (Lee 2015: 51, 84–5, fig. 2.16). The depiction of body modifications, such as male circumcision and tattoos, is another representational strategy to distinguish non-Greeks from Greeks. Various groups across the Mediterranean practised male circumcision, but Herodotus associates it with the Colchians, Phoenicians, Syrians, Ethiopians and Egyptians (Herodotus 2.36–7, 2.104), as visible in a scene of Heracles battling the Egyptian pharaoh Busiris and his priests on a red-figure pelike by the Pan Painter (Fig. 1.6; Lee 2015: 86). Although tattoos were used across the Mediterranean to brand criminals, war prisoners and the enslaved, tattooing is primarily associated with Thracians, especially Thracian women (Herodotus 5.6; Lee 2015: 84–6; Tsiafakis 2015). Thracian women are typically depicted in the mythological context of Orpheus' murder, an example of which can be seen on an Attic red-figure amphora attributed to the Phiale Painter, where the arms of the female aggressor are covered in 'V'-shaped tattoos (Fig. 1.7; Lee 2015: 84).

Non-Greek dress and items of adornment varied according to ethnic group and were highly stereotyped. Non-Greek garments differ fundamentally from Greek ones, as non-Greeks don animal skins (e.g. pre-Classical period Amazons, who pair these with short knee-length chitons) and sleeved jackets and leggings (*anaxyrides*) with elaborate patterns, and Greeks do not.[83] Sleeved jackets and leggings are most likely Persian in origin, but by ca. 530 BCE, vase-painters also use them to denote Scythians, Amazons, Trojans and generic non-Greeks (Cohen 2012: 460–4; Lee 2015: 120–6). Non-Greeks were also typified by their belting habits, which were the inverse of Greek practices. Whereas Greek men did not wear belts (with the exclusion of charioteers, whose garment required one), non-Greek men did and vice versa for women – which most likely had the effect of masculinising non-Greek women and feminising non-Greek men (Kurtz and Boardman 1986; Lee 2015: 136–7). Certain styles of headgear could also indicate the foreign origins of figures – Scythian archers wear the *kurbasia*, a cap with a tall crown, which is sometimes pointed, and long flaps to protect the cheeks and back of the neck; the Persian *kidaris* is similar to Scythian headgear, but made of a softer material; and Thracians wear the *alôpekis*, which is a cap made out of animal hide that has an intact tail dangling off the back (usually fox,

Figure 1.6 Attic red-figure pelike (ca. 460 BCE) from Thespiae, Greece by the Pan Painter depicting Heracles battling Busiris and his priests (Athens, National Museum 9683). Photo © Album/Art Resource, NY.

Figure 1.7 Detail of an Attic red-figure Nolan amphora (ca. 450–440 BCE) from Attica attributed to the Phiale Painter, depicting a Thracian woman with 'V'-shaped arm tattoos attacking Orpheus with a sword (Paris, Louvre G 436). Photo © Erich Lessing/Art Resource, NY.

and often accompanied by fawn-skin boots with turned-down tops; Cohen 2012: 469; Lee 2015: 160). Weapons likewise vary among ethnic groups – Thracians, for instance, are depicted with *peltê* (small crescent-shaped shields), Scythians are shown with double-curved composite bows, and Persians carry long bows (Cohen 2012: 469–75). It must be noted, however, that identifying figures as foreign based strictly on their dress can lead to misidentification. A variety of non-Greek headwear can be worn by Greek symposiasts and komast dancers as a form of play-acting the Other (Smith 2010: 182; Osborne 2011: 145–6). Additionally, although all constructed sleeves are Persian in origin, some sleeved garments (i.e. *cheiridôtos chitôn* and *kandys*) were adopted by the Athenian elite in the Archaic and Classical periods, so figures wearing them cannot be identified as non-Greek per se. The same is true of the *ependytês*, a short pullover originally associated with Persians but later worn by Athenians, and the Thracian *zeira*, a boldly pat-terned mantle appropriated by Athenian men as an equestrian garment in the late sixth century BCE (Lee 2015: 120–6).

Physiognomy is inconsistently used to construct ethnic identity in the visual arts. Thracians and Scythians are sometimes depicted with reddish or light-coloured hair (Lee 2015: 49–51, 84–5, fig. 2.16), while sub-Saharan Africans are often, but not exclusively, shown with furrowed brows, flattened noses, thick protruding lips and tightly curled short hair (Cohen 2012: 466).[84] For the most part, skin colour simply follows vase-painting conventions: in black-figure, men are black and women are white, all figures are the red-orange colour of the vase's clay in red-figure, and in white-ground all figures are drawn with a dark outline and skin the pale colour of the vase's clay (Cohen 2012: 464). Although these are the norms, there are, of course, exceptions. For example, white-ground alabastra attributed to the so-called Group of the Negro Alabastra represent sub-Saharan Africans with black skin, foreign dress (long sleeves and trousers) and non-Greek physiognomy (discussed below; Beazley 1963: 267–9; 1971: 352; Neils 1980; 2007; Osborne 2000: 38–9).[85] Also, on a red-figure pelike (ca. 450–440 BCE) attributed to the Workshop of the Niobid Painter, the Ethiopian princess Andromeda is being tied to a stake in preparation for her sacrifice to a sea monster (Fig. 1.8). Andromeda's skin is rendered in standard red-figure, and she is dressed in the aforementioned conventional 'foreign' dress – patterned sleeves and leggings and a soft cap. The Ethiopian enslaved persons flanking her, however, are outlined in white and represented with black skin. Although Andromeda and the enslaved shared the same ethnicity, it has been suggested that their appearances differ on account of their class disparity (Cohen 2012: 464–8). There are also Athenian sculptural (partially mould-made in the form of heads, often used as drinking vessels during symposia) and plastic vases (vases in the form of sculptural groups) that use black glaze to represent sub-Saharan Africans (Lissarrague 1995). The inconsistent use of skin colour in the visual arts is paralleled in ancient literary sources, where mention of skin colour is often omitted, suggesting that it 'was not the chief component in the construction of difference' (Haley 2009: 33).

The varying use of skin colour as a marker of ethnicity is used by some scholars, such as Frank M. Snowden Jr, to support the notion that classical antiquity was a time 'before colour prejudice' (1970; 1983; 1997; 2010). On the basis of Graeco-Roman visual and literary evidence, Snowden sees no evidence of social marginalisation or prejudicial treatment of sub-Saharan Africans, namely Ethiopians. Instead, he interprets artistic representations of Ethiopians as naturalistic and mimetic, rather than comic or grotesque, and asserts that their literary references have positive and valorous connotations (e.g. Herodotus 1.134, 2.22; Homer, *Odyssey* 19.246–8; Pseudo-Aristotle, *Problems* 898b, 909a).[86] In

Figure 1.8 Attic red-figure pelike (ca. 450–440 BCE) from the Workshop of the Niobid Painter depicting Andromeda tied to a stake by enslaved individuals (Boston, Museum of Fine Arts 63.2663). Photo © 2021 Museum of Fine Arts, Boston.

his words, 'The approach of Greek and Roman artists in their renderings of the black was evidently in the spirit of those classical authors whose comments on the Ethiopian, at home or abroad, attached no great importance to the color of a man's skin' (Snowden 2010: 250). Furthermore, Snowden notes that Greeks attributed differences in appearance and skin colour to environmental, rather than hereditary factors (e.g. Herodotus 2.22; Pseudo-Aristotle, *Physiognomics* 6.812a; Snowden 1970: 2, 172–5, 258; 1983: 7, 85–6, 112; Goldberg 1993: 21; Bérard 2000; Fredrickson 2002: 17).

Erich Gruen's (2011) analysis of ancient literature supports Snowden's position. Gruen focuses on literary representations of non-Greek groups (e.g. Persians, Egyptians), and although individual instances of prejudice and stereotyping exist, he rejects the generalisation that Greeks were xenophobic or ethnocentric. Instead of rejecting or distancing themselves from non-Greeks, Greeks transformed or reimagined them to suit their own purposes and connected themselves to non-Greeks through cultural appropriation. To support this position, he points to numerous cases in which Greeks express admiration for the skills and achievements of non-Greeks. Gruen also finds significance in the Greek desire to closely link themselves to non-Greeks, typically achieved through the invention of kinship relationships (e.g. Danaus, Pelops, Cadmus).

Gruen's monograph, however, has come under intense scrutiny. First, he has been criticised for only considering Greek attitudes towards foreign societies and avoiding the issue of how non-Greeks, as minorities, were treated within Greek society. As a result, he misses subtle indicators of alterity and marginality. For example, Gruen sees the construction of fictive kinship with non-Greeks as the opposite of 'Othering', while 'the motif of the city founded by a hero from a distant land could be interpreted as a strategy for neutralizing the potential danger posed by the "Other" to collective self-definition by incorporating it into the "Same"' (Broder 2011). Furthermore, Gruen – like Snowden before him – displays a narrow view of Blackness. The determination of the skin tone deemed dark enough to be considered black- or dark-skinned is a cultural decision – northern cultures like the Scythians, for instance, might have considered the medium-toned Athenians to be black- or dark-skinned. In the Greek context, even though Gruen maintains that only Ethiopians were understood to have black skin (2011: 202), Egyptians, Colchians and Indians are clearly described by Herodotus (2.57, 2.104, 3.101) and others (e.g. Pseudo-Aristotle, *Physiognomics* 6.812a) as having black skin. Finally, Gruen glosses over evidence of prejudice in literature and art. For instance, in Aeschylus' *Suppliant Women*, Egyptians are Othered through their Blackness and hypersexuality, but Gruen asserts that their negative depiction is rooted instead in the immoral behaviour of the sons of Aegyptus and does not apply wholesale to all Egyptians (2011: 231–3). Moreover, a passage in Pseudo-Aristotle (*Physiognomics* 6.812a) reads: 'Those who are too black are cowards, observe Egyptians and Aithiopians. And those who are too white are also cowards, look at women. The color that favors bravery is between the two of them' (as translated in Samuels 2015: 733). Although Gruen dismisses this text as exceptional (2011: 202), it is in perfect alignment with the aforementioned precepts of Athenian racial citizenship, as the author is referring to the medium-toned Athenian male citizen as the paradigm of bravery between the marginalised groups. Likewise, despite Gruen interpreting the juxtapositions of dark-skinned men and Greeks on plastic vases as positive or 'good-natured joking' (2011: 2019), the inscriptions on the vases suggest otherwise, as they label the Greeks as 'beautiful' and degrade the dark-skinned body by sarcastically stating over it 'Timyllos is beautiful like this face' (Samuels 2013).

Research on Greek art also demonstrates the existence of entrenched prejudice towards non-Greeks. There has been an increase in studies of Late Archaic/Classical period visual representations of non-Greeks that explore the images in terms of their own internal logic. Rather than examining these representations prima facie, this approach requires consideration of viewership and display contexts, as well as careful analysis of representations with similar themes in order to understand how composing elements are manipulated across scenes to convey messages. The resulting conclusion is that individuals with sub-Saharan African physiognomy (excluding the mythical figures of Andromeda and Memnon, whose features have been 'Hellenised') are excluded from roles of high status or esteem and are constructed as a negative juxtaposition to the normative adult male citizen (Raeck 1981). In contrast, other groups, such as Scythians, Thracians and Persians, are always denoted as foreign through their dress and other cultural markers, but they also share commonalities with Greeks. Scythians and Thracians are similarly depicted performing many of the same tasks as Greeks (e.g. scenes of arming, departure and battle), and sometimes tasks of lower rank (e.g. minding the horses). Representations of Persians, on the other hand, change over time. From ca. 490–470 BCE, they are often presented as inferior warriors, easily defeated by heroic Greek hoplites. In the 460s, Persian iconography is conflated with that of Amazons, which implicitly feminises them, but from the mid-fifth century onwards, their depictions are more normalised in that they perform actions similar to Greeks (and Scythians and Thracians), such as departing for battle (Tanner 2010: 27–31). Thus, a nuanced investigation of representations of non-Greeks in Greek art reveals that, although depictions fluctuated over time, they were typically portrayed as subordinate and inferior to Greeks (Xydas 2003). This understanding aligns with the prevailing view, which is based primarily on literary evidence, and described by Susan Lape:

Although this view [that the Greeks were not prejudiced against individuals of different ancestries and ethnicities] may be valid as a generalization, it does not accurately reflect all of the ancient evidence. First, the idea that ecological theories of human diversity never yield the hereditarian thinking associated with racism appears to be mistaken. For example, the Hippocratic text *Airs, Waters, Places* treats Scythian ethnic characteristics as heritable, even though these characteristics are said to have been initially formed by climate and cultural practice. More important for present purposes, not all Greeks attributed human diversity to ecological factors: the Athenians understood their exceptionalism as issuing from birth, ancestry, and heredity. (Lape 2010: 34)

This view, which is shared by others (e.g. Hoffmann and Metzler 1977; Sassi 2001: 24, n. 101–2; Isaac 2006), is reinforced by the aforementioned visual evidence, and perhaps the closest to the ancient reality in the Late Archaic/ Classical period.

Attitudes towards non-Greeks began to change in the late fourth century BCE in the wake of Alexander the Great's conquest of Asia Minor.[87] Just like the Archaic colonies before them, Hellenistic kingdoms became middle grounds in the East where Greek and non-Greek cultures hybridised in unique and variable ways (e.g. Rotroff 1997).[88] Another similarity between the two diasporas is the way in which sustained cross-cultural contact reinforced bonds of Greekness – this resulted in the development of Panhellenism during the Archaic period, whereas in the Hellenistic period it is perhaps most clearly evidenced by the development of koine Greek (Herring 2009: 130). One would expect that the strengthening of Greek bonds would be accompanied by a parallel reaffirmation of the distinctions between Greeks and non-Greeks. This dichotomy, however, began to fade in the Hellenistic period, and what we see instead is the 'barbarian' stereotype challenged in new ways.

One catalyst for change was probably Alexander's own desire to attain *homonoia*, which roughly translates to 'unity and concord', among the diverse peoples he ruled. This aim is reflected in his policies, which are described as having seven principal features:

1) shrewd attention to the welfare of the Persians, 2) respect for the Persian institutions, especially religion, 3) equal distribution of offices among Macedonians and Persians, with the Persians holding the civil positions and the Macedonians, the military, 4) the 'gradual regeneration' of Persia rather than 'progressive degradation', 5) free communication throughout the empire, 6) advocation of the blending of customs, 7) liberal extensions to the Persians of the privileges and advantages of his own country. (de Mauriac 1949: 109–10)

While these policies ultimately sought to forge *homonoia* through equality, they created instead an artificial social structure that fostered enmity among the groups. As conquerors, Macedonians resented social equality with the vanquished, while the Persians, the former ruling class of the Achaemenid Empire, were outraged to find themselves on the same social stratum as minority groups they had traditionally viewed as inferior (e.g. Bactrians, Sogdians, Syrians; de Mauriac 1949: 109–10). Despite initial resistance to these political measures, it is likely that Alexander's policies left a lasting mark on his subjects, transforming relations between Greeks and non-Greeks for centuries to come.

New attitudes towards non-Greeks are manifest in Hellenistic art. Consider, for instance, the dedicatory sculptural group commissioned by King Attalos I (ca. 241–197 BCE) at Pergamum in commemoration of his victory over the Gauls. The original monument (ca. 220 BCE), sculpted by Epigonos, does not survive, but two Roman marble copies are firmly associated with it: the Dying Gaul (Fig. 1.9) and the Gallic Chieftain and His Wife (Fig. 1.10).[89] It is clear from their appearances that the subjects are Gauls. They are recognisable by their bushy unkempt hair and moustaches, as well as the torque worn round the neck of the Dying Gaul. In both cases, the Gauls are represented not as

Figure 1.9 The Dying Gaul, a Roman marble copy of a Hellenistic Greek bronze original (Pergamum, ca. 230–220 BCE) attributed to Epigonus (Rome, Capitoline). Photo © HIP/Art Resource, NY.

Figure 1.10 The Gallic Chieftain and his Wife (Ludovisi Gaul), a Roman marble copy of a Hellenistic Greek bronze original (Pergamum, ca. 230–220 BCE) attributed to Epigonus (Rome, Museo Nazionale). Photo © Vanni Archive/Art Resource, NY.

stereotypical barbarians, but as noble, albeit defeated, heroes. The Dying Gaul, identified as a trumpeter by the broken instrument lying on the shield beneath him, has been wounded on his right side. He has collapsed, and painfully braces himself against the ground as blood liberally pours from his wound. The Gallic Chieftain, on the other hand, is a portrait of defiance. He has chosen death for himself and his wife. He has already killed her to prevent her inevitable enslavement, and as he slowly lowers her limp body to the ground, he plunges his sword into his own chest. Interestingly, both the Dying Gaul and the Gallic Chieftain are nude (Pollitt 1986: 85–90; Smith 1991: 99–104; Pedley 2012: 357–8). In Greek art, nudity is described as a costume and functions symbolically (Bonfante 1989). Although male nudity in art has various meanings (Osborne 1997; Hurwit 2007; Lee 2015: 173–82), it is clear that Greeks regarded it as a distinguishing feature of their culture (Herodotus 1.10.3; Thucydides 1.6; Bonfante 1989: 546; Hurwit 2007: 46). Here, the symbolism of the Gauls' nudity is ambiguous – it could be an element of realism, as Gauls were known to shed their clothing for battle (Polybius 2.28.7), or it could be a device meant to underscore the honourable, Greek-like nature of the Gauls, already attested by their depicted demeanour and behaviour. If the latter interpretation is correct, these sculptures represent a profound shift in Greek attitudes towards non-Greek peoples, which could be rooted in a widespread Hellenistic understanding that the fundamental similarities between Greeks and non-Greeks were far greater than their differences.

Having defined key terms that will be used throughout this book and explored ancient Greek attitudes towards individuals with physical impairments, low socioeconomic status and non-Greek ancestry and ethnicity, the focus now shifts to the bioarchaeological evidence. The following chapter discusses the documented bioarchaeological evidence of physical difference in the Late Archaic/Classical Greek world (ca. sixth to fifth/fourth centuries BCE) in order to gain a better understanding of how physical impairment might have affected social integration.

NOTES

1. As defined by the Centers for Disease Control and Prevention (USA) (2020), 'Disability and health overview', <https://www.cdc.gov/ncbddd/disabilityandhealth/disability.html#:~:text=A%20disability%20is%20any%20condition,around%20them%20(participation%20restrictions)> (last accessed 24 May 2021).
2. For a comprehensive discussion of ancient Greek words relating to physical impairments and imperfections, see Samama 2017.
3. For more on *pêros* and its derivatives, see Muller 2018.

4. Note that *penia*, the word for 'poverty' in ancient Greek, has a broader meaning than our modern understanding of poverty, which is primarily socioeconomic. The ancient Greek understanding of *penia* was the absence of *ploutos* (wealth) and can simply refer to individuals who had to work for a living. *Ptôcheia*, on the other hand, is closer to our modern meaning of poverty, as it refers to beggary and destitution and is conceived of as the worst form of *penia* (Taylor 2017: 11–14).

5. Although it has been suggested that Phocis was a poor agricultural state lacking social differentiation, Jeremy McInerney (1999: 187) points to boundary formation and militarisation as evidence of Phocis' social stratification in the fifth century BCE.

6. For more on class in the Archaic period, see Rose 2012.

7. Complete power-sharing with the lower classes was present in Athens and a few other poleis, but it was not the norm (Bintliff 2010: 31). Also, in terms of demography, the most concerted effort towards reconstructing the population of an ancient Greek city state has focused on Athens. For a historiography and appraisal of demographic approaches to Classical Athens, see Akrigg 2011.

8. For a careful treatment of Greek ethnic terminology, see Fraser 2009.

9. Peloponnesian identity was also asserted situationally (Vlassopoulos 2008). Also, for an argument against calling the range of Greek identities 'ethnicities', see Vlassopoulos 2015.

10. Note that Lynette Mitchell (2007) asserts that there was no single genesis of Panhellenic identity, but rather historical moments of its realisation. Also, see Saïd 2001 for a discussion of how the rhetoric of Panhellenism was manipulated to reinforce solidarity and collective identity at various moments from the fourth century BCE to the Roman period.

11. The reference to 'shared blood' in this passage from Herodotus has been interpreted as hereditary descent, as it does not appear that Herodotus believed in a biological definition of ethnicity. As Jonathan Hall notes, 'In attempting to establish an ethnic affinity between Egyptians and Colchians, for example, he pays scant regard to phenotypic similarities (2.104.2), and he attributes the hardness of Egyptian skulls to environmental rather than biological factors (3.12.2)' (1995: 93). For more on Herodotus' construction of ethnicity, see Thomas 2001.

12. For more on the ethnogenesis and changing nature of these groups, see McInerney 2001.

13. For the origins of Dorian, Ionian, Achaean and Aeolian ethnic identities, see J. Hall 2002: 56–89.

14. Note that regional ethnos-based identities are perceptible in Arcadia and Phocis in the late sixth and early fifth centuries BCE, but a collective Boeotian identity did not likely coalesce until the mid-fifth century (McInerney 1999; Larson 2007).

15. Bintliff (2012) demonstrates that there could easily be multiple subpopulations existing within an ethnos like Boeotia.

16. See Larson 2007 for Boeotian collective identity and Luraghi 2008 for Messenian collective identity.

17. For more on ethnonyms, see Lampinen 2019.

18. Although, note that Denise Demetriou asserts that cross-cultural contact prompted the development of collective identities: 'Being treated by others as a collective group often led Greeks and non-Greek ethnic groups to adopt these larger identities, once they recognized the similarities they shared' (2012: 238–9).

19. See St. Hoyme and İşcan 1989; Smedley and Smedley 2005; Sauer and Wankmiller 2009 for a history of thought and scholarship concerning the identification of 'race' in human remains. For a history of thought and scholarship on 'race' in archaeology, see Challis 2013.

20. Note that there has been some debate over the use of the term 'Other'. For instance, Benjamin Isaac intentionally eschewed its usage in *The Invention of Racism in Classical Antiquity* because it 'has in recent decades acquired quite a broad meaning: "Others" include women, slaves, children, the elderly, or disfigured people. It refers to any group that is not part of the establishment, but is placed on the margins or periphery of society, or does not belong to it at all' (2004: 4). For the purposes of this book, Isaac's broad definition fits precisely the topic under discussion.

21. For perspectives on disability in Greek philosophy, see Macfarlane and Polansky 2004; Meeusen 2017.

22. Note, however, that there is no evidence that disabled veterans were categorised in a military, social or economic way in the ancient Greek world (Edwards 2012).

23. Note that not all physically impaired individuals were socially marginalised in the ancient greater Mediterranean region. There are examples of individuals in Egyptian and Near Eastern contexts who, instead of being buried in an isolating manner suggestive of social marginalisation, were interred with relatively numerous and elaborate grave goods, implying that their loss evoked profound grief in their survivors. Analyses of the skeletons of these individuals also reveal that they received additional care throughout their lives, which allowed them to live longer than they otherwise would have (e.g. Boutin and Porter 2014; Boutin 2016).

24. For more on the public mockery and humiliation of disabled people, see Garland 1994; Kazantzidis and Tsoumpra 2018.

25. See Kelley 2007: 42–3 for more on physical impairment as divine punishment.

26. Deborah Kamen (2013) argues that there were not three, but ten different status groups in ancient Athens that are distinguished primarily on the basis of juridical status. In order of ascending status they are ordinary and privileged enslaved individuals, freedmen with conditional freedom, ordinary and privileged metics, bastards (*nothoi*), disenfranchised citizens, naturalised citizens, and male and female citizens.

27. Athenian citizens were divided into four property classes based on the agricultural yield of their land: *pentakosiomedimnoi* (500 *medimnoi* (dry units of measure) or *metrêtai* (liquid units of measure)), *hippeis* (300), *zeugitai* (200) and *thêtes* (less than 200; Patterson 1981: 175).

28. Note that William Thalmann (2011: 82–3) suggests that some of the figures in the harvesting scenes are enslaved.

29. Some sportsmen might have also lived in poverty. Aristocratic athletes and horse owners relied on a supporting cast of others, such as trainers (although these might be the exception, as trainers were often of high socioeconomic status), charioteers and jockeys, to secure their victories, but the roles of these individuals were often marginalised (Nicholson 2005).

30. See Thalmann 2011: 78–82 for a careful reading of the iconography of the Foundry Painter's vase that suggests that some of the figures are enslaved.

31. Metic is the anglicised form; *metoikos* literally means 'a person who has changed his *oikos*' or 'a person who lives with others of the same standing' (Garland 2014: 155). See Fraser 2009: 111–18 for metic ethnics.

32. Note that Watson (2010) and Bakewell (1997) argue that metic status did not originate in Athens until the middle of the fifth century BCE.

33. Failure to pay taxes or procure a *prostatês* likely resulted in fines. For more on these fines (and the evidence for them), see Meyer 2009. Note that Meyer provides a radical reinterpretation of inscriptions previously associated with freedmen alone.

34. See Blok 2009b for ancient literary references to the law.

35. For alternative explanations for the Citizenship Law's inception, see Blok 2009b.

36. Once granted *isoteleia*, metics in the highest tax brackets would, like wealthy citizens, be required to subsidise public works (e.g. dramatic choruses, triremes and gymnasia) and pay a special tax (the *eisphora*) during times of war or public emergency (Garland 2014: 156).

37. The fact that the metics stayed in the city and fought for the restoration of democracy was an extraordinary act, as the Thirty negatively targeted metics when they first came to power ca. 404 BCE. The Thirty, who were seeking to recast Athens after xenophobic Sparta, arrested metics and confiscated their property. Among those arrested was the orator Lysias, whose father had emigrated from Syracuse at Pericles' invitation and lived as a model metic in Athens for thirty years (Lysias 12.4; Garland 2014: 164).

38. For manifestations of 'status anxiety' exhibited by naturalised citizens (especially in the case of Apollodorus, Pasion's son), see Lape 2010: 216–20.

39. Athenians were not the only ones who were believed to be *autochthones*. See Blok 2009a: 251–2 for a list of *autochthones*. For a survey of references to autochthony in ancient literary sources, see Morgan 2015.

40. Note that Vincent Rosivach (1987) rejects the common translation of *autochthôn* as 'sprung from the earth itself' in favour of 'always having the same land' or 'a people which has lived in its homeland since time immemorial'.

41. See Fraser 2009: 103–11 for ethnics of the enslaved. Also see Wiedemann 1988; Thompson 2003: 9–33; Hunt 2011; 2018 for literary and epigraphic sources pertaining to Greek slavery. For a catalogue of Greeks who were enslaved by non-Greeks, non-Greeks who enslaved Greeks, and Greeks who enslaved other Greeks, see Garland 2014: 271–7. Also note that the term 'slave' has been eschewed in favour of 'enslaved' as it reifies that enslavement was imposed upon the individual and not a natural or inherent condition.

42. On the issue of whether ancient Greece was a 'slave society', see Finley 1959; de Ste. Croix 1981: 226; Rihll 2011: 69–72; Vlassopoulos 2016.

43. For critical approaches to Orlando Patterson's concept of social death, see Bodel and Scheidel 2017.
44. See McKeown 2011 for more on resistance among chattel slaves.
45. There were other slave sanctuaries in the Greek world, such as the Sanctuary of Zeus on Mount Ithome and the Sanctuary of Poseidon at Taenarum (Thucydides 1.128.1, 1.133; Garland 2014: 147).
46. For more on manumission in the ancient Greek world, see Zelnick-Abramovitz 2005.
47. Around the second half of the fourth century BCE, a different and more complex procedure was instituted for manumission (Rihll 2011: 56–7).
48. See Canevaro and Lewis 2014 for other obligations that freedmen would have towards their former slaveholders.
49. For more on the contested history of the conquest of Messenia, including ancient literary evidence for its reconstruction, see Luraghi 2008: 68–106.
50. For an overview and interpretation of literary texts associated with slavery, see DuBois 2008: 117–217. Also, for a discussion of popular (non-elite) Greek literary traditions (e.g. Aesop's fables, tales of runaway slave colonies etc.) as gleaned from the literature of the elite, see Forsdyke 2012.
51. For enslaved viewers of Athenian vases, see Lewis 1998/9.
52. See Thalmann 2011: 88–91 for a discussion of a bronze statuette of a bound enslaved individual with sub-Saharan African features.
53. For similar 'mistress and maid' depictions in Athenian vase-painting, see Reilly 1989; Oakley 2000.
54. In an effort to merge the mythic traditions, Apollodorus (*Library* 1.7.2) states that it was Hesiod's Bronze race that was destroyed by the flood.
55. For a summary of Greek theories on eugenics, see Galton 1998.
56. Although Edith Hall (1989: 49) denies that the *Odyssey* is ethnographic, themes of cultural contact, conflict and colonisation are all prevalent. See Malkin 1998; Dougherty 2001; Hartog 2001; Skinner 2012: 55 for more on ethnography in the *Odyssey*.
57. Thomas Harrison, however, argues that 'the institution of slavery was a major factor in fostering a discourse on the differences among foreign peoples' (2019: 37) and that the non-Greek enslaved must have served as ethnographic informants.
58. An example of Herodotus' neutrality is his statement that Egyptians call everyone who speaks a foreign language 'barbarians' (2.158.5), which of course eschews the fact that Greeks would consider the Egyptians to be barbarians (Nippel 1996: 128).
59. The literature on Greek colonisation is vast and wide-ranging (see McInerney 2018 for a bibliography). Also, note that colonies were places to dispose of socially marginalised persons. For example, the *partheniai* of Sparta (degraded or disenfranchised citizens) were sent to Tarentum (Zuchtriegel 2018: 32–3).
60. It should be noted that the use of the word 'colony' and its derivations can be misleading. Common usage of 'colony' is steeped in modern colonial analogy and implies that the colony was dependent upon the polity from which it derived. That was not the case with Archaic Greek colonies – these settlements

abroad were called *apoikia*, which means 'home away from home', and were always intended to be fully independent city states (Finley 1976). Archaic Greek colonies and modern imperial ones bear few similarities; it is simply that there were movements and settlements of people in both instances (Owen 2005: 17). Nevertheless, modern imperial analogy has influenced the study of Greek colonisation for the majority of the twentieth century and has led to a series of assumptions about the process, namely that it was a state-sponsored activity; 'land hunger' and trade were the primary, often conflicting, motivations; social conditions in metropoleis (mother cities), such as poverty, famine and civil *stasis*, were contributing factors; and the Greeks imposed their own culture upon the indigenous groups they encountered. These assumptions have been questioned in the post-colonial era, and new enquiries have reshaped our understanding of the Greek colonial phenomenon. In particular, we now recognise that the metropolis played a minor organisational role, 'land hunger' and trade are no longer seen as conflicting motives, unfavourable social conditions such as poverty or social unrest are viewed as retrojections that draw upon conventional poetic *topoi*, and interactions between Greeks and locals are understood to be multidimensional. As a result, it is clear that Greek colonisation was less like a modern colonial movement and more of a mass migration or diaspora (McInerney 2018). That being said, our broader understanding of Greek colonisation, however, does not negate the role of population pressure in the Archaic diaspora. Bioarchaeological research at Apollonia (modern Bulgaria) documented an increase in skeletal stress immediately after the arrival of the Greeks, and a corresponding decrease in levels of skeletal stress at Corinth, Apollonia's mother city. The decrease in skeletal stress at Corinth has been interpreted as evidence of an alleviation of population pressure (Kyle et al. 2016).

61. For an analysis of Greek trading systems, see Cunliffe 1988: 1–37.
62. The 'middle ground' is a physical and conceptual cultural territory that is shared by relatively equal groups. As a space of intercultural negotiation, the middle ground facilitates the development of new practices and meanings (White 1991: x). Each side plays a role, and the role is typically 'dictated by what it perceives to be the other's perception of it, resulting from mutual misrepresentation of values and practices' (Malkin 2011: 46). This role playing results in 'creative misunderstandings' which lead to the creation of an entirely new culture that does not securely belong to one group but contains elements of both. For instance, S. Rebecca Martin (2017) has argued that what we consider to be 'Phoenician art' is a construct, heavily influenced by Achaemenid, Egyptian and Greek art, and that a shared Phoenician identity only arose in the late sixth/early fifth century BCE in response to need for collective bargaining associated with their Achaemenid naval service and changes in trading patterns. Considering the Phoenician example, it is easy to see how there are some who maintain that the Mediterranean itself has served as a form of global-scale middle ground for cultural interaction, exchange and competition (e.g. Hodos 2009; 2010), but typically it is regional (e.g. Greek Sicily) and microregional (e.g. Morgantina and its surrounding territory) networks that are the focus of middle-ground research (Malkin 2002; 2004; 2011;

Antonaccio 2003; Gosden 2004; Hodos 2006; Demetriou 2012). Most often, and especially in the work of Irad Malkin, the middle ground is 'any regional cluster of networks where Greeks founded colonies or lived in *emporia* and mixed settlements' (2011: 47–8).

63. For a case study that demonstrates the equality of Greeks and locals in Sicily, see Fitzjohn 2007.

64. For evidence contrary to this position, see J. Hall 2002: 90–124.

65. At the end of the sixth century, Hecataeus (*FGrH* I fr. 119) uses the term *Hellênes* to refer to the entire population of Greece, and this is our earliest extant linguistic evidence of Panhellenism. *Hellênes* is used in the *Iliad* (2.681–5), but it specifically references the people who lived in the region south of Thessaly (Garland 2016: 46).

66. Currently, network theory is the dominant interpretive framework used to analyse Greek colonial interactions (Barney 2004; Tartaron 2014). Network theory envisions the ancient Greek world as a decentralised Mediterranean network composed of nodes (colonies, mother cities, emporia, Panhellenic sanctuaries – Delphi in particular), ties (what connects one node to another, e.g. communication, modes of transportation, shared religion and cultural practices) and flows (things that pass between nodes and through ties, e.g. raw material, currency, knowledge). The interactions among the nodes ultimately fostered the formation of a shared Greek identity (Malkin 2005; 2011; Donnellan 2016; McInerney 2018). Network theory is different from the 'world-system' model (e.g. Vlassopoulos 2007a; 2007b; Hall 2014). A world-system is comprised of 'processes, exchanges and interactions that link many groups, communities and polities: and these processes, exchanges and interactions, moving people, goods and ideas, range beyond the boundaries of a single group, community or polity . . . it can often be the case that the same agents might move people, goods and ideas/technologies at the same time' (Vlassopoulos 2007a: 94–5). The result of this is that the relationships between the three processes must be studied contextually in order to be understood. Furthermore, the world-system model does not require the participation of a whole world; rather there can be several competing world-systems (Vlassopoulos 2007a). The world-systems models have been criticised because they 'exhibit a tendency toward mechanistically reductionist, structurally overdetermined, functionalist explanations and an emphasis on core determination of process on the periphery. They are unable to accommodate culture or local agency and, in their uniformity, they deny the fundamental historicity of colonialism' (Dietler 2005: 58). Note, however, that Vlassopoulos (2007a: 93–4) maintains that the world-system model can be used without (dominant) core and (exploited) periphery assumptions. For more on the outmoded 'centre and periphery' model, see Rowlands et al. 1987; Champion 1989.

67. Clemente Marconi's work on Archaic temple architecture and iconography at Selinous also supports an Early Classical origin of the Greek/non-Greek divide. Although several scholars see Western Greek temples and their decoration as statements of Greek identity in non-Greek territory, Marconi rejects this and asserts that Archaic temple architecture and iconography in Sicily served to

broadcast a polis civic identity that was shaped by shared Greek traditions that originated in mainland Greece (2007).

68. For an alternative view of the origins of the Greek *barbaros*, see Kim 2013: 35–7.

69. Note, however, that the literary evidence is ambiguous here. Thucydides (1.3.3) states that Homer never used the term *barbaros*, and it has been argued that *barbarophonon* is a post-fifth-century alteration to the *Iliad* (Kim 2013: 29).

70. For Greek attitudes on non-Greek religion, see Rudhardt 2002.

71. It seems that there was still speculation of an impending Persian invasion of Greece, which might have been the true impetus for this call to arms (Isocrates 5.76; Mitchell 2007: 138).

72. Note that Ward (2002) maintains that Aristotle's criteria for natural slavery was simply deficiency of deliberative ability and that both Greeks and barbarians could be natural slaves on that basis.

73. Although we have the most information for Athens, there is evidence to suggest that Aegina, Chios and Corinth had comparable enslaved populations (Harrison 2019).

74. Even though it has been demonstrated that most of the enslaved were non-Greek, the percentage of non-Greek slave names is relatively low (Vlassopoulos 2010) – 20–7 per cent of all known slave names in Athens and only around 11 per cent of all known slave names at Delphi (Lewis 2018b).

75. For a catalogue of the enslaved, see Garland 2014: 271–7.

76. See Thompson 2011: 205–7 for written descriptions of enslaved individuals of African descent.

77. Hesiod (fr. 233 West), however, identifies the Pelasgians as one of the Hellenic peoples who occupied and divided Crete (McInerney 2014: 27). Also note that the Leleges were a similar, diffusive, non-Greek prehistoric people (McInerney 2014).

78. Interestingly, most of these mythical figures might have originally been Greek through the Archaic period, but were assigned foreign origins in the Late Archaic/ Classical, especially in Attic drama, in order to reinforce social subdivisions. For instance, Medea, who is originally Corinthian, is of Black Sea origin in Euripides' play (Hall 1989: 35; Miller 2005).

79. For brief commentary on these passages, see Gruen 2011: 206 n. 79.

80. Although, it is worth noting that stereotypes do not always carry negative connotations (e.g. Dench 1995: 22; Bohak 2005; Skinner 2012: 115–21): 'A form of social knowledge, they are best conceived as mobile, discursive systems of understanding that people carried in their heads. Stereotypes could find a voice in a variety of contexts: the agora, theater, or symposium. That they affected individual perception and were an important factor in defining both individual and group identities is important; that we might find their ubiquity unsettling or distasteful is not' (Skinner 2012: 121).

81. For representations of Etruscans in Athenian vase-painting, see Shapiro 2000; for Phrygians and Lydians, see DeVries 2000; for Thracians, see Tsiafakis 2000; for Persians, see Castriota 2000; and for Egyptians, see Miller 2000.

82. Munich, Staatliche Antikensammlungen und Glyptothek 2378.

83. Note that Dionysus and maenads also typically wear animal skins in Dionysiac scenes (McNally 1978).

84. Note that satyrs and centaurs are also represented with these physical features (Padgett 2003).
85. Since some of these alabastra represent Amazon archers who are identically attired, a recent reappraisal by Neils (2007) of the corpus suggests that the black archers are black Amazons from Libya (Diodorus Siculus 3.52–5). For other Greek representations of sub-Saharan Africans, see Leclant 2010; Snowden 2010; Padgett 2000: 67–8, fig. 2.10); Bérard 2000: 395–406, figs 15.3–12. For vase representations of sub-Saharan Africans inspired by myth (e.g. Busiris, Memnon and Andromeda), see Miller 2000.
86. See Mitchell 2009; Walsh 2009 for more on grotesque and comedic representations in Greek vase-painting, especially on Boeotian Cabirion vases.
87. For vestiges of the 'tradition of mocking the barbarian' in the late fourth century BCE, see Romm 1996: 134–5.
88. Hybridisation, or hybridity, is a biological term used to describe the offspring of different breeds, varieties, species or genera. When applied to cross-cultural interactions, it describes the social space between two groups, a 'third-space', where complex negotiations in cultural adoption and combination take place (Bhabha 1994). In this third-space, shared experiences and regular encounters between people from different traditions who were using different forms of material culture contributed to processes of cultural appropriation and admixture (Tronchetti and Van Dommelen 2005: 193). The term can also be applied to aspects of social identity (e.g. Sikeliote) and material culture, where in the latter case it is specifically used to describe a mixture of styles (Antonaccio 2001; 2005). Like Hellenisation, the concept of hybridity carries its own problematic assumptions. For example, it assumes that material culture carries at least some of its original significance when it is recontextualised and that there are distinct homogeneous groups (e.g. Greek and indigenous), recognised as such in antiquity, that could be blended and hybridised (Antonaccio 2005: 107; Owen 2005: 16–17; Tronchetti and Van Dommelen 2005; Van Dommelen 2006). Nevertheless, hybridity is most successful when it is 'used to investigate the nuances of interaction and exchange at all levels (looking beyond the macro-social level to the everyday contact between people on the ground) in specific localised contexts (moving away from the idea that only the colonised, indigenous population was made hybrid), and understood as a process or set of practices' (Cole 2019: 76; cf. Antonaccio 2010).
89. Pliny the Elder mentions Epigonos and praises one of his works, called 'The Trumpeter' (*Natural History* 34.88), which has been associated with the Dying Gaul (Pollitt 1986: 85).

CHAPTER 2

Disability

The concept of disability is a cultural construct. By simple definition, 'disability' can describe any number of physical, mental or medical conditions that cause someone to be labelled as 'different' or 'unfit' by other members of their society. As a result, the notion of what is disabling can vary widely over time and across cultures (Roberts 2000: 46). For instance, rickets, which is caused by prolonged vitamin D deficiency, results in bowed legs, curvature of the spine and stunted growth. In the past, rickets was seen as a disabling condition because it would have impaired an individual's mobility and aptitude for physical labour. Today rickets is rare, but when it does occur, there are surgical and therapeutic interventions widely available to help restore mobility. Furthermore, the understanding of what constitutes a disability can even differ among groups within a culture. An apt illustration of this comes from Martha's Vineyard, an island off the coast of Massachusetts. Throughout most of the United States, deafness is (and has traditionally been) viewed as a disabling and socially isolating condition, but on Martha's Vineyard, congenital deafness was endemic for approximately 250 years (the last deaf resident died in the early 1950s; Groce 1985). There, the incidence of congenital deafness was thirty-five times more common than the national average, which prompted all residents – those who could hear as well as those who could not – to use sign language. The unique bilingual nature of the island created a situation in which communication barriers and social stigmas usually associated with deafness were non-existent, thus ensuring the complete social integration of those who, in other circumstances, would most likely have been considered disabled. Deafness, therefore, was not deemed to be a disability on the Vineyard. Indeed, when asked about the status of the deaf on the island, a woman who grew up in the early twentieth century candidly remarked 'those people weren't handicapped. They were just deaf' (Groce 1985: 5).

In order to better understand ancient Greek societal attitudes towards disabled people, this chapter reviews the bioarchaeological evidence of physical difference in the Late Archaic/Classical Greek world (ca. sixth to fifth/fourth centuries BCE). Although material from the Greek mainland is the primary focus of this investigation, case studies from earlier and later periods of Greek history, as well as Greek colonial contexts, are incorporated to illustrate patterns of continuity and/or change. The chapter begins with a description of theoretical models of disability employed within the field of disability studies. Since literary accounts suggest that some individuals born with conspicuous congenital conditions were rejected shortly after birth, the next section examines the practice of infant exposure. The discussion that follows focuses on physical differences that are detectable on human skeletal remains, namely those associated with the limbs (e.g. club foot), stature (e.g. dwarfism), the cranium (e.g. craniosynostosis) and non-binary sex and gender (e.g. intersex). The bioarchaeological evidence of these conditions is surveyed and examined in the context of contemporary literary and visual sources. Conditions that primarily impact soft tissue, such as mental illness, blindness, deafness and cognitive impairment, will not be discussed since they generally do not affect the skeleton. The chapter concludes with a consideration of intersectionality and the ways in which the coalescence of multiple marginalising factors (e.g. a person who has a curved spine and is enslaved) can negatively impact social integration.

THEORETICAL MODELS OF DISABILITY

Three major theoretical models of disability have emerged from the field of disability studies.[1] The first (and the oldest) is the medical model, which understands disability to be a direct result of conspicuous biological anomalies. Within the framework of this model, anomalies inevitably lead to marginalisation because an individual with physical abnormalities cannot, by definition, meet societal standards for corporeal normality. The remedy for any stigmatising abnormality is always medical intervention, which aims to transform the disabled body and make it as close to 'normal' as possible (e.g. Brisenden 1986; Cross 1999: 10; Gosbell 2018: 32–3).[2] The second model was developed in response to the shortcomings of the medical model. Called the social model, it rejects the notion that disability is the direct result of physical impairment and argues instead that disability is caused by societal structures that promote discrimination (specifically 'ableism', or discrimination against disabled persons).[3] The social model compares disability to other forms of social discrimination (racism, sexism, homophobia, xenophobia etc.) and emphasises the need to address disability on a social level (e.g. Abberley 1987; Cross 1999: 10–12; Gosbell 2018: 33–4). It also considers disability and impairment to be dichotomous, with disability as socially constructed and impairment as biological – similar to the way in which gender studies perceives sex as biological and gender as a social construct (e.g. Davis 2000).

The social model of disability has been criticised for numerous reasons.[4] First, it 'ignores the embodied reality of impairment, to an extent delegitimising the potential pain and hardship that can be associated with an impairment' (Gosbell 2018: 35). Also, by comparing disability to other socially constructed forms of discrimination, like racism, it overlooks the physiological experience of the disabled and the reality that people with impairments would continue to navigate their environment differently from other members of society whether they faced social discrimination or not. Another point of contention is the binary construct between impairment and disability. When the two are viewed as discrete categories, it is difficult to tell where the impairment ends and the disability (and concomitant discrimination) begins. Take, for instance, a person on the autism spectrum: '[if that person] has difficulty communicating with others and/or accessing community services, to what extent is this the result of their biological or neurological "impairment" or the result of a disabling society unprepared and unwilling to embrace neurological diversity?' (Gosbell 2018: 36). Finally, the social model is seen as flawed because it intrinsically sees impairment as a 'problem' that is simply transferred from the individual (à la medical model) to social structures (Gosbell 2018: 34–6).

The third theoretical model of disability is the cultural model (e.g. Snyder and Mitchell 2006; Junior and Schipper 2013: 35). Through this interpretive lens, disability is viewed as a shifting and culturally determined phenomenon that cannot be defined by a single factor, such as an individual's medical condition (i.e. the medical model) or degree of impairment-driven social discrimination (i.e. the social model). Instead, the cultural model focuses on ways in which notions of disability and non-disability (or able-bodiedness) are constructed within a given culture, which includes the reception of the impairment and any symbolism associated with it. Accordingly, this model rejects the concept of disability as a static and unchanging global phenomenon, and promotes instead the conception that it is 'experienced, represented, and interpreted differently across various cultures and historical periods' (Gosbell 2018: 37) and that it can be locally variable. The benefit of the cultural model is that it allows us to understand how disability is represented in a given culture at a specific point in time. The cultural model is also phenomenological in that it recognises that the distinctions between biological impairment and socially constructed physical disability are not always clear and that it is more beneficial to conceive of them as different aspects of a single experience (Gosbell 2018: 36–9).

But, how does one approach disability from the vantage point of the cultural model? Broadly construed, culture 'denotes the totality of "things" created and employed by a particular people or a society at a given time in history, be they material or immaterial: objects and instruments, institutions and organisations, ideas and knowledge, symbols and values, meanings and interpretations, narratives and histories, traditions, rituals and customs, social

behaviour, attitudes and identities' (Waldschmidt 2017: 7). Using this definition of culture, the cultural model focuses on the development of a nuanced
understanding of the social positions of disabled people. It seeks to investigate
the ways in which individuals with disabilities (and those without) negotiate
their places within systems of religion, custom, law, symbolism and knowledge,
as well as within processes of categorisation and institutionalisation. It is also
concerned with the relationships between disabled people and material culture
(Waldschmidt 2017).

The cultural model is well suited to the bioarchaeological exploration of past
attitudes towards disability.[5] The various components of a burial assemblage –
the body and its position, grave goods, burial receptacle, grave/tomb type and
placement within (or away from) the cemetery – allow us not only to identify
individuals with physical impairments, but also to learn more about the ways
in which these people operated within their own cultural contexts and were
perceived by the members of their communities (discussed in more detail in
Chapter 1). Theya Molleson has boldly asserted that '[a]n understanding of
attitudes to disability in the archaeological context can really only be inferred
from the treatment of the dead' (1999: 69). Molleson might be right. Other
forms of evidence, namely literature and art, are useful and, in fact, necessary for
the reconstruction of contemporary attitudes towards the impaired, but are also
inherently biased in that none include a first-hand perspective of one who lived
with a physical impairment. Burials, however, are unique because they alone
hold the potential to shed light on individual experience. Thus, the patterns
that emerge from the current bioarchaeological study allow us to make broader
statements about the social positions of disabled people.

On the other hand, as previously discussed, archaeological evidence from
funerary contexts holds the potential to shed light on the individual experiences of disabled people in an intimate way that literary and visual sources
cannot. In particular, physical differences can be detected from the analysis
of skeletal material. These differences are visible due to the plasticity of the
human skeleton, which is shaped over the course of one's lifetime in response
to growth and development, injury and illness, and repetitive activity. Furthermore, since the dead do not bury themselves, the mortuary treatment of the
deceased can provide insight into an individual's identity and place within a
community (Knüsel 1999: 32, 35–6).

However, the bioarchaeological investigation of disability is not without its
complications. In general, the physical evidence of disability is scarce. Common explanations for this dearth include the following possibilities: occurrence was less frequent in antiquity, individuals with disabilities might have
been buried apart from the population, skeletons with pathological conditions
(especially those with metabolic or demineralising disease processes such as
osteoporosis) might not preserve as well as unaffected ones, conditions might

have been misdiagnosed or missed altogether during skeletal analysis, and the sample sizes of skeletons available for study are too small to include the rare instances of disability (Waldron 2000: 31).

Another issue is that skeletal evidence is not self-evident. For example, it is not possible to determine the degree of an individual's impairment or level of pain from skeletal material alone. Minor osteoarthritic change can produce severe pain while other, more extensive, skeletal changes may be asymptomatic. Furthermore, not all skeletal changes induce impairment (Roberts 1999). Just as it is imprudent to assume that the greater the impairment, the greater the pain, Tom Shakespeare counsels that there is danger in confusing the biological evidence with social experience (1999: 100). Likewise, Katherine Dettwyler maintains that archaeologists are not 'justified in drawing conclusions either about quality of life for disabled individuals in the past or about the motives or attitudes of the rest of the community from skeletal evidence of physical impairment' (1991: 375). Rather, skeletal evidence must be contextualised and studied in tandem with other components of the burial assemblage as well as additional extant lines of evidence (e.g. historical, literary, visual, epigraphic).

Finally, it is not possible to discern all disabling conditions from the skeletal record. For instance, many disabling conditions affect only soft tissues, and as a result skeletal remains rarely reveal evidence of mental illness, blindness, deafness, speech impediments or cognitive impairment (Roberts 2000: 48).[6] This analysis, therefore, focuses on case studies of physical impairments that can be identified from skeletal material, such as those that affect the limbs, stature, and the shape of the cranium.[7] Although skeletal adaptations that are associated with the ageing process, like those that affect joint mobility (e.g. osteoarthritis) and stature (e.g. kyphosis), are similarly perceptible in human remains, discussion of these is postponed until the end of the chapter because of their intersectionality (i.e. bodies with age-related impairments embody two marginalising characteristics – advanced age and disability).

EXPOSURE OF DISABLED INFANTS

This survey of the bioarchaeological evidence of physical impairment in the ancient Greek world begins with infants, as we must first consider that individuals born with obvious abnormalities were removed from the population shortly after birth. However, the practice of exposure, the rejection and subsequent abandonment of a newborn, complicates the archaeological investigation of disability.[8] Across the ancient Greek world, infants who were unwanted, unhealthy, disabled or deformed were candidates for exposure after birth (Plato, *Theaetetus* 149a–151c, 160c–161a; Ogden 1996: 106–10; Cohen 2000a: 4; Jenkins 2015: 22).[9] Literary sources suggest that children judged to be abnormal were especially at risk (Patterson 1985: 113–14). Plato (*Republic* 5.460c) and Aristotle (*Politics* 7.1335b), for instance, deem it necessary for members of their respective ideal city states to dispose of inferior or seemingly defective infants – Aristotle taking it as far as to suggest that there should be a law that forbids citizens from rearing deformed children.[10] Indeed, where the average Greek parents were concerned, especially those that already had healthy offspring, the worth of rearing these children was quite low, and as previously stated, physical defects were believed to be indicators of divine disfavour (Delcourt 1938; Ogden 1994: 93–6; 1997: 29–34; Garland 2010: 2, 59–72; Penrose 2015: 510).[11] As a result, we can presume that many individuals with congenital conditions were removed from the population before they had an opportunity to mature.

Those responsible for the decision to expose a newborn varied according to individual circumstance and local custom.[12] In Athens, the purview was typically the father's, but in cases of sexual assault or illegitimacy the onus would be on the mother.[13] In Sparta, the decision was made by the *Gerousia* – the council of elders (Plutarch, *Lycurgus* 16.1–2; Huys 1996; Rousselle 2001: 319; Penrose 2015: 309–10).[14] It has also been suggested that the midwife could play a role as well, as she might 'be the one to take an unwanted live infant and expose it or hand it over to someone who wanted a child' (Evans Grubbs 2013: 85). Yet, regardless of who made the choice, the process was generally the same: infants were carefully inspected for infirmities or defects, and those with obvious irregularities were placed in a pot or chest and discarded in either a deserted spot, or alternatively, a place that would allow it to be readily found by passersby, such as near a shrine, crossroads or rubbish heap.[15] Although the abandoned infant would be vulnerable to the elements, starvation and wild animals, exposure was not necessarily a death sentence – myth and tragedy (e.g. Atalanta; Euripides' *Ion* and *Alexander*; Sophocles' *Oedipus Rex*) provide us with examples of exposed infants who were reared by adoptive parents, and we can imagine that childless couples and slave traders might eagerly retrieve unwanted babies (Patterson 1985: 116, 121–2; Rousselle 2001: 305).

It cannot be assumed that *all* disabled newborns were exposed (Laes 2013). Some disabilities, for example, might not have been evident at birth, so those who were blind, deaf or non-verbal would not be immediately identified. Herodotus (1.34, 38, 85) provides us with an illustration of such a case from Lydia. Croesus, the king of Lydia, had two sons – the elder, Atys, was his heir, while the younger, whose name is never given, was born deaf and non-verbal. Although Croesus was openly disdainful of his disabled son (1.38.2), the young man remained his devoted companion and eventually saved the king's life during the Persian siege of Sardis (Garland 2010: 96–7; Laes 2013: 133). Other congenital issues, such as those related to growth or mental development, do not manifest until well after the brief window for exposure closes (Garland 2010: 13). Furthermore, some parents might have simply chosen to raise their children regardless of their physical impairments, as the aforementioned law proposed by Aristotle (*Politics* 7.1335b) insinuates that disabled children *were* being raised, otherwise there would be no need to outlaw the practice.

Archaeological evidence of exposure is rare; nevertheless, a case can be made for the infanticide of disabled newborns in the Athenian Agora.[16] Forty metres north of the Temple of Hephaestus, a well was constructed during the Classical period to serve the needs of an area of artisans' workshops (G 5:3). Over time, the well accumulated a fill that contained a variety of material, such as bronze scraps from nearby metal workshops, pottery and the skeletal remains of humans and animals, including 150 dogs.[17] One of the most striking finds, however, was a substantial Hellenistic deposit (second quarter of the second century BCE) of commingled human bone containing approximately 460 infants and foetuses.[18] Although the temptation is strong to connect these deaths to the practice of exposure, osteological analysis has shown that most of the infants and foetuses died from natural causes at or near the end of a full-term pregnancy (with the notable exception of one individual who was most likely the victim of child abuse) and were subsequently denied conventional burials on account of either their age or low social status (Liston et al. 2018).[19]

There were, nevertheless, a small number of individuals in the well with congenital conditions who were deemed to be candidates for exposure. At least seven, possibly ten, full-term infants had cleft palates, which would not only have disfigured them, but also impaired their ability to feed and breathe, as well as increased their susceptibility to infections and liquid aspiration. Two other infants were born with limb differences. One had a stunted right arm – the humerus and ulna displayed shortened bone shafts with joint abnormalities – while another had a deformed left clavicle that would ensure that its left shoulder was positioned abnormally low and angled towards the front of the chest.[20] So, even though the Agora Bone Well served predominately as a disposal site for the newborn dead, it undoubtedly doubled as a spot for infant exposure (Liston et al. 2018).

PHYSICAL DIFFERENCES

Despite widespread exposure practices that disproportionately targeted disabled infants, literary and archaeological evidence attests that some individuals with congenital physical conditions survived to adulthood. As previously discussed, this is partially due to the fact that numerous congenital conditions are not immediately apparent at birth (e.g. dwarfism; Dasen 1990: 191) and could have manifested only after the opportune window for exposure had closed one to two weeks after birth. To illustrate this with modern statistics, approximately 3 per cent of infants born in Euro-American countries have visible congenital conditions, but by the time children reach five years of age, that percentage jumps to 8 per cent (Graumann 2013: 181).

With the exposure option taken off of the table, parents might have sought other forms of intervention to aid their children. In the realm of medicine, the Hippocratic authors provide some guidance on congenital conditions and birth-related injuries. They warn that children born with dislocated limbs risk atrophy if the limbs are not reset (*On Joints* 55), and recommend appropriate vocations for those with congenital arm differences (*On Joints* 12) and impaired mobility (*On Joints* 53; Rose 2003: 38–40).[21] Furthermore, impaired mobility could be improved through the use of prosthetic devices (Herodotus 9.37; Pindar, *Olympian* 1.25–7; Bliquez 1995; Stampolidis and Tassoulas 2014: 264–7; Draycott 2019) and access ramps (Sneed 2020). Miraculous healings were also deemed to be within the realm of the possible, as evidenced by the plethora of votive offerings (anatomical or otherwise) at healing sanctuaries. These dedications are offered to healing gods, such as Asclepius, either in thanksgiving for cures for, as described by Martha Rose, 'everything from lameness to missing eyeballs' (2003: 38), or alternatively, as gifts given by petitioners in the *hope* that such a healing might occur (Roebuck 1951; Van Straten 1981: 111–12; Aleshire 1989; Forsén 1996; Vlahogiannis 2005; Horn 2013; Geroulanos 2014; Petsalis-Diomidis 2016; Hughes 2017; Draycott and Graham 2017).

The potential for acquired postnatal disabilities was also an ever-present reality. Soldiers were permanently injured in war (Herodotus 6.114.1, 6.134–6; Felton 2014), prisoners could be mutilated in captivity (Quintus Curtius 5.5.5–24; Diodorus Siculus 18.69.2–9; Justin 11; Miles 2003), metalworkers and miners were prone to debilitating industrial injuries (Burford 1972: 72; Rose 2003: 40), and surgeons were known to inadvertently damage limbs (*On Joints* 63–6; Von Staden 1990: 86, 103). Instances of acute illness, infection and injuries – athletic, accidental or episodes of interpersonal violence – could also result in permanent impairment (*On Fractures* 11; Dawson 1986; Garland 2010: 22; Pudsey 2017).[22] Likewise, malnutrition and vitamin deficiency, which are often closely tied to one another, can irrevocably change the shape of the body, as they can lead to stunted growth (e.g. malnutrition) and bowed limbs (e.g. rickets). Starvation, the most extreme form of malnutrition, occurs when an individual's body weight drops by one third, and can precipitate debilitating side effects which include blindness, muscle atrophy and oedema (Pojman 2012: 128). Indeed, the earliest description of starvation oedema is found in the writings of Hesiod, who encourages farmers to properly provision themselves for the winter 'so that the irresistible cold of winter does not take you in poverty, causing you to rub a swollen foot with a shrunken hand' (*Works and Days* 496f as quoted in Garland 2010: 21).

Regardless of whether physical impairments were acquired at birth or at some later date, they complicated the lives of those who had them. For instance, it might be difficult for the someone with a physical impairment to arrange or maintain a marriage, as Plato remarks that it can be intolerable to be married to someone who is physically or mentally impaired (*Laws* 11.925e, 926b).

Furthermore, depending on the severity of the impairment, one's ability to work might be impacted significantly. Although the Hippocratic authors, as discussed above, offered suggestions of appropriate vocations for those with physical disabilities, in the fifth and fourth centuries BCE the Athenian state made special payments to disabled citizens, which included those severely injured in war (Aeschines 1.104, 109; Aristotle, *Athenian Constitution* 49.4; Lysias 24; Dillon 1995; 2017). This practice, which might have its origins in sixth-century Solonian reforms (Plutarch, *Solon* 31.2), gained additional significance during the period of democracy, as it stymied a potential avenue of political coercion. By providing those unable to work with a means of subsistence, the Athenian state prevented them from relying on the financial assistance of wealthy patrons who might seek to exert political influence over their unfortunate wards (Dillon 1995).

In order to better understand how individuals with disabilities were affected by their conditions on both a personal and societal level, the discussions that follow focus on case studies of the various manifestations of physical difference for which we have literary, visual and bioarchaeological evidence. These conditions broadly fall into four discrete categories: associated with the limbs (e.g. club foot), stature (e.g. dwarfism), the cranium (e.g. craniosynostosis) and non-binary sex and gender (e.g. intersex).

Limb differences

Limb differences are attested in myth, especially in stories concerning Oedipus and Hephaestus. Oedipus, whose name literally means 'swollen foot', is alternately described as having either congenitally clubbed feet, or as in Sophocles' play, feet that were bound and pinned together when he was exposed shortly after birth (*Oedipus Rex* 1034; Ogden 1997: 29). The origin of Hephaestus' impairment is similarly ambiguous (Barbanera 2015). One iteration maintains that he was born with a congential foot condition (*Odyssey* 8.323–36), which prompted his mother, Hera, to fling him into the ocean (*Homeric Hymn to Apollo* 2.311–18). In the other version, his feet were severely injured when he fell on the island of Lemnos after his violent expulsion from Mount Olympus by Zeus (*Iliad* 1.589–94; Ogden 1997: 36).[23] The latter scenario would have been plausible to an ancient audience, as violent falls were known to severely impair the feet. The Hippocratic Corpus warns of the dangers of heel fractures sustained from jumping or falling from high places, as the force can cause the bones (the talus and calcaneus) to separate, which can lead to necrosis and gangrene (*On Fractures* 11; Rose 2003: 17). Furthermore, scenes of Hephaestus' return to Olympus on Greek vases, such as those depicted on an Ionian black-figure hydria from Caere (ca. 535 BCE; Fig. 2.1) and an Attic black-figure volute krater commonly called the François Vase (ca. 570/560 BCE), underscore his impairment by representing him riding a donkey, with his feet noticeably

Figure 2.1 Black-figure hydria (Ionic-Greek, ca. 525 BCE) from Caere, Italy depicting the return of Hephaestus to Olympus (Vienna, Kunsthistorisches Museum IV 3577). Hephaestus riding a mule with visibly impaired feet (centre), Dionysus (left), maenad with a snake and flute-playing satyr (right). Photo by Erich Lessing © Erich Lessing/ Art Resource, NY.

turned backward (Brennan 2016). Yet, regardless of how he acquired them, Hephaestus' impaired feet and cumbersome gait set him apart from the rest of the pantheon and made him the laughing stock of the gods (*Iliad* 1.598–600; *Odyssey* 8.256–366; Smith 2009; Bremmer 2010; Pavel 2017; Hall 2018).

Despite their rarity in the realm of myth, it is likely that limb differences were common in ancient Greek populations. Some of these are congenital conditions that are acquired in one of three ways: on account of heredity or circumstances impacting either gestation or birth. The Greeks observed that physical conditions could be passed from parents to offspring, as Aristotle remarks that physically impaired parents tend to produce physically impaired children (*History of Animals* 585b, 586a; *Generation of Animals* 721b) and a Hippocratic author notes that mobility impairments are hereditary (*Sacred Disease* 3). Even the gods were not believed to escape heredity, as Hephaestus' sons are described by later authors as being born with mobility impairments (Apollonius Rhodius, *Argonautica* 1.202–6; Apollodorus, *Library* 3.16.1). Today, we recognise that genetic factors are responsible for 90 per cent of developmental conditions (Roberts and Manchester 2007: 46). Yet, without the advantage of modern science, Greeks could not understand the nuanced differences between heredity and chromosomal mutation, nor did they have a firm grasp on what could be inherited and what could not. This imperfect understanding of heredity is reflected in Aristotle's assertion that children can inherit their parents' superficial defects, such as scars or brands (*Generation of Animals* 724a). Furthermore, Greeks could not discern whether a physical condition was caused by genetics, gestation, conditions of birth or some combination of genetic and environmental factors (Roberts and Manchester 2007: 47–8). They did, nevertheless, recognise that physical impairments could be acquired during the gestational period (Aristotle, *Generation of Animals* 772b, 773a) or in the event of a premature birth (Aristotle, *Generation of Animals* 775a; Pseudo-Aristotle, *Problems* 895a; Rose 2003: 14–16).

Club foot (or talipes equinovarus), the physical impairment that Hephaestus most likely had, is the most common congenital condition of the foot, and it is observed today in 1 in every 800–1000 births. With club foot, typically the tendons in the foot are shorter than normal, causing the foot to rotate inward and downward at the ankle. One or both feet can be affected. Although its aetiology is unknown, club foot has been determined to be more prevalent in males, and it could be transmitted as an autosomal dominant trait, since a family history is present in many cases (Aufderheide and Rodríguez-Martín 2005: 75; Roberts and Manchester 2007: 58). Club foot, and its corrective treatment, is described in the Hippocratic treatise *On Joints* (62). According to the author of the treatise, mild cases of club foot can be reversed by bending, pushing and bandaging the foot and stabilising it with corrective footwear (Horstmanshoff 2012: 3–4). These rehabilitative measures were effective because club foot is primarily a soft tissue disorder that impacts the bones of the foot only if left untreated (Aufderheide and Rodríguez-Martín 2005: 75).

Despite the existence of corrective therapies for club foot, not everyone born with the condition received treatment. As it progressed, the foot impairment would result in a limp and atrophy of the affected limb, which was generally deemed to be unattractive (Plato, *Hippias Minor* 374c; Aristophanes, *Frogs* 845–6; Edwards 1997a: 42–3), and in some cases, cause for mocking and ridicule (Garland 2010: 114). For instance, komast dancers with club foot, who are depicted primarily in the festive context of the symposion, are well attested on black-figure vases produced during the seventh and sixth centuries BCE (e.g. Fig. 2.2). Komast dancers were the first human figures to be depicted in vase-painting with any regularity, and images of them were produced in each of the major black-figure production centres (Corinth, Attica, Laconia, Boeotia, East Greece and the Greek West), although specific iconography and significance varied according to region. In general, komast dancers are disruptive, ridiculous

Figure 2.2 Corinthian alabastron (ca. 625–600 BCE) by the La Trobe Painter depicting two komast dancers engaged in a dance or struggle in the bottom register. The dancer on the viewer's left is visibly impaired (Paris, Louvre S1104). Photo by Hervé Lewandowski © RMN-Grand Palais/Art Resource, NY.

figures who are often padded to appear fat-bottomed and fat-bellied. They are occasionally depicted with large genitalia and typically display a propensity for lewd public behaviour, which includes bottom-slapping, excreting, urinating, copulating and vomiting. Most komast dancers do not have club foot, but those that do can be found in sympotic scenes and also in scenes of the Return of Hephaestus, where they are possibly present to imitate and mock the god of the forge (Smith 2009: 85–7). Indeed, it is presumed that komast dancers, and those with club foot in particular, were meant to be sources of comic relief in the same way that Hephaestus served as the brunt of Olympian jokes (Smith 2009; 2010; Hall 2018).[24]

Beyond the realm of visual arts, club foot is also perceptible in human remains. Because the skeletal adaptations produced by club foot are so slight, it is far easier to diagnose the condition in mummies than skeletons. However, if club foot is suspected (on the basis of limb atrophy, foot anomalies etc.), the best approach is to reconstruct the bones of both feet and search the suspect foot for signs of abnormal changes to the distal tibia, talus, calcaneus, cuboid, navicular and metatarsals (Aufderheide and Rodríguez-Martín 2005: 75). Very few archaeological cases of club foot have been documented, and only one of these derives from the ancient Greek world. In that case, an Adolescent male from Lerna (122 Ler., Middle Bronze Age, ca. 2000–1600 BCE; see the Introduction for the ranges of osteological age categories like Adolescent) bears noticeable abnormalities on the left calcaneo-navicular joint, and the left femur is noticeably thinner than the right, suggesting atrophy of the muscles of the left leg (Angel 1971: 55; Grmek 1991: 71).

Another condition that affects the limbs is congenital dislocation. Although the head of the radius can be congenitally dislocated, its occurrence is exceedingly rare (Aufderheide and Rodríguez-Martín 2005: 73). Rather, the dislocation most frequently observed at birth is that of the hip. Even though breech births are six times more likely to develop hip dislocation, it is also clear that genetic factors play a role in its aetiology. For example, parents who do not have hip dislocation, but have a family history of it, have a 6 per cent chance of producing offspring with a dislocated hip. If only one parent has the condition, the odds rise to 36 per cent. Congenital hip dislocation affects females more often than males and the left hip more frequently than the right. Both hips are involved in more than half of the documented cases. Due to its hereditary component, modern prevalence rates vacillate among populations from between 1 and 15–20 per 1000 live births (Aufderheide and Rodríguez-Martín 2005: 69; Roberts and Manchester 2007: 57).

Congenital hip dislocation, technically termed congenital acetabular dysplasia, is a defect in the development of the acetabulum that prevents union between the femoral head and acetabulum. Hip dislocations are discussed in the Hippocratic treatise *On Joints* (51–61, 70–8), but in antiquity, it is likely that a congenital dislocation would only be apparent when children began to walk, but by then it would have been too late for treatment. In skeletal remains, signs of hip dislocation include an underdeveloped acetabulum, the creation of a new articulation (neo-acetabulum) on the os coxa, the flattening of the femoral head, and degenerative joint disease at the site of the dysplasia (Roberts and Manchester 2007: 57–8; Waldron 2009: 211). One ancient Greek skeleton is suspected to have been born with a dislocated hip.[25] The individual, a Young Adult male (16 Arg.), was found in Argos and dates to the Geometric period (ca. 900–850 BCE). The dysplasia affected the individual's left hip, which caused an unevenness of gait that ultimately led to the development of degenerative changes on the neo-acetabulum, proximal femur and vertebrae (Charles 1958: 280, 311; Grmek 1991: 71).

Unfortunately, ancient authors are often not specific in their descriptions of physical impairments, and it is impossible to know the precise conditions of some historical personages. For example, Agesilaus II, a fourth-century king of Sparta (r. 398–359/8 BCE), is described as having an impaired leg from an early age (Xenophon, *Hellenica* 3.3.3; Plutarch, *Agesilaus* 2.3; *Moralia* 208d–e; Samama 2013: 240). The genesis and specific nature of his impairment is never disclosed, but it has been suggested that the literary evidence leans in favour of a congenital condition like hip dysplasia or club foot (e.g. Penrose 2015: 517). Despite their lack of medical details, the same literary sources provide us with a fascinating psychological portrait of Agesilaus and his attitude towards his impediments and abilities. According to Plutarch, Agesilaus tried to minimise his impairment and refused to sit for portraits (*Agesilaus* 2.4), but at the same time, he was the first to mock himself or make a joke about it (2.3). He also would not permit his impairment to prevent him from the completion of any task (2.3), including the physically demanding Spartan educational system. It seems that his own approach to overcoming personal obstacles stunted his compassion for others. Plutarch informs us that Agesilaus, having encountered a soldier with a mobility impairment who had left the battlefield in search of a horse, told the man that it was necessary for a soldier to stand his ground rather than turn and flee (*Moralia* 210f).[26] Furthermore, while on another campaign, he purportedly abandoned an ill companion. As his friend called out to him to protest his desertion, Agesilaus told the man that he, Agesilaus, could not be both compassionate and prudent (*Agesilaus* 13). Yet, even though Agesilaus was a respected and capable general, he was almost denied the kingship on account of his mobility impairment. An oracle from Apollo, produced by a seer colluding with Agesilaus' political rival, warned 'boasting Sparta not to sprout a crippled monarchy' (Garland 2010: 40). The prophecy appeared to reference Agesilaus (*Agesilaus* 3.7; Pausanias 3.8.9), but a clever reinterpretation proffered by Lysander, another respected general, shifted the focus from Agesilaus and ensured his successful election to the office of king (Xenophon, *Hellenica* 3.3.3). In an interesting reversal, however, the first interpretation of the oracle was recalled in later years, and Agesilaus' mobility impairment was ultimately blamed for the downfall of Sparta (*Agesilaus* 30; Pausanias 3.8.9; Penrose 2015: 516–20).

Returning to the aetiology of limb differences, other pathological processes can lead to physical impairments. Some infectious diseases, like tuberculosis (described in the Hippocratic treatises *Internal Affections* 10–12 and *Diseases* 2.48–50), can cause the formation of destructive lesions in joints, especially those of the hip, knee, ankle, foot and shoulder (Aufderheide and Rodríguez-Martín 2005: 139–40). Autoimmune diseases, such as rheumatoid arthritis, which affects connective tissue, can also produce erosive lesions on the joints (Roberts and Manchester 2007: 155–7; Waldron 2009: 46–53). Furthermore, rickets, a metabolic disease often caused by a vitamin D deficiency, results in bowed legs (Roberts and Manchester 2007: 237–40; Waldron 2009: 127–9). None of these conditions have been documented on extant Greek skeletal remains, and they are rarely attested in the archaeological record.

Another pathological process that can lead to significant limb impairment is gout. Gout is a metabolic disorder that results in a high concentration of uric acid in the blood. Uric acid crystals accumulate in and around joints, causing inflammatory and sometimes erosive changes. The disease begins with an acute attack of the first metatarsophalangeal joint (or big toe), then spreads to other joints (Waldron 2009: 67–70). Gout is mentioned twenty-two times in the Hippocratic treatises, and a tyrant of Syracuse, Hieron I (d. 466 BCE), supposedly had it (Pindar, *Pythian* 1.90; Grmek 1991: 376). It is often linked with intemperance, gluttony and a lack of self-control in ancient Greek literary sources (e.g. Aristophanes, *Wealth* 559), and it is possible that individuals with gout may have been subjected to some degree of social stigma for their perceived lack of moderation (Gosbell 2018: 79–80). Only one Greek skeleton, a Young Adult male from Lerna (70 Ler., Middle Bronze Age, ca. 2000–1600 BCE), has signs of gout. This individual appears to have had urate crystal deposits on his right metatarsophalangeal joint and left elbow (Angel 1971: 51, 89, 92; Grmek 1991: 72–3).

Of the pathological conditions observed on human skeletal remains, skeletal fractures are among the most common (Roberts and Manchester 2007: 84–5), and complications stemming from them most likely account for a large percentage of physical impairments acquired after birth.[27] The structure of bone allows it to tolerate a certain degree of compressive or shear force, but fractures occur when the applied force exceeds the bone's ability to withstand it (Waldron 2009: 141). The three major causes of fractures that affect the limbs are acute injury (accident or interpersonal violence), underlying disease (a disease process, like a bone tumour or osteoporosis, weakens the bone and makes it susceptible to fracture) and repeated stress (often seen in athletes today, this produces hairline fractures and is difficult to discern in archaeological material). The way in which the external force is applied to the bone determines the manner in which it will fracture (Fig. 2.3). Force applied at right angles will result in a horizontal transverse fracture in mature bones and a greenstick fracture (essentially an incomplete transverse fracture) in the immature bones of youths. Indirect or rotational force will produce a spiral fracture, an acute-angled force will create an oblique fracture, force from above or below generates a linear or longitudinal fracture that occurs along the axis of the bone, and impaction fractures occur when two ends of the bone are forced together. Lastly, an avulsion fracture occurs when a muscle associated with a bone, ligament or joint capsule is suddenly strained and pulls the portion of the bone it is attached to away from the rest of the bones (Roberts and Manchester 2007: 90). Fractures are further classified by the number of elements affected and whether they pierce the skin. When a bone breaks into two elements, the fracture is classified as 'simple'. Bones that have broken into more than two parts are called 'comminuted'. Fractures that occur beneath unbroken skin are 'closed' and those that break the skin are 'open' or 'compound' (Waldron 2009: 139).

Successful healing of a fracture depends on the affected bone element, type and position of the fracture, severity, stability of fragments during healing, age and nutritional status of the individual, presence or absence of infection or other pathological process, adequate blood supply and access to treatment. In general, compound fractures are more susceptible to infection, which can lead

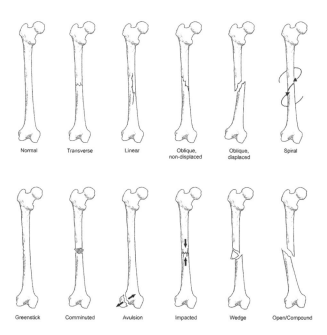

Figure 2.3 Diagram of different fracture types. Drawing by D. Weiss.

to delayed healing and even death in extreme cases. This type of fracture tends to heal neatly, but often results in loss of bone length. Comminuted fractures, on the other hand, are less likely to heal in a manner that preserves functionality. However, any fracture that is not properly set can result in non-alignment or malalignment of the fragments (this can occur even in transverse fractures when the surrounding muscles contract at the breakage site and shift the positions of the bones), shortening or deformation of the affected limb, degenerative joint disease and associated soft tissue damage (including damage to the nerves and blood supply; Roberts and Manchester 2007: 89–92).

Ancient Greek medical practitioners were capable of properly treating fractures. The fifth-century BCE Hippocratic treatise *On Fractures* explains how to set breaks, place them in traction, and immobilise them with bandages and devices. The knowledge compiled in the Hippocratic treatise was most likely perfected over time, as well-healed fractures have been documented on skeletons dating to as early as the Middle Bronze Age (e.g. 58 Myc. from Grave Circle B at Mycenae, mid-shaft humeral fracture on a Middle Adult female, ca. 1650–1450 BCE), but it has been suggested that effective methods for treating fractures were not widespread until the Iron Age (e.g. Tomb 93 from the Kerameikos at Athens, ulnar fracture on an Old Adult Male, twelfth to tenth centuries BCE and multiple examples from the Athenian Agora). Aligned and well-healed fractures have also been observed in the Hellenistic (ca. 323–31 BCE) population of Abdera. In addition to these cases where medical intervention was likely, there are also some Early Bronze Age (ca. 3000–2000 BCE) archaeological examples of fractures that healed naturally (e.g. greenstick femoral fractures on subadults from Karataş in western Anatolia, 117 and 122 Ka.; Angel 1945; 1973; 1976; Grmek 1991: 60–1; Agelarakis 2000: 17; Liston 2017: 525).

However, not all ancient fractures were treated successfully, and some bear evidence of malalignment and infection. Medical practitioners recognised the potential complications of fractures, as the Hippocratic Corpus warns that atrophy and shortening of limbs can occur if the proper recuperative measures are not observed (*On Fractures* 14, 16), that some fractures inevitably result in limb differences (*On Fractures* 8, 19–20), and that certain leg injuries will cause mobility impairments (*On Joints* 63). Archaeological skeletons bear witness to these statements. Although not meant to be an exhaustive list, the following examples illustrate the permanent results of malaligned fractures. At Asine, a male (110 As.) from the Middle Bronze Age (ca. 2000–1450 BCE) sustained a mid-shaft humeral fracture that healed with a 15° angulation, causing a shortening of the limb and prompting osteoarthritic changes at the shoulder and elbow. Another male (52 As.) from that period had a mid-shaft tibial fracture with a 10° angulation, as did a male (71 As.) from the Protogeometric period (twelfth to eighth centuries BCE), except in this case the angulation was 5° and there was a 10 mm shortening of the bone (Angel 1982; Grmek 1991: 59–60).

Middle Bronze Age (ca. 2000–1600 BCE) examples from Lerna consist of an Old Adult male (73 Ler.) who fractured the distal ends of his right radius and ulna. A blood clot formed and ossified in the membranous space between the two bones, fusing the radius and ulna together and slightly pronating the lower arm. A similar injury is witnessed on a Young Adult female (207 Ler.) whose distal radial and ulnar fractures healed in a manner that produced a dorsal deviation of the wrist and a shortening of the forearm. A Middle Adult male (127 Ler.), on the other hand, has a 'flail', or immobile, ankle and leg shortening possibly caused by a heel fracture (Angel 1971; Grmek 1991: 60–1). At the Late Archaic/Classical (sixth to third centuries BCE) colonial cemetery of Metaponto in southern Italy, three cases of unset fractures were observed. The displaced fragments of a double-fractured left femur of an Old Adult male (T 80) healed in a manner that left the femur 6 cm shorter than the right one. There are also perceptible asymmetries on the lumbar vertebrae of this individual, which most likely point to postural compensation for the shortened left leg. The remaining two cases involve fractures of the distal forearm. The fusion of the radius and ulna occurred in an Old Adult female (T 258–5). Another Old Adult female (SAV 4A) experienced lateral displacement of the wrist and shortening of the radius and ulna (Henneberg and Henneberg 1998: 527).

Although all fractures are susceptible to infection, open fractures are more vulnerable than closed ones (approximately 3–25 per cent of open fractures become infected). Relatively few archaeological fractures show signs of infection, but those that do bear evidence of osteomyelitis – a non-specific infection of bone and bone marrow that causes an inflammatory destruction of the bone that can persist for many years and eventually lead to death if left untreated (Waldron 2009: 85–7, 143–4).[28] Osteomyelitis is associated with fractures in individuals belonging to the Late Bronze Age (ca. 1600–1400 BCE) population of Pigi Artemidos in northern Greece (tibial fracture in a Young Adult male, Gr 2), the Late Minoan IIIC (twelfth to eleventh centuries BCE) population of Kavousi on Crete (radial fracture in an Old Adult male, Burial 5–7) and the Early Iron Age (ca. 1100–700 BCE) population of Pydna in northern Greece (humeral fracture in a Young Adult male, burial number 56 prim/947; Liston 1993: 147; Triantaphyllou 1998; Tritsaroli and Koulidou 2018).

In antiquity, the standard treatment for osteomyelitis was amputation. However, amputation is rarely attested in the archaeological record (Roberts and Manchester 2007: 123), and there are no known examples from a Greek context.[29] In fact, the Hippocratic Corpus gives the impression that Classical Greeks did not practise preventative amputation to stem the progression of infection. Rather, 'amputation' (if one can indeed call it that in this context) was viewed as a natural consequence of necrosis or gangrene, where the limb would either fall off on its own or be pulled off when it was ready (*On Fractures* 33; *On Joints* 69; *Prognostic* 9; Rose 2003: 20; Garland 2010: 134). Nevertheless, if an individual were to lose a limb, prosthetic devices could be fashioned to replace what was lost.[30] Although limb prostheses have not been recovered from Greek archaeological contexts (Bliquez 1995: 2264; Draycott 2019), they are mentioned in literature. For instance, Pindar describes Pelops' ivory shoulder (*Olympian* 1), Herodotus mentions Hegesistratus of Elis' wooden foot (9.36–7), and Aristotle tells us of Pythagoras' purportedly golden thigh (fr. 191). Other aids, such as staffs, crutches (e.g. *Odyssey* 17.203, 336–8; Aeschylus, *Agamemnon* 79–80; Lysias 24) and corrective shoes (*On Joints* 62), could also be used by the impaired to improve their mobility (Rose 2003: 24–7).

As previously mentioned, fractures typically result from acute injuries caused by accidents or interpersonal violence. Herodotus (2.129–30) recounts that Darius, the Persian king, injured his foot while dismounting his horse, and the injury was so serious that Darius gave up hope of ever using his foot again. A fourth-century BCE dedicatory inscription from the sanctuary of Asclepius at Epidaurus records another accident, describing how Cephasias' foot was injured after he was thrown from his horse. It is insinuated that Cephasias' injury was divine punishment for his ridiculing Asclepiadic cures for mobility impairments, and that he was cured only after he recanted his previous position on the god's efficacy (Rose 2003: 17). Accidents can also cause joint dislocations. Shoulder dislocations occur more frequently than those of the hip and other joints, but they are difficult to discern from human skeletal remains (Waldron 2009: 155–6). Long-term hip (Angel 1945: 293, 303; Papathanasiou 2005: 384) and foot (Papathanasiou 2005: 384) dislocations, on the other hand, are easier to identify and have been found on ancient Greek skeletons from Neolithic (ca. 5000–3200 BCE) and Submycenaean/Protogeometric (ca. 1150–1000 BCE) contexts. Although there is a paucity of skeletal material displaying dislocation, hip dislocations were observed frequently enough for the Hippocratic authors to catalogue the various gaits that are caused by them, including crawling (*On Joints* 52, 56, 58, 60; Rose 2003: 19).

Like accidents, war injuries could also cause debilitating limb impairments. Ancient literary sources discuss a number of memorable wounded warriors. The earliest accounts are found in Homer's *Iliad*, which contains strikingly precise anatomical descriptions of battlefield injuries (Grmek 1991: 27–33; Kömürcü et al. 2014). For example, when a stone was thrown into Aeneas' hip, it hit

> where the thighbone turns
> In the socket that medics call the cup.
> The rough stone shattered this joint and severed
> Both tendons, ripping open the skin. The hero
> Sank to his knees, clenching the dirt with one hand,
> While midnight settled upon both his eyes. (5.331–5 as translated in Lombardo 1997: 92–3)

With the help of his divine mother Aphrodite, as well as Apollo, Artemis and Leto, Aeneas fully recovered from his injuries and returned to the battlefield at dawn the next day (5.336–43, 481–4, 547–54), but the typical soldier was not so fortunate. So severe, for instance, was Diomedes' foot injury that he was forced to physically withdraw from the fight (11.369–400, 14.26–130; Christensen 2015). The unfortunate Philoctetes, on the other hand, was wounded before even reaching Troy. During the voyage, he was bitten on the foot by a snake (2.729–36), and his comrades marooned him on the small desert isle of Chryse off the coast of the island of Lemnos because they could not bear the foul smell of his infected wound or his unrelenting screams of pain (Sophocles, *Philoctetes*; Edwards 2012).[31]

Ultimately, the fate of wounded warriors lies with their commanding officers. Injured soldiers could be carried by litter, cart or wagon, slung over a pack mule or loaded onto a ship (Sternberg 1999: 192). Noble commanders such as Xenophon and Alexander the Great (that is, until the unbearable stress of the Gedrosian Desert: Arrian, *Anabasis* 6.25.2) personally ensured that their wounded were assisted (Xenophon, *Anabasis* 4.5.7–8, 16, 22, 5.8.6–11; Quintus Curtius 7.3.17, 8.3.9), whereas Xerxes, the Persian king, and Nicias, the Athenian general, both abandoned their injured when it came time to make hasty retreats (Herodotus 8.115.3; Thucydides 7.75.2–5; Sternberg 1999). Although there is no compelling evidence that 'wounded veterans' constituted their own social category, there is evidence to believe that those fortunate enough to return home might have received financial assistance from the state. Heracleides of Pontos (ca. fourth century BCE) asserts that Solon and Peisistratus both passed laws in the sixth century BCE that provided financial aid to individuals who were wounded in battle and incapable of working, similar to the dole (ca. fifth century BCE) mentioned in Chapter 1 that was established for other disabled citizens who could not work (Dillon 1995: 30; 2017: 171–8).

It is difficult to positively identify combat injuries in the archaeological record. Without a revealing burial context, such as a commemorative polyandreia (e.g. Agelarakis and Zafeiropoulou 2017; Agelarakis 2017) or another form of mass grave (e.g. Kyle et al. 2018; Lonoce et al. 2018), or pointed biological evidence, such as wounds attributable to (and containing fragments of) weapons (e.g. Agelarakis 2014a; 2014b), one cannot definitively say whether skeletal evidence of trauma was attributable to combat, some other form of interpersonal conflict or an accident.[32] For instance, a young woman from the Kerameikos (early third century BCE) had a metal object embedded in her forehead long enough for the bone to heal around the point of entry. The metal would have been visible to anyone looking at her – but we cannot determine whether it was embedded accidentally (e.g. she could have fallen onto the metal object or been pushed into it) or during a siege or skirmish (Bisel 1990; Nikita et al. 2016).

However, a Young Adult female from Abdera (ca. second half of the seventh century BCE) who was wounded in the head, presumably by a slingshot, and subjected to life-saving surgical intervention, could have been a civilian injured in aggressions between the Clazomenaean colonists of Abdera and the local Thracians (Agelarakis 2006; 2014a). Even though we cannot say with certainty that these women acquired their wounds in a combat setting, Homer (*Iliad* 8.517–19, 18.514–15) mentions that cities could be defended by women and other non-combatants (e.g. children and the elderly). Aeneas Tacticus' treatise *How to Survive Under Siege* (fourth century BCE) corroborates Homer, informing us that women could aid in the defence of a city under siege (40.4–5) and were sometimes the subjects of targeted attacks (4.8–12). A concrete example of female defenders comes from Argos, where a female musician-poet named Telesilla roused the women of the city to defend their home from Spartan attack in 494 BCE (Pausanias 2.20.8–9; Plutarch, *Moralia* 245c). Although there are many mythical examples of women warriors (e.g. the goddesses Athena and Artemis, the Amazons and the heroine Atalanta), it is less likely that the women served as soldiers, as this was an exceedingly rare occurrence in the ancient Greek world, with the notable exceptions of queens of Caria (ca. fifth to fourth centuries BCE; MacLachlan 2012: 180–6; Fabre-Serris and Keith 2015). The final example, also from Abdera, is an Old Adult male (early fourth century BCE) who was most likely a wounded veteran. His right frontal bone revealed evidence of healed sharp force trauma where an arrowhead had embedded and was subsequently surgically removed (Agelarakis 2014b). Another arrowhead was embedded in his left ulna, but only a portion of it could be removed surgically. The bone healed around the remaining fragmented arrowhead without trace of infection, but it is likely that the individual's mobility and grip strength were impeded (Pinto 2013).[33]

Philip II (ca. 382–336 BCE), king of Macedon and father of Alexander the Great, is a rare example of a person whose war-related injuries are documented in both literature and the archaeological record. Unlike the ideal or 'wise' general who eschews the risk of life and limb (Plutarch, *Pelopidas* 2.6; Samama 2013: 233), Philip's approach was to lead from the front of the battle and actively participate in the melee. As a result, he sustained serious injuries on multiple occasions (Demosthenes, *Philippics* 1.10–1; *On the Chersonese* 35–6; Samama 2013: 235). According to Demosthenes, Philip lost an eye, fractured his clavicle, and both his hand and leg were permanently injured (18.67; Riginos 1994; Samama 2013: 236).[34]

In 1977 at Vergina, Manolis Andronikos discovered four built tombs inside a large burial mound he called the Great Tumulus. Vergina (ancient Aegae) was the first Macedonian capital and the place where Philip II was assassinated; therefore, the tombs within the tumulus are believed to belong primarily to Macedonian kings, and Andronikos identified Tomb II as Philip's (Andronikos 1984). Although it was generally agreed that Philip rested within one of the tombs, there has been robust scholarly debate concerning whether he was interred in Tomb I (Bartsiokas 2000; Bartsiokas et al. 2015; Brandmeir et al. 2018) or Tomb II (Musgrave 1985; Musgrave et al. 1984; 2010; Delides 2016). The most recent analysis of the human remains in Tomb II, which included Computerised Tomography (CT) scans and X-Ray Fluorescent scanning (XRF), support the hypothesis that Philip was indeed buried in Tomb II (Antikas and Wynn-Antikas 2016). Tomb II is a barrel-vaulted ashlar construction with a painted temple-facade. The interior space is partitioned into two rooms: an antechamber and a main burial chamber, both containing grave goods and cremated remains interred in gold larnakes that are housed in marble sarcophagi. The larnax in the main burial chamber contained a golden oak-leaf crown and the cremains of a Middle Adult male corresponding to Philip's age (he was 46 when he died). The larnax in the antechamber contained a golden diadem and the cremains of a Young Adult female. Both individuals possessed degenerative changes to their legs and spines consistent with habitual horse riding. Turning to the male burial, sharp force trauma visible on the dorsal surface of the left fourth metacarpal is the only osteological evidence that aligns with the four recorded injuries of Philip. Aside from this wounded hand, there was no indication of eye injury, a previously broken clavicle or a maimed leg. But, the healed fracture could have been on a portion of bone that does not survive, because only the right clavicle and a small fragment of the left were available for study. Furthermore, it is possible for debilitating eye and leg injuries to affect soft tissue alone, and therefore not be perceptible on skeletal remains. The female burial, on the other hand, had experienced a severe left leg fracture at some point in her life. Called a Schatzker type IV fracture, these fractures are typically the result of bad falls. The medial condyle of the femur shatters the medial portion of the tibial plateau, which causes the tibia to break and results in severe damage to the ligaments of the knee joint, the peroneal nerve and popliteal vessels. Fractures of this type bear bad prognoses, and often the consequences are leg shortening, atrophy, knee disfigurement and impaired mobility. Based on this leg injury, the grave goods found in the antechamber are believed to be the female's and shed light on her identity (discussed in more detail in Chapter 4). In particular, there is a set of gilded bronze greaves: the left one is shorter and narrower than the right and most likely custom-made to fit her. Together with the greaves, the Scythian gorytus, arrowheads, spearheads, linothorax and pectoral also placed in the antechamber suggest that she was Scythian, as archaeological evidence from Scythian tombs between the Danube and Don Rivers indicates that almost 25 per cent of Scythian horseback archers were women. Philip was engaged in diplomatic relations with King Atheas of Scythia, so it is hypothesised that the woman interred in the antechamber is his daughter and the wife/concubine of Philip II (Antikas and Wynn-Antikas 2016).

Limited available archaeological evidence suggests that individuals with limb differences did not encounter social marginalisation. Of the case studies discussed here, few individuals with limb differences date to the Classical period, and a survey of their burial contexts reveals that none were buried in a non-normative fashion that would signal social marginalisation. Only the burials of Philip II and his Scythian companion were non-normative, but theirs were consistent with wealth and high social status rather than rejection and exclusion. To determine whether other, more conspicuous, physical differences could impact an individual's social position, the next section considers stature differences.

Stature differences: Dwarfism, pygmies and curved spines

While limb differences can be cleverly masked with clothing and might not be apparent to the casual viewer, height differences are strikingly conspicuous. 'Dwarfism' is a term used to describe exceptionally short stature.[35] There are approximately 200 types of dwarfism (Waters-Rist and Hoogland 2013: 243). Among the most common causes are inadequate nutrition, Turner's syndrome, achondroplasia and lack of growth hormone (pituitary dwarfism), each having different skeletal manifestations. Bones stunted by severe malnutrition typically have normal proportions, but show signs of stress (e.g. growth arrest lines) and evidence of osteoporosis. Turner's syndrome, a genetic condition resulting from the absence, or partial absence, of one of the X chromosomes, occurs only in females. Skeletal indicators of this syndrome are short stature, delayed epiphyseal fusion, osteoporosis, cubitus valgus (turned-out elbows), cranio-facial abnormalities and shortening of the metacarpals, metatarsals and phalanges. Achondroplasia is inherited as an autosomal dominant trait, which produces abnormal spinal curvatures, spinal stenosis, short stature, distinctive proportions (e.g. disproportionate head, large space between the third and fourth fingers, frontal bossing, and excessive shortening of the arms and legs) and bowed legs (Waldron 2009: 195–206; Sulosky Weaver 2015: 148–9).

Growth arrest due to lack of growth hormone is a more complex cause of dwarfism. Growth, in general, is regulated by growth hormone, which is produced by the anterior pituitary gland in response to stimulus from the hypothalamus (Waldron 2009: 196). A lack of growth hormone in early life results in 'hypopituitarism', leading to the creation of bones that are reduced in terms of both length and width, but still retain normal physiological proportions. Due to the synergism that exists between the pituitary and thyroid glands, hypopituitarism is often accompanied by hypothyroidism, which is caused by a deficiency of thyrotrophic hormone (Ortner 2003: 422). Overall, this combination of hormone deficiencies produces stunted bones, delayed development of secondary ossification centres (i.e. epiphyseal and apophyseal growth plates remain open longer than usual, with fusion occurring as late as older adulthood), delayed closure of cranial sutures and unaffected (i.e. unstunted) crania. The catalyst of this chain of events is the destruction of the

functioning pituitary in childhood, most frequently by a tumour (either a cra-
niopharyngioma or an adenoma) located in the cranium either within or above
the sella turcica (Ortner 2003: 422; Aufderheide and Rodríguez-Martín 2005:
328–9).[36] In skeletal remains, the enlargement, erosion or destruction of the
sella turcica, or the presence of an aperture in the sella floor, can indicate the
existence of a tumour (Ortner 2003: 422; Aufderheide and Rodríguez-Martín
2005: 330; Sulosky Weaver 2015: 149).

Greeks were familiar with dwarfism. The writings of Aristotle (*History of
Animals* 6.577b 26, 29; *Problems* 10.892a; *On the Generation of Animals*
2.749a.4–6; *On the Parts of Animals* 4.686b25f.) include multiple references to
dwarfism, and most notably make a distinction between persons with dwarfism
who are disproportionate (i.e. on account of achondroplasia or other skeletal
dysplasia) and those whose limbs are like those of children; the latter condition
he attributes to malnourishment (Dasen 1993: 214–20). Throughout the Greek
world, persons with dwarfism were depicted in both vase-painting and sculpture. Persons with dwarfism are more common on Athenian red-figure vases
than black-figure ones, especially drinking vessels (e.g. Fig. 2.4; Dasen 1990:
193–202). They are shown as servants, entertainers and religious celebrants
in both Dionysian rites and the *kômos* (Smith 2009). Persons with dwarfism
also appear in mundane scenes of Athenian street life and activities at the

Figure 2.4 Attic red-figure skyphos (fifth century BCE) in the manner of the Sotades
Painter from Capua, Italy depicting a nude person with dwarfism crouching (Paris,
Louvre G617; Beazley Archive no. 209513). Photo by Hervé Lewandowski © RMN-
Grand Palais/Art Resource, NY.

palaestra (Dasen 1993: 214–42). Fascination with dwarfism increased over time and culminated in the Hellenistic period (ca. 323–146 BCE). For example, the Hellenistic interest in physical difference and social diversification provided the ideal artistic climate for the production of a series of highly individualised bronze sculptures of persons with dwarfism (Garland 2010: 116–17; Sulosky Weaver 2015: 151).

Dwarfism is uncommon in palaeopathological literature, but three published examples exist in the ancient Greek world. One skeleton dating to the Bronze Age has been recovered from Greece (Gouvalar, near Pylos, ca. 1500 BCE). This Middle Adult female skeleton was born without clavicles, and its dwarfism is probably the result of cleidocranial dysplasia, a congenital condition marked by skeletal, cranial and dental abnormalities and the virtual absence of the clavicles (Bartsocas 1977; 1982: 11–12, fig. 10; Grmek 1991: 70–1; Dasen 1993: 320–3; Garmaise 1996: 178–230). A second skeleton (W3760) was found in the Western necropolis (ca. 648–409 BCE) at Himera, a Greek colony in Sicily, and it is currently under study (Bertolino et al. 2015: 29–30). Preliminary reports indicate that this individual is a Young Adult (30–5 years; ca. 525–409 BCE) with achondroplasia (Desnick et al. 2019: 154). Also from Sicily, the third skeleton (T883) was discovered in the Classical necropolis of Passo Marinaro (ca. fifth to third centuries BCE) at the Greek colony of Kamarina. Despite its poor state of preservation, its physical characteristics are suggestive of pituitary dwarfism – the cranium was the expected size for an adult, the long bones have shortened diaphyses but otherwise normal proportions, all cranial sutures are open, and all skeletal elements are gracile (Fig. 2.5). The burial context suggests societal integration rather than marginalisation, as it was positioned in the grave in the same manner as many other Passo Marinaro deceased. In particular, it was flexed (6% of Passo Marinaro burials were flexed – an interment choice that might have been an assertion of non-Greek ethnicity: Shepherd 2005; Sulosky Weaver 2015: 225–6) with head facing east (53%), grave oriented east to west (70%), no perceptible burial container (72%) and no grave goods (54%; Sulosky Weaver 2015: 148–53, 179, 202–10).

Artistic evidence also suggests that persons with dwarfism enjoyed a climate of relative acceptance in the Classical period, at least in Athenian society (Dasen 1993: 245). Véronique Dasen sees significance in the mere fact that they do appear on vases, especially since Classical Athenians seemed to avoid representations of physical difference. In her opinion, 'This suggests that dwarfism was not perceived as an irreducible monstrosity but as a tolerable physical anomaly that did not deprive from human quality' (Dasen 1988: 269). This tolerant attitude, however, lasted only until the Hellenistic and Roman periods, when the previous climate of relative acceptance was replaced by one of rejection (Dasen 1993: 247; Garmaise 1996: 173–7; Sulosky Weaver 2015: 153).

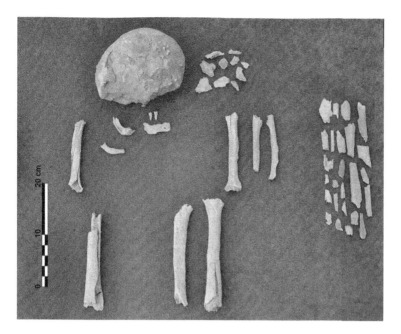

Figure 2.5 Extant skeletal remains of a presumed person with pituitary dwarfism (T883) from the Passo Marinaro necropolis (ca. fifth to third century BCE) at Kamarina, Sicily. Photo by author, use authorised by the Polo Regionale di Ragusa per i Siti Culturali.

Though also of abnormally short stature, pygmies were considered to be separate from, yet conspicuously related to, persons with dwarfism.[37] Greeks believed that the pygmies were a tribe of short-statured men who lived at the edge of the inhabited world and engaged in combat with migratory cranes over their crops (*Iliad* 3.2–6; Aristotle, *History of Animals* 8.597a; Ctesias, *Indica* 72.45b; Pliny, *Natural History* 6.187, 7.26–7; Pomponius Mela 3.81; Strabo 1.2.28, 17.2.1). Indeed, they are often depicted in art in the context of this epic struggle, called the geranomachy (Harari 2004), as illustrated by an Attic rhyton from the British Museum (460–450 BCE) in the form of a pygmy carrying a dead crane (Fig. 2.6). Most ancient authors accepted pygmies' existence as ethnographic fact, and it is certainly possible that some aspects of the myth might be rooted in reality (e.g. Ovadiah and Mucznik 2017). Their precise origins aside, Dasen suggests that the parallels between the exotic pygmies and real-life persons with dwarfism were intentional and poignant (Dasen 1993: 175–88). She maintains that the 'stories of pygmies may have emerged to account for the presence of pathologically short people in Greek cities' (Dasen 1993: 178–9). She further asserts that the existence of pygmies served another purpose, namely to alleviate archetypal fears: 'The myth demonstrates that remote countries contain no danger . . . and accounts for the presence of pathological dwarfs at Athens . . . Dwarfs appear thus as liminal, wild, but inoffensive beings, like powerless pygmies' (Dasen 1993: 188).

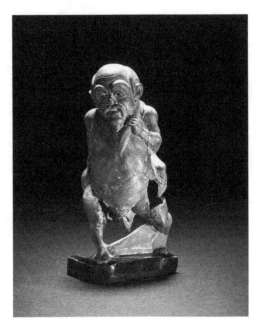

Figure 2.6 Red unvarnished ware Attic rhyton (ca. 560–550 BCE) by Sotades (potter) from Ruvo, Italy (London, British Museum 1873,0820.289). The upper portion is damaged, the lower portion is in the form of a nude, bald and bearded pygmy carrying a dead crane. The crane's head and neck are visible over the pygmy's left shoulder. Photo © The Trustees of the British Museum.

Unlike persons with dwarfism and pygmies, whose overall appearances are stunted, persons with curved spines would be of normative height but for their severe spinal conditions. The appearance of a 'hunched' back and the concomitant decrease in stature is often the result of either kyphosis or scoliosis. Kyphosis is the forward curvature of the spine, typically caused by diseases that damage the vertebral bodies (e.g. tuberculosis, osteomyelitis, brucellosis, trauma, osteoporosis). Scoliosis is the lateral deviation of the spine accompanied by the rotation of the vertebrae and spinous processes towards the concavity of the curvature. Although there are several causes of scoliosis, the most common form is idiopathic, of which there are three types: infantile (occurs before age 3, is more frequent in males, curvature usually on the left side, spontaneously corrects), juvenile (occurs between ages 4 and 9, equally distributed between the sexes, curvature usually on the right side, typically progresses in severity and causes pulmonary dysfunction) and adolescent (the most frequently occurring of the three, predominantly affects females older than 10 years, curvature usually on the right side, increases in severity; Ortner 2003: 463–7; Aufderheide and Rodríguez-Martín 2005: 66–9; Waldron 2009: 215).

It is difficult to identify ancient cases of kyphosis and scoliosis because one must have a skeleton that is relatively complete and well preserved in order to make an accurate diagnosis (Waldron 2000: 39–41; Aufderheide and Rodríguez-Martín 2005: 67–8). The necessary convergence of pathology, preservation and completeness is rare, but illustrated most notably by the recent discovery of King Richard III's (r. 1483–5) burial in Leicester, England, where the lateral deviation of the spine was clearly visible *in situ* (Buckley et al. 2013: 532–3, 536; Appleby et al. 2014). Nevertheless, it is likely that the prevalence of kyphosis and scoliosis is under-reported in the literature due to the poor condition of the human remains recovered from many Greek contexts (e.g. Sulosky Weaver 2015). Indeed, the earliest example of scoliosis is found on an Early Iron Age (ca. 900–850 BCE) Middle Adult female from Argos (Tomb 14; Charles 1958: 277–8), and the earliest example of kyphosis from the Aegean is visible on the spine of a Young Adult female from Lesbos dating to the Early Byzantine period (ca. fourth to seventh centuries CE; Tsaliki 2004). Modern parallels, nevertheless, inform us that those with kyphosis and scoliosis would have experienced back pain, and those with severe cases of scoliosis could have had impaired mobility and severe cardiac and pulmonary complications (Waldron 2009: 216–17).

Despite the paucity of skeletal evidence, there are numerous descriptions of persons with curved spines in Greek literature. The Hippocratic Corpus discusses curved spines, their aetiologies and corrective measures (*On Joints* 41–7). The first intervention involves a ladder – if the curvature is high on the back, the patient should be bound to the ladder with feet facing down, but if it is low, then the head should face down. The ladder should then be suspended from a tall structure and released, and it is of utmost importance that the ladder fall smoothly and evenly to prevent the patient from sustaining unintended injuries. Another method of back-straightening requires the patient to lie face-down on a board covered with cloaks that is fixed to the wall. A plank, inserted on one end into a groove in the wall, is placed crosswise over the curvature and pressure is applied by the physician to straighten it (Vasiliadis et al. 2009; Garland 2010: 127–8).

Two historical persons with curved spines are named in literary sources. Myskellos (ca. late eighth century BCE), the oikist of Croton, purportedly had a curved spine and impaired legs (Strabo 6.1.12; Zenobius, *Proverbs* 3.42; Ogden 1997: 62–72). The formerly enslaved satirist Aesop is also identified as a person with a curved spine. Born in either Thrace or Phrygia, Aesop purportedly lived in the sixth century BCE and died ca. 564 BCE at Delphi. He is mentioned in literary accounts by fifth-century BCE authors such as Herodotus (2.134–5) and Aristophanes (numerous references in *Wasps*; *Peace* 129; *Birds* 470), but most of the details surrounding his life, whether fact or fiction, are known from the *Vita Aesopi* (Lissarrague 2000: 132–3).[38] The *Vita Aesopi* has its origins in earlier oral and written traditions, but it has been suggested that the initial texts of the *Vita* were written in the fourth century BCE, while the majority were compiled in the fourth century CE (Lissarrague 2000: 133). Through the information conveyed in the *Vita* and other *testimonia*, we learn that Aesop was quick-witted and wise, but also physically impaired. Himerios (*Orationes* 13.5; fourth century CE) describes him as the ugliest man alive – uglier than Thersites – with a pointed head, snub nose, short neck, protruding lips, pot belly, knock knees, a stoop (i.e. a curved spine) and abnormally slow speech (Perry 1952; Lissarrague 2000: 135–6; Sulosky Weaver 2019b). Despite his physical imperfections, ancient authors tell us that his literary achievements prompted the Athenians to erect a sculpture of him in their city sometime in the fifth century BCE (Phaedrus 2.9; *Palatine Anthology* 16.332; Tatianus, *Ridicule of the Statues Erected by the Greeks* 34), and the individual with the curved spine in the private collection of the Villa Albani-Torlonia is often identified, albeit contestably, as a Roman marble copy of this statue (Fig. 2.7; Trentin 2009).

No extant literary sources describe the appearance of Aesop's sculpture, but if he were indeed depicted with a curved spine, it would be an anomalous occurrence in the corpus of Classical art. Although there are numerous Greek representations of persons with curved spines (e.g. Fig. 2.8), they all date to the Hellenistic period, when a preferential shift occurred in Greek art. Moving away from the idealisation of the Classical period, Hellenistic art embraced individualism, including the dramatic and the physically different (Pollitt 1986:

Figure 2.7 Marble bust of a person with a curved spine (ca. second century CE; Rome, Villa Albani 964). Photo © Alinari/Art Resource, NY.

Figure 2.8 Hellenistic ivory figure of a person with a curved spine made in Alexandria, Egypt (ca. first century BCE; London, British Museum 1814,0704.277) © The Trustees of the British Museum/Art Resource, NY.

1–16; Mitchell 2017). Interpretations of figures with curved spines abound, as they have been viewed as apotropaic (Wace 1903–4; Binsfeld 1956: 43–4), representations of mimic actors (Richter 1913), votives to Asclepius (Perdrizet 1911: 58), indicators of sexual potency (Shapiro 1984: 391–2), sympotic entertainers (Giuliani 1987) and belonging to the world of Dionysus (Wrede 1988). However, Lisa Trentin's recent study (2015) advocates for a more complex read of the extant material. She finds that depictions of persons with curved spines did function as apotropaic devices, lucky talismans and comic devices, but that they also served a broader psychological purpose. Trentin notes that these representations generally feature not one, but rather a series of conspicuously marginalising traits – stunted stature, a curved spine, and non-Greek facial features (stereotypically sub-Saharan African) – in order to accentuate their Otherness. By highlighting their Otherness, representations of persons with curved spines served as powerful stimuli for conversation and introspection, and 'recognizing the Otherness in the hunchback necessitated a recognition of the Self in relation to that Otherness, whether in opposition *or* in alignment . . . and contemplation – about the place of this deformed body, and all bodies, including a viewer's own, in contemporary society' (Trentin 2015: 92–3). She applies this conclusion not only to Hellenistic material, but also to Roman representations as well.

As this survey demonstrates, skeletal evidence of short-statured individuals is sparse. For the Late Archaic/Classical period, no human remains with visible signs of dwarfism or severe spinal conditions have been found on the Greek mainland. The only fully published skeleton with dwarfism that dates to this time frame comes from a colonial context – Greek Sicily – and this individual was buried in a fashion that befits social integration rather than marginalisation. Conclusions, however, can hardly be drawn from a solitary burial, especially from this region, since literary and archaeological evidence suggest that Sicilian Greek city states were more diverse and tolerant polities than many mainland ones (Thucydides 6.17.2–4; Sulosky Weaver 2015: 77, 223–9; 2019b).

Cranial differences: Craniosynostosis and artificial headshaping

Like stature differences, cranial differences are obvious at first glance. Yet, whereas stature differences might take years to manifest, cranial differences typically occur in infancy. At birth, a newborn's calvarium, or cranial vault, consists of the frontal, parietal and occipital bones, which are united by fibrous sutures consisting of dense connective tissue. The connective tissue is flexible and allows for movement, mechanical stress and brain growth. As the need for cranial flexibility declines around age 2, the amount of connective tissue decreases and the sutures begin to close (Aufderheide and Rodríguez-Martín 2005: 52; Slater et al. 2008).[39] However, when one or more of the six cranial sutures fuses prematurely, this condition is called craniosynostosis (or craniostenosis). Premature suture closure prevents the associated bones from growing, which leads to compensatory overgrowth of other cranial bones and cranial asymmetry (Waldron 2009: 209; Sulosky Weaver 2015: 144; 2019b).[40]

The final shape of the skull is dependent upon which sutures have fused (Fig. 2.9). The premature fusion of the metopic suture causes trigonocephaly, which is characterised by a pointed, elongated protrusion that forms a ridge in the centre of the forehead and by bossing (i.e. abnormal enlarging or bulging) on the parietal-occipital region. Early fusion of the sagittal suture leads to scaphocephaly – the elongation of the cranium that results in bitemporoparietal narrowing and bossing of the frontal and occipital bones. Cranial appearance after fusion of the coronal suture is more variable, as it depends upon the nature of the closure. If only the right or left side is involved, the cranium is frontal plagiocephalic, marked by a flattening of the forehead on the affected side and contralateral frontal bossing. However, if the entire coronal suture fuses prematurely, then the cranium is brachycephalic, meaning that it bears a circular shape with a prominent frontal bone, flattened occiput and anterior displacement of the vertex. Acrocephaly occurs when the coronal and sagittal sutures fuse and form a bulge in the upper occipital region where the occipital and parietals meet. Finally, the fusion of the right or left lambdoid suture results in

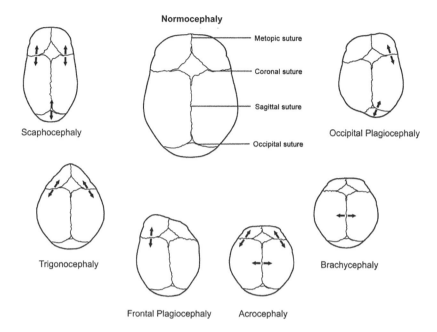

Figure 2.9 Diagram of various types of craniosynostosis. Drawing by D. Weiss.

occipital plagiocephaly, the ipsilateral occipitoparietal flattening of the cranium with contralateral parietal and frontal bossing (Waldron 2009: 209–10; Sulosky Weaver 2015: 144–5; 2019b).

Today, craniosynostosis occurs in 1 in 2,500 children, and it usually presents as an isolated condition that is unassociated with other pathologies (Morriss-Kay and Wilkie 2005: 637). Although several factors appear to contribute to the development of craniosynostosis, including genetic errors, birth trauma and intrauterine infection, aetiology can only be assigned in less than one third of known cases (Aufderheide and Rodríguez-Martín 2005: 52; Roberts and Manchester 2007: 154–5). Furthermore, the relationship between craniosynostoses and cognitive or neurological development is not always discernible, but both have the potential to be adversely affected. For instance, in modern cases of severe deformation (i.e. when more than one suture is involved), rising intracranial pressure is documented, and this can negatively impact development (Aufderheide and Rodríguez-Martín 2005: 52; Waldron 2009: 209; Sulosky Weaver 2015: 145; 2019b).

It is clear from literary sources that ancient Greeks were familiar with craniosynostosis. The Hippocratic treatise *On Injuries to the Head* (1.1–4) begins with a discussion of variable head shapes and sutural arrangements. Also, Plutarch (*Pericles* 3.2) describes Pericles as having an unnaturally long head, and claims that his portraits were always helmeted so that attention would be drawn away from the shape of his cranium. Indeed, fifth-century depictions of Pericles (post-429 BCE) depict him as a general with a Corinthian helmet perched atop his head (Fig. 2.10). Upon close inspection of these representations, paediatric neurosurgeon Concezio Di Rocco (2005) finds corroborating evidence in the general's facial features. In particular, Di Rocco notes that Pericles' physical traits reveal mild hypothelorism (abnormally close eyes) and a noticeably reduced latero-lateral cranial diameter, both suggestive of sagittal synostosis, or scaphocephaly (Sulosky Weaver 2015: 146; 2019b).

Although sagittal synostosis is not typically associated with mental impairment, other synostoses, such as that of the metopic suture, frequently are. At least one third of patients with metopic synostosis display cognitive and behavioural impairments (Sidoti et al. 1996). Thersites, described in the *Iliad* (2.211–24) as the ugliest of the Achaeans, had a limp, rounded shoulders, and most importantly, a 'pointed head'. His physical appearance, coupled with his bouts of inappropriate behaviour, fit the profile of a trigonocephalic individual.[41] Even though it is possible that this character is a literary scapegoat (Ogden 1997: 38–41), his appearance and behaviour could be rooted in fact and the result of metopic synostosis (Di Rocco 2005; Sulosky Weaver 2015: 146; 2019b).

Figure 2.10 Roman marble copy (ca. second century BCE) from Tivoli, Italy of an earlier Greek portrait bust of Pericles (died ca. 429 BCE) (London, British Museum GR 1805,0703.91). Photo © The Trustees of the British Museum/Art Resource, NY.

Aesop might also have exhibited the telltale signs of craniosynostosis. As previously discussed, Himerios' description of Aesop (*Orationes* 13.5) states that he had a pointed head and links him to Thersites – specifically proclaiming that he is uglier than Thersites. Although no artistic representations of Aesop can be securely identified (including the aforementioned sculpture from the Villa Albani-Torlonia), the one that most likely depicts the fabulist can be found on the tondo of an Attic red-figure kylix from Vulci (Fig. 2.11).[42] Here a seated man with an enlarged and disproportionate head is shown wrapped in a cloak and holding a stick. His mouth is open, suggesting that he is engaged in conversation with the fox seated opposite him, whose mouth is also open as it gestures towards the man with its paw.[43] Based on the cranial shape of the man (albeit without any trace of a pointed portion) and his verbal exchange with the fox, this figure has been identified as Aesop (Lissarrague 2000: 137–8, fig. 5.1; Garland 2010: 111, pl. 32; Sulosky Weaver 2019b).[44]

In terms of skeletal evidence, only two individuals with craniosynostosis have been recovered from the Aegean region (Ortner 2003: 460–3; Aufderheide and Rodríguez-Martín 2005: 52–4). The first, an adult male, was found in an Early Minoan (ca. 3000–2100 BCE) rock shelter at Kephala Petras in eastern Crete.

Figure 2.11 Tondo of an Attic red-figure kylix (ca. 450 BCE) attributed to the Painter of Bologna 417 from Vulci, Italy depicting Aesop(?) conversing with a fox (Vatican, Museo Gregoriano Etrusco inv. 16552; Beazley Archive no. 211120). Drawing by D. Weiss.

This individual had an abnormally narrow and long skull that was most likely caused by the premature fusion of the sagittal suture (Triantaphyllou 2012: 165–6). The second example was discovered in 1893 by Münter, a Danish civil servant. Using *De vitae Sophoclis poetae* as a guide, Münter was searching for the tomb of Sophocles, who was purportedly buried in a family plot 11 stades outside of the walls of Deceleia on the road connecting Deceleia and Acharnai (modern Menidi). At the 11 stades mark, Münter uncovered three sarcophagi that were without any trace of identifying inscriptions. The most elaborate of the three was made of marble and contained grave goods dating to the fifth century BCE – namely an iron strigil, a wooden stick, and some alabaster and terracotta vases. Based on the date and ostensible expense of the sarcophagus, Münter assumed that the individual interred in it was Sophocles. Although it is unlikely that the occupant of the marble sarcophagus is Sophocles, the cranium of this individual displays a discernible flattening of the left occipitoparietal region, probably caused by either the premature fusion of the left lambdoid suture or of the left parietal and temporal bones (Virchow 1893; Grmek 1991: 65–7; Sulosky Weaver 2015: 145; 2019b).

Even though these are the only known examples of craniosynostosis from the Aegean, two additional cases have been discovered in the Passo Marinaro necropolis (ca. fifth to third centuries BCE) at the Greek colony of Kamarina on Sicily. The first, T413 (Fig. 2.12), is an individual of indeterminate age who exhibits signs of occipital plagiocephaly, while the second, T539 (Fig. 2.13), is an Adult (20+ years of age) with acrocephaly (Sulosky Weaver 2015: 144–8; 2019b). The burial contexts of these individuals do not suggest that they were socially marginalised, as they do not deviate from established cemetery norms. The variables examined, namely grave orientation, grave type, amounts and types of grave goods, body position, head orientation and position within the cemetery are all consistent with patterns witnessed throughout the necropolis. While it is certainly possible that these individuals could have experienced social marginalisation at some point in their lifetimes, their unremarkable burial contexts do not support their continuous, or perpetual, marginalisation (Sulosky Weaver 2019b).

Caution is called for when attempting to apply conclusions made in colonial contexts to material from the Greek mainland. As previously discussed, the populations of Sicilian Greek city states were probably more diverse and tolerant than other Greek polities. Nevertheless, the extant evidence from the mainland does appear to support the conclusions made at Kamarina. There is nothing in the extant biographies of Pericles to suggest that he was marginalised on account of his cranial shape – on the contrary, Thucydides, his contemporary, referred to him the 'First Citizen of Athens' (Thucydides 2.65). Likewise, the aforementioned individual interred in the marble sarcophagus, mistakenly identified as Sophocles, was buried in an extraordinary manner that is suggestive of wealth

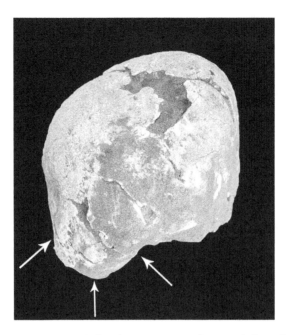

Figure 2.12 Craniosynostosis in T413 (posterior view of cranium) from the Passo Marinaro necropolis (ca. fifth to third century BCE) at Kamarina, Sicily. Bilateral cranial asymmetry (indicated by arrows) caused by premature fusion of the right lambdoid suture (occipital plagiocephaly). Photo by author, use authorised by the Polo Regionale di Ragusa per i Siti Culturali.

rather than exclusion. The only secure evidence for the marginalisation of those with cranial differences is literary. In both cases, namely that of Thersites as well as Aesop, the source of their marginality might not have been their cranial differences alone, but rather their intersectionality – a concept to which we will return at the end of this chapter.

As opposed to craniosynostosis, which is a naturally occurring phenomenon, artificial cranial modification requires human intervention. Also known as 'headshaping', this widespread practice has been attested worldwide across time and cultures (Anton 1989; Tubbs et al. 2006; Lorentz 2009: 75; Bonogofsky 2011: 6–7). Headshaping is purposeful cranial manipulation that is performed in infancy, when the cranium is cartilaginous and malleable, and achieved through the use of devices such as boards, pads or stones. Although the rationale for headshaping tends to be culture-specific, it is often performed for reasons related to aesthetics or health, or to denote gender, ethnicity, social status or group affiliation (Lorentz 2009: 75). Ultimately, it results in the permanent modification of the bones of the cranium, including the

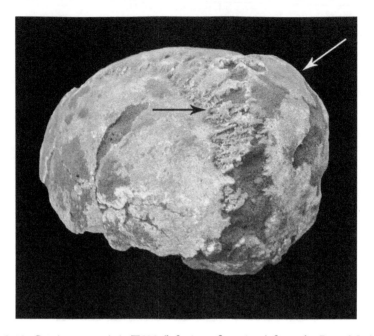

Figure 2.13 Craniosynostosis in T539 (left view of cranium) from the Passo Marinaro necropolis (ca. fifth to third century BCE) at Kamarina, Sicily. There is a bulge in the upper occipital region (indicated by white arrow), accompanied by a band of ossicles across the lambdoid suture (indicated by black arrow). These skeletal changes are caused by premature fusion of the coronal and sagittal sutures (acrocephaly). Photo by author, use authorised by the Polo Regionale di Ragusa per i Siti Culturali.

face (Cheverud et al. 1992; Anton 1989; Bonogofsky 2011: 6), and can cause cognitive impairment (Lekovic et al. 2007).

It is generally difficult to determine whether cranial differences were caused by external forces, such as headshaping or positional moulding (i.e. posterior flattening of the cranium caused by prolonged contact between the back of the infant's head and a flat surface), or by intrinsic disorders (i.e. true cranio-synostosis). Although modern clinical features (i.e. macroscopic appearance, radiographical findings and pathological studies) are often unable to distinguish between the two (Di Rocco et al. 1998), biological anthropologists (e.g. Dean O'Loughlin 1996) have had measured success in differentiating between cranio-synostosis and artificial cranial deformation on the basis of endocranial structures, particularly venous sinus patterns. Furthermore, other morphological observations have been made that are helpful in distinguishing between pathological, positional and intentional causes. In particular, crania with reduced volumes tend to be pathologically modified, and those affected by pathological premature suture closure appear markedly different from those that have been shaped by position or intent, while at the same time crania that are shaped by position or unintentional cultural practices vary in appearance and are not uniform. Intentional headshaping, on the other hand, tends to be uniform and patterned within a population and can involve differential degrees of alteration (Lorentz 2009: 79–80).

There are, nevertheless, clear archaeological instances in which crania were indeed shaped by external forces. Numerous examples have been found in the greater Mediterranean region, primarily from Egypt (but only dating to the 18th Dynasty ca. 1549/1550–1292 BCE – Dingwall 1931), Cyprus (Angel 1953; 1961; 1972; Schulte-Campbell 1979; 1983a; 1983b; 1986; Domurad 1986: 219–20; Fox Leonard 1997; Lorentz 2003; 2004; 2005; Harper and Fox 2008: 8–10) and the Near East (e.g. Strouhal 1973; Kurth and Röhrer-Ertel 1981; Molleson and Campbell 1995; Fletcher et al. 2008).[45] However, the only evidence for headshaping in the western Aegean are crania (Tharrounia 8, 9 and 10) from a Late Neolithic (ca. 4300–3200 BCE) cave cemetery in Euboea. These crania exhibit premature suture closure that appears to have been artificially induced. Headshaping is suspected here because the fusion of these sutures did not produce the modifications that are associated with an intrinsic disorder such as craniosynostosis (e.g. early fusion of the sagittal suture did not form a crest, but depression instead). Rather, the crania appeared to conform to the shaping device (Lorentz 2009: 84).

Archaeological examples of artificially modified crania have not been recovered from mainland Greek Late Archaic/Classical contexts. This lack of evidence could be meaningful, as it could indicate that Greeks of this period did not perform artificial cranial modification. Extant literary sources support this interpretation, suggesting that the practice was known at the time, but associated with non-Greeks. In *On Airs, Waters, Places* (14), the Hippocratic authors describe a foreign group called the Macrocephali ('Longheads') who purportedly lived along the Phasis River in the Black Sea region at the edge of the known world.[46] The Macrocephali differed substantially from the Greeks in terms of appearance and culture; indeed, *On Airs, Waters, Places* remarks that no other ethnic group bears a cranial shape quite like theirs. For the Macrocephali, long heads were both aesthetically pleasing and indicative of nobility. In the beginning, they turned to artificial means to achieve this desired look. Immediately after the birth of a child, the infant's soft spherical cranium was manipulated by hand and massaged into place, then bound with bandages and other devices to achieve permanent elongation. Over time, the need for human intervention was no longer necessary, as their aesthetic preference transformed into a heritable trait (NB although this is what the Greeks believed, it does not accurately reflect the reality of how traits are inherited). Children began to be born naturally with long heads, and the Macrocephali retained this unique physical characteristic until they adopted the practice of intermarriage. The offspring of these mixed unions bore heads that had reverted to a spherical shape (Kennedy 2016: 21–2). Thus, the legendary Macrocephali played a variety of roles within Greek society. Specifically, their 'existence' substantiated the understanding that people living at the edges of the known world were exotic and often monstrous, they served as evidence for the Greek belief of the heritability of acquired traits, and most importantly for our purposes, they provided a palatable explanation for the foreign custom of headshaping.

Non-binary sex and gender: Intersexuals and eunuchs

Just as tales of the Macrocephali offered the Greeks an ontological basis for the unusual practice of headshaping, the myth of Hermaphroditus underpinned their complicated relationship with intersex persons. The earliest references to Hermaphroditus come from Attica and date to the fourth century BCE. These include an early fourth-century dedicatory base from Vari and a literary reference in the late fourth-century work of Theophrastus (*Characters* 16; Ajootian 1997: 220–1). The most complete version of the myth, however, is found in Ovid's *Metamorphoses* (4.274–388; ca. 8 CE). The male child of Hermes and Aphrodite, Hermaphroditus happened upon a nymph named Salmacis who lived by an eponymous spring. The nymph attempted to seduce him, but he rejected her advances. When Hermaphroditus thought Salmacis had left, he began to swim nude in the spring. She leapt in after him and forcibly wrapped herself around his body, praying that they would never part. The gods granted her wish, and the two bodies merged into one. A distraught Hermaphroditus, realising that he was now a being of dual sex, prayed in turn to his divine parents that any man who should enter the spring should suffer the same fate as he. Moved by his plight, his parents acquiesced and bestowed transformative powers upon the waters. Thousands of years later, the fact that the term 'hermaphrodite' has come to be synonymous with 'intersex' attests to the enduring potency of the myth (Delcourt 1961; Robinson 1999; Brisson 2002: 42–60; Androutsos 2006; Graumann 2013).

The myth of Hermaphroditus is not the first Greek literary reference to an intersex individual. Pherecydes, a philosopher writing in the mid-sixth century BCE, and later poems of the Orphic tradition dating as early as 500 BCE, describe early intersex primordial deities (West 1971: 29–36; 1983: 203).[47] However, the intersex persons that appear in the fifth-century texts of Empedocles (Wright 1981: 212–5) and Plato (*Symposium* 189b–190c) are not deities, but rather beings who represented an early stage of mortal evolution. It is possible that these figures were precursors of Hermaphroditus, whose myth and representations seem to date to the fourth century BCE, as previously discussed (Ajootian 1997: 226–7).

By the Hellenistic period, cultic devotion to Hermaphroditus was linked to fertility and popular throughout Greece, Italy and Anatolia. Since the earliest artistic representations and literary evidence of Hermaphroditus derive from Athens and Attica, it has been suggested that the cult had its origins in Athens and developed in response to the demoralising and destabilising events of the late fifth century, namely the Peloponnesian War, two plagues and an earthquake.[48] Indeed, in the aftermath of the Peloponnesian War a religious shift appears to have occurred, as cults to numerous new deities (e.g. Isis, Cybele and Adonis) were instituted and new religious building projects proliferated throughout Attica. Beyond Athens, an inscription from an altar (third century BCE) at Cos mentions Hermaphroditus in a list of deities associated with healing, fertility and childbirth. In addition to the altar, other material evidence, such as marble sculptures of Hermaphroditus found at Cos and elsewhere in Anatolia (e.g. Fig. 2.14), speak to the presence of a well-established cultic tradition in the region (Ajootian 1997: 227–9; Romano 2009).

While Hermaphroditus was venerated, actual intersex individuals were persecuted. Despite the fact that Hermaphroditus embodied, in the words of Aileen Ajootian, 'both male and female elements, [he] was considered not a monstrous aberration, but a higher, more powerful form, male and female combining to create a third, transcendent, gender' (1997: 228). Even though one would expect that reverence for a divine intersex figure would mollify, or even negate, powerful adverse reactions to living intersex persons, this does not appear to be the case. Instead, not only is it suspected that infants born intersex would be candidates for exposure (Brisson 2002: 7–15), but Diodorus Siculus (32.12.3) describes an instance where an intersex individual was burned alive in Athens in the first century BCE, even though he himself seems to recognise that intersex features are naturally occurring physical abnormalities (4.6.5–7; Ajootian 1997: 229). Diodorus Siculus (32.11) also recounts the story of the orphaned Callo from Epidaurus, who initially identified as a female until a tumour appeared on her genitals. When an apothecary lanced the tumour, it was found to contain male genitalia, which the apothecary freed from the surrounding tissue. After the procedure, Callo changed her name to Callon and began to live as a man. Callon's story, however, ends tragically, as he was brought to trial for impiety on the theory that Callo, who had been a priestess of Demeter, had witnessed things that were not to be seen by men.[49]

Although intersex features are indeed flagged as physical abnormalities, they are more common than one might think. Sex is often constructed dichotomously as male or female, but it is more accurately conceived as a continuum of expressed masculine and feminine features. Hormone levels can influence the eventual development of secondary sexual characteristics that are either associated with the opposite sex or androgynous (Gilchrist 1999: 57; Aufderheide and Rodríguez-Martín 2005: 334; Knüsel 2015). This complicates sex determination in skeletal remains, which relies primarily on the macroscopic assessment of conspicuous secondary sexual characteristics (Bass 2005: 19–21).[50] On the

Figure 2.14 Hellenistic marble sculpture of Hermaphroditus (Pergamum, third century BCE; Istanbul, Archaeological Museum inv. no. 363 T). Photo © Vanni Archive/Art Resource, NY.

surface, the analysis of nuclear DNA (nDNA) appears to provide a solution to the sex determination quandary, but it is also fraught with perils (Brown and Brown 2011: 151–67; Geller 2017). First, archaeological samples are prone to degradation, but even if nDNA is successfully extracted and analysed, sex chromosomes are not as straightforward as commonly believed. In addition to XX (normative female) and XY (normative male), there are numerous other categories (Nordbladh and Yates 1990: 225) with frequency rates as high as 1 in 1,000 (Joyce 2008: 44). Second, there is no guarantee that genotypic sex matches phenotypic expression, or appearance. When the two are at odds, this is a rare occurrence known as sex reversal. Typically, the female phenotype is determined by the absence of the Y chromosome (e.g. XX, XO, XXX, XXXX, XXXXX). However, 1 in 20,000–25,000 individuals with an XX genotype are phenotypically male, and in the majority of cases this is due to translocation. Specifically, one of the individual's X chromosomes carries a copy of the SRY gene that was transferred from the Y chromosome at some stage in the person's ancestry. Likewise, 1 in 20,000 individuals who are phenotypically female have an XY genotype – in some, this is because the SRY gene has been deleted from their Y chromosome, but in others it is due to either the X chromosome having two copies of the DAX gene instead of one or androgen insensitivity (Brown and Brown 2011: 160–2).

Intersex individuals deviate from the aforementioned examples in that they display both male and female phenotypic characteristics. Some have internal gonads that contain structures consisting of testicular tissue as well as ovarian tissue, whereas others have mixed components of external genitalia – unsurprisingly, most intersex individuals are infertile. The two primary genetic causes of intersexuality are congenital adrenal hyperplasia and Klinefelter's syndrome. Congenital adrenal hyperplasia is caused by a defect in steroid hormone synthesis, and affected persons can be phenotypically male, female or intersex with a male or female genotype that typically does not agree with the phenotype. Klinefelter's syndrome, on the other hand, results in an XXY genotype and a phenotype that is either male or intersex. Persons with Klinefelter's syndrome usually have infantile male genitalia, gynecomastia and female pubic hair distribution (Aufderheide and Rodríguez-Martín 2005: 334; Brown and Brown 2011: 161; Knüsel 2015). There are no characteristic skeletal features associated with Klinefelter's syndrome, but it has been observed that stature is commonly more than 180 cm, the lengths of the trunk and limbs are disproportionate, and there is a predisposition towards long-bone synostoses and vertebral anomalies (Aufderheide and Rodríguez-Martín 2005: 369). To date, no intersex individuals have been identified in the archaeological record. However, Christopher Knüsel suggests that some might be hiding in plain sight. Quite often, the sex of a skeleton is labelled 'indeterminate', usually because it is fragmented, incomplete or bears ambiguous secondary sexual characteristics. Knüsel proposes that ambiguous characteristics of largely complete skeletons might point to intersex, especially if the grave goods interred with the individual are similarly ambiguous or gender neutral (Knüsel 2015).[51]

Although skeletal material is lacking, there are myriad artistic representations of intersex persons.[52] The earliest known depiction, a fragment of a clay mould for a terracotta figurine, dates to the last quarter of the fourth century BCE and comes from a well deposit in the Athenian Agora (Garland 2010: 119).[53] The mould would have produced figures of the *anasyromenos*, or revealing, type. Figures of this type, mostly small-scale works of marble or terracotta, stand frontally with breasts visible beneath, or partially exposed by, their drapery as they raise their garments to reveal that they are ithyphallic.[54] These figurines, as well as other intersex types, are believed to represent Hermaphroditus and function both apotropaically and as votive offerings. The best-known type is the so-called 'sleeping' one, illustrated by the Borghese Hermaphroditus in the Louvre (Fig. 2.15). Also dating to the Hellenistic period, but known to us through Roman marble copies, these sculptures, like the aforementioned individuals with curved spines, embody the Hellenistic predilection for the dramatic and the physically different. This sculptural type is a visual surprise – at first glance, the subject appears to be a young woman, nude and vulnerable as she slumbers soundly. Voyeurism inevitably overcomes the viewer and encourages movement around the sculpture, ensuring that the figure's exposed phallus will be plainly visible from the back side (Fig. 2.16). It is possible that the marble sleeping sculptures are copies of a famous bronze hermaphrodite created by Polycles in the second century BCE, but the original is lost and only referenced by Pliny the Elder (*Natural History* 34.80), who does not provide a detailed description of it (Ajootian 1997: 220–5, 230–1; Garland 2010: 119–20).

Castrated males, or eunuchs, represent another non-normative androgynous class of gender. Unlike intersexuals, eunuchs are not depicted in Greek art, but they do appear in early myth.[55] Uranus (Sky) was the consort of Gaea (Earth), but was cruel and disdainful towards their children whom he had imprisoned. Angered by the treatment of her children by their father, Gaea fashioned a sickle and goaded her children into seeking revenge. Her son, Cronus, agreed to do so and waited until Uranus came to lie with Gaea. When the opportune moment arose, Cronus castrated his father with the sickle and eventually assumed his position as ruler of the gods. Uranus, in turn, was rendered impotent – in every sense of the word – and faded away from the mythic centre stage (Hesiod, *Theogony* 154–206, 491; Gantz 1993: 10–12, 41; Clay 2003: 17–19).

To castrate an adult male as Cronus did would mean almost certain death for the eunuch. The pubic area is highly vascular, and the swift removal of the penis, testicles and scrotum (i.e. total castration) with a sharp instrument was undoubtedly associated with a high mortality rate. For this reason, it has been hypothesised that castration of this sort was only performed to signify the

Figure 2.15 Frontal view of the Sleeping Hermaphroditus (Borghese Hermaphroditus) from Rome, Italy. Roman marble copy of a Hellenistic Greek original (ca. second century BCE), cushion and mattress by Gian Lorenzo Bernini ca. seventeenth century (Paris, Louvre MA 231). Photo by Erich Lessing © Erich Lessing/Art Resource, NY.

Figure 2.16 Rear view of the Sleeping Hermaphroditus (Borghese Hermaphroditus) from Rome, Italy. Roman marble copy of a Hellenistic Greek original ca. second century BCE, cushion and mattress by Gian Lorenzo Bernini ca. seventeenth century (Paris, Louvre MA 231). Photo by Erich Lessing © Erich Lessing/Art Resource, NY.

symbolic (or actual) killing of any enemy. This belief is further bolstered by the writings of the Hippocratic authors and Aristotle, who seem to encounter only eunuchs who were castrated prepubescently (*On the Nature of the Child* 20; Aristotle, *Generation of Animals* 784a; Erlinger 2016: 31–4). Furthermore, it is assumed that when castration did occur in the ancient world, its aim was not total castration, but rather the removal (or crushing) of the testicles and the scrotum for the purposes of reproductive sterilisation (Bullough 2002: 1–5).

Beyond reproductive sterilisation, men were castrated for a variety of reasons. In his biography of Cyrus the Great, Xenophon advances that the Persians' observations of the natural world, and their concomitant need to control enslaved men, encouraged them to implement the practice of castration:

> For instance, vicious horses, when gelded, stop biting and prancing about, to be sure, but are none the less fit for service in war; and bulls, when castrated, lose somewhat of their high spirit and unruliness but are not deprived of their strength or capacity for work. And in the same way dogs, when castrated, stop running away from their masters, but are no less useful for watching or hunting. And men, too, in the same way, become gentler when deprived of this desire, but not less careful of that which is entrusted to them. (Xenophon, *Cyropaedia* 7.5.62–3 as quoted in Bullough 2002: 5–6)

Since, as Xenophon notes, castration resulted in more pliable men, it was often associated with the eastern Mediterranean slave trade. In particular, enslaved eunuchs were highly prized in the Achaemenid Empire, where they served in royal courts and were often entrusted to safeguard and attend to women (Llewellyn-Jones 2002). Unsurprisingly, Persian preferences impacted the wider slave market, and Herodotus provides us with a glimpse of their unintended consequences. He tells the tale of the slave trader Panionius of Chios (ca. fifth century BCE), who castrated men and sold them to the Persians in Ephesus and Sardis. Panionius, however, met an ironic fate at the hands of one of his victims, a Carian named Hermotimus of Pedasa, whom he had purchased as a prisoner of war. After his castration and subsequent sale, Hermotimus had become the chief eunuch of Xerxes. By chance, Hermotimus ran into Panionius in the city of Atarneus, whereupon he feigned gratitude and thanked him profusely for making him a eunuch since his castration had afforded him a comfortable life in the court of the Persian king. Hermotimus invited Panionius and his family to relocate to Atarneus so that he might repay his former owner with a share of his luxuries. Panionius agreed to this, but the repayment he was expecting was meted out in the form of retaliation – Panionius was forced to castrate his four sons, and they were, in turn, coerced to castrate their father (Herodotus 8.105–6). This story sheds light on yet another aspect of castration: its punitive use. Assyrian laws, for instance, deemed castration to be a fitting punishment for perpetrators of sex crimes (Driver and Miles 1935: 389; Bardel 2002: 53–4), and a monument of Pharaoh Merneptah (19th Dynasty, r. 1213–1203 BCE) publicly declared that he harvested 6,359 trophy penises from a defeated Libyan invasion force and other dissenters. It is unclear whether the castrated were alive, dead or a combination of both when the trophies were taken (Bullough 2002: 6). Nevertheless, a later relief from the Temple of Medinet Habu in Egypt (ca. 1180 BCE) shows that the practice was a long-entrenched one, as a pile of enemy hands and genitals is conspicuously present in a scene depicting captives and spoils of war from Ramses III's campaign against the Libyans (Fig. 2.17; Bardel 2002: 54).[56]

Virtually all of the eunuchs who appear in the writings of Classical Greek authors are either Persian or in Persian territory. Eunuchs appear in drama as early as 476 BCE in Phrynichus' *Phoenissae* (Bardel 2002: 51), a play about the Greek victory over the Persians at Salamis and the distress it caused in Xerxes' court. In addition to the aforementioned story of Panionius and Hermotimus,

Figure 2.17 Detail of a relief from the main temple of Ramses III (r. 1193–1162 BCE), outside the temple walls, at Medinet Habu, Thebes. Bound captives are led to the right by an Egyptian soldier, while scribes presumably tally the numbers of enemy dead based on the severed hands and genitals piled before them. Photo by Erich Lessing © Erich Lessing/Art Resource, NY.

Herodotus describes eunuchs in the employ of King Astyages, the biological father of Cyrus the Great (1.108.5–17.5), and as guards of the false king Smerdis who are killed by Darius and his co-conspirators (3.77–80). Some Greeks also find themselves in danger of castration, as Herodotus refers to an incident in which the Corinthian tyrant, Periander, captured 300 boys of prominent Corcyraean families and sent them to Sardis to be castrated (3.48–53). Luckily, the boys were waylaid and thereby rescued on the island of Samos, but others did not fare quite as well – Herodotus also reveals that the Persians castrated and enslaved all of the male Ionian children when they conquered Ionia and suppressed the revolt (6.9.4, 32.2; Erlinger 2016: 46–58). The next author to mention eunuchs, Ctesias of Cnidus, was the primary physician of King Artaxerxes II, who ruled from ca. 404–360 BCE. His fragmented work, *Persica*, features scheming eunuchs who attend to the royal family, exert influence over powerful people and participate in court intrigue (Lenfant 2012; Erlinger 2016: 58–73). Xenophon's *Cyropaedia* discusses a eunuch named Gadatas, a major ally of Cyrus the Great in his war against the Assyrians (5.2–4, 7.5), and provides the reasoning behind Cyrus' institution of an all-eunuch royal guard (7.5.58–65; Erlinger 2016: 73–82).[57] During his conquest of Persia, Alexander did not discontinue the use of courtly eunuchs (purportedly a eunuch named Bagoas was his lover), and if anything, it appears that the practice spread southward to Egypt during this period (Jonckheere 1954; Erlinger 2016: 23, 89–128).[58] Finally, the one exception to this trend, the only eunuch who is *not* associated with Persia, is the doorman in the household of Callias in Athens who is mentioned in Plato's *Protagoras* (314c).

Castration is a transformative process that impacts an individual both socially and physically. Socially, 'it takes a boy or a man, excludes them from their main social or cultural group, puts them in a liminal position . . . and then reincorporates them into the social sphere, but *not in the same cultural or social group from which they had been removed*' (Reusch 2013: 31, original emphasis). As a result, boys cannot become men or participate in male social spheres and must, instead, form new social groups that often consist of other castrates. The physiological effects of castration, on the other hand, are less uniform than its social ones and vary depending on the time that castration occurs. Those castrated prepubescently lack many male secondary sexual characteristics due to androgen deprivation, as these hormones are primarily synthesised in the testes. The medical condition resulting from androgen deprivation is called hypogonadism, and it is characterised by a dearth of facial and body hair; fat deposits on the hips, buttocks and breasts (and sometimes around the eyelids); swollen and wrinkled skin from loss of elasticity; disproportionately long limbs (contributing to increased height); a large barrel-shaped chest; an infantile penis (when present); a high-pitched voice; an enlargement of the pituitary gland; cardiovascular and pulmonary changes; and a reduction or absence of the prostate

(Peschel and Peschel 1986; Eng et al. 2010: 108–9; Erlinger 2016: 27–8). Men who are castrated postpubescently, however, are physically indistinguishable from those who are not castrated. Where they primarily differ is in sex drive and potency, or namely lack thereof (Wille and Beier 1989; Erlinger 2016: 28–30).

As a result of the careful analyses of the remains of eunuchs from the Ming Dynasty (1368–1644 CE) of imperial China and castrated European opera singers (called *castrati* and popular from ca. the sixteenth century CE until the pope banned the practice in 1903), the effects of prepubescent castration on the human skeleton are well documented (Eng et al. 2010; Belcastro et al. 2011; Reusch 2013; Zanatta et al. 2016). All of the observed skeletal changes are related to androgen deprivation, which generally affects bone growth and composition. The epiphyseal closure of bones that fuse around or after puberty is delayed, which lengthens the growth period and creates elongated bones. Excessive growth is most visible in the limbs, as they are disproportionately long. The bones of the mid-face region, which grow substantially during puberty, are stunted rather than elongated and retain a child-like appearance, the nose is deep-set over a protruding mandible, and the unaffected mandible seems heavier and more robust in contrast. Regarding the architecture of the pelvis, the sciatic notch and subpubic angle bear typical male characteristics, while the wings of the ilia flare outwards in a typical female fashion (Reusch 2013: 36–8). Castrates are also susceptible to osteoporosis, kyphosis of the spine and hyperostosis frontalis interna (HFI), the last a condition commonly seen in postmenopausal women but rare in men that causes the symmetrical thickening of the inner table of the frontal bone of the cranium (Eng et al. 2010: 108; Belcastro et al. 2011).

Although the skeletal indicators of prepubescent castration are clear and conspicuous, castrates, like intersexuals, have not been positively identified in any Greek skeletal assemblages. It is possible that recovery rates are negatively influenced by taphonomic factors. The skeletal material of individuals, like castrates, with osteoporosis/osteopenia (loss of bone mass) tends to decay faster than their more robust, unaffected counterparts (Weaver 1998; Roberts 2009, 58–9). Preservation of castrates also could be impacted by disposal methods. For example, if a body is wrapped in a textile and placed in a grave, it is more susceptible to insects and microorganisms than a body that is interred in a lead coffin (Chamberlain and Parker Pearson 2001: 11–45). Since most, if not all, castrates in the Greek world were enslaved, they are likely to have been buried inexpensively with either no burial container or one made of a cheap, perishable material such as wood (see Chapter 3 for burials of the enslaved). Furthermore, it is difficult to detect castrates *in situ* because some of their most conspicuous abnormalities, those related to height and body proportions, might go unnoticed during excavation, and thus detection will most likely occur not in the field, but during laboratory analysis (Reusch 2013: 38).

INTERSECTIONALITY

The case studies discussed here represent the limited bioarchaeological evidence of physical difference in the ancient Greek world, but very few derive from the Late Archaic/Classical Greek mainland – the time and region that is the focus of this broader study of social marginalisation. This dearth, however, is neither unique nor unexpected, especially since it has already been noted by Martha Rose (2003: 5). As previously discussed, the lack of skeletal remains of disabled individuals is a common archaeological problem. Furthermore, even though the paucity of evidence prevents a focused synchronic study of the social ramifications of physical impairment, it provides us instead with a diachronic glimpse into the ways in which the disabled were treated over time in ancient Greek society. One common denominator among the burials is that none of the individuals were buried in a non-normative fashion that would suggest social marginalisation. Although a number of literary passages discussed in Chapter 1 allude to the derision and mockery of the physically impaired, an individual can be ridiculed for an unusual or undesirable physical trait without experiencing social marginalisation (Rose 2003: 43; Garland 2010: 73–86), which appears to be the case in the ancient Greek world. Thus, the bioarchaeological evidence, though sparse, supports the position (discussed in Chapter 1) of scholars like Martha Rose (e.g. 2003) and Robert Garland (e.g. 2010) who maintain that the physically impaired were fully integrated into society and not marginalised.

Although physical impairment alone was not sufficient cause for social marginalisation, there is evidence to suggest that the intersectionality of multiple marginalised factors was, and myriad literary examples support this interpretation. Consider Oedipus, for instance. If he did indeed have a club foot, it was not enough to marginalise him, as Oedipus was not marginalised until he was also blind and ritually polluted (Garland 2017: 159). Thersites and Aesop are intersectional figures as well. Thersites is physically impaired, prone to inappropriate behaviour and has an acerbic personality (*Iliad* 2.231–44), whereas Aesop, a foreigner and freedman, is physically impaired and has a speech impediment (Himerios, *Orationes* 13.5). In the case of Thersites, from the moment he appears in the Achaean assembly, it is clear that he is not a welcome member of the group, but rather a figure whose ugly appearance and brutish antics have set him apart from the others. His marginal status is reinforced by the public humiliation and beating he sustains at the hands of Odysseus (*Iliad* 2.266–99). Aesop, on the other hand, is more complex. Greek authors discuss his literary achievements, but never comment on his physical appearance (Herodotus 2.134–5; Plato, *Phaedo* 60c–d; Aristotle, *Rhetoric* 2.1393a; Aristophanes, *Wasps* 566, 1446; *Peace* 129; *Birds* 470), while in a later source, Plutarch's *Symposium of the Seven Sages* (10), jokes are made at the expense of Aesop's former servile status, not his physical appearance (Trentin 2009: 138).[59] Aesop's life, nevertheless, ended when he was thrown from a cliff at Delphi after his sharp wit angered influential people there, who ultimately sentenced him to death on trumped-up charges of temple robbery (Plutarch, *Moralia* 556f–557a; Kurke 2003).

The public beating and execution of Thersites and Aesop, respectively, have prompted scholars to identify them as scapegoats. The scapegoat ritual – which required a marginal individual to be ritually expelled (and occasionally executed) in order to purify a community – suggests that it was rather desirable for a Greek polis to have some imperfect residents (Ogden 1997: 15–23; Garland 2010: 23–6). A scholiast to Aristophanes maintains that this was the case at Athens: 'For the Athenians used to keep some excessively feeble and poor and useless people, and when some disaster fell upon the city, e.g. a famine or some such thing, they used to sacrifice these men to be purified of the pollution and their own evil . . .' (Scholiast, Aristophanes, *Knights* 1136 as quoted in Ogden 1997: 16). Although scapegoat preferences could vary according to city (enslaved individuals were selected at Abdera and Chaeronea, Leucas and Rhodes chose criminals, and Massilia designated the destitute), a scholiast to Aeschylus explains the general Greek practice, indicating that disabled people were favoured for the task, especially those with leg and foot impairments:

> . . . when a famine or something else of things which are deprecated occurred among the Greeks, they would take the man who was most odious and a cripple, a victim of nature, a lame man, people of that sort, and they would sacrifice him to be rid of the evil that was troubling them. (Scholiast, Aeschylus, *Seven Against Thebes* 680 as quoted in Ogden 1997: 16–17)

Jan Bremmer (1983) notes that a common denominator among all scapegoats is that they are selected from the ranks of the socially marginalised. Another commonality among many scapegoats, be they physically impaired, criminals or foreigners, is low socioeconomic status, which implies that their intersectionality made them the perfect scapegoats.[60]

Low socioeconomic status often intersects with disability in the ancient Greek world. The Athenian state supported physically impaired people who were impoverished and incapable of work (Lysias 24; Penrose 2015: 506–7; Dillon 2017: 176–7), and the enslaved were frequently disabled. Castrates, for instance, are almost always enslaved, and Robert Garland remarks that the enslaved 'ran an enormously high risk of becoming crippled, bow-backed or in some other way deformed. Indeed, a physical deformity, however mild, was their distinguishing hallmark, as Aristotle noted (*Pol.* 1.1254b 27–31)' (Garland 2010: 22). The connection between disability and slavery is likewise underscored by the story of the mutilated Greeks at Persepolis.[61] When Alexander the Great reached the Achaemenid capital of Persepolis in 330 BCE, he encountered a group of Greeks who had been severely mutilated during Persian enslavement (Quintus Curtius 5.5.5–24; Diodorus Siculus 18.69.2–9; Justin 11; Miles 2003).[62] These men, recently released by the Persians, were those

> who had been punished in captivity by mutilation of their bodies, and who entreated that, 'as he [Alexander] had delivered Greece, he would also release them from the cruelty of their enemies'. Permission was given to them to go home, but they preferred receiving portions of land in Persia, lest, instead of causing joy to their parents by their return, they should merely shock them by the horrid spectacle which they presented.
> (Justin 11 as quoted in Miles 2003: 865–6)

Regarding their physical appearance, Diodorus Siculus (18.69.2–9) notes that the Greeks were mutilated on a case-by-case basis. During their captivity, the men acquired practical skills or crafts, so their captors preserved the extremities that each man needed for his trade, but amputated the rest. As a result, the mutilations varied from man to man, with some lacking hands or feet, while others were deprived of ears or noses. Quintus Curtius (5.5.5–24) provides us with additional information, stating that the Greeks were also branded with letters from the Persian alphabet (possibly as marks of ownership) and that their Persian captors mutilated them in order to amuse themselves and humiliate their captives. The Persians' plan evidently worked, and even though Alexander was apparently prepared to arrange – both logistically and financially – for the repatriation of these mangled men, the demoralised formerly enslaved opted to remain together in Asia rather than live out the rest of their days as social pariahs at home (Miles 2003).

According to Diodorus Siculus (18.69.2–9), most of the mutilated Greeks at Persepolis were elderly, and their advanced age likely served as a compounding marginalising characteristic (Gilleard 2007). On account of the high mortality rates associated with childbearing, war and infectious disease in the ancient world, the average life expectancy for Greeks was relatively low by modern standards: 36 years for women and 45 years for men (Angel 1970: 94). Yet, the age at which one was considered 'old' is unclear, and it is likely that the threshold between youth and old age was nebulous, as no official rite of passage marked its commencement (Lee 2015: 47). One can argue, however, that women would have transitioned to old age around the time of menopause, which would have occurred between ages 40 and 50 (Amundsen and Diers 1970), and men were most likely considered elderly when they were discharged from military service around age 60 (Finley 1981: 156).[63] This corresponds to the age range given in the lyric poem attributed to Solon which separates human life into ten stages of seven years. The author remarks that the seventh and eighth stages (ages 49–62) are when a man's speech is the best in his life, but in the ninth stage (ages 63–9) there is a weakening in his ability to think and speak (Lattimore 1960: 23).

The ancient Greeks regarded old age as a double-edged sword. On the one hand, old age is associated with wisdom, experience and honour, and the elderly had special status. For instance, older men had earned the right to counsel younger generations (*Iliad* 4.323), men over the age of 59 could legislate in the *Gerousia* (Spartan council of elders), and many city states mandated that children provide food, shelter and care for their aged parents (Aristotle, *Athenian Constitution* 55.3, 56.6; Aeschines, *Against Timarchus* 28, 103, 105; Xenophon, *Memorabilia* 2.2.12; Isocrates 19.24–9; Finley 1981; Harokopos 2019: 9). Although the formulation of these laws might give the impression that elder abuse was rampant (and there is a third-century BCE petition that describes a case of a daughter allegedly refusing to care for her blind and frail ageing father: *Selected Papyri* 2.268; Rose 2003: 27–8), we also have examples of filial devotion, such as the Argive brothers, Cleobis and Biton, who yoked themselves to a cart to transport their elderly mother to the Temple of Hera (Herodotus 1.31). On the other hand, there was also an understanding that old age was sorrowful, destructive and difficult (e.g. *Iliad* 8.53, 8.103, 10.79, 14.487, 18.434, 23.623; *Odyssey* 11.196, 24.249–50). The elderly, with their sparse grey hair, stooped backs and physical impairments, were staples in Attic tragedy, where they were objects of pity (e.g. Aeschylus, *Agamemnon* 74–5; Euripides, *Heracles* 639–41), and comedy, where they were mocked (e.g. Aristophanes, *Acharnians* 687–91; the character of Demos in *Knights*; Garland 2017: 163–5; Harokopos 2019: 8–9). Both of these attitudes towards the elderly – respect and derision – are also perceptible in Athenian Classical art (Meyer 1989; Bergemann 1997: 102–16; Birchler Émery 1999; Matheson 2009; Lee 2015: 47–8; Harokopos 2019: 24–5).

Humans gradually deteriorate as they age, and the Greeks recognised that old age precipitated physical impairment and weakness (*Iliad* 23.627–8). Xenophon remarks that old men forfeit their hearing, sight, wit and memory as they age (*Memorabilia* 4.7.8; Rose 2003: 72), but there are other debilitating physical changes that can occur as well. For instance, osteoporosis, a metabolic disease process resulting in the reduction of total bone mass, can lead to increased risk of fracture (Roberts and Manchester 2007: 242–7), and ante-mortem tooth loss, which increases with age and could be caused by periodontal disease, trauma, extraction or scurvy, can make it difficult to eat and potentially result in malnutrition (Waldron 2009: 238–9).[64]

Of the degenerative processes that affect the skeleton, one of the most painful and disabling is the deterioration of the joints. Degenerative joint disease (also referred to in the literature as osteoarthrosis, osteoarthritis, arthropathies and rheumatism) is caused by the gradual disintegration of articular cartilage (also discussed in Chapter 3; Roberts and Manchester 2007: 133). This deterioration is a three-step process: the first two phases only affect soft tissue, but in the third stage, the advanced breakdown of cartilage stimulates new bone growth in an attempt to repair the damage. New bone (called osteophytes) often forms around the margins of joints and on the joint surfaces. As the condition progresses, pitting (porosity) of the joint surface, the widening and flattening of the joint contour, and eburnation (highly polished area on the joint surface caused by complete disintegration of the cartilage, i.e. bone-on-bone contact) can also be present (Waldron 2009: 26–8). Although the exact causes of degenerative joint disease are difficult to ascertain, advancing age, genetic predisposition, biological sex, obesity, trauma, repetitive movement and related systemic conditions (e.g. Paget's disease, osteoporosis) are all known to contribute to its development. As a result, the aetiology of degenerative joint disease can be complicated and multifactorial (Waldron 2009: 28–9, 39–40).

It is at the intersection of advanced age and disability that we find a non-normative burial from Athens that is suggestive of social marginalisation. It dates to the Late Helladic IIIC–Submycenaean periods (ca. 1190–1000 BCE) and was found in the cemetery along the north bank of the Eridanos. The individual, an Old Adult male (AA 340, Tomb 82) was buried in the prone (face down) position. During life, he sustained fractures to the left tenth and eleventh ribs that had healed before death, and there was another healed fracture at the head of the first metacarpal (the base of the thumb). It is not possible to determine whether the rib fractures were acquired on account of an accident or interpersonal violence, but the thumb fracture, called a Bennett's fracture, typically occurs when an individual strikes someone or something with a closed fist. Furthermore, this individual's mobility was most likely impaired by the advanced degenerative joint disease that was observed on the shoulders, elbows, wrists, hips, knees, ankles and every vertebra in the spinal column. Based on the pattern of joint involvement and the severity of the spinal lesions, it is probable that the degenerative changes were caused by a systemic disease – most likely calcium phosphate deposition disease (Liston 2017: 557–8).

It is possible that intersectionality also led to the purposeful burial of skeletons in wells. The deposition of skeletons in wells has been attested in Greek archaeological contexts since the Bronze Age at Corinth (Early Helladic), Eleusis (Middle Helladic), Argos and Mycenae (Late Helladic). Given the early dates of these excavations (1890s through the 1970s), careful attention was not always paid to the skeletal material, and as a result, full palaeopathological analyses were not conducted. The excavators of these sites, nevertheless, recognised the significance of non-normative deposition, and speculated that the bodies represented casualties of war, epidemic, siege, famine, flood or earthquake, among other potential causes (Little and Papadopoulos 1998; Papadopoulos 2000; 2017: 602–6). It is at Athens, however, where careful osteological analysis of skeletons from wells allows for a more cogent interpretation of the phenomenon. An Early

Iron Age (ca. 900–850 BCE) Young Adult male (Tomb 29, U–V 19:1, AA 288) was placed in a flexed position in a well situated north of the Acropolis in the area that would later become the Athenian Agora. This individual had compression fractures on the first and third lumbar vertebrae, an elliptical depression fracture on the upper right side of the cranium and a more substantial compound depression fracture on the left side of the cranium. All of the fractures were remodelled and healed prior to death, suggesting that the individual lived for some time after receiving these injuries, which subsequently impacted his life in various ways. The vertebral fractures could have induced chronic pain and affected the man's mobility to some degree, but did not cause paralysis, as musculoskeletal markers indicate that the individual was mobile and using his legs at the time of death. The depression fractures, on the other hand, constitute the more serious injuries, as they carry a high potential for transitory or permanent neurological impairment that could have manifested as behavioural or functional abnormalities, aphasia or post-traumatic epilepsy. As a result, the intersection of physical and neurological impairments most likely led to this individual's non-normative burial (Little and Papadopoulos 1998; Papadopoulos 2000; 2017: 602–3; Liston 2017: 542–3).[65] Similarly, a later example of a Middle Adult male (AA 24) buried in a Hellenistic well (G 5:3, second quarter of the second century BCE) in Athens bears skeletal evidence of severe degenerative joint disease, osteoporosis and hereditary hemochromatosis, as well as a healed circular depression fracture on the right frontal bone and healed nasal bone fractures. Hereditary hemochromatosis, which most likely caused the degenerative joint disease and osteoporosis, is an autosomal recessive disease that promotes the accumulation of toxic levels of iron, resulting in visceral and metabolic complications. In this case, severe degenerative joint disease, which includes the anklyosis (fusion) of the eighth and ninth thoracic vertebrae and the fifth lumbar vertebra and the sacrum, as well as extensive damage to joints in the knees, elbows, neck and hands, would have been physically debilitating. Furthermore, the cranial depression fracture might have led to a traumatic brain injury – providing us with yet another example of an individual in the well who might have exhibited both physical and neurological differences (Liston et al. 2018: 26–9).

Despite the general lack of skeletal evidence of physical difference in the ancient Greek world, the diachronic case studies surveyed in this chapter reveal that physical impairments were not sufficient cause for social marginalisation. Rather, social marginalisation most likely occurred with intersectionality, when physical impairment was only one of multiple marginalising factors (i.e. advanced age, low socioeconomic status, non-Greek ethnicity etc.) embodied by a single individual. Continuing the investigation of the marginalising factors, the next chapter discusses how low socioeconomic status might have impacted social integration.

NOTES

1. For more on theoretical models in disability studies, see Gosbell 2018: 31–43. Also, for a historiography of disability studies (both in general and for the ancient world), see Anderson and Carden-Coyne 2007; Laes 2017b; Gosbell 2018: 4–8.
2. For a recent approach to the medical model, see Roush 2017.
3. Note that Edwards (1997b) refers to the social model as the 'community model'. The social model continues to predominate disability studies and has been adopted by bioarchaeologists as well (e.g. Southwell-Wright 2013).
4. For a critique of the social model, see Riddle 2013.
5. Although they are not employed in this study, note that other recent theoretical models, such as the Bioarchaeology of Personhood (Boutin 2016) and the Bioarchaeology of Care (Tilley and Oxenham 2011; Tilley 2015; Powell et al. 2016), have been used by archaeologists to reconstruct the lived experiences of past persons who had physical impairments. Also, see Stodder 2017 for a quantitative approach to impairment and disability and Battles 2011 for a holistic anthropological approach. See Byrnes and Muller 2017b; Shuttleworth and Meekosha 2017 for historiographies of bioarchaeological approaches to impairment and disability.
6. Disabling conditions that are not perceptible on skeleton remains have been studied elsewhere (note that this list is meant to be representative and not exhaustive): deafness/non-speaking – Edwards 1997b; Laes 2011b; Rose 2003: 66–78; blindness – Rose 2003: 79–94; Garland 2017; mental illness/ neurodiversity – Gourevitch 1983; Harris 2013; Rose 2017; cognitive/intellectual impairment – Berkson 2004; Goodey 2005; Bosman 2009; Goodey and Rose 2013; Rose 2017. At the same time, note that there is some skeletal evidence that might serve as indicators of the aforementioned conditions. For instance, at Apollonia Pontica (ca. fifth to third centuries BCE), unilateral aural atresia in an adult female skeleton might have resulted in hearing impairment and the déformation of the external ear (Keenleyside 2011), and occipitalisation of the atlas in two adult females might have restricted head and neck movements and caused neurological complications (Keenleyside 2015). Also, some cases of trepanation observed in the archaeological record might have been performed to assuage symptoms associated with mental illness (Bourbou 2013: 341–3).
7. For more on the role of case studies in palaeopathological research, see Mays 2012a.
8. Note that exposure, where the infant is abandoned and could potentially be retrieved by a third party, differs from infanticide, which exclusively refers to the deliberate death of an infant. Although some cases of exposure undoubtedly resulted in the death of the infant, and thus infanticide, the two terms must be used carefully and not interchangeably (Patterson 1985).
9. For a historiography of exposure and infanticide, see Oldenziel 1987; Evans Grubbs 2013; Bonnard 2018. Also, it is reductionist to assume that all Greek city states favoured infant exposure, especially as Aristotle (*Politics* 7.1335b) implies that some did not. Even though Isocrates denies that infant exposure

was practised at Athens (12.121–3), scholars have generally dismissed this claim (Rousselle 2001: 313). See Amundsen 1987: 9 for Jewish and Egyptian customs, which appear to forbid exposure and infanticide.

10. See Amundsen 1987 for an analysis of pertinent passages in the works of Plato and Aristotle.

11. See Rose 2003: 29–49 for a refutation of this assertion.

12. For a discussion of Greek emotional responses to the loss of a child, see Golden 1988; Bourbou 2013. Also, note that the Gortyn law code (ca. fourth century BCE) permitted the exposure of perfectly healthy children (Dillon 2017: 169).

13. Although Garland is uncertain of whether exposure was definitively practised in Athens, he maintains that it must have been conducted before the *amphidromia*, the naming ceremony that took place five to ten days after the child's birth (2001: 81). For more on the *amphidromia* (and the *dekatê*), see Ogden 1994: 88–91.

14. Not all scholars accept the evidence supporting Spartan exposure practices. For arguments for and against, see Laes 2008: 92–3; Dillon 2017: 168–9.

15. See Ogden 1997: 13 for evidence of vessels used for infant exposure (pots in particular).

16. Skeletal assemblages from Roman contexts at Ashkelon, Israel (Smith and Kahlia 1992) and in Britain (Mays 1993; 2003; Mays and Faerman 2001; see Scott 1999: 110; 2001a; 2001b; Gowland and Chamberlain 2002 for the opposing view) have also been interpreted as containing evidence in support of infanticide (see Liston et al. 2018: 109–13 for a critical review and refutation of these interpretations). However, note that although Mays (1993: 887) asserts that infanticide was practised in Roman Britain, he was unable to discern any skeletal abnormalities in any of the infant remains he studied.

17. Dogs are associated with kourotrophic deities, like Hecate, and children are often interred with dogs in Graeco-Roman funerary contexts. For more on the interpretation of the dogs in the Agora Bone Well, see Liston et al. 2018: 53–63, 105–9, 134–9.

18. Similar contemporaneous deposits of infants and dogs in wells have also been discovered at Messene (late third century BCE; Bourbou and Themelis 2010) and Eretria (third century BCE; Chenal-Velarde 2006; Bourbou and Themelis 2010: 113).

19. A child aged 16–18 months (AA26a), one of the oldest in the assemblage, possessed a cranial fracture on the posterior right parietal. The absence of callous formation at the fracture indicates that the child survived for about 12 to 21 days after receiving the injury. The child also had three broken ribs, which had healed at the time of death, and a mandibular fracture that occurred 4–5 days before death. Furthermore, the child's long bones have asymmetrical deposits of periosteal bone that were likely caused by trauma as they are analogous in appearance and distribution to those of abused children from forensics contexts (Liston et al. 2018: 32–6). According to Liston and Rotroff (2013: 71) these lesions occur '[w]hen a child's arms or legs are grabbed roughly or the child is shaken while being gripped by the limbs, the bruising of the periosteal membrane results in new bone formation'.

20. Another infant could also have been a candidate for exposure – this child was born with a class IV cervical rib which could have caused impaired arm motion due to compression of the brachial nerves (Liston et al. 2018: 50).

21. Plato also recommends commercial/retail vocations for those who are not capable of performing other types of labour (*Republic* 2.371c–d).

22. For a critical discussion on degree of mobility after fracture, see Gilmour et al. 2019.

23. Some have suggested that Hephaestus' physical differences derive from some form of dwarfism – either achondroplastic or diastrophic (Aterman 1965a; 1965b; Silverman 1965; Ogden 1997: 35). Furthermore, he is often accompanied by persons with dwarfism in his workshop (e.g. the Cabeiri, the Telchines and the Dactys) and on his Return to Mount Olympus (Ogden 1997: 36–7). For the connection between Hephaestus and physically impaired komast dancers in Archaic black-figure vase-painting, see Smith 2009; 2010: 28, 192.

24. Note that Ziskowski (2012) asserts that the appearance and disappearance of komast dancers in Corinth (ca. 630–570 BCE) is tied to the tyrannical reign of the Cypselids, who controlled Corinth from the mid-seventh century to the first quarter of the sixth century BCE, and had a family history of mobility impairments (see also Smith 2010). This family history is recorded by Herodotus (5.92), who explains how the first tyrant, the eponymous Cypselus, was the son of a woman with a mobility impairment named Labda (for more on Labda, see Garland 2010: 98–9).

25. J. Lawrence Angel (1946: 82) briefly mentions a Greek skeleton with congenital hip dislocation, but fails to provide context or chronology for the individual.

26. Plutarch appears to be enamoured with the literary trope of the mobility impaired soldier who is admonished to stand and fight rather than flee, as different versions of it are scattered throughout his *Moralia* (210f, 217c, 234e, 241e, 331b; Rose 2003: 44).

27. An oft-cited statistic asserts that 10 per cent of all known ancient Greek skeletons possess at least one ante-mortem fracture (Grmek 1991: 91; Garland 2010: 19), and this figure has been used as proof to support the claim that 'a large part of the population suffered from a visible disability' (Samama 2017: 121). This conclusion is a non sequitur based on the flawed assumption that all skeletal fractures lead to physical impairment.

28. Note, however, that periostitis can also be present at a fracture site (Roberts and Manchester 2007: 92). Also, there are many different types of bacteria that can result in osteomyelitis, but the majority of recorded cases are caused by *Staphylococcus aureus* (Waldron 2009: 84–5).

29. Amputation is difficult to discern archaeologically. For instance, signs of perimortem amputation on the human skeleton can be mistaken for post-mortem damage, while healing amputations can be mistaken as healing fractures with delayed union or non-union (Roberts and Manchester 2007: 123).

30. The best-attested prosthetics are dental ones (*On Joints* 32–4; Bliquez 1995: 2642–62; Stampolidis and Tassoulas 2014: 264–7).

31. Philoctetes' wound has also been interpreted as having been caused by a poisoned arrow, such as those he carried from Heracles (Mayor 2008: 48–54).

32. However, even after careful analysis the purpose of mass graves can be elusive. Osteological analysis of skeletons interred in a Late Classical/Early Hellenistic

mass grave at Chania (Crete) revealed that the ca. forty deceased individuals were mostly males between 17 and 35 years of age. There were no pathological indicators of their cause of death, and certainly no evidence of trauma that might point to injuries sustained during combat (Bourbou and Niniou-Kindeli 2009).

33. Note that Agelarakis has identified numerous wounded warriors (e.g. 2014b; 2016).

34. Demosthenes lists these injuries in chronological order, as it is presumed that Philip's eye was wounded at Methone (ca. 354 BCE), his collarbone was broken while he was fighting the Illyrians (ca. 344 BCE), and his leg and arm were permanently injured by the Thracians after he returned from battle with the Scythians (ca. 339 BCE; Riginos 1994: 105). Although other biographical facts and details concerning these injuries are provided by later authors, it is suspected that they were fabricated (Riginos 1994).

35. 'Short stature' is defined as a height below the fifth percentile on a growth chart or at least three standard deviations from the mean height for age (Waldron 2009: 195).

36. Ortner (2003: 422) also remarks that malformation or traumatic destruction of the pituitary rarely leads to hypopituitarism, and craniopharyngiomas are most often the cause.

37. Note that other mythological and literary references to short-statured beings include the Cercopes, daemons associated with Hephaestus and the forge (the Cabeiri, the Telchines and the Dactys) and anonymous kourotrophic daemons (Dasen 1993: 175; for more on these daemons, see Blakely 2000).

38. For additional fifth-century BCE sources, see Perry 1952: 211–41; for *Vita Aesopi*, see Perry 1952: 1–208.

39. The average adult experiences full suture closure between ages 30 and 40 on the inner (endoseal) surface of the cranium and ten years later on the external surface. This chronology excludes the metopic suture which fuses between an individual's first and fourth years (Scheuer and Black 2000: 107).

40. When one suture is involved, the condition is referred to as 'simple', and it is called 'compound' when two or more are affected (Waldron 2009: 209).

41. Note, however, that Bartsocas (1973) proposes an alternative diagnosis, namely that Thersites had cleidocranial dysplasia, a congenital condition that causes the deformation of the skull, collarbones and vertebral arches (see also Simms 2005).

42. On potential representations of Aesop and Aesopic themes, see Lissarrague 2000: 137–47.

43. For more on vocalisations and speech in Greek art, see Himmelmann 1998: 37; Steiner 2001: 30–2. Note that there is a contemporaneous unattributed Attic red-figure askos, ca. 440 BCE (Paris, Musée du Louvre G 610), that depicts a bald male figure, nude and leaning on a stick wrapped in a cloak, who bears an enlarged head and markedly pointed forehead (which, if taken literally, might be indicative of trigonocephaly). A crouching lion stands before the man, but nothing suggests that the two figures are in dialogue with one another, and this is why the bald man has not been identified as Aesop (Lissarrague 2000: 138, fig. 5.2).

44. The identification of the man as Aesop was first made by Jahn (1843: 434). Although Lissarrague acknowledges that this identification is plausible, he also

notes that the image on the tondo is unique for the Classical period as it depicts a disproportionate individual (subject matter not popularised until the Hellenistic period, ca. 323–31 BCE) and that the composition 'falls within a dual tradition of human caricature and anthropomorphized animals' (2000: 137). Hermann (1949: 435–7), however, does not think that the figure is Aesop since he does not have a curved spine and is not dressed as an enslaved individual. He identifies the figure as Phaedrus, a Cynic fabulist, instead.

45. For a more extensive list of bibliographical sources concerning headshaping in the ancient Near East, see Lorentz 2009: 90.

46. Hesiod also mentions the Macrocephali in a lost work entitled *Periodos ges* (Strabo, *Geographica* 7.3.6; Garland 2016: 57).

47. For Pherecydes, there were three primordial forces, namely Zas (Zeus), Chthonie (Ge or Gaea) and Chronos, and Chronos is described as intersex and capable of procreating with itself. The Orphic tradition also includes an intersex being able to procreate with itself, referred to variously as Phanes, Protogonos, Bromios, Zeus and Eros (Ajootian 1997: 226; Brisson 2002: 72–114).

48. However, note that on Cyprus there was a bearded statue of a male Aphrodite called Aphroditus (Macrobius, *Saturnalia* 3.8), and a terracotta plaque featuring Aphroditus and dating to the seventh century BCE was found in Perachora (Ustinova 1998: 106).

49. A third intersex person described by Diodorus Siculus (32.10) was a person of Macedonian descent named Heraïs from Abae in Arabia, who lived life as a woman until a surgical procedure was performed to free and modify her previously encapsulated male genitalia. Heraïs then traded her female garb for men's clothing and changed her name to Diophantus. Two other individuals with ambiguous bodies are described in the Hippocratic treatise *Epidemics* (6.8.32). In both cases, the women – Phaethousa of Abdera and Nanno of Thasos – spontaneously 'masculinised' by ceasing to menstruate, growing body hair all over (including beards) and developing deeper voices (King 2015). A related case is mythical. There are different versions of the story, but at its core the maiden Caine was transformed by Poseidon into an invulnerable man named Caineus (Brisson 2002: 62–3; Bremmer 2015). Also, the historical figures of Alcibiades and Menander and the mythical figures of Dionysus and Paris, among others, are often described as androgynous and effeminate, and effeminacy is often associated with hypersexuality and even pansexuality (Shapiro 2015). For transvestitism in art, especially as it relates to depictions of komast dancers, see Miller 1999; Smith 2002; 2010: 64–5.

50. Note that sex, which is biological (and not binary), is distinguished from gender, which is culturally constructed (Hollimon 2011; 2017; Wesp 2017). Also, morphological sex determination in subadults under 18 years of age is problematic. Although scholars have attempted to establish sex diagnostic criteria for younger individuals (Mays and Cox 2000: 121–5; Lewis 2007: 47–55), none of the current methods are reliable, and thus sex determination in subadults is not recommended (Scheuer and Black 2000).

51. Although archaeologists have historically assigned biological sex to an individual based on their gendered grave goods (e.g. weapons are gendered male, while

needles and cosmetic boxes are gendered female), it is well established that this practice leads to serious errors, as biological sex evidenced in skeletal remains and gender expressed by artefact assemblages do not always agree (e.g. Knüsel and Ripley 2000; Brown and Brown 2011: 165–6).

52. Miranda Green (1997) argues that figural representations of intersex individuals were produced as early as the prehistoric period in Europe (e.g. the Neolithic wooden figurine known as the 'god-dolly' from Westhay, UK, ca. 3040–2450 BCE) and that they were viewed as liminal beings connected to the spirit world.

53. The well deposit in which the mould was discovered was associated with coroplastic activity that has been connected to the Eleusinion on the North Slope of the Acropolis, suggesting that the figurines produced by the mould could have served as fertility votives (Ajootian 1997: 227–8).

54. *LIMC* V (1990), 'Hermaphroditos *anasyromenos*', pp. 274–6, nos 30–55 (A. Ajootian).

55. For eunuchs in Achaemenid art, see Llewellyn-Jones 2002; N'Shea 2016.

56. Though they are not discussed in detail here, note that there were also self-castrated sacred eunuchs who served as attendants to the Syrian goddess in Anatolia during the Hellenistic and Roman periods (Lightfoot 2002).

57. Also note that Socrates claims that eunuchs educated Cyrus' children (Plato, *Laws* 695a–b). In general, it has been argued that eunuchs primarily served as literary devices in Classical Greek works. Edith Hall maintains that 'the palace eunuch of the Greeks' imagination encapsulates their systematic feminization of Asia; emotional, wily, subservient, luxurious, and emasculated, he embodies simultaneously all the various threads in the fabric of their orientalist discourse' (1989: 157). Christopher Erlinger, on the other hand, asserts that their presence in Greek literature is used to 'erode distinctions between ethnicities' (2016: 1).

58. The popularity of eunuchs increases substantially during the Roman period (Stevenson 1995; Hales 2002; Lightfoot 2002; Erlinger 2016: 129–242).

59. Lisa Trentin (2009: 138) asserts that 'Aesop's extraordinary intelligence seems to have redeemed his "Otherness" and his ugliness is associated with wisdom, much like the philosopher Socrates, a figure with whom Aesop is regularly associated'. For more on the connections between Aesop and Socrates, see Plato, *Phaedo* 60; Lissarrague 2000: 136.

60. There are, of course, exceptions to this, as there are instances of young aristocratic men and women and a king functioning as scapegoats (Bremmer 1983).

61. Many scholars have questioned the authenticity of the story (summarised in Miles 2003: 871–2), and although its veracity cannot be proven definitively, Mandc Miles (2003) presents evidence supporting its credibility.

62. The number of mutilated Greeks varies according to source. Quintus Curtius states that there were 4,000, while Diodorus Siculus claims that there were only 800 (Miles 2003: 866).

63. The age limit for military service did not apply to generals. Pericles was still a general when he died at age 66, and King Agesilaus of Sparta died at the end of his tour of mercenary service in Egypt at age 84 (Finley 1981: 156–7). Although his specific age is never given, Timoleon continued to serve in combat until he

was completely blind from cataracts (Plutarch, *Timoleon* 37.6–8). Also note that older individuals have been identified in polyandreia (e.g. Agelarakis 2013: 384).

64. An Old Adult female from Eleutherna (Lady 'G', ca. mid-seventh century BCE) and an Old Adult female from Athens (AA314, Tomb 61, LHIIIC–Submycenaean, ca. 1190–1000 BCE) are appropriate examples of the deleterious processes of age – both appear to have had osteoporosis, ante-mortem tooth loss and degenerative joint disease (Agelarakis 2012).

65. Another Early Iron Age (ca. 900–850 BCE) Young Adult male (Tomb 83, AA 362a) recovered from a different Athenian well exhibited signs of similar injuries. This individual had evidence of healed severe traumatic injuries to his spine which consisted of crush fractures on the posterior portions of the vertebral bodies of T10 and S1. In both places, portions of the vertebral body were pushed into the spinal canal, occluding it by 20–30 per cent. This occlusion likely caused chronic pain and impairment of sexual and excretory functions, but no serious loss of mobility (Papadopoulos 2017: 602–3; Liston 2017: 558–60). Perhaps the combination of sexual/excretory and mobility impairment (due to pain) was the intersectional impetus for the individual's non-normative burial.

CHAPTER 3

Socioeconomic Status

It was of utmost importance to the ancient Greeks to be remembered after death. Visits to graves were mandated by funerary ritual, and family members would visit the resting places of their loved ones at various points throughout the year in order to maintain the graves and leave offerings, such as libations, ribbons, garlands and food (Garland 2001: 104–6). Although the majority of cemetery goers were intimately connected to the deceased, others were encouraged to visit as well. Greek cemeteries were positioned outside of their defensive walls, flanking the roads that led to the gates of their cities. This placement was strategic, as it ensured that grave monuments would be visible to travellers as they moved in and out of the city (Kurtz and Boardman 1971: 92–3; Garland 2001: 104–7; Mirto 2012: 95).

Some cities, like Athens, took additional measures to ensure that their cemeteries were attractive sites for visitors. Thucydides (2.34) tells us that the Athenians placed their public cemetery, the *dêmosion sêma*, in a picturesque district of the city and implies that visitors were actively encouraged to visit the graves of those who were interred there. Skilfully wrought sepulchres and stelae (upright gravestones) further enhanced the beauty of the landscape. Archaeological excavations in and around the public cemetery of Athens have revealed sculpted grave markers and cenotaphs that are among the finest examples of High Classical art, such as the 'Stele of Hegeso' (ca. 400 BCE; Fig. 1.4) and the 'Cenotaph of Dexileos' (ca. 390 BCE; Fig. 3.1). Thus, through the use of cultivated landscape and exceptional funerary art, the Athenians encouraged travellers to linger among the monuments, gazing upon their sculpted forms and contemplating their inscriptions, ensuring that the memory of the dead would be preserved among the living (Kurtz and Boardman 1971: 68–71, 84–90, 92–3, 130–41; Wolfe 2013: 23–43).

Yet, as Plato so aptly reminds us, 'in every city there are two cities: the rich and the poor' (*Republic* 422e as translated in Vickers 1990: 613), and conspicuous commemoration of this sort was cost prohibitive for the poor. Beginning with

Figure 3.1 Cenotaph of Dexileos (ca. 390 BCE) from Athens, Greece. Photo © Marie Mauzy/Art Resource, NY.

the grave plots, those parallel to the road and highly visible were more expensive than those situated farther back or aligned in other directions (e.g. Salibra 2003: 53–5). Furthermore, a sculpted monument like the Stele of Hegeso probably cost between 300 and 400 drachmas, which was equivalent to the cost of a sizeable house in Classical Athens. To put this into perspective, the average soldier or skilled labourer earned around one drachma per day, while an unskilled labourer earned approximately three obols per day (Vickers 1990; Wünsche 2007: 89).[1] Thus, without the economic means to commemorate their dead in an obvious and ostentatious manner, it was relatively easy for the lives of the poor to be forgotten. In death, as in life, the poor faded into obscurity to the point where they are largely invisible in the archaeological record.

In order to better understand ancient Greek societal attitudes towards individuals of lower socioeconomic status, this chapter reviews the available bioarchaeological evidence of the non-elite in the Late Archaic/Classical Greek world (ca. sixth to fifth/fourth century BCE). Although material from the Greek mainland is the primary focus of this investigation, case studies from earlier and later periods of Greek history, as well as Greek colonial contexts, are incorporated to illustrate patterns of continuity and/or change. The chapter begins by discussing the ways in which socioeconomic status can be discerned from burial contexts. Then the focus shifts to the bioarchaeological evidence of low socioeconomic status, beginning with the under-representation of poor infants and children. Next, burials that are believed to belong to impoverished individuals (both free and enslaved) are identified and interpreted in the context of contemporary literary and visual sources. The chapter concludes with a consideration of intersectionality and the ways in which the coalescence of multiple marginalising factors (e.g. a person who is both non-Greek and enslaved) can negatively impact social integration.

DISCERNING SOCIOECONOMIC STATUS FROM BURIAL ASSEMBLAGES

Burials that are notably impoverished, or conversely lavish, do not necessarily reflect the social status of the deceased. Mourners could prefer to bury their loved one without grave goods, and make conscious display of their wealth during other phases of the funerary ritual, such as the *prothesis* (lying-in-state) or the *perideipnon* (funerary banquet). On the other hand, mourners of lower socioeconomic status might choose to spend their scarce resources on prestige burial containers or grave goods as a way of honouring the deceased. Also, there are some valuable gifts, such as textiles, that are perishable and leave behind no traces in the archaeological record. Therefore, attempting to discern the social status of the deceased from burial assemblages alone is a precarious endeavour (Parker Pearson 2005: 78–9). Nevertheless, it is evident that some burial containers and objects are intrinsically more valuable than others, and burials which contain them represent displays of wealth that are relative to the culture and settlement from which they derive.[2]

Various modes of interpretation have been suggested for burial assemblages. The processual approach assumes that a society's burial complexities are directly related to its social organisation. For example, the grave of an individual from a sedentary agricultural community should be more complex than that of a person from a hunter-gatherer tribe – in other words, graves from agricultural communities should contain more formal organisation and material culture, and thus more information, than those of their tribal counterparts. Also, details about the deceased's social persona (defined as 'the composite of the social identities maintained in life and recognized as appropriate for consideration at death') are communicated through specific treatments of the body (e.g. type of grave or grave orientation) and the inclusion of particular grave goods (Binford 1971: 17 after Goodenough 1965). Sumptuous grave-good assemblages, for instance, indicate wealth, while certain other grave goods can be associated with age, gender, profession or other social identities. Essentially, processualists maintain that 'who you are affects how you get buried and the separate bits that make up your identity get represented in different ways' (Parker Pearson 2005: 29). Adherents to this approach were traditionally concerned with recording quantity, quality and typology of grave goods and the implications of their characteristics (Baker 2012: 27).

Postprocessualists understand funerary rituals to be an indirect reflection of society (Hodder 1980; 1982; Härke 1997: 21). Postprocessualists tend to take two separate approaches to mortuary studies, one that focuses on the symbolic and contextual genesis of funerary practices and another that emphasises their sociological origins. Symbolic, or contextual, interpretation is based on the understanding that human action is expressed in symbols. Although the actions themselves are ephemeral, their symbolic patterns are preserved in the archaeological record. The remnant of symbolic action, material culture, is like language or text in that it is composed of signs (signifiers) and their meanings (the signified), which can be deciphered when placed in the proper context (Tilly 1989: 186; Härke 1997: 21). Archaeologists who take a symbolic/contextual approach to mortuary analysis are not concerned simply with quantity, quality or typology of grave goods. Instead, they are interested in relationships, such as the locations of grave goods within the burial and the correlation of grave-good sizes and decorations with age and gender of the deceased (e.g. Pader 1980; 1982; Richards 1987). On the other hand, the sociological approach relies heavily upon social theory, especially structuration theory, which posits that 'society is not a given framework in which individuals play pre-ordained roles, but an interplay of rules (structuring principles) and actions (social practices), with ideology providing the legitimation for the former . . . [therefore] burial ritual is not a mere passive reflection of society, but the result of actions which contribute to shaping society itself' (Härke 1997: 21). As a result, adherents of this approach understand that grave goods are not a reflection of wealth or social status, but rather a manifestation of the survivors' claims regarding the deceased's property and position in society (Parker Pearson 1982: 101; Samson 1987; Härke 1997: 21).

The concept of materiality, which serves as an interpretive framework for this book (as discussed in the Introduction), bridges processual and postprocessual approaches (Oestigaard 2004: 48). Materiality is generally concerned with the processes by which people of the past created meanings and identities through the active use of material culture. Objects, although inanimate, 'interact' with people and are able to reinforce, reinvent and renegotiate social relationships because the acts of making, using, transforming and depositing objects have social consequences. In other words, objects both embody and reflect relationships (Hurcombe 2007: 103). Social relationships are inherently multifaceted, and they exist on communal and individual levels. Therefore, in order to fully understand the ways in which material culture is actively used, elements of methodological collectivism (a processual principle stating that human behaviour can be deduced from 'laws' that apply to a specific social system as well as descriptions of the positions or functions of an individual within the social system) and methodological individualism (a postprocessual theory stating that human processes can be deduced from principles governing the behaviour of individuals and descriptions of their unique situations) are both considered to determine how materiality shapes and constructs human beings and societies (Oestigaard 2004: 31, 48). As a result, the objects interred with the deceased are purposefully placed and are capable of revealing not only relationships between the living and the dead, but also those that are shared among the living. Specifically, grave-good assemblages contain information about the deceased and their relationships with their culture (e.g. items related to funerary ritual, such as oil-bearing vessels), their families (e.g. statements of wealth, prestige or affiliation can be made through the inclusion of unique or sumptuous grave goods), their communities (e.g. artefacts which denote ethnic or political alignment) and themselves (e.g. objects related to gender or occupation; Fahlander and Oestigaard 2008b: 7–9).

'Wealth' can be calculated from grave-good assemblages in a variety of ways. The simplest method is based on counts where the graves that contain the most goods are considered to be the wealthiest. Alternatively, a 'scale of value' could be developed for each object based on its raw material and labour investment. The values of each item in a grave are then added together, with the sum representing the wealth score of the burial (Parker Pearson 2005: 78–9). Ian Morris (1987: 141–3; 2001: 106–7; 2011: 182), on the other hand, has calculated grave-good wealth statistically using Gini's coefficient of inequality. Gini's coefficient (G) provides a measure of 'the evenness of the distribution of a trait, from 0 (all graves contain exactly the same number of objects, whether pots or metal ornaments) to 1 (all known pots were in one grave, and no other graves held any examples)' (Morris 2011: n. 20). Essentially, the higher the number (G), the greater the degree of income inequality.[3]

Another technique for calculating burial wealth is to identify culture-specific grave goods that reflect economic differences and 'expenses borne by the living in favor of the dead' (Prohászka 1995: 194; see also Gill 1988). In Late Bronze Age Athens (ca. 1550–1050 BCE), for instance, Susan Kirkpatrick Smith (2000) found that skeletons in graves with one or more non-pottery goods (e.g. jewellery, objects made of ivory or bronze) displayed fewer signs of skeletal and dental stress (discussed below) than those in graves lacking non-pottery goods. Since non-pottery objects are normally more expensive than pottery, and the absence of skeletal and dental stress markers can be taken as a proxy for good health (relatively speaking), the individuals buried in graves with at least one non-pottery good were deemed to belong to a higher social rank than those without non-pottery goods. Moreover, objects made of metal (with the exception of lead, which was a cheap by-product of silver-refining process) were valuable throughout Greek history because metal in its raw form served as currency and objects made of metal were typically more costly than ceramics (Prohászka 1995: 194–5, 207). Not all metals, however, were deemed to be equal, as gold had the greatest worth, followed by silver, and then bronze and other alloys (Vickers 1990). Nevertheless, prestige metal objects such as mirrors, cauldrons and jewellery have been interpreted as signifiers of wealth in Classical contexts (Prohászka 1995).

As previously discussed, any calculation of wealth must be performed with the caveat that burials are arranged by mourners whose motives we cannot reconstruct. It is generally thought that burials adhere to unwritten laws of decorum, so in theory, burial components should be appropriate to the socio-economic status of the deceased. Since Greek funerary rituals are performa-tive in nature, an indecorous funerary display would have had negative social ramifications, as Ian Morris notes: 'Failure to provide an adequate amount [of grave goods] would probably have incurred the same kind of disappoint-ment as being stingy with the dowry of a dependent kinswoman; inappro-priate lavishness would, equally probably, have been seen as a kind of social climbing' (2001: 125). However, there are numerous reasons why survivors might choose to bury their loved one with a lavish burial assemblage. The sim-plest explanation is that the grand display befits the deceased's elite status. Yet, regardless of whether it is viewed as 'social climbing', there are demonstrable instances in which people of modest means are buried in a manner that makes them appear greater, or wealthier, in death than they actually were in life (e.g. Sulosky Weaver 2019a). Presumably, this act can also bolster the public image of the deceased's survivors by association. Furthermore, the construction of expensive burial assemblages can be tied to elite competition. In the Black Sea region, especially during the Classical and Hellenistic periods, there is clear evidence for elite competition in the elaborate nature of the tombs and the wealth of the grave goods (Petersen 2010: 259–66; Rempel 2011). Additional-ly, excessive displays of wealth can be attributed to profound expressions of grief, especially when the deceased was a child. Grave-good practices connected with children often differ from those associated with adults, and cases where children are provided with grave goods that are more plentiful or expensive than adults have been interpreted as 'a personal desire by grieving adults to express the importance of the child' (Crawford 2000: 177–8). Likewise, there are numerous explanations for why graves might appear impoverished. Again, the simplest answer is that the display, or lack thereof, reflects the status of the deceased. Wealthy individuals, however, could be interred without valuable grave goods, as their survivors might choose to display their status through ephemeral ritual displays or perishable grave goods, like textiles. There have also been historical moments where funerary displays were restricted or forbid-den by anti-sumptuary legislation (e.g. for Athens – Solon and Cleisthenes ca. sixth century BCE: Cicero, *On the Laws* 2.26.64, 2.59, 2.64; Demetrius of Phaleron ca. late fourth century BCE: *Marmor Parium* B.13).

Graves without goods might be typical when examined within their proper sociocultural context.[4] Consider grave-goods patterns in Attica, for example. In the Archaic period (ca. 700–480 BCE), emphasis was placed on the outward appearance of graves rather than grave goods. The erection of ostentatious monumental earth mounds, built tombs and funerary sculptures was a popular trend among the elite, but the graves themselves often contained few to no goods. In the Classical period (ca. 480–323 BCE), grave goods generally increase in number and type, but by the end of the period, Late Classical (ca. 400–323 BCE) and Hellenistic (ca. 323–86 BCE) graves feature few to no goods (Kurtz and Boardman 1971: 75–9, 164–6; Morris 1994; 1998: 220; 2001: 108–55).

Since one cannot infer socioeconomic status from material remains alone, any assessment of status should include the analysis of human skeletal remains. Social status significantly impacts health. In general, individuals of lower socioeconomic status are more susceptible to skeletal trauma and disease because they eat a less nutritious diet, live in poor-quality housing and operate under difficult or dangerous working conditions (Link and Phelan 1995; Roberts and Manchester 2007: 42). Thus, evidence of social inequality can be revealed through the presence of skeletal and dental stress markers, stunted growth, stable isotopic analysis of diet and musculoskeletal stress markers. Focusing first on markers of skeletal and dental stress, multiple indicators of stress must be considered in order to gain a comprehensive understanding of an individual's health, which is ultimately a compilation of nutrition, disease and other aspects of life history (Larsen 2015: 8–9). Stress markers can be either specific or non-specific. Stress caused by specific deficiencies include metabolic diseases like scurvy (vitamin C deficiency) or rickets (vitamin D deficiency). Non-specific stress markers have multifactorial aetiologies and can be attributed to periods of severe illness and/or malnutrition (i.e. vitamin and dietary deficiencies). Examples of non-specific stress markers include cribra orbitalia (porous lesions on the upper margins of the eye orbits), porotic hyperostosis (porous lesions on the cranial vault), Harris lines (lines of growth arrest on long bones), linear enamel hypoplasia (lines of growth arrest on the teeth), periostitis (infection of the bone periosteum) and osteoporosis (Parker Pearson 2005: 81–2; Larsen 2015: 30–60).

Growth rate is considered to be 'a highly sensitive indicator of [the] health and well-being of a community or population' (Larsen 2015: 9). An individual's height, or stature, is dictated by genetic potential and environmental factors that are present during periods of bone growth, such as health, nutrition, exposure to sunlight and physical or emotional stress. As a result, stature can be stunted by adverse environments, poor nutrition and episodes of infectious disease. Children raised in impoverished or stressed conditions, for instance, are generally smaller than those who were not, and this trend can continue through adolescence, ultimately impacting terminal stature (Kron 2005; Larsen 2015: 9). Though rare, there can be exceptions to this general rule, and these are most likely attributed to genetic factors. For example, the analysis of the skeletal remains of Prince Spytihněv, Duke of Bohemia, and his wife (875–915 CE) revealed that their statures fell within the average range of the rest of the population who were of lower social rank (Becker 2017).

Nutrition impacts not only stature, but other aspects of health as well. Notably, the relationship between nutrition and disease is synergistic: poorly nourished individuals are more susceptible to infectious disease, and once contracted, infectious disease inhibits the body's ability to absorb nutrients (Larsen 2015: 9). Diet can be reconstructed through the analysis of stable isotopic ratios of carbon and nitrogen in collagen, the major protein in bone and teeth. Carbon and nitrogen both have two stable isotopic forms: $^{12}C/^{13}C$ and $^{14}N/^{15}N$. Since the isotopes have different masses, they fractionate in natural processes, resulting in the variation of isotopic ratios across biological materials and parts of the natural environment. The differences in isotopic ratios are measured in delta units (δ), which represent the deviation in the isotopic ratio from that in an accepted standard material, and expressed as parts per thousand (‰). The $\delta^{13}C$ is generally negative because most biological materials contain less ^{13}C than the standard, while $\delta^{15}N$ is typically positive because most biological tissues contain more ^{15}N than the standard (Mays 2000b: 425).

It follows that each class of food differs in its stable isotope ratios. During photosynthesis, terrestrial plants convert carbon dioxide (CO_2) from the air and water into organic chemicals, which alters the ratio of ^{12}C to ^{13}C by discriminating against ^{13}C to varying degrees. For example, temperate plants (e.g. trees, shrubs, leafy plants, temperate grasses such as wheat and rice, nuts and fruits) convert carbon into a three-carbon molecule, and these C_3 plants contain less ^{13}C. Tropical and subtropical plants (e.g. tropical grasses, maize and sugar cane, millet, some amaranths and some chenopods) produce a four-carbon molecule, and C_4 plants contain more ^{13}C. Marine plants differ from terrestrial ones in that their source of carbon during photosynthesis derives from dissolved bicarbonate, which is enriched in ^{13}C and yields a $\delta^{13}C$ value that falls between the ranges of C_3 and C_4 plants. Marine and terrestrial plants also differ in $\delta^{15}N$, with marine plants containing more ^{15}N than terrestrial ones because a greater amount of denitrification occurs in oceans. $\delta^{15}N$ can also be used to discern dietary preferences between legumes, which have less ^{15}N, and non-leguminous plants like peas, which have more ^{15}N on account of the nitrogen-fixing bacteria in their roots. Additionally, values of $\delta^{13}C$ and $\delta^{15}N$ must be analysed together, otherwise they can be ambiguous and misleading. Terrestrial plants grown in the same area acquire virtually the same $\delta^{15}N$, reflecting the fixed nitrogen they acquired from shared soil, so $\delta^{13}C$ must also be measured to determine whether they are C_3 or C_4 plants. A similar issue occurs when freshwater and marine plants are compared, as their $\delta^{15}N$ values are very close and $\delta^{13}C$ values are required to distinguish between the two (Mays 2000b: 425–6; Brown and Brown 2011: 82–4; Schepartz et al. 2017: 156).

The $\delta^{13}C/\delta^{15}N$ values of humans and animals are a reflection of the $\delta^{13}C/\delta^{15}N$ values of the food they consume. Since bone collagen replaces itself slowly – in adult humans, complete turnover can take ten to thirty years – the stable isotopic ratios of collagen provide a long-term indicator of diet (Mays 2000b: 426). However, the relationships between stable isotopic ratios and diet are not one-to-one, and they require some calculation:

> In large herbivorous mammals, for example, muscle proteins have a $\delta^{13}C$ value some 3‰ higher than the $\delta^{13}C$ content of the diet, and bone collagen is 2‰ higher again. Hence, if a large herbivore is grazing on C_3 plants, its diet will have a $\delta^{13}C$ of about −26.5‰, but in muscles will give a figure of −23.5‰ and in bone collagen a value of −21.5‰. The basis of this ^{13}C enrichment when going from dietary carbon to body carbon is not understood, but presumably resides in the way in which dietary amino acids are converted into protein. Similar effects are seen with nitrogen isotopes, the shift in $\delta^{15}N$ being +2–6‰ from diet to body protein, probably due to the excretion of nitrogen in urea, which is depleted in ^{15}N. (Brown and Brown 2011: 84)

In human bone collagen, the $\delta^{13}C$ is 5‰ greater than diet and the $\delta^{15}N$ is 2–3‰ greater than diet (Mays 2000b: 425–6).

Isotopes continue to shift in accordance with trophic level. If the muscle protein of a herbivore that consumed C_3 plants is ingested by a primary carnivore and converted into bone collagen, the carnivore's $\delta^{13}C$ value will be 1–2‰ higher than the herbivore's and the $\delta^{15}N$ value will be 3–4‰ higher. The pattern continues as you move up the food chain, with top carnivores having the highest $\delta^{13}C$ and $\delta^{15}N$ values. Humans, who are generally omnivorous, tend to have isotope values that are closer to plants because the land animals they consume are either herbivores or primary, rather than top, carnivores. Although the isotope shifts are relatively small compared to a plant diet, they are substantial enough to discriminate between individuals whose diets include a heavy meat component from those whose do not. One interesting exception to this pattern are nursing infants. An infant essentially consumes part of its mother, which places it on a higher trophic level than its mother with greater values of $\delta^{13}C$ and $\delta^{15}N$. These values fall once the infant is weaned and ingesting a typical diet (Brown and Brown 2011: 84–5).

Although diet must be studied on the biomolecular level, evidence of habitual and strenuous activity is visible to the naked eye. Force and repetitive activity cause changes to human bone. The magnitude, direction and frequency of force applied to bone, as well as strenuous and repetitive movements, all promote the production of new bone growth. Over time, cortical bone dimensions increase in order to accommodate heavy loads, and they can likewise decrease in response to reduction in physical activity, serious injury and/or age (Knüsel 2000: 382–4). For example, a study of Native American populations in pre- and post-Spanish-contact Florida reveal that the cortical bones of post-contact Native Americans were substantially thicker than those of their pre-contact ancestors. This change in cortical diameter indicates that the post-contact Native Americans, who were living in and around Spanish missions, were stronger and had adapted to more physically demanding labour, which was possibly imposed on them by the Spanish (Ruff and Larsen 2001).

Specific repeated activities can cause modifications to tendon and ligament attachment sites (entheses). These changes to the cortical bone, called entheseal markers or musculoskeletal stress markers (MSMs), take the form of bony crests, spicules or sulcus-like depressions, and their formation is prompted by the increased development of muscles that are frequently recruited to perform repetitive tasks. Activity and behavioural patterns can be reconstructed through observation of the patterns of MSM development, and they are often used to provide insight into broader societal trends, such as those concerned with gender- or status-based labour division (e.g. Hawkey and Merbs 1995; Kennedy 1998; Karakostis et al. 2017).[5] For example, a group of males (ca. fifth to third centuries BCE) interred near the western shore on the island of Thasos displayed similar patterns of robust MSMs, traumatic injuries and joint degeneration, suggesting that they were engaged in the same occupation. On the basis of ethnographic analogy, it is likely that the males were engaged in wooden boat building and repair. Furthermore, one of these individuals also had bilateral external auditory exostosis, sometimes referred to as 'surfer's ear', a condition in which bony growths form in the external ear canal along the suture lines of the tympanic, temporal and mastoid bones in response to repeated exposure to cold water. Boat repair teams require a diver to guide and position the boat during the hauling process, and it is possible that the man with the external auditory exostoses was the diver (Agelarakis and Serpanos 2010).

Repetitive activities, however, can also lead to the gradual degeneration of joints. Habitual strenuous loading of the vertebral column, for instance, can cause disc degeneration and vertebral compression, especially in the lower thoracic and lumbar vertebrae. Disc degeneration is often evidenced by the formation of Schmorl's nodes, which are smooth-walled depressions centrally placed on the vertebral body (Knüsel 2000: 387–92). In the vertebral column and other joints throughout the body, degenerative joint disease (DJD, often called osteoarthritis and also discussed in Chapter 2) is caused by the gradual disintegration of articular cartilage, which takes place in approximately three stages. The first two phases affect soft tissue and have no impact on bone. During the third stage, the advanced breakdown of cartilage prompts the production of new bone growth to repair the damage, among other adaptations. These adaptations consist of the formation of new bone (osteophytes) around the margins of joints, formation of new bone on the joint surface, pitting (porosity) of the joint surface, widening and flattening of the joint contour, and eburnation (highly polished area on the joint surface caused by complete disintegration of the cartilage and bone-on-bone contact). The exact causes of DJD are often difficult to determine because, in addition to repetitive activities, advancing age, genetic predisposition, sex, obesity, trauma and related systemic conditions (e.g. Paget's disease, osteoporosis) are all known to contribute to its development (Waldron 2009: 26–9, 39–40).

It is important to note that none of the skeletal markers discussed are stand-alone indicators of socioeconomic status. For instance, in their analysis of ninety-four burial assemblages from Pontecagnano (Italy, seventh to third centuries BCE), John Robb and colleagues (2001) found that typical stress markers (e.g. linear enamel hypoplasia, cribra orbitalia and stunted adult stature) did not correlate to social status, while indicators of repetitive activity (e.g. Schmorl's nodes) and physical stress (e.g. skeletal trauma and periostitis) did. To further complicate the matter, health does not necessarily equal wealth, and individuals who appear robust and healthy might have lived in poverty. For this reason, all available mortuary evidence – material as well as biological – must be interpreted together in its proper sociocultural context in order to discern an individual's social status (Morris 2001: 200; Klaus et al. 2017: 15).

The success of discerning socioeconomic status from both biological and material evidence is demonstrated by recent research into Late Bronze Age (ca. 1675–1050 BCE) burial assemblages at Pylos. The hierarchical structure of Mycenaean culture at Pylos is materially manifest in tomb type, with elite tombs consisting of shaft graves (graves at the bottom of shafts ranging in depth from 1–4 m – only one example of this tomb type has been found at Pylos), tholos tombs (built beehive-domed structures covered with earthen mounds) and chamber tombs (chambers cut into the soft bedrock on a hillside reached through a narrow rock-cut passageway). In addition to being architecturally complex, these tomb types typically contain prestige goods, which reinforces their identification as the resting places of the elite. Also, these built tombs were often reopened, reused and arranged in clusters that most likely reflected kin groupings or 'family plots'. Pit graves and cist graves (slab-lined graves) are found at Pylos as well, and based on the poorer quality of the grave goods interred in them, they have been interpreted as the burials of members of the lower strata of society. Using tomb type as a proxy for hierarchical rank, the analysis of human remains revealed distinct patterns in diet and health disparities across sex and socioeconomic class. Members of the lower social strata ate a poorer diet than those of the upper social strata who had greater access to animal protein. Also, females tended to have poorer oral health than males, which could reflect differential sex-based dietary practices or indicate that females were subjected to more biological stressors than their male counterparts (Schepartz et al. 2009b; 2017).[6]

BIOARCHAEOLOGICAL EVIDENCE OF LOW SOCIOECONOMIC STATUS

The manner in which socioeconomic status is denoted in burial contexts can be highly variable and apt to change. Ian Morris, for instance, observes widespread shifting patterns in the assertion of socioeconomic status over time. Throughout much of the Early Iron Age (i.e. the so-called Dark Age) and Archaic period (ca. 1050–750 BCE and ca. 700–525 BCE), burials in central Greece reflected a stark divide between the rich and the poor, to the degree that it seems only the elite members of society were afforded formal burial (1987; 2000: 195–256).[7] Morris defines 'informal burial' as 'still constituting a rite of passage for all the actors, but in a manner very different from that of the observed burials, and leaving little or no identifiable material residue' (1987: 105). This practice begins to change ca. 500 BCE in many parts of Greece, where socioeconomic distinctions fade and are replaced by 'citizen cemeteries', which Morris refers to as 'a symbolic system privileging a vision of the community as an internally homogeneous, egalitarian, restrained group of men', where in Athens in particular 'citizens [in their deployment of material culture] systematically denied the very real social distinctions within their polis: between men and women, free and slave, adult and child, rich and poor' (1998: 220). Another shift occurs around ca. 400 BCE in Athens when the elite emerge again as an archaeologically distinct group (1994; 2001: 108–55).

Morris' conclusions (especially the concept of 'citizen cemeteries') have not been universally accepted, and although the patterns he describes are self-evident, there is currently no scholarly consensus on their interpretation (Garland 1989; Humphreys 1990; D'Agostino and D'Onofrio 1993; Papadopoulos 1993; Houby-Nielsen 1995; Sourvinou-Inwood 1995: 413–44; Sørensen 2002; Patterson 2006). Nevertheless, the present bioarchaeological study of low socioeconomic class in the Late Archaic/Classical period is complicated by the general lack of social distinctions in burials, especially Athenian burials, ca. 480–400 BCE. This complication is further compounded by the dearth of infant and juvenile burials in the archaeological record.

Under-representation of infant and juvenile burials

Burials of infants and juveniles, particularly those from lower social strata, are under-represented in ancient Greek cemeteries (Morris 1987; 2001: 75–80;

Shepherd 2018). Mortality, or the frequency with which death occurs in a population, is closely connected to age, and the probability of death is typically highest in the very young and the very old. Specifically, infants and juveniles experience the highest rate of mortality because they are socially and physically dependent upon adults (among other reasons discussed below). From late adolescence to early adulthood, these rates fall, only to increase again with age. This age-structure is referred to as a standard, or 'attritional', mortality profile, and when an archaeological sample deviates from this profile, it indicates that cultural, pathological or taphonomic processes have biased the sample (Chamberlain 2006: 3, 7, 17, 25). Infants and juveniles are typically under-represented in archaeological samples on account of cultural (e.g. they are often the recipients of differential burial treatment) and taphonomic (e.g. immature bones are small, fragile and prone to rapid decay as well as misidentification by excavators) processes (Lewis 2007: 20–37). In ancient Greek assemblages, cultural practices, such as infant exposure and differential burial treatment, are most likely the primary sources of sample bias (Shepherd 2018).

Some infants born to the impoverished might have been removed immediately from the population because their families chose not to invest in their care and rearing. Children could be economically burdensome, and poor families might have availed themselves of the practice of exposure, which was the socially sanctioned rejection and abandonment of a newborn (see Chapter 2 for a detailed discussed of exposure). Illegitimate children and babies born to enslaved women, *pornai* (prostitutes) and *hetairai* (courtesans) were also prime candidates, and presumably females were disproportionately exposed among the lower socioeconomic classes, as their future marriage dowries would have been seen as major expenses (Beaumont 2012: 91). Once the decision to expose was made, the infant was placed in a pot or chest and discarded either in a deserted spot or a place where it could be readily found by passersby (e.g. a shrine, crossroads or rubbish heap; Patterson 1985; Rousselle 2001; Golden 2015: 146–7).

Even if a family decided to keep an infant, the threat of premature death was high (Lewis 2007: 81–96). Aristotle notes that infant deaths tended to occur within the first week of life (*History of Animals* 588a), and these would most likely be attributed to stillbirth, birth and maternal complications (e.g. infant trauma), pneumonia (caused by aspiration of amniotic fluid), respiratory distress syndrome (especially in preterm or low-birthweight perinates with immature lungs), poor hygiene (e.g. parasites, infections from bathing in contaminated water, tetanus from dirty instruments), gastric distress and disease (Gilmore and Halcrow 2014). Although we are unable to reconstruct ancient Greek rates of infant mortality, if they compare to those of premodern preindustrial societies, they could be as high as 50 per cent within the first year of life (Beaumont 2012: 86–7).

Infant and juvenile mortality rates were most likely highest among families of low socioeconomic class. For instance, injuries and illnesses sustained in unsanitary environments could readily lead to infection and death.[8] Children, with their developing immune systems, would be particularly vulnerable to the effects of poor sanitation and infectious disease. Furthermore, weaning is perhaps the most dangerous period in the life of a young child (Lewis 2007: 100). Switching from breastmilk to solid foods increases a child's exposure to bacterial and parasitic infections, which in turn increases susceptibility to diarrhoeal disease – a situation called 'weanling's dilemma'. Diarrhoeal disease prevents the absorption of nutrients, causing malnourishment, predisposition to disease, stunted growth and even death. If a weaning child were to escape parasitic or bacterial infection, malnourishment could still occur if supplementary foods were of poor nutritional value. Malnourished children are at high risk for infection and also find themselves less resistant to future infections (Lewis 2007: 100; Moffat and Prowse 2018).

The only extant instructions concerning weaning date to the second century CE, but they seem to represent the codification of centuries-old practices. Soranus of Ephesus (*Gynaekia* 2.21.46) recommends breastmilk for the first six months of life, followed by a mixed diet of breastmilk supplemented by solid food for the next eighteen to twenty-four months. Stable isotopic data ($\delta^{13}C$ and $\delta^{15}N$ values) from a Middle Bronze Age assemblage from Lerna (Greece), Classical burials at Apollonia Pontica (Bulgaria), Imperial and Late Roman samples from Italy (Isola Sacra), Egypt (Dakhleh Oasis) and Britain (Queenford Farm), and populations across Byzantine Greece corroborate Soranus' timetable, as it has been determined that weaning occurred between the ages of 2 and 4 during the Bronze Age, Classical, Roman and Byzantine periods. The process of weaning was gradual, often lasting years rather than months, which prolonged the period of time that children would be susceptible to weaning-related health complications (Triantaphyllou et al. 2008; Bourbou and Garvie-Lok 2009; Bourbou et al. 2013; Kwok and Keenleyside 2015).

Stable isotopic studies have not been performed on Late Archaic/Classical Greek child burials from mainland Greece, but it has been suggested that they may have been weaned within the same time frame of 2–4 years of age (e.g. Beaumont 2012: 54). Evidence for Greek weaning is primarily material, in the form of feeder bottles (*bombylioi*) interred in the graves of small children. These ceramic spouted cups sometimes were capped with strainers, suggesting that they could also be used to filter out food particulates that were too large for weaning children. The types of foods that would be placed in feeder bottles is unclear, but honey is a leading candidate. Soranus advocates for diluted honey (*Gynaekia* 2.11.17), and honey residue has been found in a Mycenaean feeder bottle from Midea in the Argolid (Beaumont 2012: 54–6).[9] If honey was given to weaning children, it could have had serious negative effects on infant health.

Honey is unsafe for infants, as it is often contaminated with the spores of *Clostridium botulinum*, a bacterium that secretes botulinum neurotoxin. Botulinum neurotoxin can cause botulism, a severe form of food poisoning that can result in death through the paralysis of respiratory muscles. In infants, the spores of the bacterium can colonise the intestinal tract, causing infant botulism. Although they vary in severity, symptoms of infant botulism include a reduction in muscle tone, difficulty suckling, respiratory problems and death from respiratory failure (Bourbou and Garvie-Lok 2009; Bourbou et al. 2013).

Having established the high potential for infant and juvenile mortality – especially for those born into poverty – it seems counterintuitive that infant and child burials are under-represented in the archaeological record (Dasen 2013: 33; Shepherd 2018). Their under-representation, however, implies that they were typically excluded from formal burial alongside adults (e.g. Mycenaean Achaea, ca. 1800–1065 BCE: Jones 2018), possibly because children were not considered to be full members of society until approximately 3 years of age (this understanding is certainly true for Classical Athens, but has been found to vary according to time and space: Lagia 2007; Golden 2015: 141–53). Instead, children are often buried in age-specific clusters within a cemetery (e.g. Borgo necropolis at Gela, seventh to fifth centuries BCE: Orsi 1906), interred in domestic contexts (e.g. Oropos in Attica, ca. late eighth to early seventh centuries BCE: Vlachou 2007), placed in independent cemeteries (e.g. Kylindra on Astypalaia, ca. 600–400 BCE: Hillson 2009) or deposited in wells (e.g. Athens, ca. second quarter of the second century BCE: Liston and Rotroff 2013; Liston et al. 2018). Maria Liston and colleagues suggest that deposition in wells (e.g. the Agora Bone Well discussed in Chapter 2) and other marginal places (e.g. rubbish heaps) provided a solution for families that were unable or unwilling to devote much-needed financial resources to infant interment:

> Many of the free poor must have lived at close to subsistence levels, often one catastrophe away from serious deprivation, and they were not in a position to invest significant resources in the burial of infants who enter the life of the family so briefly . . . and the Agora Bone Well would have offered a pragmatic solution to the all-too-common phenomenon of perinatal infant death. (Liston et al. 2018: 139)

It is virtually impossible to discern socioeconomic status from infant and child burials. Although there are some, albeit few, examples of lavish child burials, they cannot be taken as assertions of class identity, because even though these displays could be connected to social status, they could also be material expressions of profound grief. These wealthy burials, however, are the exception, as the majority of infants and young children were buried in a simple, standardised manner (Shepherd 2007). In Classical Athens and elsewhere, most infants under the age of 1 were interred in amphorae (called *enchytrismos* burials), often with feeder bottles, while older infants up to the age of 3 were placed in terracotta tubs (called larnakes), typically with small animal figurines. These children, aged 3 and younger, were buried apart from adults (e.g. in independent cemeteries, domestic contexts etc.), but children older than 3 were interred among adults with similar burial treatments and grave goods that were indicative of identity (i.e. gender- and class-specific; Houby-Nielsen 1995; 2000; Golden 2015: 15).

The free poor: Citizens and metics

Shifting to adults, it is highly probable that the poor were not well represented in the funerary landscape of Classical Athens. Thomas Heine Nielsen and colleagues have argued that 'even poor citizens could easily afford a [modest] grave monument inscribed with their name' and that 'many of the sepulchral inscriptions must in fact commemorate ordinary citizens of little distinction and slender means, and that wealthy citizens – though perhaps represented in more than their due proportion – probably count for a fairly small fraction of the funeral monuments we have' (1989: 412). On the basis of one piece of epigraphic evidence, they estimated that a simple grave marker with short inscription and a small standard relief would have cost between 10 and 20 drachmas (1989: 414). This, they maintained, would have been affordable to Athenians of lower socioeconomic status since, as previously discussed, the average soldier or skilled labourer earned around one drachma per day, while an unskilled labourer earned approximately three obols per day (Vickers 1990; Wünsche 2007: 89). However, it is likely that Nielsen and colleagues' cost estimate is far too low. Graham Oliver (2000) has demonstrated that a 'cheap' burial must have cost upwards of 40 drachmas when all costs (e.g. grave marker, inscription and/or sculpted relief, burial plot, deposition etc.) are taken into consideration. As a result, wealthier Athenians were more likely to erect funerary monuments than poorer ones.[10]

Since funerary monuments are incapable of pointing us in the direction of the impoverished, we must turn to the contents of graves themselves. As previously discussed, Classical period burials across the mainland generally possess fewer material manifestations of wealth than those belonging to the periods immediately before (i.e. the Archaic period) and directly after (i.e. the Hellenistic period; Morris 1998). In other words, Classical graves appear relatively egalitarian; however, a slight difference has been observed in graves belonging to individuals of higher socioeconomic status in the northern Peloponnese. In particular, burials that have been identified as lower status contain no gender-specific grave goods, while those that appear to be higher status bear goods connected to gender roles. On this basis, Nikolas Dimakis (2016: 62, 75–6) suggests that the expression of gender in burial assemblages appears to be a prerogative of the elite in the northern Peloponnese.

Even though the material record is relatively silent on the issue of socioeconomic status, social distinctions are more readily apparent in human skeletal remains. Anna Lagia (2014) has demonstrated that health disparities are evident among individuals of upper and lower socioeconomic statuses in Classical Athens. Two cemeteries dating to the Classical period, the Kerameikos and Plateia Kotzia, are believed to contain populations that represent different social strata. The Kerameikos is located immediately outside of the western city wall of Athens and contains a relatively large proportion of individuals of high socioeconomic status, as evidenced by the grand monumentalisation of the cemetery. The Kerameikos was also the spot selected for the burial of eminent politicians, aristocratic family plots and the commemoration of the Athenian war dead. Although there were undoubtedly individuals of lower socioeconomic status interred in the Kerameikos, a greater proportion of them were buried at Plateia Kotzia. Positioned 40 m outside of the western city wall of Athens, Plateia Kotzia catered primarily to individuals of lower socioeconomic status, as evidenced by its rural setting and lack of monumentalisation.

Lagia's study (2014) focused primarily on non-specific indicators of physiological stress – namely cribra orbitalia and porotic hyperostosis. These skeletal lesions can be caused by prolonged iron-deficiency anaemia, blood loss, deficiencies in vitamin B12 and/or folic acid and hereditary hemolytic anaemias (e.g. sickle-cell anaemia or thalassaemia; Grmek 1991: 245–75; Walker et al. 2009; Oxenham and Cavill 2010; Rothschild 2012; McIlvaine 2015). When prevalence rates of cribra orbitalia and porotic hyperostosis were compared, it was found that subadults showed the greatest lesion frequencies and they were essentially the same in both cemeteries. This could indicate that early stress episodes negatively impacted a younger person's ability to survive. Another trend visible in both cemeteries is sex-specific health disparities, as there was a higher prevalence of skeletal stress in females when compared to males. Finally, adult males at Plateia Kotzia displayed an overall higher frequency of physiological stress than those at the Kerameikos, which was most likely connected to physical and environmental stressors associated with their lower socioeconomic class.

In Classical Thebes (fifth century BCE), dietary differences were linked to socioeconomic status (Vika 2011). Socioeconomic status has been discerned through mode of burial and grave-good assemblages, and the human remains in those burials were subjected to stable isotopic analysis. The stable isotopic values of carbon and nitrogen from individuals in pit graves (lower status) were compared to those in tile graves (higher), and statistically significant differences were found in their $\delta^{13}C$ and $\delta^{15}N$ values. When individuals were separated into lower- and higher-status burials on the basis of grave goods, statistically significant differences in their $\delta^{13}C$ and $\delta^{15}N$ values were also noted. It seems that the individuals who were either buried in pit graves or with relatively lower-status grave-good assemblages had more varied diets. These patterns have been interpreted as a sign of opportunistic food choices. Presumably, the high-status members of society were able to consume a regular diet of foods they preferred, whereas those of lower status were relegated to diet defined by availability.

Although we can be reasonably certain that the burials in the aforementioned case studies from the northern Peloponnese, Athens and Thebes represent individuals of lower socioeconomic status, we still cannot discern their political statuses. Because all of the burials were normative and bear no evidence of social marginalisation, it is assumed that they belong to free individuals (i.e. citizens or metics) and not the enslaved, but the possibility that some burials contain enslaved individuals cannot be ruled out.

The enslaved

Despite the ubiquity of the enslaved in the ancient Greek world, their burials are virtually undetectable (see Chapter 1 for a detailed discussion of slavery in the ancient Greek world). There are approximately thirty burials of skeletons that are either shackled or associated with shackles from half a dozen Classical and Hellenistic sites (see the Introduction for the shackled burials at Phaleron; Thompson 2003: 222).[11] We know that the enslaved were shackled (e.g. leg shackles with ankles bones still attached were allegedly recovered from a mine in the Laurion district: S. P. Morris 2018), and that shackles were used for punishment (e.g. Morris 2011: 189). Furthermore, the enslaved's former shackles were deemed appropriate offerings to the gods upon manumission, and an example of this can be found at the Sanctuary of Demeter at Heraclea in southern Italy (Zuchtriegel 2018: 71).[12] Although it is a distinct possibility that shackled burials belonged to the enslaved, this identification is not definitive, as these individuals might also have been prisoners. Nevertheless, the general lack of burials of the enslaved suggests that either the enslaved were buried non-normatively or we cannot differentiate the graves of the enslaved from those of impoverished individuals. Moreover, Donna Kurtz and John Boardman (1971: 198–9) suggest that the enslaved might have been buried in family plots and indistinguishable from free members of the family.

A small percentage of burials of the enslaved are conspicuous. Even though grave markers commemorating the enslaved are rare, a few have been recovered from Classical contexts in Attica. Most of these are for wet nurses who were presumably memorialised in such an expensive fashion because they grew close to the families they served. These sculpted monuments depict the wet nurses in a manner similar to those of higher-status Athenian women (Wrenhaven 2012: 92–100), but as previously discussed in Chapter 1, this is not necessarily unique, as it is often difficult to differentiate between the enslaved and their slaveholders on sculpted grave stelae from Athens. The most conspicuous burials of the enslaved, however, are reserved for those who died in service of the city state. In particular, Athenian enslaved individuals who fell at the Battle of Marathon were buried in the tumulus at the site with the Plataean war dead (Pausanias 1.32.3), and the names of the enslaved appear on the Peloponnesian War casualty lists (Arrington 2011: 184 n. 33; 2015: 96–7, 187).

It has been hypothesised that a fourth-century BCE mass grave at Pydna in northern Greece contained enslaved individuals (Triantaphyllou and Bessios 2005). One hundred and fifteen individuals were recovered from a rectangular rock-cut shaft approximately 4 m deep. The bodies appeared to have been thrown haphazardly into the shaft in four distinct depositional phases (first 11 bodies, then 45, then 2 and finally 57). Four of these individuals had restraining devices (i.e. neck bands, arm and leg shackles), and aside from these, there were additional unique features of the assemblage that point to the likelihood that the dead were enslaved. First, males and females occur in nearly equal frequencies, which starkly contrasts with contemporary cemeteries in Macedonia, where males are typically over-represented. Also, the majority of the individuals in the grave died young – there were some subadults under the age of 18 (16% of the study sample), but most of the individuals were adults who died before the age of 30 (55%), while the remaining adults died between the ages of 40 and 50 (29%). Despite the exceptionally young age of the study sample, the individuals displayed a high incidence of lesions and skeletal markers associated with the musculoskeletal system. Degenerative joint disease was present in 62% of the study sample. As previously discussed, degenerative joint disease is typically age-progressive, but at Pydna, Young Adults of both sexes exhibited degenerative joint disease in their wrist and foot joints, which indicates mechanical stress and habitual overuse of the joints. Robust musculoskeletal stress markers were present in 62% of the sample and enthesopathies (inflammation or pathological changes at the sites of tendon and ligament attachments) were visible on 60% of the individuals. Both of these skeletal markers are consistent with high levels of physical, repetitive activity. A small percentage (7%) of the deceased had evidence of trauma, primarily in the form of healed rib fractures. Individuals of both sexes also displayed high incidences of physiological stress markers, such as non-specific infection (periostitis of the lower limbs: 52%), indicators of non-specific stress (cribra orbitalia and/or porotic hyperostosis: 55%) and linear enamel hypoplasia (33%). As previously discussed, these physiological stress markers are signposts of low levels of health, and are typically caused by malnutrition and/or periods of acute illness. All of the skeletal evidence – the inclusion of subadults, roughly equal distribution of males and females, low average age at death and high incidence of physical and physiological stress markers – suggest that the individuals deposited in the shaft were of low socioeconomic status and engaged in hard labour. The likelihood that these individuals were enslaved is further supported by the material evidence (i.e. their non-normative burial and the presence of restraining devices) and comparison to contemporary cemeteries in Macedonia. For instance, in Amphipolis, the average age at death was higher (between 30 and 40 years of age) and there was a significantly lower incidence of physical and physiological stress markers (Malama and Triantaphyllou 2001; Triantaphyllou and Bessios 2005).

One would expect to find burials of the enslaved in areas that were primarily inhabited by the enslaved, such as the dwellings around the mines at Laurion.[13] The Athenian silver mines at Laurion were among the most productive in antiquity (Morin et al. 2012: 9). These vertical shafts, which could be as deep as 100 m, produced 20 metric tons of silver a year at their height of operation (Vickers 1990: 618; Morin et al. 2012: 9), and the work associated with this massive haul was largely carried out by the enslaved (e.g. Xenophon, *Ways and Means* 4.14–15, 23–5; Rihll 2011: 68–9). It appears that cupellation of silver (the process of separating silver from lead) began as early as the ninth century BCE, and large-scale extraction was under way in the late sixth century BCE. The facilities continued to expand throughout the fifth and fourth centuries, and by the 340s BCE there were tens of thousands of enslaved individuals at Laurion. Ian Morris (1998) describes Laurion as the 'wild west of Attica'. Any participation in mining was perceived as a stain on a citizen's virtue (Demosthenes 21.167, cf. 23.146), and the fiercely competitive nature of the region is reflected in the special legislation that governed business there. For instance, there were laws that forbade lease holders from cutting into, attacking or smoking out their rivals' mines (Demosthenes 37.35–6; Morris 1998).

It stands to reason that the buildings and quarters associated with silver production at Laurion, as well as the objects inside of them, would have been associated with the enslaved. Enslaved individuals would have lived at Laurion with their families, as literary sources indicate that they were permitted to live near their work with their families, to practise their religious rites and to be buried with their families (Kurtz and Boardman 1971: 198; Lagia 2015a: 122). Epigraphic evidence suggests that many of these enslaved persons came from Asia Minor and the Balkans (Pritchett 1956: 276–86; 1961; Lauffer 1979: 123–32). There are, however, no material traces of social class or non-Greek identity in any of the extant artefacts or architectural remains (Morris 1998).

It is the burials at Laurion that teach us the most about the enslaved individuals who mined Attica's silver. Most of the graves date to the middle of the fifth century (ca. 470–440 BCE), and the cemetery was hypothesised to be the final resting place of miner-slaves based on its proximity to the mines, the simplicity of the burials, the haphazard spatial arrangement of the graves and the lack of grave goods. Ian Morris' (2011: 181–8) study of 219 burials from Laurion found that they differed in several ways from contemporary burials across Attica. Although numbers of subadults and adults are roughly equal in a typical cemetery, there were far fewer subadults at Laurion. Only one in every five burials contained a subadult, which Morris interprets as a sign of child labour in the mines. Furthermore, the graves were noticeably poorer, as they held less than one fifth as many grave goods as a typical grave from Attica. There were also fewer cremations (presumably a more expensive funerary rite) and more cases of multiple inhumation (an economical form of burial and a rarity in Classical Attica). Although Morris rightly cautions that we cannot be absolutely certain that these were the graves of enslaved individuals, the evidence suggests that the people buried in the Laurion cemetery were non-elite at the very least.

On a biomolecular level, stable isotopic studies of $\delta^{13}C$ and $\delta^{15}N$ compared bone samples from Laurion to contemporary burials from Athens and discovered that the people of Laurion were consuming a diet that was relatively similar to that of the people of Athens. Although one might expect the diet of the Laurion enslaved to be poorer and less nutritious, this would not be practical, as the enslaved needed to be well nourished in order to endure the arduous tasks required of them. Interestingly, where the diets differed was in regard to protein sources, as the Laurion diet incorporated broader sources of protein than the Athenian one. This dietary diversity might be the result of non-Greek enslaved persons continuing to practise their ethnic foodways at Laurion, or it could alternatively reflect the presence of socioeconomic class distinctions within the Laurion sample (Lagia 2015a).

INTERSECTIONALITY

The material presented here represents our limited bioarchaeological evidence pertaining to lower socioeconomic status on the Greek mainland during the Late Archaic/Classical period. For the most part, individuals of lower socioeconomic status are archaeologically invisible for a number of reasons: (1) infants and juveniles are typically under-represented, and it is exceedingly difficult to discern socioeconomic status from the graves of infants and children; (2) the poor were often afforded differential burial treatment; and (3) although there are notable exceptions – especially in Athens – Classical period burials trend towards the egalitarian. Despite these challenges, subtle indicators of low socioeconomic status have been perceived. In particular, grave-good patterns have emerged in the northern Peloponnese to suggest that higher socioeconomic status was indicated by the inclusion of gender-specific objects. Health and dietary disparities have also been identified. At Athens, individuals of lower socioeconomic status had a higher prevalence of non-specific physiological stress markers, while at Thebes, individuals of lower status had a more varied diet which most likely reflected opportunistic eating patterns dictated by availability rather than choice. All of these burials are normative and do not reflect social marginalisation. It is assumed that they belong to free individuals – either citizens or metics – but it is also possible that some enslaved people are represented as well.

There are few securely identified burials of the enslaved in the archaeological record. Because there are so many missing burials of the enslaved, it is reasonable to assume that a substantial percentage of the enslaved population was buried non-normatively in a manner that rendered them invisible in the archaeological record. It is also possible that their graves are indistinguishable from those of free impoverished individuals or that the enslaved are undetectable because they were buried in family plots in the same manner as free members of the household. There are, however, some clear examples of burials that contain enslaved individuals. It is probable that some burials of persons with shackles belonged to the enslaved, although it is also possible that these individuals could have been prisoners. The clearest instance of shackled burials belonging to the enslaved comes from a mass grave at Pydna where all the skeletal (roughly equal distribution of males and females, low average age at death, high incidence of physical and physiological stress markers) and material evidence (presence of restraining devices) suggests that the deceased were enslaved. Moreover, at Laurion, where one would expect to find large numbers of the enslaved, the burials deviate from the funerary norms of Attica in that there were fewer subadults, grave goods and cremation burials and some instances of multiple inhumation, a rarity in Attica. Furthermore, the diets of people from Laurion were more varied than those closer to the urban centre of Athens, possibly signifying that the enslaved, who literary sources tell us were primarily non-Greek, maintained their ethnic foodways.

Of the burials surveyed in this chapter, the only ones that are non-normative and suggestive of social marginalisation are those belonging to the enslaved. The enslaved, in general, are liminal and uniquely intersectional individuals, which probably accounts for their marginality. As previously discussed in Chapter 1, the enslaved have no identity, no freedom and no agency, rendering them non-persons and 'socially dead'. Their non-personhood was reflected by the Greek pejorative term for the enslaved (*andrapoda*), which translates to 'human-footed things'. Moreover, the activities of the enslaved, namely servile and banausic activities, were distasteful to Greeks of higher social standing. Furthermore, with the notable exception of the Helots, the enslaved were typically non-Greek. The preference for non-Greek enslaved persons was rooted in widespread beliefs concerning the inferiority of non-Greeks and the understanding that enslaved individuals who were linguistically and culturally distinct from one another would not be apt to organise and rise up in revolt. Thus, the marginalising factors of non-Greek ethnicity and low socioeconomic status coalesce in the body of the enslaved, and it is their intersectionality that serves as the catalyst for their social marginalisation.

Sex-specific health disparities were evident in the Kerameikos and Plateia Kotzia, suggesting that gender provides an additional point of intersection with low socioeconomic status that presumably compounded the degree of an individual's social marginalisation. Moreover, the marginalisation of impoverished females began at birth. Infant females from poor citizen families were most likely exposed at a higher rate because of their burdensome marriage dowries in comparison with elite families, who might have exposed more males (non-firstborn sons in particular) on account of inheritance practices (Beaumont 2012: 91).

The social marginalisation of intersectional women is further supported by Greek literary sources. With the exception of wet nurses, who seem to have been beloved by families, enslaved women would have been socially marginalised for all the reasons enslaved men were, namely their objectification and their servile, often non-Greek origins. Other groups of women would have also experienced prejudice and social marginalisation. For instance, three additional types of women are identified in Demosthenes' *Against Neaera*: 'For we have courtesans (*hetairai*) for pleasure, and concubines (*pallakai*) for the daily service of our bodies, but wives (*gynaikes*) for the production of legitimate offspring and to have a reliable guardian of our household property' (122 as translated in Lee 2015: 48).[14] Of all of these types, aside from citizen women, we know the most about *hetairai*. As a group, *hetairai* were of relatively high social status. Paradoxically, they were able to achieve a greater degree of independence than citizen women, as *hetairai* were typically educated (in poetry and music in particular) and could amass fortunes with the support of wealthy patrons. Furthermore, *hetairai* were typically foreign-born metics, and thus not appropriate marriage partners, especially after the passage of the Citizenship Law of ca. 451/450 BCE (Neils 2000: 206–7; Lee 2015: 48).

Even though they were not appropriate marriage partners, the allure of foreign women was both strong and renowned. Foreign women and their erotic potential were viewed as threats to the household and the state, and in tragedy they were stereotyped as 'diseases' with the potential to infect the citizen body (Kennedy 2014: 38–49). If one questioned the danger of metic women, they need look no further than the negative examples provided by Aeschylus' *Suppliant Women* and Euripides' *Medea* (Bakewell 2008/9: 106–7; 2013; Kennedy 2014: 26–67).

The perceived threat posed by foreign metic women is illustrated by Demosthenes' mid-fourth-century BCE oration *Against Neaera*. The prosecutor's version of the story alleges that Neaera was purchased as a small child by a freedwoman, Nicarete, who trained her to be a prostitute in Corinth. Neaera was purchased from Nicarete by two unmarried men for their exclusive use, but she eventually bought her freedom with the help of a wealthy patron. After a series of misfortunes, she married Stephanos, an Athenian citizen. While married, financial constraints required her to work as a *hetaira*, purportedly enabling her and Stephanos to blackmail any wealthy young men who solicited sexual favours from her. It was not, however, for prostitution or blackmail that she was brought to trial, but rather for fraudulently living in a citizen marriage and feigning the legitimacy of her children. The charges were serious, as there was a law (most likely passed in the 380s BCE) that prohibited foreigners from marrying Athenian citizens, and the penalty was enslavement and confiscation of property, which was the same penalty given to persons who were convicted of illegally exercising citizen rights (Lape 2010: 220–39; Deene 2011: 159). Neaera was perceived to be a danger to Athenian society because her behaviour 'strikes at the heart of Athenian privilege . . . [she has] taken what even the demos does not allow itself to give, the privilege of native birth' (Patterson 1994: 210), and it appeared that 'the safety of a foreign whore like Neaira came at the expense of some respectable citizen girl's marriage' (Kennedy 2014: 106). Although we do not know the verdict, her intersectionality – female, low socioeconomic status, formerly enslaved, sex worker, non-Athenian – probably sealed her guilt in the minds of the Athenian citizen jury before the case was even presented (Johnstone 1998).

From a survey of extant literary sources, one could assume that all metic women were engaged in sex work. Although some certainly were, others undoubtedly were not, as literary and epigraphic evidence insinuates that metic women engaged in a broad range of activites. For instance, they sold goods in the Agora and worked as nurses, manual labourers, musicians, tavern-keepers, nurses, midwives, priestesses and in the textile industry (Kennedy 2014: 123–53). Their conflation with sex workers is most likely rooted in the Athenians' fear of metic women. As Rebecca Futo Kennedy explains:

> Metic women who interacted with citizen men were slandered and reviled in the courts and on stage and in other public fora in the manner best suited to demonstrate their mercenary natures and their unsuitability to becoming citizen wives. They became prostitutes. Not real prostitutes, but imaginary ones. As the Athenians further developed a sense of ethnic and social superiority over the course of the fifth century, metic women found themselves the victims of a form of ideological warfare. They became the ultimate enemy of the Athenian state, and thus found themselves spoken of and represented only as courtesans, concubines, and slaves. (2014: 59)

Furthermore, Kennedy maintains that the role of the *hetaira*, which has traditionally been misinterpreted as that of a courtesan, or high-class prostitute, does not entirely make sense in context and should be reconceived.[15] What fits the evidence better is the understanding that '*hetaira*' was a 'name used to refer to elite women, sometimes of foreign birth, who participated in sympotic and luxury culture'; understood in this way, 'the appearance of these women in both sympotic and political discourse makes more sense, as does the way we have come to identify *hetairai* as foreign women of renown, wealth, and access to the political elite' (2014: 74). Although it was certainly possible that some *hetairai* engaged in casual sex or prostitution, the proportion would have been a subset of the whole. *Hetairai*, Kennedy argues, only became associated with prostitution over the course of the fifth century BCE: 'In the wake of the Citizenship Law, when citizen women's sexual behavior had become more important to the citizen body in general, the term *hetaira* . . . transformed, perhaps, into a term of denigration and used of women who stood outside of the newly idealized citizen family or whose behavior challenged or was viewed as disruptive to the family' (2014: 86).

Aspasia, metic from Miletus and consort of Pericles, serves as an illustration of the public abuse metic women were forced to endure. Sometime after the passage of the Citizenship Law of ca. 451/450 BCE, Pericles (the proposer of the law, as discussed in Chapter 1) began a long-term relationship with Aspasia and fathered at least one of her children – a son, sometimes referred to as Pericles Jr (Kennedy 2014: 74). On its face, Pericles' personal situation served as a problematic paradigm for the Athenians, as Alan Shapiro notes:

> His transgression was to become too emotionally attached to a woman who was not his wife and not even an Athenian – Aspasia – to the point where he divorced his legal wife in order to share his household with Aspasia. The punishment as it were was that Perikles lived to see the sons by his citizen wife die in the plague, while his son by Aspasia was denied citizenship under the terms of the very legislation that Perikles himself had proposed in 451 BCE. (2015: 292; Plutarch, *Life of Pericles* 37.3–5)

As discussed in Chapter 1, Pericles successfully engineered an amendment to the Citizenship Law that allowed his son to be naturalised and ultimately launch his own political career. Aspasia, on the other hand, was publically targeted and slandered over the course of several decades in order to defame Pericles and their son. She was sexualised and demonised, particularly in the comic and Second Sophistic traditions, which spin her as a successful courtesan and madam, both highly trained and educated, who manipulated Pericles until his death, when she returned to the business of running brothels. Although she is often referred to as a *hetaira* in scholarship, there is only one ancient example where she is explicitly called a *hetaira*, which can be found in Athenaeus (59) in a quote from Heracleides of Pontus' *On Pleasure* (ca. fourth century BCE). In reality, she very well may have been a *hetaira*, but in the sense that she engaged in sympotic and luxury culture, not sexual acts with strangers. Moreover, the real story of Aspasia, as reconstructed by Rebecca Futo Kennedy from epigraphic evidence, is much more interesting than the fabricated one. She appears to have immigrated to

Athens from Miletus with her sister and aristocratic brother-in-law (Alcibiades the Elder) and their children. Far from impoverished or controversial, her Alcmaeonid connections would have permitted Aspasia to move among elite Athenian circles – including intellectual ones, as Plato, Xenophon and Aeschines all seem to portray her as a Sophist (Kennedy 2014: 74–87).

Aspasia, however, was an exception, and life was most likely harsher for the majority of metic women. As previously discussed, all metics, including metic men, were politically and legally disenfranchised and probably experienced discrimination because many were non-Greek, formerly enslaved or impoverished (or all three). Metic women were particularly vulnerable because, in addition to potentially embodying all of those marginalising factors, they were targets of slander and had recourse to even fewer rights than men (Kennedy 2014: 106–12). For instance, there was no permanent path to citizenship for metic women. Even after their husbands were enfranchised, metic women could be citizens only so long as their husbands lived, after which their status reverted to that of metic (Carey 1991; Kennedy 2014: 100). Furthermore, metic women without male family members lacked physical and legal protection, rendering these women easy targets for rape and violence, as there was little in the law code that held men accountable for attacking or murdering them (Demosthenes 47; Kennedy 2014: 101–6).

The bioarchaeological evidence from the Late Archaic/Classical Greek mainland suggests that low socioeconomic status alone was not sufficient cause for the social marginalisation of free individuals. Rather, social marginalisation most likely occurred with intersectionality, when low socioeconomic was only one of multiple marginalising factors (i.e. non-Greek ethnicity, gender etc.) embodied by a single individual. Continuing the investigation of marginalising factors, the next chapter discusses how non-Greek ancestry and ethnicity might have impacted social integration.

NOTES

1. 1 mina = approximately 1 lb of silver, 100 drachmas = 1 mina, 6 obols = 1 drachma. Also note that 60 minae are equivalent to 1 talent (Vickers 1990: 613–14).
2. This is also true of burial rites. For instance, in the fourth century BCE, Macedonian aristocrats preferred cremation burial over inhumation (Musgrave 1990).
3. The formula for Gini's coefficient is: $G = A/A+B$; $G = 2A$; $G = 1-2B$ (given that $A+B = 0.5$, or the line of perfect equality), where A is defined as the area that lies between the line of equality and the Lorenz curve and B is defined as the area that lies beneath the Lorenz curve. A Lorenz curve must be calculated before Gini's coefficient. To calculate a Lorenz curve, list each grave by number of grave goods from low to high (Ian Morris separates ceramic goods from metal goods and

calculates them separately). Then calculate the total number of grave goods, and from there calculate the lowest 1% of grave goods, as well as the lowest 1% as a percentage of the total number of grave goods just calculated. Do the same for the lowest 2%, 3%, 4% etc. Place these points on a graph with the fraction of the graves as the x-axis (horizontal axis), and the fraction of grave goods is the y-axis (vertical axis). The curve that results when all the points are plotted is the Lorenz curve. For the necessary assumptions made when applying this calculation to burial contexts, see Morris 1987: 141–3.

4. For grave goods (namely lack thereof) at Greek colonies in southern Italy, see Zuchtriegel 2018: 76–8.
5. For a study that questions this association, see Nikita et al. 2019.
6. The bioarchaeological investigation of Middle to Late Bronze Age (ca. 1620–1500 BCE) burials from Pigi Athenas (Macedonian Olympus) also found evidence of social inequalities between males and females indicated by greater instance of biological stress and morbidity in females than in males (Tritsaroli 2017).
7. An exception to this is the Geometric period cemetery of Agios Dimitrios (ca. 850–740 BCE), where there was evidence of equal burial treatment of all ages and sexes, and no dietary or pathological differences according to sex or status. However, all the other osteological evidence indicates that the population was stressed, malnourished, living in substandard conditions and thus unable to reach its biological potential. In particular, stable carbon and nitrogen isotopic data revealed that they consumed a C_3 low-protein plant diet, the infant mortality rate was high, stature estimates were low and there was a high prevalence of dental disease and non-specific physiological stress (Papathanasiou 2013).
8. For a history of sanitation and hygiene in the ancient Greek world, see Antoniou and Angelakis 2015; Yannopoulos et al. 2017.
9. For a diachronic survey of weaning based on stable isotopic data, see Pearson 2018.
10. In her survey of Attic epitaphs, Elizabeth Meyer (1993) specifically links Classical commemorative practices in Athens to a conspicuous assertion of citizenship.
11. Commonly cited examples of 'slave' burials in southern Italy and Sicily are T100 at Gela, T1771 at Acragas (an individual buried with iron shackles from the Pezzino necropolis), skeletons extended upon the lids of sarcophagi at Syracuse (e.g. Tombs 204, 205, 320, 425, 471) and finally, the Archaic Ponte di Ferro necropolis at Poseidonia might be a slave cemetery (Shepherd 2005: 122 n. 21).
12. The enslaved were also placed in neck chains, as illustrated on the stelae of a freedman slave trader from Amphipolis ca. 100 BCE to 100 CE. The inscription reads 'Aulus Capreilius Timotheus, freedman of Aulus, slave trader', and the bottom of three registers carved in low relief depicts a file of ten enslaved individuals linked by neck chains led by an overseer (Morris 2011: 191). Another register depicts men transporting large vats and an amphora, presumably linked to wine manufacture, so it has been suggested that Aulus Capreilius Timotheus made wine on his estate and traded it for enslaved persons (Coleman 1997: 181).
13. Sarah Morris and John Papadopoulos (2005) argue that stone towers built in rural and urban Classical and Hellenistic contexts in Greece might have served as places

to secure enslaved persons in instances of slave-run operations (e.g. farms, mines) with absentee landlords.

14. Aside from wives, the other women listed in Apollodorus' speech in *Against Neara* are traditionally interpreted as sex workers, but note that two types of sex workers, common prostitutes (*pornai*) and state-owned prostitutes (*dikteriades*), were omitted from the list (Neils 2000: 206). For alternative interpretations of *pallakai* ('marriage by sale of the bride to the groom', creating a slave bride) and *hetairai* ('single woman'), see M. Morris 2018. Rebecca Futo Kennedy (2014: 72–4) also argues that *hetairai* were not engaged in sex work.

15. Although it has been often assumed in scholarship that female *aulos* players were prostitutes, Max Goldman (2015) has demonstrated that some *aulos* players might have prostituted themselves, but *aulos* playing is far from synonymous with sex work.

CHAPTER 4

Ancestry and Ethnicity

Matters related to ancestry and ethnicity are among the most complex and contested issues in archaeology. Ancestry and ethnicity are facets of social identity, and each person has multiple strands of social identities that influence or dictate their roles in society. These strands are often connected with age, gender, class, status, rank, profession and sexuality, among others, and they all function differently in social group contexts. Rank and gender, for instance, are often cited as the causes of division among social groups, whereas ethnicity and ancestry are more cohesive in nature and have the capacity to bring groups together and strengthen bonds (MacSweeney 2009). Although ancestry and ethnicity are commonly understood as immutable and rooted in biology, the reality is far more complicated. Genealogy, for example, can be fabricated, and ethnic affiliations can shift in response to sociopolitical stimuli such as conflict, violence and changing constellations of power. Ancestry and ethnicity are always defined in response to political systems, and like many other social identities, they are cultural constructs characterised by their dynamism, flexibility and self-definition (Smedley and Smedley 2005: 17; Derks and Roymans 2009b: 1–2).

Two prominent historical figures, Herodotus and Philip II, illustrate the complexity of ethnic identity. Herodotus was born in the 480s BCE in Halicarnassus (modern Bodrum, Turkey) in the geographical region of Caria. Historically, the people of Caria did not speak Greek – indeed, Homer describes the Carians fighting for Troy as *barbarophonos*, or 'of incomprehensible speech' (*Iliad* 2.867). However, it was in this land of non-Greeks, approximately 500 years prior to Herodotus' birth, that the polis of Halicarnassus was founded by Doric-speaking Greeks. It did not remain a strictly Dorian city throughout its history, as there is strong evidence that a significant portion of the population identified as Ionian in the fifth century BCE when the city was a member of the Delian League. At this point, official documents from Halicarnassus were issued in Ionian, and Herodotus composed his *Histories* in Ionic Greek. So, the population of Halicarnassus was of heterogeneous

Greek ethnicity. It is also safe to assume that Halicarnassus was home to people of non-Greek ancestry and ethnicity, as it would have been a zone of contact for Greeks, Carians and Persians (Cartledge 2002: 52–3; Herda 2013). Carians and Greeks had been intermarrying for generations (Herodotus 1.146.2–3; Lohmann 2012). Herodotus himself was the most likely product of intermarriage, as the names of his father and uncle (or cousin) are Carian, or Carian-derived.[1] Furthermore, Halicarnassus and the people of Caria were subjects of the Achaemenid Empire and within the jurisdiction of the satrapy (province) of Lydia at the time of Herodotus' birth. Persian occupation undoubtedly left an indelible cultural and genetic mark on the city and its population (Cartledge 2002: 52–3). Today, we would be quick to identify the Father of History as Greek, but how would he have self-identified? Possibly as an Ionianised Dorian of Carian descent, as some have suggested (Herda 2013: 424).

Philip II (ca. 382–336 BCE), king of Macedon and father of Alexander the Great, is another complicated example, as ancient authors do not agree on whether he was Greek or non-Greek. Demosthenes describes Philip as 'neither a Greek nor a remote relative of the Greeks, nor even a respectable barbarian, but one of those cursed Macedonians from an area where in former times you could not even buy a decent slave' (Demosthenes 9.31 as translated in Hall 2001: 159). Isocrates (5.32–4, 76–7), on the other hand, draws our attention to Philip's Greek ancestry, noting that his ancestors were from Argos and that he purportedly descended from Heracles. Striking a middle ground, Thucydides (2.80.5–6, 2.99.3, 4.124.1, 4.126.3) accepts the Greek descent of Macedonian rulers, but not their subjects, while Herodotus (5.20, 22; 6.44; 7.9a–b; 8.137; 9.45) maintains that all Macedonians and their kings are Greek (Hall 2001). Although Philip's son is responsible for the diffusion of Greek culture throughout western Asia, it is uncertain how Philip himself would have identified, and it is highly probable that his ethnic identity was protean, shifting in response to audience and circumstance.

Individuals who identified as non-Greek would have been minorities on the Greek mainland. As is often the case with minorities, they might have found themselves disenfranchised and unable to attain economic and social justice (Scham 2001: 189). In order to better understand ancient Greek societal attitudes towards individuals of non-Greek ancestry and ethnicity, this chapter reviews the bioarchaeological evidence of non-Greeks in the Late Archaic/Classical Greek world (ca. sixth to fifth/fourth century BCE). Although material from the Greek mainland is the primary focus of this investigation, case studies from earlier and later periods of Greek history, as well as Greek colonial contexts, are incorporated to illustrate patterns of continuity and/or change. The chapter begins with a discussion of the archaeology of ethnicity and ancestry, which specifies the ways in which migration, ethnicity and ancestry can be identified in burials. Then, burials believed to belong to individuals of non-Greek ethnicity or ancestry are identified and interpreted in the context of contemporary literary and visual sources. The chapter concludes with a consideration of intersectionality and the ways in which the coalescence of multiple marginalising factors (e.g. a person who is both non-Greek and enslaved) can negatively impact social integration.

THE ARCHAEOLOGY OF ETHNICITY AND ANCESTRY

As discussed in Chapter 1, ethnic and ancestral identities are dynamic and often have both social and biological components.[2] It is their dynamism, however, that complicates their identification and interpretation in the archaeological record. Although there are some scholars who maintain that ethnicity is not an appropriate subject of archaeological enquiry (e.g. Trigger 1977: 22–3; Hall 1997: 111–42), Siân Jones maintains that it can be recognised in context. She understands ethnic expression to be grounded in what Pierre Bourdieu refers to as the *habitus*, 'a system of lasting, transportable dispositions which, integrating past experiences, functions at every moment as a *matrix of perceptions, appreciations and actions* and makes possible the achievement of infinitely diversified tasks' (Bourdieu 1977: 82–3, original emphasis). Furthermore, the *habitus* is governed by 'principles of generation and structuring of practices and representation which can be objectively "regulated" and "regular" without in any way being the product of rules' (Bourdieu 1977: 72). Essentially, *habitus* is the way that individuals perceive their social world and react to it. Their reactions are usually shaped and shared by their social groups (e.g. ethnic groups) and have material expression. As Jones explains:

> . . . the way in which particular styles of material culture are meaningfully involved in the articulation of ethnicity may be arbitrary across cultures, *but it is not random within particular socio-historical contexts.* Ethnic symbolism is generated, to varying degrees, from the existing cultural practices and modes of differentiation characterizing various social domains, such as gender and status differentiation, or the organization of space within households. (1997: 125, original emphasis)

So, even though there is not a direct relationship between material culture and ethnicity, material culture still plays a meaningful role in the way that ethnicity is expressed and reinforced (Hakenbeck 2007: 25). David Mattingly (2010: 287) pseudo-mathematically describes material culture's role as follows: $I = mc(p)$, where 'I' equals an aspect of social identity (e.g. ethnicity), 'mc' equals material culture, and 'p' equals practice (i.e. the performative aspect of identity). This process is especially visible in the mortuary sphere, where aspects of the deceased's identity – including ethnic identity – are constructed and communicated by their survivors (Metcalf and Huntington 2005: 24).

Most archaeological enquiry concerning non-Greek ethnicity has taken place in the colonial sphere. Mixed burial traditions, the presence of non-Greek names in funerary inscriptions and the inclusion of non-Greek grave goods have been traditionally cited as evidence of either foreign residents or intermarriage and hybridity between Greeks and locals (e.g. Shepherd 1999; 2005; Lomas 2000; Zuchtriegel 2018: 70). In some cemeteries, such as those at Pithekoussai, multiculturalism is pervasive. Founded by Euboeans on the island of Ischia in the early to mid-eighth century BCE, Pithekoussai supported large populations of Greeks, locals and Phoenicians, and grave assemblages often consist of an assortment of Euboean, East Greek, Phoenician and local objects. For instance, a late eighth-century BCE cremation burial (tumulus 168) of a subadult approximately 12–14 years of age (Becker 1999b) contained a locally derived silver serpentine fibula, a type typically worn by men, and twenty-six Late Geometric vases, including Protocorinthian globular aryballoi, other globular aryballoi which appear to have been made at Ialysos on Rhodes by Phoenicians and the 'Cup of Nestor', a Late Geometric Rhodian kotyle (Buchner and Ridgway 1993: 212–23, pls 67–75; Shepherd 2007; Osborne 2009: 109; Tartaron 2014).[3] This, and other graves at Pithekoussai, demonstrate how Greek settlements beyond the Aegean functioned as middle grounds for cultural interaction and exchange.

Special attention has been placed on intermarriage and the detection of local women in the cemeteries of Greek colonies, especially at Pithekoussai and Sicily (Saltini Semerari 2016). Based on evidence from the cemeteries at Pithekoussai, for instance, it has been hypothesised that the presence of locally produced fibulae and metal ornaments in female graves is indicative of intermarriage between Greek men and native women, who must have continued to wear native dress (Buchner 1975; Coldstream 1993; Hodos 1999; Shepherd 1999: 275). Although this theory is widely cited in the literature, it cannot be applied to all colonial regions, or even throughout Magna Graecia, as Tamar Hodos' and Gillian Shepherd's respective research has revealed that the fibula phenomenon does not apply to Sicily (Hodos 1999; Shepherd 1999).

As previously discussed, wholesale adherence to these traditional interpretations of material culture is a slippery slope, as a single object cannot, in itself, be connected to an ethnic identity. As Lieve Donnellan notes, the archaeological community now recognises 'that "pots do not equal people" and that material cultures cannot be equated with monolithic, uniform and harmoniously organised groups' (2016: 112), and recent work at Pithekoussai demonstrates this. For instance, Olivia Kelley (2012) maintains that the fixation on fibulae and intermarriage has overshadowed the clear evidence of the ways in which local Italic agency actively shaped the material culture of Pithekoussai, especially in male graves. Lieve Donnellan (2016) comes to a similar conclusion in her network analysis of the Archaic necropolis. Donnellan rejects the common narrative that locals lived in Pithekoussai with Greeks and occupied a lower rung on the social hierarchy than their Greek counterparts. Her research suggests that the people of Pithekoussai maintained strong, meaningful links with surrounding indigenous groups, which are manifest in terms of dress, bodily adornment, foodways (storage, preparation, consumption) and funerary rituals. There was also palpable economic, social and political influence from the Aegean and Levant, especially in regards to wine consumption, production and trade.

Furthermore, it has been demonstrated that foreign material and visual culture can be purposefully chosen for its exotic and prestigious connotations rather than its ethnic ones (Owen 2005: 8; Riva 2010; Burgers 2012). Lieve Donnellan observed this practice at Istros in modern Romania, where elite burials in the Greek necropolis are modelled on the burials of local elites. By appropriating local elite funerary practices, the Greek colonists were able to integrate 'into the local elitarian landscape, and could express status and power to their indigenous counterparts, and lower-class fellow citizens as well' (2011: 68). Greek integration into the networks of local elites also allowed them to acquire new territory, and their legitimate possession of this territory was reinforced by their strategic outward display of a local identity. Moreover, in Tauric Chersonesus (northern coast of the Black Sea), Kamarina (Sicily) and Lucanian Heraclea (southern Italy), Gabriel Zuchtriegel (2018: 95–7) notes that burials with non-Greek components belong exclusively to elite members of the population and none reflect any trace of social marginalisation.

Since ethnicity is situational and constantly negotiated, the conscious choice can be made to embrace the traditions and practices of a different cultural group to varying degrees. For example, in the south-eastern Iberian Peninsula (ca. sixth to fourth centuries BCE), it was local agency that spurred the widespread adoption of Greek culture. Despite the dearth of substantial Greek settlements, indigenous elites enhanced their own prestige and social status by broadcasting their foreign affiliations. This association was given tangible expression by the acquisition of foreign objects through trade with Greeks and Phoenicians, imitation of Greek sculptural funerary monuments, the adoption of sympotic culture, and the use of Greek script for economic transactions (Domínguez 2002). Shifting to an example from the mortuary sphere, the Sicilian Greek city states had more in common with one another than with their mother cities in Greece *or* with any neighbouring indigenous settlements. The colonists chose to create 'an independent burial tradition for themselves . . . [one] specific to the new settlement which could not readily be associated with any one city in Greece, but which served to define that settlement culturally' (Shepherd 2005: 132). This invented burial tradition was not strictly an amalgamation of Greek practices, but rather a product of cultural exchange, as it also included elements, such as multiple inhumation and flexed burial positions, which are considered to be locally derived. Furthermore, the adoption of this novel burial tradition was symbolic: it was a material and tangible assertion of a Sicilian Greek identity

(Shepherd 1995: 67; 2005: 118–23).[4] The act of forging a new hybrid ethnic identity was not limited to Sicily; it was a widespread by-product of Greek colonisation. Irad Malkin asserts that the phenomenon can be attributed to young settlers who were 'less constrained by tradition and the authority of their elders. They were less prone to simply replicate previous social patterns and, both by necessity and choice, were freer to abstract and implement their own social and political order' (2015: 31).[5]

Analysis of the human skeleton can also shed light on ethnic affiliations. Some forms of body modification, such as headshaping and foot-binding, are cultural in origin. These changes to the body are artificially induced and have special significance or symbolism within an ethnic group. There are also other bodily traits that can indicate group membership and biological affinity. These consist of measurements of specific anatomical parts (metric traits) and the presence of particular skeletal and dental anomalies (non-metric traits). Metric and non-metric traits, for the most part, cannot be externally manipulated, as they are products of genetic and environmental triggers (Zakrzewski 2011). Although their aetiology is complicated and multifactorial, these traits have been used to successfully demonstrate biological affinities among population groups, as group members often share generational genetic and environmental commonalities (Berry and Berry 1967; Finnegan 1978; Turner et al. 1991; Scott and Turner 1997). Yet, herein lies the catch-22 of bioarchaeological investigations of ethnicity – recognising ethnicity frequently requires the identification of biological affinities in order to hypothesise ethnic groupings, but group membership is not predicated on biological affinity (Zakrzewski 2011).

Reconstruction of an individual's physiological stress can also provide insight into ethnicity. There are some genetic diseases that are linked to specific ethnic groups – especially ethnic groups that have traditionally had lower rates of gene flow. For instance, Tay-Sachs disease is a genetic disorder that has the highest incidence in Irish and Ashkenazi Jewish populations. Sickle-cell anaemia is another example, but this genetic disorder disproportionately affects individuals of African, Mediterranean and Southeast Asian descent. Furthermore, ethnic cultural practices can lead to health disparities. Based on sex, age or socioeconomic status (among other factors relating to social identity), members of some groups might be treated differently and barred from the consumption of nutritious foods or forms of medical care. Thus, physiological stress is yet another indicator that can aid in the identification of ethnic affiliation when considered together with other corroborating evidence (Roberts and Manchester 2007: 42–3).

Since information derived from a single class of evidence is ultimately one-sided and identity is multifaceted, studies of ethnicity should include multiple lines of evidence. It is only by studying biological and material components in tandem that we can better understand the many factors that contributed to an individual's embodied experiences, as the recent reconsideration of Tomb II at Vergina demonstrates. Vergina (ancient Aegae) was the Macedonian capital of Philip II. In 1977, four built tombs were discovered beneath a large burial mound, which the excavators called the Great Tumulus (Andronikos 1984). These tombs were believed to belong to Macedonian kings, and although it is generally agreed that Philip rested within one of the tombs, scholars disagree as to whether he was interred in Tomb I (Bartsiokas 2000; Bartsiokas et al. 2015; Brandmeir et al. 2018) or Tomb II (Musgrave 1985; Musgrave et al. 1984; 2010; Delides 2016). The most recent analysis of the human remains in Tomb II, which included Computerised Tomography (CT) scans and X-Ray Fluorescent scanning (XRF), support the Tomb II hypothesis (Antikas and Wynn-Antikas 2016). Tomb II is a barrel-vaulted ashlar construction with a painted temple-facade. The interior space is partitioned into two rooms: an antechamber and a main burial chamber, both containing grave goods and cremated remains interred in gold larnakes (small box-like containers) housed in marble sarcophagi. The larnax in the main burial chamber contained a golden oak-leaf crown and the cremains of a Middle Adult male, identified as Philip (see Chapter 2 for a detailed discussion of Tomb II and the burial identified as Philip's). The larnax in the antechamber contained a golden diadem and the cremains of a Young Adult Female who had experienced a severe left leg fracture at some point in her life – probably the result of a bad fall – that resulted in limb atrophy and shortening. It is tempting to suggest that she fell from a horse, since she also possessed degenerative changes to her legs and spine that are consistent with habitual horse riding, but the cause of her fall is unknown (Antikas and Wynn-Antikas 2016).

Even though they primarily consist of arms and armour, the grave goods found in the antechamber most likely belonged to the young woman. These items consist of a set of custom-made gilded bronze greaves (the left one was shorter and narrower than the right), a Scythian gorytus (combination bow-case and quiver), arrowheads, spearheads, linothorax (breastplate made of reinforced linen) and Scythian-style pectoral (a leather-backed protective neck-covering plated with iron and a gilded silver frontal covering). The martial nature of the assemblage as well as the inclusion of the gorytus and pectoral suggest that she was Scythian (Jacobson 1995: 102; Antikas and Wynn-Antikas 2016). Widely regarded as the genesis for the mythical Amazons (Tyrrell 1984: 23–4; Blok 1995: 83–102; Mayor 2014: 34–51), Scythian women rode horses and wielded weapons (*On Airs, Waters, Places* 17; Kennedy et al. 2013: 37–8). Archaeological evidence confirms this, as the contents of tombs between the Danube and Don Rivers indicate that almost 25 per cent of Scythian horseback archers were women (Antikas and Wynn-Antikas 2016). Although there is no extant account of Philip having married a Scythian, he purportedly engaged in diplomatic relations with King Atheas of Scythia (Gardiner-Garden 1989), and it is hypothesised that the woman interred in the antechamber is Atheas' daughter and a wife or concubine of Philip II (Antikas and Wynn-Antikas 2016). One explanation for why she was buried with Philip, while his other wives were not, could be that she died contemporaneously. Mortuary and literary evidence reveals that Scythian widows and concubines were killed upon the deaths of their men so that they could accompany them to the afterlife (Herodotus 4.71.4; Rolle 1980: 29; Kennedy et al. 2013: 315). Thus, without careful consideration of the material *and* biological evidence from Tomb II, and an understanding of the tomb's historical and cultural contexts, a credible identification of the woman in the antechamber would not have been possible.

Material indicators of ethnicity

Although the ideal scenario is one in which material and biological evidence align to mutually confirm ethnic identity, there are some instances in which only material evidence is available. This is especially true for older excavations where the skeletal remains were discarded and in cases where funerary monuments were spoliated and moved from their original context. It is, however, through extant funerary inscriptions that we know with certainty that non-Greeks were buried in mainland Greek cemeteries in the Late Archaic/Classical period. For example, the base of a Late Archaic marble funerary monument reused in the Piraeus Gate of the Themistoclean city wall of Athens bears a bilingual inscription (*IG* 1³ 1344). The partially preserved inscription, written in Attic Greek and Carian, commemorates Tyr[, son of Skylax, and seems to have supported a kouros statue sculpted by a local artist named Aristocles, who is named in the last line of the inscription. Kouroi – conventional nude figures of striding male youths – were costly grave markers that also served as a venue for competition among Greek aristocratic families (Pedley 2012: 174). The choice of a kouros in this context is an interesting commemorative strategy, because it broadcasts salient information about the deceased's identity to the Athenian viewer, namely 'young man', 'wealthy' and 'Greek'. It is not until the viewer read (if they were literate) the inscription that they would notice that it was bilingual and that the deceased is identified as Carian, while his father, despite having a Greek name, is a Carian metic. By choosing to memorialise his son in the manner of the Athenian aristocracy, Skylax was able to simultaneously make an aspirational claim to social belonging while still asserting his Carian identity (Herda 2013: 423–4).

In Athens, it was relatively common for metic funerary monuments to be visually indistinguishable from those commemorating Athenians (Osborne 2011: 149; see Chapters 1 and 3 for discussions of metics). Another example of this is the sculpted stele of a metic named Eirene from Byzantium (ca. 375–350 BCE). The stele is the common naiskos type with a pediment framed by antae. The figural scene features a woman seated in a high-back chair to the right, looking at the viewer and tugging at her veil. Opposite her to the left is a standing woman holding an infant (*IG* 2^2 8440). This seated matron/standing woman composition is common in Athenian funerary art, but what is uncommon is the bilingual inscription written in Attic Greek and Phoenician. A bilingual inscription is a fitting commemoration for Eirene, who hailed from the Greek city of Byzantium, which was a much more ethnically diverse city than Athens. Presumably its location on a major trading route near Greek, Persian, Scythian and Phoenician spheres of influence, as well as its relaxed policy towards immigrants, fostered the multiethnic composition of its population (Kennedy 2014: 107, 110). Furthermore, a survey of extant funerary inscriptions reveals that approximately 40 per cent belonged to metics who desired to be commemorated in an Athenian fashion (Meyer 1993). In these cases, although the inscriptions denote the deceased as non-Athenian, 'the graves and monuments themselves are less revealing of variant identities' (Shepherd 2013: 552).

Conversely, there are other instances where the form or iconography of funerary monuments clearly derive from non-Greek precedents. One interesting stele (mid-fourth century BCE), often referred to as the 'Kamini stele', was produced in an Attic workshop, but features Achaemenid Persian iconography similar to motifs found on inscribed gems and monumental relief sculptures at Persepolis (Miller 1997: 56). There is no inscription on the Kamini stele that might indicate how the deceased ethnically identified, but given the stele's date, there is a high probability that the individual was Athenian. Fourth-century Attic elites often sought to self-aggrandise by appropriating Achaemenid iconography and modelling their final resting places after the tombs of Carian dynasts or Persian kings. In rare instances, metics also occasionally chose to commemorate themselves in this fashion, and a prime example is the monumental tomb of Nikeratos and his son Polyxenos (ca. second half of the fourth century BCE). These men were metics from Istros, a Greek colony in the Black Sea region, and their tomb is reminiscent of the Mausoleum at Halicarnassus (and Anatolian monumental tombs in general), and aspects of its iconography are Graeco-Persian in origin (Boardman 1995: 27–31; Allen 2003). This unique tomb aside, it seems that we have a paradoxical situation where metics were choosing to commemorate themselves in an Athenian manner, while elite Athenians were opting for more exotic, non-Greek motifs. This pattern serves as a reminder that art and material culture alone, uncorroborated by other lines of evidence, are inaccurate indicators of ethnicity.

One has to look closely at funerary monuments to distinguish between metics and citizens in Athens. There does not appear to have been any anti-sumptuary laws directed at metics, as their grave markers could be situated in highly visible and conspicuous places and comparable to – or even more elaborate than – those of citizens (Gray 2011: 49–50). In terms of spatial organisation, patterning differs according to cemetery conventions. The graves of metics and citizens were interspersed rather than segregated in the Kerameikos. Even on casualty lists, the names of non-Greeks, denoted as 'barbarian archers', appear with those of fallen Athenian soldiers (Low 2012: 16–17; Arrington 2015: 96), and Thucydides (2.34.1–7) tells us that foreigners were permitted to join the processions of state funerals for the war dead. In other Athenian cemeteries, namely the East, West, Piraeus and Sikelia Hill cemeteries, the opposite is true. Non-Greek metic communities opted to be buried together, as the inscriptions on funerary monuments indicate metics were clustered in plots on the basis of their geographic origins (Shea 2018: 194–208).

Beyond Attica, there is scant material evidence connected to non-Greek ethnicity in Late Archaic/Classical non-colonial contexts. Nothing exists but funerary monuments, and none can be matched with skeletal remains. Furthermore, the potential ambiguity of the Attic monuments reinforces the need to explore multiple lines of evidence when seeking to answer questions about ethnic identity. Since the search for material indicators of non-Greek graves has yielded few conspicuous indicators of ethnicity, it is prudent to shift to another avenue of enquiry. In particular, biomolecular analyses performed on human skeletal remains, such as stable isotope analysis, are capable of identifying migrants whose status might have otherwise gone undetected.

Identifying evidence of migration

Arguably, human history is a history of migration (Burmeister 2017). Migration involves the movement of individuals or groups, and these movements can be classified by pattern (local, circular, chain) or impetus (career, colonising, coerced; Tilly 1978; Anthony 1997).[6] As people move, they bring their cultural practices with them, leaving measureable traces in the cultural, linguistic and skeletal record (Adams et al. 1978: 486). Traditionally, archaeologists have used ancient literary accounts and linguistic diffusion, in addition to archaeological indicators like sudden changes in material culture, technology, settlement patterns, subsistence patterns and cultural practices (especially in the funerary sphere), as evidence pointing towards migration.[7]

Material culture can be a valuable tool for the study of migration, cultural transfer and acculturation, but it also can be ambiguous, especially because it is not always clear whether it is objects and ideas or people (or both) that are moving. As discussed in the Introduction, material culture is a mode of communication that can be used to embody and reflect relationships. Like any form of communication, the significance of material culture is dynamic, rather than static, and foreign objects can serve different functions and hold different meanings in new contexts. For instance, when immigrant societies face new ecological, social and economic environments, they prove to be flexible in their cultural practices and often adopt new ones in order to adapt (Burmeister 2017). In the

Greek city states of the Black Sea region, elite burials typically incorporated local Scythian funerary elements such as the use of kurgans (burial mounds) and the inclusion of weapons, horse equipment and elaborate jewellery among the grave goods (Petersen 2010: 304–5). Indigenous societies are likewise adaptive and flexible as they respond to the arrival of new groups and communities (Burmeister 2017). In Scythian contexts, Greek sympotic vase shapes are found in kurgans, and this trend has been interpreted as the Scythian aristocratic adoption of the connotations of wealth and leisure embodied by the symposion (Jacobson 1995: 188; Námerová 2010). In both of these examples from the Black Sea, local and immigrant elites emulated one another's cultural practices to varying degrees for reasons we may never know. These processes of cultural exchange are often complex and intricate, and they can be difficult to perceive, reconstruct and interpret in the archaeological record (Burmeister 2017).

The so-called 'Dorian invasion' is an example of a migratory event that was investigated through the use of traditional literary, linguistic and archaeological methods.[8] Later Greek tradition, preserved through the writings of Tyrtaeus (fr. 2 West, lines 12–5), Herodotus (9.26), Thucydides (1.12) and Pausanias (2.18.6), maintains that the Dorians invaded mainland Greece from the north at the end of the Bronze Age (ca. 1170 BCE), causing the destabilisation and ultimate collapse of Mycenaean society.[9] The Dorian invasion is linked to the Greek mythological tradition of the *nostoi* – the Returns of the Greeks. The *nostoi* paint a picture of large migratory waves and rampant sociopolitical instability in the wake of the Trojan Wars:

> If one reads the mythological narrative of the *nostoi* as straight history, as many Greeks of later centuries did, one would conclude that their ancestors *c.* 1100 BCE were in a very bad way. Hardly anyone had returned from Troy, and most of those who had were killed or evicted. Some survivors didn't even try to get home, going instead to Italy or other far-off places to build new towns. The old mainland kings and their families were all gone. Thebes was still in ruins. Hordes of so-called Thessalians had swept across the Pindos and pushed whole populations southwards. The Dorians had come from the north and taken over the Peloponnese. They claimed to be Heraklid, returning to their ancestral home; whatever the truth or comfort of that explanation, they had caused complete upheaval in Messenia, Lakonia, and Argos. The old Achaians were restricted to the north shore of the peninsula, at the expense of the poor Ionians who were forced out. Some of these put down roots in Attica, but others were trying to make a new start overseas. Many groups joined the exodus: Minyans, Abantes, Dryopes, Kadmeians, Pelasgians, and more. In their new homes they often met stiff resistance from the indigenous peoples. (Fowler 2018: 43)

Early scholars had no reason to doubt the *nostoi* narrative, and their linguistic and archaeological research seemed to support the historical understanding of later Greek authors. Nineteenth-century linguists asserted that all of the major Greek dialects were brought to the mainland by three migratory waves, with the Dorian migration being the latest. According to this model, proto-Ionians arrived first, followed by proto-Achaeans (who later split into a northern proto-Aeolic branch and a southern proto-Arcado-Cypriot branch), and then proto-Dorians (Hall 1995). Early Iron Age material culture and technological achievements were also attributed to the Dorians, such as the introduction of iron metallurgy, single burial in cist graves, spectacle fibulae and a type of pottery called 'Handmade Burnished Ware', or 'Barbarian Ware' (Chadwick 1976; Cline 2014: 149). However, it has since become clear that there was no fabled northern invasion. Since Linear B was deciphered in the 1950s, it has been apparent that all Greek dialects, including Dorian, had developed within the Mycenaean world (Hall 1995). In terms of material culture, none of the purported evidence is imported or unexplainable: iron technology developed in response to the collapse of trade networks and access to bronze, single burial in cist graves was a revival of a pre-Mycenaean burial practice that had never completely fallen out of use, spectacle fibulae appear for the first time in the tenth century BCE, and Early Iron Age pottery has Mycenaean origins (Chadwick 1976; Snodgrass 2001: 44, 177–84, 217–39, 256).

Unlike traditional lines of linguistic and archaeological evidence, which can be misleading and ambiguous, biomolecular analysis is capable of identifying migrants with a high degree of accuracy. The analysis of ancient DNA is not as applicable as one might suspect, as it is much better at discerning components of biological ancestry and patterns of gene flow (see the discussion of ancestry at the end of this chapter; Brown and Brown 2011: 168–9). Stable isotope analysis, on the other hand, provides critical information regarding the mobility of individuals and groups, as it allows us to identify migrants and infer their geographical places of origin. Stable isotopes of strontium ($^{87}Sr/^{86}Sr$), oxygen ($^{18}O/^{16}O$), sulphur ($\delta^{34}S$) and lead ($^{206}Pb/^{207}Pb$, $^{208}Pb/^{206}Pb$) exist in geographical rock formations and fresh water sources.[10] Each locale bears a unique isotopic signature, so humans acquire the isotopic signature of their environment by eating and drinking locally. For example, strontium from bedrock is present in soil and groundwater. Plants absorb bedrock strontium from soil and water, and animals acquire strontium from ingesting plants, water and other animals. As it moves through the food chain, the isotopic composition of strontium is unchanged by these biological processes because the relative mass differences of strontium isotopes are very small. As humans eat and drink locally, strontium isotopes are incorporated into the mineral matrix of their hard tissues, namely bones and teeth, ensuring that the strontium isotopic composition of hard tissues will reflect an individual's diet and habitat. Bones and teeth, however, each provide different insights into migratory practices. Since teeth only grow and change in childhood, the isotopic signature recorded in an individual's teeth will reflect childhood residence, while the signature of bones, which constantly grow and remodel throughout life, will reflect residence around the time of death (Brown and Brown 2011: 79–88, 266–86; Larsen 2015: 338–47).

Although stable isotope analysis is capable of identifying non-locals in the archaeological record, it does so in a limited fashion. Only childhood and peri-mortem residences are perceptible, while multiple migrations or short-term residencies are undetectable. Furthermore, behaviour can skew isotopic signatures. Oxygen values can be affected by drinking water from a non-local source (e.g. water transferred from a mountain source to a city via aqueducts), food preparation practices (boiling, brewing, stewing etc.) and breastfeeding. Strontium values, on the other hand, can be impacted by the consumption of shellfish and non-local food. Another complication of strontium analysis is that some areas are geologically similar and do not bear sufficient variabil-ity to detect mobility. Since each analysis has its limitations, both strontium and oxygen isotopes (and others, such as sulphur and lead) should be studied together in order to minimise error and best discern an individual's place of origin (Sperduti et al. 2018: 151–2).

For ancient Greek populations, there are an increasing number of stable isotopic studies performed for the purpose of reconstructing mobility.[11] Bio-available strontium (derived from archaeological and modern faunal bone/tooth enamel and modern snail shells) and the isotopic composition of spring water have been mapped for large portions of mainland Greece and the Aegean (Nafplioti 2011; Dotsika et al. 2018).[12] Strontium isotope analysis of Early to Late Neolithic (seventh to fifth millennium BCE) populations across seven sites in northern Greece (n = 36) has revealed broad migratory patterns. Virtually all of the individuals in the diachronic sample were local to the area (or alternatively, to an isotopically homogeneous environment), suggest-ing limited mobility. Three individuals from a Late Neolithic population at Kleitos, however, bore isotopic signatures that lie outside of the bioavailable local range, implying that they spent a portion of their young lives in another environment. Although the sample size is small, the results of this study are in alignment with patterns of mobility and exchange attested by analyses of pottery circulation. In particular, there were low levels of mobility during the Early and Middle Neolithic and greater movement in the Late Neolithic (Whelton et al. 2018).

Strontium isotopes have also been used to identify potential migrants in Bronze Age assemblages. At Mycenae, eleven individuals from Grave Circle A (ca. sixteenth to fifteenth centuries BCE) were analysed and only two are clearly local, three are definitively migrants and the remaining six are ambiguous. The only two females identified in the sample are part of the migrant group, and the non-local origins of these females might reflect marital patterns, specifically marriage alliances between families of high social rank. The six ambiguous individuals might have skewed isotopic signatures on account of diet. Sources of food deriving from approximately 5–10 km away from the acropolis of Mycenae bear a higher strontium isotope ratio. Furthermore, Mycenae's palace economy was based on mobilisation. Surpluses from the wider territory under its control were collected to finance the operations of the state, and Mycenae itself served as a central repository and distribution centre (Nakassis et al. 2010: 244–5). Presumably, Mycenae's higher-ranking individuals – such as those buried in Grave Circle A – would have had easy access to non-local food, including seafood (Nafplioti 2009). At Knossos, on the other hand, strontium isotopic ratios were used to answer the question of whether a Mycenaean invasion caused the widespread destruction across Crete during the Late Minoan period (ca. 1490/1470 BCE). Individuals from burials at Knossos (n = 30) that were deemed to be 'Mycenaean' in character ('warrior burials', burials with bronze objects, and mainland-style single-chamber tombs) and post-Late Minoan were analysed, and they were all found to be local to Knossos. These results raise more questions than answers, as numerous plausible scenarios could account for them – for instance, the individuals studied represent a new generation of Mycenaeans on Crete and not the invaders, or the widespread destruction was caused by Minoans themselves, and the subsequent new Minoan leaders adopted a Mycenaean symbolic system to legitimise or justify their rule (Nafplioti 2008).

For assemblages dating to the Early Iron Age, immediately following the collapse of Mycenaean society, strontium isotopes have been used to detect trends in population movement. The disintegration of the Mycenaean palatial system (ca. thirteenth to twelfth centuries BCE) prompted a variety of social changes, which significantly altered social organisation, trade and interaction, production and technology, material culture and burial practices. Traditional models of population movement (including the now disfavoured 'Dorian invasion' theory) have sought to explain these widespread cultural shifts, and those that are currently favoured propose scenarios in which small-scale movements of individuals or groups across the Aegean provided the impetus for social and cultural change (Morris 2007). To detect instances of population movement in southern Thessaly, strontium isotope analysis of human tooth enamel, combined with evidence derived from funerary contexts and osteological analyses, were examined from three sites (ca. eleventh to ninth centuries BCE): the cemetery of Voulokaliva at Alos (n = 13), the cemetery of Chloe at Pherae (n = 10) and two cemeteries at Pharsala (n = 13). Burial practices varied on a site-by-site basis: tholoi with multiple inhumations (excluding subadults under the age of 5) were used at Chloe, while simple pit and cist graves and a circular structure (probably an imitation of a tholos tomb) with single and double inhumations of all ages were observed at Voulokaliva. The burial practices witnessed at Pharsala were more diverse. Two cemeteries, designated Site 1 and Site 2, were studied. Site 1 had some cremations, but primarily single and multiple inhumations in pits, cists, burial enclosures, tholoi and tumuli, while Site 2 consisted of tholos tombs containing multiple adults. At Chloe, stable isotope analysis revealed that all of the sample individuals were indigenous to the area, and most from Voulokaliva were local, with the exception of three individuals who were either obtaining food from a wider area around Alos or were simply non-local. The implications of the finds from Chloe and Voulokaliva suggest that these populations were utilising geographically constrained food production and procurement strategies. At Pharsala, on the other hand, a group of non-locals from areas that were geologically and isotopically distinct were identified at Site 2. These non-locals were buried in a different location from their local counterparts at Site 1, but they shared similar burial practices, implying that they either came from an area that was culturally similar to that of Pharsala or they assimilated to the customs of Pharsala. Overall, this study provides evidence for small-scale migration of individuals or families who did not prompt social change, but rather adopted the cultural practices of their new communities (Panagiotopoulou et al. 2018).

In a Greek Sicilian context, stable isotopic ratios of strontium and oxygen were used to determine the geographic origins of soldiers who participated in the Battles of Himera. The Battles of Himera were fought between the Carthaginians and Greek Sicilians in 480 BCE and 409 BCE respectively. Eight mass graves containing 132 adult male individuals have been associated with these battles on the basis of their location on the documented battlefield site, stratigraphic position, dates and the presence of weapons in the graves. Seven mass graves (FC 1–7) date to 480 BCE, and one (FC 8+9) dates to 409 BCE. It is highly probable that the individuals interred in the mass graves were soldiers, since weapons are present in the graves, they are all adult males, and many skeletons bear evidence of violent trauma. Taking their identification a step further, it is likely that these soldiers fought (and ultimately died) for Himera because they were buried intentionally, in an orderly and respectful manner. Ancient literary accounts of the battles (Herodotus 7.165–7; Diodorus Siculus 11.20–1, 13.62) allowed for the formulation of two hypotheses that were tested through isotopic analysis, namely that the Greek combatants who fought in 480 BCE hailed from various Greek cities across Sicily, while the Greek combatants who fought in 409 BCE were primarily from Himera. The strontium and oxygen values of tooth enamel of sixty-two individuals (fifty-one from 480 BCE and eleven from 409 BCE) were analysed and compared to those of twenty-five adult individuals from Himera's western necropolis, a nearby cemetery understood to contain the contemporaneous, general population of Himera. In the mass graves dating to 480 BCE, approximately two thirds of the sampled individuals were non-local, with many of these individuals originating from regions beyond Sicily. Extant literary sources attest to a coalition of Sicilian Greek allies fighting together at

Himera 480 BCE, but the individuals who originated beyond Sicily could represent migrants to Greek Sicily or foreign mercenaries hired by Sicilian Greek tyrants. Shifting to the mass grave from 409 BCE, only one fourth of the sample was non-local, which supports the ancient authors who claim that Himera was unaided and ultimately defeated in 409 BCE (Reinberger et al. 2021).

Another form of stable isotope analysis, namely that of sulphur, was used to identify migrants in a Bronze Age mass burial in Thebes (ca. 2200 BCE). Like strontium, sulphur composition is dictated by local bedrock and atmospheric depositions, and it is also influenced by microbial processes in the soil. Plants, for instance, receive sulphate through their roots from the weathering of bedrock as well as through precipitation (e.g. droplets from sea evaporation or precipitation containing dissolved sulphur gases). Then, through ingestion of local foods, human hard tissues reflect the sulphur composition of the local environment. The mass grave in Thebes was deposited in the ruins of an apsidal building, and a burial mound was erected over it. The grave contained twelve individuals of both sexes and all age groups. None of the individuals bore any clear evidence of trauma or chronic pathologies, and it is unclear why they were buried in this extraordinary fashion. Stable isotopic evidence identified only one non-local outlier in the group, an Adult Female. Her place of origin cannot be identified with certainty, but it is clear that she was not born in Thebes (Vika 2009).

What stable isotope analysis has revealed in the ancient Aegean is that it is difficult, if not impossible, to detect migrants through burial contexts alone. For instance, on Crete, burials that were deemed to be Mycenaean in character were found to contain locals, and in Thessaly, all of the isotopically identified migrants were placed in normative burials. Based on their normative burials, one could conclude that migrants were not socially marginalised in the Bronze Age and Early Iron Age, at least not in the select communities that were studied from Crete, Mycenae, Thebes and southern Thessaly. This observation also applies to the extraordinary context of the fifth-century BCE mass graves from Greek Sicily. Although mass graves are non-normative per se, it can be argued that these are circumstantially 'normative' since the mass graves at Himera are associated with specific battles, the aftermath of which undoubtedly required mass graves for the expedient interment of the war dead. Furthermore, within the mass graves, the isotopically identified migrants and/or mercenaries were buried in the same manner as the Greek Sicilian soldiers, which could be attributed to a unifying *esprit de corps* forged through participation and death in battle or simply their lack of social marginalisation.

The observation that migrants were buried normatively and were unlikely to have been socially marginalised generates more questions than answers, especially since the migrants' places of origin were never ascertained in any of the aforementioned studies, and the only conclusion that could be drawn was that the migrant individuals were not local. Therefore, it is possible that all of the migrants identified in these studies shared cultural affinities with the locals, and that is why they were placed in normative graves. Had they hailed from different cultures or ethnic groups, would they still have been buried normatively? This is a question that we currently cannot answer. Furthermore, to date there are no published stable isotopic studies of the Late Archaic/Classical period assemblages from the Greek mainland, so we likewise cannot determine whether earlier migrant burial patterns persisted or diverged.[13] It is hoped that future, more expansive stable isotopic testing will provide answers to the questions posed here.

Biological affinity: An aspect of biological identity

Evidence derived from stable isotope analysis may provide information about population mobility, but it does not necessarily correspond to biological relatedness, or 'affinity'. The determination of biological affinity has often relied on the analysis of the variation of morphological skeletal and dental traits among and between populations. The degree of relatedness among individuals and populations is referred to as biological distance, or 'biodistance' (Buikstra et al. 1990). Studies of biodistance presuppose that 'variation in morphological traits of the skeleton reflects underlying genotypic variation' and that 'a greater frequency of shared attributes indicates closer genetic affinity than a lower frequency of shared attributes' (Larsen 2015: 357). Insights derived from biodistance analysis allow us to reconstruct population history, especially in regards to population shifts (i.e. formation/introduction of new populations and social groups) and stasis (i.e. lack of local biological change; Larsen 2015: 357).

Skeletal variation, especially as it relates to the analysis of biodistance, can be assessed metrically and non-metrically. When it comes to metric variation, the skull is often regarded as an indicator of biological affinity. The physical dimensions of the skull are influenced by genetic, cultural, climatic and diet-related factors, and measurement of the skull is precise and repeatable, as cranial dimensions are measured as a series of linear distances between standardised morphological landmarks (Mays 2000a; Pietrusewsky 2014). Advocates of craniometric analysis argue that genetics is one of the strongest determinants of skull form – so much so that craniometric data can be used as a proxy for genetic data (e.g. Pietrusewsky 2014). This position, however, ignores the fact that other factors, such as climate (especially extreme cold: Betti et al. 2010) and widespread shifts in dietary patterns (Katz et al. 2017), can profoundly influence cranial shape. Moreover, like ancestry analysis, craniometric analysis is another scientific tool that has historically been used to perpetuate the myth of biological racial classification (Perrin and Anderson 2013). Because of this association, the use of craniometrics is controversial, and its utility is limited to the potential identification of broad population trends (e.g. Algee-Hewitt 2017).

208   MARGINALISED POPULATIONS IN THE ANCIENT GREEK WORLD

Very few biodistance analyses have explored craniometric variation in ancient Aegean populations. This dearth is most likely due to the controversy surrounding the method as well as lack of suitable samples, as many ancient remains are fragmentary and craniometric analysis requires complete skulls. Nevertheless, craniometrics were used to suggest that shifting immigration patterns changed the ethnic composition of Lerna throughout the course of the Bronze Age (ca. 3000–1150 BCE; Angel 1971). Another analysis of craniometric traits was performed to answer the question of whether there was clear evidence of a Mycenaean invasion of Crete during the Late Minoan period (ca. 1700–1450 BCE). The sample from Crete consisted of individuals from various sites and time periods: Chalcolithic (ca. 3300–3000 BCE) Palaikastro, Middle Minoan (ca. 2100–1700 BCE) Fourni cemetery (near Archanes) and Knossos, and Late Minoan (ca. 1700–1450 BCE) Knossos (and sites around Knossos) and Archanes. The craniometric traits from Crete were statistically compared via Discriminate Function Analysis to those of Late Bronze Age (ca. 1600–1100 BCE) individuals on mainland Greece from the Argolid, Attica and Messenia. The results suggest that there is no measurable biodistance between the individuals from Chalcolithic and Middle Minoan Crete, but a shift is perceptible in the Late Minoan samples. This shift could be explained by the genetic introduction of a new population, such as the Mycenaeans from mainland Greece, whose craniometric traits proved to be measurably different from those of the Chalcolithic and Middle Minoan individuals, or by a substantial and widespread dietary change (Manolis 2001).

Non-metric traits are minor skeletal and dental variants that have been successfully used to demonstrate biodistance. The development of non-metric traits is influenced by genetic and environmental factors (e.g. Konigsberg et al. 1993), as well as habitual activity (e.g. Sanchez-Lara et al. 2007). The multifactorial aetiology of these traits complicates their interpretation, but they are, nevertheless, compelling indicators of relatedness, and comparisons of non-metric trait and ancient DNA (aDNA) analyses indicate that the two types of data bear similar relationships to one another (Cheverud 1988; Hubbard et al. 2015; Sodini et al. 2018). Due to the strong hereditary component of their development, non-metric traits have been used to strengthen claims of genetic relationships within cemeteries, such as the identification of family plots (e.g. Rubini 1996). They are, however, best utilised to determine biological affinities among population groups, as members of past population groups are presumed to share generational genetic and environmental commonalities (Berry and Berry 1967; Finnegan 1978; Turner et al. 1991; Scott and Turner 1997; Tyrrell 2000).

Although single traits have been identified as having special significance to Greek and non-Greek populations respectively, single traits in themselves are not accurate measures of biodistance. For example, three dental traits have traditionally been associated with Italic populations (Becker and Salvadei 1992;

Pinto-Cisternas et al. 1995). Italic peoples typically have a higher incidence of shovel-shaped incisors (i.e. incisors with posterior surfaces shaped like the blade of a shovel) and bifurcated roots on the maxillary first premolars (i.e. maxillary premolars possessing a double rather than a single root) than Greeks. Thus, it has been suggested that the presence of those traits in Greek burial contexts indicates that locals were integrating and intermarrying into Greek communities (Becker and Salvadei 1992; Becker 1995: 280). Similarly, the 'Etruscan upper lateral incisor', a concavity on the mesio-lingual border of the crown of the upper lateral incisor, has a restricted geographical distribution (i.e. the Italian peninsula and surrounding islands) and is present in approximately 30 per cent of Etruscans from the seventh to the first centuries BCE (Pinto-Cisternas et al. 1995). Since 18 per cent of the population of Metaponto, a Greek colony in southern Italy, bears this trait, researchers suggest that its presence is most likely the product of intermarriage and/or integration with local Italic peoples (Pinto-Cisternas et al. 1995: 337; Henneberg and Henneberg 1998: 518).

Upon closer inspection, it is unlikely that any of these traits are true indicators of biodistance. Due to its alleged exclusivity and restricted geographical distribution, the 'Etruscan upper lateral incisor' appears to be best suited for studies of biological affinity. However, the 'Etruscan upper lateral incisor' has also been observed in non-Italic populations and is often recorded as an 'interruption groove' (Turner et al. 1991). Interruption groves have been found in high frequencies in ancient Illyrian and Corinthian populations (McIlvaine et al. 2014), so it is doubtful that the 'Etruscan upper lateral incisor' exclusively denotes Italic heritage. Likewise, shovel-shaped incisors have also been attested in early Italic populations (Fabbri and Mallegni 1988: 172; Becker and Salvadei 1992), but they are seen in skeletal assemblages from mainland Greece and the Aegean as well (e.g. Lerna, Crete and Lefkandi; Angel 1944; 1971; Carr 1960; Musgrave and Popham 1991).[14] Finally, double-rooted maxillary first premolars have similarly been observed in ancient Aegean skeletons (e.g. Carr 1960). As a result, one cannot successfully argue that any of these singular traits, present in both Italic and Greek populations, are reliable indicators of biological affinity (Sulosky Weaver 2015: 100–5). These examples illustrate how non-metric trait analysis cannot rely on solitary traits, and that it is most effective when multiple traits are compared.

In colonial contexts, the analysis of multiple non-metric traits has discerned distinctions among regional populations. When compared statistically, archaeological sites with significant Greek influence, and presumably populations, tend to group separately from non-Greek ones (Sulosky Weaver 2015: 89–100; Sulosky Weaver and Kyle forthcoming). For instance, in Sicily and Illyria, the relative frequencies of non-metric cranial traits were compared using optimal scaling multivariate statistical tests. From Sicily, fourteen populations were compared: four were local pre-colonial (ca. seventeenth to fourteenth centuries BCE), six were post-colonial Greek (ca. eighth to third centuries BCE), three were local, non-Greek and post-colonial (ca. eighth to sixth centuries BCE), while the fourteenth population derived from a Greek site that sustained a large local non-Greek contingent (Morgantina, ca. eighth to fifth centuries BCE).[15] From Illyria, five populations were compared. Two populations were local pre-colonial: Lofkënd (fifteenth to eighth centuries BCE) and pre-colonial Apollonia (twenty-second to seventh centuries BCE). Two populations were post-colonial Greek: one from Apollonia (sixth century BCE and first century BCE) and one from Epidamnus (fifth to first centuries BCE). Another population, designated 'peripheral Apollonia' (fourth to first centuries BCE), was post-colonial, but of unknown ethnic composition. The test performed on the Sicilian sites success-fully grouped the populations into 'Greek' and 'Non-Greek' groups, the latter of which included the Greek site of Morgantina. The inclusion of Morgantina with the non-Greek groups is unsurprising, as it is well known that the city, though Greek, sustained a large local population (e.g. Tsakirgis 1995; Walsh 2011/12). The test performed on the Illyrian sites yielded similar results. The pre-colonial and colonial Apollonia populations grouped with Lofkënd. This association most likely reflects a significant Illyrian contribution to the genetic composition of Apollonia, a conclusion that is supported by ancient literary evidence and other biodistance studies (e.g. McIlvaine et al. 2014). Epidam-nus and peripheral Apollonia, however, did not cluster with the other groups. This separation suggests that Epidamnus had a larger Greek population than Apollonia. Peripheral Apollonia, on the other hand, is most likely an outlier on account of its small sample size. When all of the populations in the study (with the exception of peripheral Apollonia) were compared in a single test, no obvi-ous patterns could be discerned. What this reveals is that optimal scaling tests are best suited for regional studies and may not be capable of identifying Greek populations and/or multiple ethnic groups that are separated by considerable geographical distances (Sulosky Weaver and Kyle forthcoming).

Similar outcomes derive from other non-metric studies of biodistance in colonial contexts.[16] Cranial and dental non-metric traits were used to compare pre-colonial Illyrians (ca. 1100–900 BCE) to colonial Apollonians (ca. 800–30 BCE) and Greeks from Corinth (ca. 1600–30 BCE). The results suggest that approximately 90 per cent of the individuals buried in the Apollonian necropo-lis were more phenotypically similar to Illyrians than Corinthian Greeks. When considered in the context of funerary practices, these results align with the material record. The use of tumulus burial, a traditional Illyrian burial form, persists after colonisation in the necropolis at Apollonia. Although the burial type is Illyrian, inside the tumuli there are large numbers of Greek grave goods and burial positions that might indicate cultural hybridity and/or intermar-riage between Greeks and Illyrians (McIlvaine et al. 2014). Dental non-metric traits were also used to study biodistance between two populations from the

Greek colony of Metaponto in southern Italy (ca. 700–250 BCE) and those of three surrounding local sites (ca. 900–350 BCE). It was found that the three local Italic populations were similar to one another, but biologically removed from the Metaponto populations. The Metaponto samples, which represented rural and urban populations respectively, do not display phenotypic similarities, suggesting that Metaponto was comprised of sizeable groups of people with diverse geographical origins, while the surrounding Italic communities were relatively homogeneous (Rathmann et al. 2017). A subsequent study of the region focused on dental metric and non-metric variation among a larger sample of pre-colonial (ca. 900–700 BCE) and post-colonial populations (ca. 700–200 BCE). The results reveal that pre-colonial southern Italy was typified by low levels of mobility, but notable biological difference among groups. These patterns shifted post-colonisation, when mobility increased, but biological differences decreased. The results further suggest that approximately 18 per cent of post-colonial individuals were of Greek ancestry and that they lived alongside local Italic peoples in not only Greek colonies but also indigenous villages (Rathmann et al. 2019).

No biodistance studies of ethnicity have been performed on assemblages from Late Archaic/Classical non-colonial mainland contexts. Even though biodistance studies are formulated more easily in Greek colonial contexts, or in time periods of significant population shift (e.g. the purported Mycenaean invasion of Crete), research questions can also be formulated for Greek cemeteries in the mainland. For instance, intracemetery biodistance studies could compare a random sample of burials to those that are suspected to belong to non-Greeks, such as non-normative burials and grave clusters or individual graves that contain evidence of a non-Greek identity (e.g. non-Greek names, grave goods, funerary iconography, burial rites or tomb styles).

Estimating ancestry

As discussed in the Introduction, traditional methods of estimating ancestry from cranial, postcranial and dental morphology are currently eschewed because they perpetuate the harmful fallacy of biological racial categorisation. Furthermore, many of the morphological characters that are purportedly indicative of ancestry have been proven to be either ambiguous or inaccurate. Genetic testing, on the other hand, has been touted as a more precise method for the estimation of ancestry, but it also bears the stigma of biological racial categorisation (Hakenbeck 2019). As Kim TallBear explains:

> [Genetic, or molecular, origins] are inferred for an individual based on
> a specific set of genetic markers, a specific set of algorithms for assessing
> genetic similarity, and a specific set of reference populations. But each of

those constitutive elements operates within a loop of circular reasoning. Particular, and particularly pure, biogeographic origins must be assumed in order to constitute the data that supposedly reveals those same origins. Native American DNA as an object could not exist without, and yet functions as a scientific data point to support the idea of, once pure, original populations. Notions of ancestral populations, the ordering and calculating of genetic markers and their associations, and the representation of living groups of individuals as reference populations all require the assumption that there was a moment, a human body, a marker, a population back there in space and time that was a biogeographical pinpoint of originality. This faith in originality would seem to be at odds with the doctrine of evolution, of change over time, of becoming. (2013: 6)

Instead of providing the definitive answer to the question of ancestry, DNA is simply one small piece in the complicated puzzle of human kinship and should be treated with caution and used in conjuction with other lines of archaeological evidence (Ensor 2021).

Moreover, it is notoriously difficult to recover aDNA from ancient human remains because it is subject to degradation and contamination (Evison 2001). Over time, physical and chemical processes destroy most of the DNA molecules contained in human skeletal remains from archaeological contexts. In some cases, no aDNA can be derived from archaeological samples (e.g. Bouwman et al. 2009). When aDNA is successfully extracted, the small amounts that remain intact are typically damaged, broken and difficult to analyse (Yang and Watt 2005). The Polymerase Chain Reaction (PCR) technique remedies this problem because it is sensitive enough to detect minuscule amounts of DNA molecules and amplify them quickly (Saiki et al. 1988; Stone 2008: 466). Its hypersensitivity is also a drawback of this technique, because modern contaminating DNA (e.g. skin cells, sweat and saliva) can also be found and amplified, so great care must be taken not to contaminate the samples during excavation, transport and analysis (Yang and Watt 2005).

Despite the difficulty of extracting aDNA, genome-wide data have been recovered and analysed from approximately 342 prehistoric individuals from findspots across the Aegean. Iosif Lazaridis and colleagues (2017) compared the aDNA via Principal Component Analysis to samples taken from 1,029 present-day West Eurasians in order to better understand the genetic coherence and ancestral origins of Aegean peoples. Samples from Minoan (ca. 2900–1700 BCE) and Mycenean (ca. 1700–1200 BCE) contexts in Crete and mainland Greece are genetically homogeneous and closely related to those from southwestern Anatolia, while modern Greek genetic profiles are closest to those of the Myceneans. A subsequent genetic study yielded similar results. Whole genomes were sequenced for samples from three Aegean Bronze Age cultural contexts: Cycladic (two individuals from the Cycladic islands, ca. 3200/3000–1100 BCE), Minoan (one individual from Crete, ca. 3200/3000–1100 BCE) and Helladic (three individuals from mainland Greece, ca. 3200/3000–1100 BCE, encompassing Mycenaean culture ca. 1600–1100 BCE). In addition, mitochondrial DNA (discussed in detail below) was recovered from eleven individuals across all three cultural contexts. Comparison to documented genomic data from diachronic Aegean samples suggests that the various Aegean populations were genetically homogeneous in the Early Bronze Age (ca. 3000 BCE). However, a shift occurred in the Middle Bronze Age (ca. 2600–2000 BCE), when the Aegean may have functioned as a type of 'genomic crossroads' as the region was shaped by 'Caucasus-like' and 'Pontic-Caspian Steppe-like' gene flow. It was also observed that modern Greeks are genetically similar to Middle Bronze Age (ca. 2000 BCE) individuals from northern Greece (Clemente et al. 2021).

Genome-wide analyses of ancient Aegean peoples, nevertheless, are relatively rare, and studies of mitochondrial DNA are far more common. Mitochondrial DNA (mtDNA), found in the mitochondria of cells, is inherited solely through the maternal line. Due to its high degree of preservation, strict matrilineal transmission and slow rate of evolution, mtDNA has been used as an indicator of maternal relatedness (Torroni et al. 1996: 1835; Fernández et al. 2006). For instance, mtDNA has been used to establish biological relatedness among individuals in Grave Circle B at Mycenae (ca. 1675–1550 BCE; Bouwman et al. 2008). MtDNA analysis targets two hypervariable regions of the mitochondrial genome that lie adjacent to one another. Based on mitochondrial sequence variants (i.e. haplotypes), the individual is assigned to one of approximately ninety mitochondrial haplogroups (i.e. one of the major sequence classes of mtDNA present in humans). In order to belong to a haplogroup, one must possess a small set of shared-sequence polymorphisms that are unique to the haplogroup and present in every member (Brown and Brown 2011: 24, 177–8).

MtDNA haplogroups (as well as Y-chromosome haplogroups, discussed later) are most frequently used to provide a glimpse into an individual's 'deep' ancestry and geographical origins (Nelson 2016). Population geneticists have created a system of letters and numbers to determine when a person's remote ancestors migrated out of Africa, and the spatiotemporal narrative is as follows: all humans share a common sub-Saharan African ancestor belonging to haplogroup L. Although the exact dispersal routes are not currently known, members of haplogroup L3 (a branch of haplogroup L) migrated out of Africa approximately 60,000 years ago (Macaulay et al. 2005; Mellars 2006; Torroni et al. 2006; Wells 2006: 179–80; Behar et al. 2008; Soares et al. 2012). Somewhere between East Africa and the Persian Gulf, haplogroup L3 bifurcated into haplogroups M and N (Wells 2006: 180–2, 186–7), which encompass the mtDNA pool of all ancient non-Africans (Torroni et al. 2006: 340). Descendants of haplogroup N began to spread across Europe around 40,000–50,000 years ago, coinciding with interstadial 12, which was the twelfth warm period during the quaternary glaciation (Torroni et al. 2006: 341). Haplogroup N eventually subdivided into haplogroups H, I, J, K, T, U, V, W and X, which, together with haplogroups N and M, comprise virtually all European mtDNA lineages (Torroni et al. 1996; Lacan et al. 2013).

The mtDNA results of only two individuals from a Classical context have been published. Both individuals (T118 and T313) are from the necropolis of Passo Marinaro (ca. fifth to third centuries BCE) at the Greek colony of Kamarina in Sicily, and they belong to European haplogroups I and H respectively (Sulosky Weaver 2015: 102–5). Today, haplogroup I is found throughout Europe with high concentrations in northern Eurasia, Greece and western Turkey. Haplogroup H is more widespread, as approximately 40–60 per cent of most European populations belong to this haplogroup (Loogväli et al. 2004; Wells 2006: 190–1, 197–8; Roostalu et al. 2007; Irwin et al. 2008). Although ancient and modern people from the same locale can display different haplogroups (Levy-Coffman 2005), mtDNA studies of archaeological human remains reveal distribution patterns for groups H and I that are similar to those of their modern counterparts. For instance, members of haplogroup H also have been found in Grave Circle B at Mycenae (ca. 1675–1550 BCE; Bouwman et al. 2008). So, what do these haplogroup designations and dispersal patterns tell us about the ancestry of individuals from the Passo Marinaro necropolis? They tell us very little, because even though mtDNA passes virtually unchanged between mothers and their offspring, it typifies an individual's remote ancestry. Moreover, mitochondrial genetic lineage comprises less than 1 per cent of a person's total ancestry (Nelson 2016).

Individuals who do not belong to European mitochondrial haplogroups are assumed to be of non-European matrilineal descent. Beginning with Africa, haplogroup L (also referred to as L0) and its derivatives L1 and L2 are primarily associated with sub-Saharan Africa, while another derivative, L3, is found in high frequencies in North and West Africa. As previously discussed, haplogroup M descended from members of haplogroup L3. Members of this group eventually left the continent, but the haplogroup still persists in East Africa (Wells 2006). Although individuals of African haplogroups have not yet been recovered from a Greek context, a Roman period Adult Male (F96a; ca. first to second centuries CE) belonging to haplogroup L was found at Vagnari in southern Italy. Oxygen isotope analysis indicated that the individual was not born locally (Prowse et al. 2010), but his strontium values are within the expected range for the Italian peninsula (see previous discussion for more on stable isotope analysis and migration; Emery et al. 2018). The burial does not differ significantly from other members of the cemetery, which was associated with a Roman villa. Nevertheless, his position within the household is uncertain, and excavators suggest that he could have worked at the estate as an enslaved person, freedman or tenant (Prowse et al. 2010). In this case, we have an individual from a Roman villa in southern Italy who is a member of haplogroup L, most likely born on the Italian peninsula, buried in a normative fashion. Despite the excavators' musings, there is no concrete evidence to suggest this person's position within the household, nor can we reconstruct his ethnic or ancestral identity. All we know is that his remote matrilineage stretches back to an African haplogroup.

Shifting to the Asian haplogroups, M and its derivatives C, D and Z are diffused throughout Asia, as are haplogroups A, B and F, which are derivatives of haplogroup N (Wells 2006). No individuals of clear East Asian identity have been recovered from Greek contexts, but an Adult Female (F37; ca. second to third centuries CE) from the aforementioned Roman cemetery at Vagnari belongs to haplogroup D. Like the other Vagnari burial, this individual also was not buried conspicuously; rather, '[h]er burial treatment was consistent with the other individuals in the cemetery, suggesting that her social identity was similar to the other "locals" at Vagnari, but it is certain that she or her maternal ancestors came from lands far to the east of the empire' (Prowse et al. 2010: 191).

In contrast to mtDNA, which is passed from a mother to all of her offspring, Y-chromosome genetic markers are patrilineal and transmitted virtually unchanged from fathers to sons. As with mtDNA, Y-chromosome haplogroups have been categorised according to geographical region and likewise comprise less than 1 per cent of a person's total ancestry (Nelson 2016). Approximately 80 per cent of European and Mediterranean Y chromosomes are primarily from two lineages: R1-M173 (i.e. haplogroup R1, genetic marker M173) and I-M170. It is likely that the R1-M173 lineage and its subclades, R1a and R1b, represent an ancient Eurasian marker that arrived in the Mediterranean region about 37,000 years ago, while the I-M170 lineage was introduced through a second migratory wave that occurred approximately 24,000 years ago and originated in the Near East (Quintana-Murci et al. 2003; Sazzini et al. 2014). Although there is considerably more geographical overlap among Y-chromosome haplogroups than among mtDNA haplogroups, primarily African lineages include A-M91 (the oldest and most diverse lineage which provides a link to the common male ancestor of all humans), B-M60, YAP, E-M96 (also attested in the Mediterranean) and E3a-M2, while East Asian lineages include C-M130, C3-M217, D-M174 (and subclades D1 and D2), L-M20, M-M4, O-M175 (and subclades O1a, O2 and O3) and Q-M242 (and subclade Q3-M3; Wells 2006).

Given the geographical overlap among haplogroups, Y-chromosome analysis is best suited for detecting migratory patterns (e.g. Mitchell et al. 1997; Francalacci et al. 2003). For instance, Cornelia Di Gaetano and colleagues used Y-chromosomal data from modern Sicilians to establish that there is a common genetic heritage between Sicilians and Greeks. They estimated that the Time to Most Recent Common Ancestor is approximately 2,380 years ago, which roughly corresponds to the traditionally accepted dates of Greek colonisation. Furthermore, they also perceived genetic heterogeneity between the eastern and western regions of the island, which could reflect differential ethnic settlement patterns over time (2009). Another study, by Sergio Tofanelli and colleagues, analysed both Y-chromosomal and mtDNA data from modern individuals from mainland Italy, Sicily, Greece, Albania, Croatia and western Anatolia in order to understand gene flow patterns related to the Greek colonisation of Sicily. They too found a clear signature of Greek ancestry (especially in eastern Sicily), and they also inferred sex-bias in the numbers of individuals involved in colonisation. They estimate that a few thousand (breeding) men and a few hundred (breeding) women comprised the original migrant wave (2015).

As this survey of the available evidence reveals, genetic tests have not been performed on individuals from Late Archaic/Classical mainland contexts, and few have derived from colonial ones. This is primarily because of the difficulties inherent in genetic testing. The challenges of recovering samples of replicable aDNA have already been discussed, but it must also be noted that genetic testing is expensive and destructive (i.e. the sample that is taken must be destroyed to extract the aDNA). Because of the destructive nature of the testing, it can be hard to obtain permission for DNA analyses. When permission is granted, the costs associated with genetic testing can deter archaeologists whose excavations run on a tight budget. Nevertheless, as illustrated by the biomolecular analyses from the Roman cemetery at Vagnari, genetic testing is one of multiple lines of evidence that must be considered together in order to shed light on aspects of ancient identity and behaviour, such as remote ancestry and migratory patterns. For this reason, it is hoped that DNA analysis, and other forms of biomolecular testing, will become standard procedure in the excavation and interpretation of non-normative burials so that we might have an additional source of information to better understand marginal burial treatment.

INTERSECTIONALITY

The case studies discussed here represent the limited bioarchaeological evidence of non-Greek ethnicity on the Greek mainland during the Late Archaic/Classical period. This dearth can most likely be attributed to small sample size and imprecise methods of detection. As explained in the Introduction, most mainland skeletal assemblages date to the prehistoric period, and Late Archaic/Classical populations are under-represented. Furthermore, methods for identifying non-Greeks in funerary contexts have tended to focus on material culture and burial rituals, and these would not have detected non-Greeks buried in normative Greek fashion. Indeed, funerary monuments from Athens demonstrate the high probability of this, as many non-Greeks chose to commemorate themselves in an Athenian manner, while elite Athenians were opting for non-Greek motifs. To address this deficit, Late Archaic/Classical mainland assemblages would benefit from reanalysis, especially the performance of bio-molecular studies, which are particularly well suited for the identification of migrants and non-Greeks that would have otherwise gone unnoticed.

Nevertheless, the bioarchaeological evidence we do have falls into different categories. The only instance in which there are clear material and biological indicators of non-Greek ethnicity is the female interred in the antechamber of Tomb II at Vergina. Material evidence of non-Greeks comes from Athens primarily in the form of funerary monuments, but these were removed from their original contexts and unassociated with human remains. The presence of human remains, however, is necessary for stable isotope, biodistance and ancestry analyses. Stable isotopic studies of strontium, oxygen and sulphur, coupled with the analysis of mortuary contexts, have yet to be performed on Late Archaic/Classical period assemblages from the Greek mainland. Studies of material from earlier periods have demonstrated shifts in Neolithic migratory patterns, aristocratic exogamy in Grave Circle A at Mycenae, and small-scale migration in Early Iron Age Thessaly. In a Greek Sicilian context, migrants/ foreign mercenaries were identified in a mass grave associated with the Battle of Himera, ca. 480 BCE. Likewise, there are no biodistance analyses of Late Archaic/Classical mainland assemblages, but studies of metric traits of Bronze Age populations have pointed to shifting settlement patterns in Lerna and supported the possibility of a Mycenaean invasion of Crete. In terms of non-metric traits, most studies derive from Late Archaic/Classical period colonial contexts, and these have been quite successful in separating populations with significant Greek influence from those that are predominantly non-Greek. Finally, studies of aDNA in Late Archaic/Classical assemblages are lacking, and it is yet another potential avenue for future research, as it can reveal information concerning migration and remote ancestry when used in conjunction with other forms of evidence.

Although non-Greeks were generally represented as inferior in ancient art and literature, the available funerary evidence does not indicate that they were socially marginalised. The probable Scythian female in the antechamber of Tomb II at Vergina was buried in an extraordinary way, but one that connoted wealth and prestige rather than marginalisation. Regarding the Athenian funerary monuments, the only status non-Greeks could have held in Athens was that of metic, and metic monuments are often difficult to distinguish from those of citizens. Moreover, metics are buried in accordance with cemetery conventions – interspersed among citizen monuments in the Kerameikos and clustered by geographical origins in the East, West, Piraeus and Sikelia Hill cemeteries. Likewise, all of the individuals flagged as migrants or non-Greeks in the biomolecular studies were buried in a normative manner. This pattern suggests that the Greek/non-Greek polarity might not have been as stark a divide as previously thought.

If non-Greek ethnicity alone was not sufficient cause for social marginalisation, the intersectionality of multiple marginalised factors may have been. The most obvious example of this is slavery, where non-Greek ethnicity and low socioeconomic status coalesce. As previously discussed, slavery was widespread, and most of the enslaved were non-Greek (Harrison 2019: 36). The preference for non-Greek enslaved individuals was rooted in widespread beliefs concerning the inferiority of non-Greeks (Aristotle, *Politics* 1254b19–1255b) and the understanding that enslaved persons who were linguistically and culturally distinct from one another would not be apt to organise and rise up in revolt (Plato, *Laws* 777d; Wrenhaven 2013: 2–4).

Over the course of the Late Archaic/Classical period, hundreds of thousands of enslaved individuals would have lived and died, but burials of the enslaved are virtually undetectable in the ancient Greek world. As discussed in Chapter 3, there are approximately thirty burials of skeletons that are either shackled or associated with shackles from half a dozen Classical and Hellenistic sites (Thompson 2003: 222). There is a possibility that the shackled burials contained enslaved people, but this identification is not definitive, as these individuals might also have been prisoners. The general lack of burials of the enslaved suggests that either slaves were buried non-normatively or we cannot distinguish the graves of the enslaved from those of impoverished individuals. If the latter is true, then there are three possibilities that account for our inability to distinguish free from enslaved: the buriers might have signified the difference in ephemeral rituals that leave no archaeological trace; the buriers might have signified status materially, but we are unaware of how they constructed their symbols; or it might not have been deemed important to differentiate between enslaved and free in the context of death. Although these hypotheses could be tested on cemeteries with large enslaved populations, the results of Ian Morris' attempt to do this at Laurion, where the enslaved were employed in the silver mines and elsewhere, were inconclusive (1998; 2011). Nevertheless, because there are so many missing burials of the enslaved, it is reasonable to assume that a substantial percentage of the enslaved population was buried non-normatively in a manner that underscored their social marginalisation and rendered them invisible in the archaeological record.

Despite the general lack of bioarchaeological evidence of non-Greek ethnicity in the Late Archaic/Classical Greek mainland, the small number of cases surveyed in this chapter suggest that non-Greek ethnicity or ancestry was not sufficient cause for social marginalisation. Rather, social marginalisation most likely occurred with intersectionality, when non-Greek ethnicity or ancestry was only one of multiple marginalising factors (e.g. low socioeconomic status) embodied by a single individual. These findings and their broader implications are explored further in the Conclusion.

NOTES

1. Herodotus' lineage is discussed in the *Suda*, the tenth-century Byzantine lexicon by Suidas.
2. For a historiography of ethnicity in archaeological thought, see Jones 1997.
3. The kotyle is called the Cup of Nestor because it is inscribed with an Euboean graffito: 'I am the cup of Nestor, good to drink from. Whoever drinks from this cup, may desire of fair-crowned Aphrodite seize him' (Osborne 2009: 109). The inscription references a story in the *Iliad* (11.632–7) about a golden cup that only Nestor could lift (Tartaron 2014). For a summary of the evidence of cultural hybridity in the graves of subadults at Pithekoussai, see Turfa 2018: 8–9.
4. Cultural hybridity is also evident in dietary practices. For instance, Laurie Reitsema and colleagues (2020) analysed stable carbon and nitrogen isotopes (see Chapter 2 for more on these analyses) from individuals interred in the East and West necropoleis (ca. seventh to fifth centuries BCE) at Himera (Sicily). They discovered that the diet consumed at Himera (primarily C_3 plants – cereals supplemented by plant 'relishes') was relatively uniform irrespective of socioeconomic status or ethnicity. This finding 'supports models of cultural hybridity in Greek colonization, wherein elements of different cultures mingled and recombined in new ways specific to the colony, rather than simple admixture or assimilation' (Reitsema et al. 2020).
5. For more on regional colonial identities, see Lomas 2004.
6. For catalogues of Greek exportation and expulsion, see Hansen and Nielsen 2004: 1363–4; Garland 2014: 253–63. For a catalogue of Greek exiles, see Garland 2014: 264–70.
7. See Anthony 1990 for a critique of this approach.
8. For linguistic methods associated with an earlier hypothesised migratory event (e.g. Drews 1988), see literature related to Proto-Indo-European (PIE). PIE is the linguistic reconstruction that represents the original language from which all Indo-European languages (including Greek) derived (J. Hall 2002: 36–8; Skomal and Polomé 1987; George et al. 2008). It is believed to have originated in the Pontic-Caspian steppe of Eastern Europe (ca. 4500–2500 BCE). As people migrated out of the region and became isolated from one another, the regional dialects they spoke slowly transformed into the Indo-European languages (Fortson 2004: 16). For more on Greek dialects, see Davies 2002.
9. Ancient authors refer to this event as the 'Return of the Heraclids', Dorian kings who were the descendants of Heracles (Rubinsohn 1975; Hooker 1979). Also, note that Philip Kaplan (2016) has demonstrated that most Greek origin stories involve displacement of some sort (the autochthonous Athenians are a notable exception) from either outside or within the Greek world.
10. Lead (Pb) isotope analysis has been used successfully to identify migrants (e.g. Montgomery et al. 2010; Shaw et al. 2016) and cultural affinity (e.g. Carlson 1996) in populations with known exposure to lead.
11. More stable isotopic studies have been performed on skeletal remains dating to the Roman period, and the proportion of migrants can range from as high as one third of the population (Portus Romae, ca. first to third centuries CE: Prowse et al. 2007;

also see Bruun 2010; Killgrove 2010; Prowse 2016) to approximately 7 per cent (Vagnari, ca. first to fourth centuries CE: Emery et al. 2018).

12. Note that Nafplioti's (2011) methods have been criticised. First, the majority of the measurements were made on archaeological tooth enamel and bone, and it should not be assumed that these are local to the depositional environment. Second, even though modern shells were also measured at some of the sites, these 'results were not correlated to the underlying geological formations, rather to "isopic zones", which are made up of geologies of varying ages' (Vaiglova et al. 2018).

13. Note, however, that non-locals have been identified in a colonial context through oxygen stable isotope analysis in Late Archaic/Classical period assemblages from Apollonia Pontica in Bulgaria (Keenleyside et al. 2011).

14. Note that shovelling is an ancient dental trait commonly seen on European Neanderthals and other fossil members of the genus *Homo* (Schwartz and Tattersall 2002: 93; Bailey 2006). Today, shovel-shaped incisors are often used to discern ancestry in modern populations because modern Asians and Native Americans have been found to have the highest frequencies of this trait (Scott and Turner 1997: 182–5; Sauer and Wankmiller 2009: 194).

15. Four of the Sicilian populations were local pre-colonial: Castiglione (seventeenth century BCE), Cefalù (seventeenth century BCE), Thapsos (sixteenth to fourteenth centuries BCE) and Plemmyrion (sixteenth to fourteenth centuries BCE). Six populations were post-colonial Greek: two from Syracuse (eighth century BCE and third century BCE), Carlentini (fifth to fourth centuries BCE), Leontini (fifth to fourth centuries BCE), Piscitello (fifth to fourth centuries BCE) and Kamarina (fifth to third centuries BCE). Three populations were local, non-Greek and post-colonial: two from Castiglione (eighth to sixth centuries BCE and seventh to sixth centuries BCE) and Monte Casasia (seventh to sixth centuries BCE). The fourteenth population derived from a Greek site that sustained a large local non-Greek contingent: Morgantina (eighth to fifth centuries BCE; Sulosky Weaver and Kyle forthcoming).

16. Biodistance studies have also been conducted on Scythian populations. For instance, craniometric data were compared among three groups: North Pontic Scythians of the steppe, North Pontic Scythians of the forest-steppe and non-Scythians (ca. fifth to third centuries BCE). The results indicated, among other conclusions, that Scythians of the North Pontic area were morphologically heterogeneous. This is unsurprising, as it has long been understood that the Scythian people were comprised of independent nomadic groups (Kozintsev 2007). A study of cranial non-metric variation, on the other hand, perceived morphological homogeneity among Late Scythian (third century BCE to fourth century CE) groups, and posited that the Scythian population was composed of local and Central Asian genetic components (Movsesian and Bakholdina 2017).

Conclusion: Marginality at the Intersections

The archaeological reconstruction of marginalised populations is complicated by a number of significant factors. This study, which focused on the Greek mainland during the Late Archaic/Classical period, was primarily impeded by a lack of known skeletal assemblages dating to the time frame under consideration. Another serious challenge was the general 'invisibility' of burials belonging to marginalised persons, as the marginalised are generally absent from Greek cemeteries. Although the reasons for their invisibility are not entirely clear, this lacuna most likely stems from the widespread practice of burying the marginalised outside of common burial grounds. As a result, these non-normative burials are left undiscovered when cemeteries are excavated.

This study focused exclusively on marginalising factors that can be discerned from burial contexts, namely physical disability, low socioeconomic status and non-Greek ethnicity or ancestry. It was found that traditional methods used to identify these characteristics could be ambiguous. For instance, methods for detecting non-Greeks in funerary contexts have tended to focus on material culture and burial rituals, but these would not have detected non-Greeks buried in normative Greek fashion and would have misidentified Greeks who embraced *en vogue* non-Greek motifs or objects. Funerary monuments from Athens, for example, demonstrate that many non-Greeks chose to commemorate themselves in an Athenian manner, while some elite Athenians were opting for non-Greek motifs. Complexities such as these illustrate the greater need for the contextual analysis of burial assemblages and careful consideration of all forms of available evidence. It is also clear that previously studied skeletal material would benefit from re-examination, especially in the area of biomolecular studies. In particular, stable isotopic studies of carbon and nitrogen can reveal dietary patterns, and stable isotopes of strontium, oxygen, sulphur and lead can identify migrants and potential non-Greeks.

Though sparse, there is bioarchaeological evidence of marginalising factors in burial assemblages from the Greek mainland dating to the Late Archaic/ Classical period. There are very few examples of physical impairment that derive from a Late Archaic/Classical context in the Greek mainland. Although the paucity of evidence prevents a focused synchronic study of the social ramifications of physical difference, widening the scope and considering case studies from different time periods allows for a diachronic glimpse into the ways in which disabled people were treated over time in ancient Greek society. One common denominator among the burials is that none of the individuals were buried in a non-normative fashion that would suggest social marginalisation. Although a number of previously discussed literary passages allude to the derision and mockery of the physically impaired, an individual can be ridiculed for an unusual or undesirable physical trait without experiencing social marginalisation, which appears to be the case in the ancient Greek world. Thus, the bioarchaeological evidence, though limited, suggests that the physically impaired were fully integrated into society and not socially marginalised.

Classical period burial assemblages are similar to one another and trend towards the egalitarian. There are, nevertheless, subtle indicators of low socioeconomic status present in some contexts. In particular, grave-good patterns have emerged in the northern Peloponnese to suggest that higher socioeconomic status was indicated by the inclusion of gender-specific objects. Health and dietary disparities have also been identified through stable isotopic analyses of carbon and nitrogen. At Athens, individuals of lower socioeconomic status had a higher prevalence of non-specific physiological stress markers, while at Thebes, individuals of lower status had a more varied diet which most likely reflected opportunistic eating patterns dictated by availability rather than choice. All of these burials are normative, and none reflect social marginalisation. It is assumed that they belong to free individuals – either citizens or metics – but it is also possible that some enslaved persons are represented as well.

There are few securely identified burials of the enslaved in the archaeological record, and it is reasonable to assume that a substantial percentage of the enslaved population was buried non-normatively in a manner that rendered them invisible in the archaeological record. It is also possible that their graves are indistinguishable from those of free impoverished individuals or that the enslaved are undetectable because they were buried in family plots in the same manner as free members of the household. There are, however, some clear examples of burials of the enslaved, and they are all non-normative. It is probable that some burials of persons with shackles belonged to enslaved persons, such as those interred in a mass grave at Pydna, where all the skeletal (roughly equal distribution of males and females, low average age at death, high incidence of physical and physiological stress markers) and material evidence (presence of restraining devices) suggests that the deceased were enslaved. Moreover, at Laurion, where one would expect to find large numbers of enslaved individuals associated with silver-mining, the burials deviate from the funerary norms of Attica in that there were fewer subadults, grave goods and cremation burials and some instances of multiple inhumation, a rarity in Attica. Furthermore, the diets of people from Laurion were more varied than those closer to the urban centre of Athens, possibly signifying that the enslaved, who literary sources tell us were primarily non-Greek, maintained their ethnic foodways.

The majority of the evidence of non-Greeks comes from Athens in the form of funerary monuments that were often removed from their original contexts and unassociated with human remains. As a result, these monuments are limited in what they can reveal, because human remains are necessary for the morphological and biomolecular studies that have successfully identified non-Greeks and other migrants in cross-cultural and colonial settings (i.e. stable isotope, biodistance and aDNA analyses). The only instance in which there are clear material and biological indicators of non-Greek ethnicity is the female interred in the antechamber of Tomb II at Vergina, who most likely identified as Scythian. She was buried non-normatively, but in a manner that connoted wealth and prestige rather than social marginalisation. Likewise, the non-Greek Athenian funerary monuments found *in situ* are typically not segregated, but interspersed among citizen monuments. This pattern suggests that the Greek/non-Greek polarity might not have been as stark a divide as previously thought.

From the small body of available evidence, what is clear is that the presence of just one culture-specific marginalising factor was not sufficient to warrant non-normative burial. Rather, it was the intersection of two or more marginalising factors that precipitated non-normative burial, which serves as an indicator of social marginalisation. The most obvious example of this is slavery, where non-Greek ethnicity, low socioeconomic status and physical difference coalesce. Most enslaved individuals (with the notable exception of Helots) were non-Greek, because non-Greeks were deemed to be inferior to Greeks and it was understood that enslaved persons who were linguistically and culturally distinct from one another would have difficulty organising a revolt. The enslaved occupied the lowest rung on the socioeconomic ladder, as they were bereft of identity, freedom and agency, rendering them non-persons and 'socially dead'. Indeed, they were often categorised as subhuman, which is reflected by the Greek pejorative term for the enslaved, *andrapoda*, meaning 'human-footed things'. Furthermore, the activities of the enslaved, typically servile and banausic in nature, were distasteful to Greeks of higher social standing and often led to accidents and permanent injuries. Indeed, physical impairment was often a distinguishing characteristic of the enslaved in the Greek world. For instance, Aesop, a non-Greek and formerly enslaved individual, was physically impaired and had a speech impediment, and Greeks who had been enslaved by the

Persians at Persepolis were severely mutilated by the time they were liberated by Alexander ca. 330 BCE.

Most of the mutilated Greeks at Persepolis were elderly, and their advanced age probably contributed to their social marginalisation. The age at which one was considered 'old' is unclear, but it can be argued that women transitioned to old age around the time of menopause (ca. ages 40–50), and men were most likely considered elderly when they were discharged from military service around age 60. Old age was a double-edged sword for the ancient Greeks, for even though it was associated with wisdom, experience and honour, it was also sorrowful, destructive and difficult. These contrasting attitudes towards the elderly – respect and derision – are also perceptible in Athenian drama and art. Yet, humans inevitably deteriorate as they age, and the Greeks recognised that old age precipitated physical impairment and weakness. At the intersection of advanced age and disability, we find an early (ca. 1190–1000 BCE) non-normative burial from Athens that is suggestive of social marginalisation. The individual, an Old Adult male, was buried in the prone position and displayed evidence of healed trauma that was most likely caused by interpersonal violence. Most notably, this individual's mobility was impaired by advanced degenerative joint disease that was probably caused by a systemic condition, such as calcium phosphate deposition disease.

It is also clear that gender served as a compounding marginalising characteristic. Sex-specific dietary and health disparities were evident in the Kerameikos and Plateia Kotzia, and the social marginalisation of intersectional women is supported by Greek literary sources. With the exception of wet nurses, who seem to have been beloved by families, enslaved women would have been socially marginalised for all the reasons enslaved men were (e.g. their non-Greek origins, low socioeconomic status, servile occupations and physical impairments). Other groups of free women would have also experienced prejudice and social marginalisation, especially metic women, whose foreign origins and erotic potential were often viewed as threats to the household and the state.

Literary sources reveal that intersectional individuals were targeted as scapegoats. The scapegoat ritual required a marginal person to be ritually expelled or executed in order to purify a community. While scapegoat predilections varied according to city – for example, enslaved individuals were selected at Abdera and Chaeronea, Leucas and Rhodes chose criminals, and Massilia designated the destitute – there was a widespread preference for disabled individuals, especially those with leg and foot impairments. Nevertheless, the common denominators among all scapegoats were that they were selected from the ranks of the socially marginalised and were of low socioeconomic status, which implies that it was their intersectionality that made them the perfect scapegoats. Indeed, the most oft cited scapegoats in ancient Greek literature, Thersites and Aesop, are clearly intersectional. Thersites was physically impaired, was prone to inappropriate behaviour and had an acerbic personality. From the moment he appeared in the Achaean assembly, it was clear that he was not a welcome member of the group, but rather a figure whose ugly appearance and brutish antics set him apart from the others. His marginal status is reinforced by the way in which he is scapegoated, namely through the public humiliation and beating he sustained at the hands of Odysseus. Aesop, on the other hand, was non-Greek, formerly enslaved, physically impaired (he had a curved spine and a 'pointed' head) and had a speech impairment. Despite his literary achievements, his life purportedly ended when he was thrown from a cliff at Delphi after his sharp wit angered influential people, who sentenced him to death on trumped-up charges of temple robbery.

Beyond scapegoating, it is possible that intersectionality also led to the purposeful burial of skeletons in wells. The non-normative deposition of skeletons in wells has been attested in Greek archaeological contexts from the Bronze Age through the Hellenistic period. Although full palaeopathological analyses are not available for all of the individuals interred in wells, comprehensive analyses of diachronic examples from Athens reveal striking commonalities. In particular, these skeletons appear to have had physical and neurological (e.g. from cranial trauma that could lead to traumatic brain injuries) abnormalities, which probably accounts for their non-normative burial in wells.

This study has shown that social marginalisation was more complex than previously thought. There is little evidence, at least in the burial record, to support the assertion that an individual would be socially marginalised in the ancient Greek world for a single reason, such as non-Greek ethnicity. Instead, social marginalisation was coupled with intersectionality, and only occurred when a person embodied two or more marginalising factors. Furthermore, social marginalisation had deleterious effects on the lives of intersectional individuals that typically manifest as health and dietary disparities. Thus, at a time when we are grappling with the magnitude of the effects of intersectionality on living persons, it is clear that intersectional individuals in the ancient Greek world were relegated to the margins of society in death as well as in life.

Bibliography

Abberley, P. (1987), 'The concept of oppression and the development of a social theory of disability', *Disability, Handicap and Society*, 2: 5–21.

Acsádi, G. and J. Nemeskéri (1970), *History of Human Life Span and Mortality*, Budapest: Akadémiai Kiadó.

Adams, W. Y., D. P. Van Gerven and R. S. Lewis (1978), 'The retreat from migrationism', *Annual Review of Anthropology*, 7: 483–532.

Agarwal, S. C. and B. A. Glencross (eds) (2011), *Social Bioarchaeology*, Oxford: Wiley-Blackwell.

Agarwal, S. C. and J. K. Wesp (eds) (2017), *Exploring Sex and Gender in Bioarchaeology*, Albuquerque: University of New Mexico Press.

Agelarakis, A. (2019), *Execution by Styrax in Ancient Thasos*, Oxford: Archaeopress.

Agelarakis, A. (2017), *Parian Polyandreia: The Late Geometric Funerary Legacy of Cremated Soldiers' Bones on Socio-Political Affairs and Military Organizational Preparedness in Ancient Greece*, Oxford: Archeopress.

Agelarakis, A. (2016), *A Dignified Passage Through the Gates of Hades: The Burial Custom of Cremation and the Warrior Order of Ancient Eleutherna*, Oxford: Archeopress.

Agelarakis, A. (2014a), '124. Woman's cranium with traces of surgical intervention', in Stampolidis and Tassoulas, pp. 256–9.

Agelarakis, A. (2014b), 'Veterans' wounds: Traces of ancient Greek surgeon-physicians', in Stampolidis and Tassoulas, pp. 76–85.

Agelarakis, A. (2013), 'On the anthropology project of 35 Salaminos Street site of Kerameikos, Athens: A brief account', in *Archaeologikes Symboles, Museum of Cycladic Art, Athens, Volume B: Attika, A' and G' Prehistoric and Classical Antiquities Authorities*, Athens: Museum of Cycladic Art, pp. 369–86.

Agelarakis, A. (2012), 'Arcane whispers echoed from funerary building M at Orthi Petra in Eleutherna: Contributions of anthropological research', in N. C. Stampolidis and M. Giannopoulou (eds) *Princesses' of the Mediterranean in the Dawn of History*, Athens: Museum of Cycladic Art, pp. 189–204.

Agelarakis, A. (2006), 'Early evidence of cranial surgical intervention in Abdera, Greece: A nexus to *On Head Wounds* of the Hippocratic Corpus', *International Journal of Mediterranean Archaeology and Archaeometry*, 6: 5–18.

Agelarakis, A. (2002), 'Appendix: Physical anthropological report on the cremated human remains of an individual retrieved from the Amphipolis agora', in M. Stamatapoulou and M. Yeroulanou (eds) *Excavating Classical Culture: Recent Archaeological Discoveries in Greece*, British Archaeological Reports International Series 1031, Oxford: Beazley Archive and BAR Publishing, pp. 72–4.

Agelarakis, A. (2000), 'Aspects of demography and palaeopathology among the Hellenistic *Abderetes* in Thrace, Greece', *Eulimene*, 1: 13–24.

Agelarakis, A. (1995), 'An anthology of Hellenes involved with the field of physical anthropology', *International Journal of Anthropology*, 10: 149–62.

Agelarakis, A. and Y. C. Serpanos (2010), 'Auditory exostoses, infracranial skeleto-muscular changes and maritime activities in Classical period Thasos island', *Mediterranean Archaeology and Archaeometry*, 10: 45–57.

Agelarakis, A. and F. Zafeiropoulou (2017), 'Parian *polyandreia* and the military legacy of Archilochus' forebears', in D. Mulliez and Z. Bonias (eds) *Thasos: Métropole et colonies. Actes du symposion international à la mémoire de Marina Sgourou, Thasos, 21–22 septembre 2006*, Paris: École française d'Athènes, pp. 47–64.

Ajootian, A. (1997), 'The only happy couple: Hermaphrodites and gender', in A. O. Koloski-Ostrow and C. L. Lyons (eds) *Naked Truths: Women, Sexuality, and Gender in Classical Art and Archaeology*, London: Routledge, pp. 220–42.

Akrigg, B. (2011), 'Demography and Classical Athens', in Holleran and Pudsey, pp. 37–59.

Akrigg, B. and R. Tordoff (eds) (2013), *Slaves and Slavery in Ancient Greek Comic Drama*, Cambridge: Cambridge University Press.

Aleshire, S. B. (1989), *The Athenian Asklepieion: The People, Their Dedications, and the Inventories*, Amsterdam: J. C. Gieben.

Alexander, R. T. (1998), 'Afterword: Toward an archaeological theory of culture contact', in J. G. Cusick (ed.) *Studies in Culture Contact*, Carbondale: Center for Archaeological Investigations, pp. 476–95.

Alexandridou, A. (2017), 'Special burial treatment for the "heroized" dead in the Attic countryside: The case of the elite cemetery of Vari', in X. Charalambidou and C. Morgan (eds) *Interpreting the Seventh Century BC: Tradition and Innovation*, Oxford: Archaeopress, pp. 281–91.

Alexandridou, A. (2015), 'Θάνατος: Review of publications on mortuary practices in Greece (10th–4th c. BC)', *AntCl*, 84: 237–58.

Alexandridou, A. (2013), 'Destructions at the grave: Ritual burning and breaking in 7th-century BC Attica', in J. Driessen (ed.) *Destruction: Archaeological, Philological and Historical Perspectives*, Louvain: Presses universitaires de Louvain, pp. 271–86.

Alexandridou, A. and O. Kaklamani (2018), 'Θάνατος II: Review of publications on mortuary practices in Greece (10th–4th c. BC)', *AntCl*, 87: 225–66.

Algee-Hewitt, B. F. B. (2017), 'Geographic substructure in craniometrics estimates of admixture for contemporary American populations', *Am J Phys Anthropol*, 164: 260–80.

Allen, K. H. (2003), 'Becoming the "Other": Attitudes and practices in Attic cemeteries', in Dougherty and Kurke, pp. 207–36.

Allman, D. (2013), 'The sociology of social inclusion', *SAGE Open*, January–March 2013: 1–16.

Almagor, E. and J. Skinner (eds) (2013), *Ancient Ethnography: New Approaches*, London: Bloomsbury.

Alston, R., E. Hall and L. Proffitt (eds) (2011), *Reading Ancient Slavery*, London: Bristol Classical Press.

Amundsen, D. W. (1987), 'Medicine and the birth of defective children: Approaches of the ancient world', in R. C. McMillan, H. T. Engelhardt Jr and S. E. Spicker (eds) *Euthanasia and the Newborn: Conflicts Regarding Saving Lives*, Boston: D. Reidel Publishing Company, pp. 3–22.

Amundsen, D. W. and C. J. Diers (1970), 'The age of menopause in Classical Greece and Rome', *Hum Biol*, 42: 79–86.

Anderson, J. and A. Carden-Coyne (2007), 'Enabling the past: New perspectives in the history of disability', *EurRHist*, 14: 447–57.

Andreau, J. and R. Descat (2011), *The Slave in Greece and Rome*, Madison: University of Wisconsin Press.

Andronikos, M. (1984), *Vergina: The Royal Tombs and the Ancient City*, Athens: Ekdotike Athinon.

Androutsos, G. (2006), 'Hermaphroditism in Greek and Roman antiquity', *Hormones*, 5: 214–17.

Angel, J. L. (1982), 'Ancient skeletons from Asine', in S. Dietz (ed.) *Asine II: Results of the Excavations East of the Acropolis 1970–1974*, Stockholm: Swedish Institute of Classical Studies in Athens, pp. 105–38.

Angel, J. L. (1976), 'Early Bronze Age Karataş: People and their cemeteries', *AJA*, 80: 385–91.

Angel, J. L. (1973), 'Human skeletons from grave circles at Mycenae', in G. E. Mylonas (ed.) *Ho Taphikos Kyklos ton Mykenon*, Athens: Athenais Archaiologikes Hetaireias, 379–97.

Angel, J. L. (1972), 'Late Bronze Age Cypriotes from Bamboula: The skeletal remains', in J. L. Benson, J. F. Daniel and E. Porada (eds) *Bamboula at Kourion: The Necropolis and the Finds*, Philadelphia: University of Pennsylvania Press, pp. 148–65.

Angel, J. L. (1971), *The People of Lerna: Analysis of a Prehistoric Aegean Population*, Princeton: American School of Classical Studies at Athens.

Angel, J. L. (1970), 'Ecology and population in the eastern Mediterranean', *WorldArch*, 4: 88–105.

Angel, J. L. (1961), 'Neolithic crania from Sotira: Appendix I', in P. Dikaios (ed.) *Sotira: A Neolithic Settlement in Cyprus*, Philadelphia: University of Pennsylvania Press, pp. 223–9.

Angel, J. L. (1953), 'The human remains from Khirokitia: Appendix II', in P. Dikaios (ed.) *Khirokitia: Final Report on the Excavation of a Neolithic Settlement in Cyprus on Behalf of the Department of Antiquities, 1936–1946*, Oxford: Oxford University Press, pp. 416–30.

Angel, J. L. (1946), 'Skeletal change in ancient Greece', *Am J Phys Anthropol*, 4: 69–97.

Angel, J. L. (1945), 'Skeletal material from Attica', *Hesperia*, 14: 279–363.

Angel, J. L. (1944), 'Greek teeth: Ancient and modern', *Hum Biol*, 16: 283–97.

Anthony, D. W. (1997), 'Prehistoric migration as a social process', in J. Chapman and H. Hamerow (eds) *Migrations and Invasions in Archaeological Explanation*, British Archaeological Reports International Series 664, Oxford: BAR Publishing, pp. 21–32.

Anthony, D. W. (1990), 'Migration in archaeology: The baby and the bathwater', *American Anthropologist*, 92: 895–914.

Antikas, T. G. and L. K. Wynn-Antikas (2016), 'New finds from the cremations in Tomb II at Aegae point to Philip II and a Scythian princess', *IJO*, 26: 682–92.

Anton, S. C. (1989), 'Intentional cranial vault deformation and induced changes of the cranial base and face', *Am J Phys Anthropol*, 79: 253–67.

Antonaccio, C. M. (2010), '(Re)defining ethnicity: Culture, material culture, and identity', in Hales and Hodos, pp. 32–53.

Antonaccio, C. M. (2005), 'Excavating colonization', in H. Hurst and S. Owen (eds) *Ancient Colonizations: Analogy, Similarity and Difference*, London: Duckworth, pp. 97–114.

Antonaccio, C. M. (2003), 'Hybridity and the cultures within Greek culture', in Dougherty and Kurke, pp. 57–74.

Antonaccio, C. M. (2001), 'Ethnicity and colonization', in Malkin, pp. 113–57.

Antoniou, G. P. and A. N. Angelakis (2015), 'Latrines and wastewater sanitation technologies in ancient Greece', in P. D. Mitchell (ed.) *Sanitation, Latrines and Intestinal Parasites in Past Populations*, Burlington, VT: Ashgate, pp. 41–68.

Appleby, J. et al. (2014), 'The scoliosis of Richard III, last Plantagenet king of England: Diagnosis and clinical significance', *Lancet*, 383: 1944.

Archibald, Z. H. (2000), 'Space, hierarchy, and community in Archaic and Classical Macedonia, Thessaly, and Thrace', in Brock and Hodkinson, pp. 212–33.

Armelagos, G. J. and A. H. Goodman (1998), 'Race, racism, and anthropology', in A. H. Goodman and T. L. Leatherman (eds) *Building a New Biocultural Synthesis: Political-Economic Perspectives on Human Biology*, Ann Arbor: University of Michigan Press, pp. 359–77.

Armelagos, G. J. and D. P. Van Gerven (2003), 'A century of skeletal biology and paleopathology: Contrasts, contradictions, and conflicts', *American Anthropologist*, 105: 53–64.

Arrington, N. T. (2015), *Ashes, Images, and Memories: The Presence of the War Dead in Fifth-Century Athens*, Oxford: Oxford University Press.

Arrington, N. T. (2011), 'Inscribing defeat: The commemorative dynamics of the Athenian casualty lists', *ClAnt*, 30: 179–212.

Arrington, N. T. (2010), 'Topographic semantics: The location of the Athenian public cemetery and its significance for the nascent democracy', *Hesperia*, 79: 499–539.

Aspöck, E. (2008), 'What actually is a "deviant burial"? Comparing German-language and Anglophone research on "deviant burials"', in Murphy, pp. 17–34.

Aterman, K. (1965a), 'Why did Hephaestus limp?', *American Journal of Diseases of Children*, 110: 704–5.

Aterman, K. (1965b), 'Why did Hephaestus limp?', *American Journal of Diseases of Children*, 109: 381–92.

Atkin, A. (2017), 'Race, definition, and science', in Zack, pp. 139–49.

Aufderheide, A. C. and C. Rodríguez-Martín (2005), *The Cambridge Encyclopedia of Human Paleopathology*, Cambridge: Cambridge University Press.

Baba, K. (1984), 'On Kerameikos Inv. I 388 (Seg. XXII, 79): A note on the formation of the Athenian metic-status', *BSA*, 79: 1–5.

Bäbler, B. (1998), *Fleissige Thrakerinnen und wehrhafte Skythen: Nichtgriechen im klassischen Athen und ihre archäologische Hinterlassenschaft*, Stuttgart: B. G. Teubner.

Bailey, S. (2006), 'Beyond shovel-shaped incisors: Neandertal dental morphology in a comparative context', *Periodicum Biologorum*, 108: 253–67.

Bakewell, G. W. (2013), *Aeschylus's Suppliant Women: The Tragedy of Immigration*, Madison: University of Wisconsin Press.

Bakewell, G. [W.] (2008/9), 'Forbidding marriage: Neaira 16 and metic spouses at Athens', *ClJ*, 104: 97–109.

Bakewell, G. [W.] (1999a), 'Εὔνους καὶ πόλει σωτήριος / μέτοικος: Metics, tragedy, and civic ideology', *Syllecta Classica*, 10: 43–64.

Bakewell, G. [W.] (1999b), 'Lysias 12 and Lysias 31: Metics and Athenian citizenship in the aftermath of the Thirty', *GrRomByzSt*, 40: 5–12.

Bakewell, G. W. (1997), 'Μετοικία in the *Supplices* of Aeschylus', *ClAnt*, 16: 209–28.

Baker, J. L. (2012), *The Funeral Kit: Mortuary Practices in the Archaeological Record*, Walnut Creek, CA: Left Coast Press.

Barbanera, M. (2015), 'The lame god: Ambiguities of Hephaistos in the Greek mythical realm', in Boschung et al., pp. 177–210.

Bardel, R. (2002), 'Eunuchizing Agamemnon: Clytemnesta, Agamemnon and *maschalismos*', in Tougher, pp. 51–70.

Barney, D. D. (2004), *The Network Society*, Cambridge: Polity Press.

Barth, F. (ed.) (1969), *Ethnic Groups and Boundaries: The Social Organization of Cultural Difference*, Boston: Little and Brown.

Bartsiokas, A. (2000), 'The eye injury of King Philip II and the skeletal evidence from the royal tomb II at Vergina', *Science*, 288: 511–14.

Bartsiokas, A. et al. (2015), 'The lameness of King Philip II and Royal Tomb I at Vergina, Macedonia', *Proc Natl Acad Sci U S A*, 112: 9844–8.

Bartsocas, C. S. (1982), 'An introduction to ancient Greek genetics and skeletal dysplasias', in C. J. Papadatos and C. S. Bartsocas (eds) *Skeletal Dysplasias: Proceedings of the Third International Clinical Genetics Seminar, Held in Athens, Greece, May 9–13, 1982*, New York: A. R. Liss, pp. 3–13.

Bartsocas, C. S. (1977), 'The stature of Greeks of the Pylos area during the second millennium B.C.', *Hippocrates*, 2: 157–60.

Bartsocas, C. S. (1973), 'Cleidocranial dysostosis in Homer', *Archeia Hellin Pediátr Hetair*, 36: 107–9.

Bass, W. M. (2005), *Human Osteology: A Laboratory and Field Manual*, fifth edition, Columbia, MO: Missouri Archaeological Society.

Battles, H. (2011), 'Exploring the prospects for an integrated anthropology of disability', *vis-à-vis: Explorations in Anthropology*, 11: 107–24.

Baughan, E. P. (2008), 'Lale Tepe: A late Lydian tumulus near Sardis. The klinai', in N. D. Cahill (ed.) *Love for Lydia: A Sardis Anniversary Volume Presented to Crawford H. Greenewalt, Jr.*, Cambridge, MA: Harvard University Press, pp. 49–79.

Baziotopoulou-Valavani, E. (2002), 'A mass burial from the cemetery of Kerameikos', in M. Stamatopoulou and M. Yeroulanou (eds) *Excavating Classical Culture: Recent Archaeological Discoveries in Greece*, British Archaeological Reports International Series 1031, Oxford: The Beazley Archive and BAR Publishing, pp. 187–202.

Beauchesne, P. and S. C. Agarwal (eds) (2018), *Children and Childhood in Bioarchaeology*, Gainesville: University Press of Florida.

Beaumont, L. A. (2012), *Childhood in Ancient Athens: Iconography and Social History*, London: Routledge.

Beaumont, L. A. (2000), 'The social status and artistic presentation of "adolescence" in fifth century Athens', in Sofaer Derevenski, pp. 39–50.

Beaumont, L. A. (1994), 'Constructing a methodology for the interpretation of childhood age in Classical Athenian iconography', *Archaeological Review from Cambridge*, 13: 81–96.

Beazley, J. D. (1971), *Paralipomena: Additions to Attic Black-Figure Vase-Painters and to Attica Red-Figure Vase-Painters*, second edition, Oxford: Clarendon Press.

Beazley, J. D. (1963), *Attic Red-Figure Vase-Painters*, second edition, Oxford: Clarendon Press.

Beck, H. and P. J. Smith (eds) (2018), *Megarian Moments: The Local World of an Ancient Greek City-State*, Montreal: McGill University Library and Archives.

Becker, H. S. (1973), *Outsiders: Studies in the Sociology of Deviance*, New York: The Free Press.

Becker, M. J. (2017), 'Spytihněv I (875–915 CE), Duke of Bohemia: An osteobiographic perspective on social status and stature in the emerging Czech state', in Klaus et al., pp. 82–110.

Becker, M. J. (1999a), 'Calculating stature from in situ measurements of skeletons and from long bone lengths: An historical perspective leading to a test of Formicola's hypothesis at 5th century BCE Satricum, Lazio, Italy', *Rivista di Antropologia*, 77: 225–47.

Becker, M. J. (1999b), 'Human skeletons from the Greek emporium of Pithekoussai on Ischia (NA): Culture contact and biological change in Italy after the 8th century B.C.', in R. H. Tykot, J. Marter and J. E. Robb (eds) *Social Dynamics of the Prehistoric Central Mediterranean*, London: Accordia Research Institute, pp. 217–29.

Becker, M. J. (1995), 'Human skeletal remains from the pre-colonial Greek emporium of Pithekoussai on Ischia (NA): Culture contact in Italy from the early VIII to the II century BCE', in N. Christie (ed.) *Settlement and Economy in Italy, 1500 BC–AD 1500*, Oxford: Oxbow Books, pp. 273–81.

Becker, M. J. and L. Salvadei (1992), 'Analysis of the human skeletal remains from the cemetery of Osteria dell'Osa', in A. M. Bietti Sestieri (ed.) *La necropoli Laziale di Osteria dell'Osa*, Rome: Quasar, pp. 53–191.

Behar, D. M. et al. (2008), 'The dawn of human matrilineal diversity', *Am J Hum Genet*, 82: 1130–40.

Belcastro, M. G. et al. (2011), '*Hyperostosis frontalis interna* (HFI) and castration: The case of the famous singer Farinelli (1705–1782)', *J Anat*, 219: 632–7.

Bendann, E. (1930), *Death Customs: An Analytical Study of Burial Rites*, New York: Alfred A. Knopf.

Bérard, C. (2000), 'The image of the Other and the foreign hero', in Cohen, pp. 390–412.

Bergemann, J. (1997), *Demos und Thanatos: Untersuchungen zum Wertsystem der Polis im Spiegel der attischen Grabreliefs des 4. Jahrhunderts v. Chr. Und zur Funktion der gleichzeitigen Grabbauten*, Munich: Biering & Brinkmann.

Berkson, G. (2004), 'Intellectual and physical disabilities in prehistory and early civilization', *Ment Retard*, 42: 195–208.

Bernal, M. (2006), *Black Athena: The Afroasiatic Roots of Classical Civilization, Volume III: The Linguistic Evidence*, New Brunswick, NJ: Rutgers University Press.

Bernal, M. (and D. C. Moore, ed.) (2001), *Black Athena Writes Back: Martin Bernal Responds to his Critics*, Durham: Duke University Press.

Bernal, M. (1991), *Black Athena: Afro-Asiatic Roots of Classical Civilization, Volume II: The Archaeological and Documentary Evidence*, New Brunswick, NJ: Rutgers University Press.

Bernal, M. (1987), *Black Athena: Afro-Asiatic Roots of Classical Civilization, Volume I: The Fabrication of Ancient Greece, 1785–1985*, New Brunswick, NJ: Rutgers University Press.

Berry, A. C. and R. J. Berry (1967), 'Epigenetic variation in the human cranium', *J Anat*, 101: 361–79.

Bertolino, F. F. Alaimo and S. Vassallo (2015), 'Battles of Himera (480 and 409 B.C.): Analysis of biological finds and historical interpretation. Experiences of restoration in the ruins of Himera 2008–2010', *Conservation Science in Cultural Heritage*, 15: 27–40.

Betti, L. et al. (2010), 'The relative role of drift and selection in shaping the human skull', *Am J Phys Anthropol*, 141: 76–82.

Bhabha, H. (1994), *The Location of Culture*, London: Routledge.

Billson, J. M. (2005), 'No owner of soil: Redefining the concept of marginality', in R. M. Dennis (ed.) *Marginality, Power, and Social Structure: Issues in Race, Class, and Gender Analysis*, Oxford: Elsevier, pp. 29–47.

Bindman, D. and H. L. Gates (eds) (2010), *The Image of the Black in Western Art, Volume I: From the Pharaohs to the Fall of the Roman Empire*, new edition, Cambridge, MA: Harvard University Press.

Binford, L. R. (1971), 'Mortuary practices: Their study and their potential', in J. Brown (ed.) *Approaches to the Social Dimensions of Mortuary Practices: Memoir of the Society for American Archaeology 25*, Washington, DC: Society for American Archaeology, pp. 6–29.

Binsfeld, W. (1956), 'Grylloi: Ein Beitrag zur Geschichte der antiken Karrikatur', PhD diss., University of Cologne.

Bintliff, J. (2012), 'Are there alternatives to "red-figure vase people"? Identity, multi-ethnicity, and migration in ancient Greece', in Cifani and Stoddart, pp. 51–63.

Bintliff, J. (2010), 'Classical Greek urbanism: A social Darwinian approach', in Rosen and Sluiter, pp. 15–41.

Birchler Émery, P. (1999), 'Old-age iconography in Archaic Greek art', *MeditArch*, 12: 17–28.

Bisel, S. (1990) 'Anthropologische Untersuchungen', in W. Kovacsovics (ed.) *Die Eckterrasse an der Gräberstrasse des Kerameikos*, Berlin: De Gruyter, pp. 151–9.

Blaikie, P. and H. Brookfield (eds) (1987), *Land Degradation and Society*, London: Methuen.

Blakely, S. (2000), 'Madness in the body politic: Kouretes, korybantes, and the politics of shamanism', in Hubert, pp. 119–27.

Bliquez, L. J. (1995), 'Prosthetics in Classical antiquity: Greek, Etruscan, and Roman prosthetics', in W. Haase and H. Temporini (eds) *Aufstieg und Niedergang der Römischen Welt*, Berlin: De Gruyter, pp. 2640–76.

Blok, J. H. (2009a), 'Gentrifying genealogy: On the genesis of the Athenian autochthony myth', in U. Dill and C. Walde (eds) *Antike Mythen: Medien, Transformationen, und Konstruktionen*, Berlin: De Gruyter, pp. 251–75.

Blok, J. H. (2009b), 'Perikles' Citizenship Law: A new perspective', *Historia*, 58: 141–70.

Blok, J. H. (1995), *The Early Amazons: Modern and Ancient Perspectives on a Persistent Myth*, Leiden: Brill.

Boardman, J. (2014), 'Teaching in the west', *AncWestEast*, 13: 213–14.

Boardman, J. (1999), *The Greeks Overseas: Their Early Colonies and Trade*, fourth edition, London: Thames and Hudson.

Boardman, J. (1995), *Greek Sculpture: The Late Classical Period*, London: Thames and Hudson.

Boardman, J. (1994), *The Diffusion of Classical Art in Antiquity*, Princeton: Princeton University Press.

Boardman, J. (1991), *Athenian Black Figure Vases*, corrected edition, London: Thames and Hudson.

Bodel, J. and W. Scheidel (eds) (2017), *On Human Bondage: After Slavery and Social Death*, Chichester: John Wiley & Sons.

Boegehold, A. L. (1994), 'Perikles' Citizenship Law of 451/0 B.C.', in Boegehold and Scafuro, pp. 57–66.

Boegehold, A. L. and A. C. Scafuro (eds) (1994), *Athenian Identity and Civic Ideology*, Baltimore: Johns Hopkins University Press.

Boëldieu-Trevet, J. (2018), 'Des nouveau-nés malformés et un roi boiteux: histoires Spartiates', *Pallas*, 106: 213–28.

Bohak, G. (2005), 'Ethnic portraits in Greco-Roman literature', in Gruen, pp. 207–37.

Bonfante, L. (ed.) (2011), *The Barbarians of Ancient Europe: Realities and Interactions*, Cambridge: Cambridge University Press.

Bonfante, L. (1989), 'Nudity as a costume in Classical art', *AJA*, 93: 543–70.

Bonnard, J.-B. (2018), 'L'exposition des nouveau-nés handicapés dans le monde grec, entre réalités et mythes: un point sur la question', *Pallas*, 106: 229–40.

Bonogofsky, M. (2011), 'Contextualizing the human head: An introduction', in M. Bonogofsky (ed.) *The Bioarchaeology of the Human Head: Decapitation, Decoration, and Deformation*, Gainesville: University Press of Florida, pp. 1–47.

Borrego, J. Jr, E. Ortiz-González and T. D. Gissandaner (2019), 'Ethnic and cultural considerations', in S. N. Compton, M. A. Villabø and H. Kristensen (eds) *Pediatric Anxiety Disorders*, Cambridge, MA: Academic Press, pp. 461–97.

Boschung, D., A. Shapiro and F. Wascheck (eds) (2015), *Bodies in Transition: Dissolving the Boundaries of Embodied Knowledge*, Paderborn: Wilhelm Fink.

Bosman, P. (ed.) (2009), *Mania: Madness in the Greco-Roman World*, Pretoria: Classical Association of South Africa.

Bourbou, C. (2013), 'The imprint of emotions surrounding the death of children in antiquity', in A. Chaniotis and P. Ducrey (eds) *Unveiling Emotions II. Emotions in Greece and Rome: Texts, Images, Material Culture*, Stuttgart: Franz Steiner, pp. 331–50.

Bourbou, C. (2005), 'Let the bones talk: The study of human skeletal collections in Greece', in N. M. Kennell and J. E. Tomlinson (eds) *Ancient Greece at the Turn of the Millennium: Recent Work and Future Perspectives. Proceedings of the Athens Symposium, 18–20 May 2001*, Athens: Publications of the Canadian Archaeological Institute at Athens 4, pp. 173–86.

Bourbou, C. and S. J. Garvie-Lok (2009), 'Breastfeeding and weaning patterns in Byzantine times: Evidence from human remains and written sources', in A. Papaconstantinou and A.-M. Talbot (eds) *Becoming Byzantine: Children and Childhood in Byzantium*, Washington, DC: Dumbarton Oaks, pp. 65–84.

Bourbou, C. and V. Niniou-Kindeli (2009), 'A Hellenistic mass burial in the city of Chania, Crete (Greece): What can we infer about the fate of the individuals buried?', in L. Buchet et al. (eds), *Vers une anthropologie des catastrophes: actes du 9eme Journées Anthropologiques de Valbonne (Valbonne, 22–24 mai 2007)*, Antibes: Éditions APDCA/INED, pp. 273–83.

Bourbou, C. and P. Themelis (2010), 'Child burials at ancient Messene', in A.-M. Guimier-Sorbets and Y. Morizot (eds) *L'enfant et la mort dans l'Antiquité I: nouvelles recherches dans les necropoles grecques. Le signalement des tombes d'enfants*, Paris: De Boccard, pp. 111–28.

Bourbou, C. et al. (2013), 'Nursing mothers and feeding bottles: Reconstructing breastfeeding and weaning patterns in Greek Byzantine populations (6th–15th centuries AD) using carbon and nitrogen stable isotope ratios', *JAS*, 40: 3903–13.

Bourdieu, P. (1977), *Outline of a Theory of Practice*, Cambridge: Cambridge University Press.

Boutin, A. T. (2016), 'Exploring the social construction of disability: An application of the bioarchaeology of personhood model to a pathological skeleton from ancient Bahrain', *IJPP*, 12: 17–28.

Boutin, A. T. and B. W. Porter (2014), 'Commemorating disability in early Dilmun: Ancient and contemporary tales from the Peter B. Cornwall Collection', in B. W. Porter and A. T. Boutin (eds) *Remembering the Dead in the Ancient Near East: Recent Contributions from Bioarchaeology and Mortuary Archaeology*, Boulder: University Press of Colorado, pp. 97–132.

Bouwman, A. S. et al. (2009), 'Kinship in Aegean prehistory? Ancient DNA in human bones from mainland Greece and Crete', *BSA*, 104: 293–309.

Bouwman, A. S. et al. (2008), 'Kinship between burials from Grave Circle B at Mycenae revealed by ancient DNA typing', *JAS*, 35: 2580–4.

Bradley, K. and P. Cartledge (eds) (2011), *The Cambridge World History of Slavery, Volume I: The Ancient Mediterranean World*, Cambridge: Cambridge University Press.

Brah, A. and A. Phoenix (2004), '"Ain't I a woman?" Revisiting intersectionality', *Journal of International Women's Studies*, 5: 75–86.

Brandmeir, N. et al. (2018), 'The leg wound of Philip II of Macedonia', *Cureus*, 10: e2501.

Braund, D. (2011), 'The slave supply in Classical Greece', in Bradley and Cartledge, pp. 12–33.

Bredberg, E. (1999), 'Writing disability history: Problems, perspectives and sources', *Disability and Society*, 14: 189–201.

Bremmer, J. N. (2015), 'A transsexual in Archaic Greece: The case of Kaineus', in Boschung et al., pp. 265–86.

Bremmer, J. N. (2010), 'Hephaistos sweats or how to construct an ambivalent god', in J. N. Bremmer and A. Erskine (eds) *The Gods of Ancient Greece: Identities and Transformations*, Edinburgh: University of Edinburgh Press, pp. 193–208.

Bremmer, J. N. (1983), 'Scapegoat rituals in ancient Greece', *HSCP*, 87: 299–320.

Brennan, M. (2016), 'Lame Hephaistos', *BSA*, 111: 163–81.

Briant, P. (2002), 'History and ideology: The Greeks and Persian "decadence"', in Harrison, pp. 193–210.

Brisenden, S. (1986), 'Independent living and the medical model of disability', *Disability, Handicap and Society*, 1: 173–8.

Brisson, L. (2002), *Sexual Ambivalence: Androgyny and Hermaphroditism in Graeco-Roman Antiquity*, Berkeley: University of California Press.

Brock, R. and S. Hodkinson (eds) (2000), *Alternatives to Athens: Varieties of Political Organization and Community in Ancient Greece*, Oxford: Oxford University Press.

Broder, M. (2011), 'Review of Erich S. Gruen, *Rethinking the Other in Antiquity*', *BMCR*, 2011.08.24 <https://bmcr.brynmawr.edu/2011/2011.08.24> (last accessed 11 May 2020).

Brown, K. (2000), 'Ancient DNA applications in human osteoarchaeology: Achievements, problems and potential', in Cox and Mays, pp. 455–73.

Brown, T. and K. Brown (2011), *Biomolecular Archaeology: An Introduction*, Oxford: Wiley-Blackwell.

Browning, R. (2002), 'Greeks and Others: From antiquity to the Renaissance', in Harrison, pp. 257–77.

Brück, J. (2021), 'Ancient DNA, kinship and relational identity in Bronze Age Britain', *Antiquity*, 95: 228–37.

Bruun, C. (2010), 'Water, oxygen isotopes, and immigration to Ostia-Portus', *JRA*, 23: 109–32.

Buchner, G. (1975), 'Nuovi aspetti e problemi posti degli scavi di Pitecusa con particolari considerazioni sulle oreficerie de stile orientalizzante antico', in *Contribution à l'étude de la société et de la colonisation eubéennes*, Naples: Cahiers du Centre Jean Bérard 2, pp. 59–86.

Buchner, G. and D. Ridgway (1993), *Pithekoussai*. Monumenti Antichi dei Lincei 55. Rome: Giorgio Bretschneider.

Buckley, R. et al. (2013), '"The king in the car park": New light on the death and burial of Richard III in the Grey Friars church, Leicester, in 1485', *Antiquity*, 87: 519–38.

Buikstra, J. E. and A. Lagia (2009), 'Bioarchaeological approaches to Aegean archaeology', in Schepartz et al., pp. 7–29.

Buikstra, J. E. and D. H. Ubelaker (eds) (1994), *Standards for Data Collection from Human Skeletal Remains*, Fayetteville: Arkansas Archaeological Survey Research Series.

Buikstra, J. E., S. R. Frankenberg and L. W. Konigsberg (1990), 'Skeletal biological distance studies in American physical anthropology: Recent trends', *Am J Phys Anthropol*, 82: 1–7.

Bullough, V. L. (2002), 'Eunuchs in history and society', in Tougher, pp. 1–18.

Bundrick, S. D. (2019), *Athens, Etruria, and the Many Lives of Greek Figured Pottery*, Madison: University of Wisconsin Press.

Burchardt, T., J. Le Grand and D. Piachaud (2002), 'Introduction', in J. Hills, J. Le Grant and D. Piachaud (eds) *Understanding Social Exclusion*, Oxford: Oxford University Press, pp. 1–12.

Burford, A. (1972), *Craftsmen in Greek and Roman Society*, Ithaca, NY: Cornell University Press.

Burgers, G.-J. (2012), 'Landscape and identity of Greek colonists and indigenous communities in southeast Italy', in Cifani and Stoddart, pp. 64–76.

Burkert, W. (1992), *The Orientalizing Revolution: Near Eastern Influences of Greek Culture in the Early Archaic Age*, Cambridge, MA: Harvard University Press.

Burmeister, S. (2017), 'The archaeology of migration: What can and should it accomplish?', in H. Meller et al. (eds) *Migration and Integration from Pre-history to the Middle Ages*, Halle: Landesmuseums für Vorgeschichte Halle, pp. 57–68.

Burns, K. A. (1999), *Forensic Anthropology Training Manual*, Upper Saddle River: Prentice Hall Publishing.

Byrnes, J. F. and J. L. Muller (eds) (2017a), *Bioarchaeology of Impairment and Disability: Theoretical, Ethnohistorical, and Methodological Perspectives*, New York: Springer International.

Byrnes, J. F. and J. L. Muller (2017b), 'Mind the gap: Bridging disability studies and bioarchaeology – An introduction', in Byrnes and Muller, pp. 1–15.

Calame, C. (2005), *Masks of Authority: Fiction and Pragmatics in Ancient Greek Poetics*, Ithaca, NY: Cornell University Press.

Canevaro, M. and D. Lewis (2014), '*Khoris oikountes* and the obligations of freedmen in Late Classical and Early Hellenistic Athens', *Incidenza dell'Antico*, 12: 91–121.

Carawan, E. (2008), 'Pericles the Younger and the Citizenship Law', *CJ*, 103: 383–406.

Carey, C. (1991), 'Apollodoros' mother: The wives of enfranchised aliens in Athens', *ClQ*, 41: 84–9.

Carlson, A. K. (1996), 'Lead isotope analysis of human bone for addressing cultural affinity: A case study from Rocky Mountain House, Alberta', *JAS*, 23: 557–67.

Carr, H. G. (1960), 'Some dental characteristics of the Middle Minoans', *Man*, 60: 119–22.

Carter, J. C. (ed.) (1998), *The Chora of Metaponto: The Necropoleis*, vols 1 and 2, Austin: University of Texas Press.

Cartledge, P. (2011), 'The Helots: A contemporary review', in Bradley and Cartledge, pp. 74–90.

Cartledge, P. (2002), *The Greeks: A Portrait of Self and Others*, second edition, Oxford: Oxford University Press.

Castriota, D. (2000), 'Justice, kingship, and imperialism: Rhetoric and reality in fifth-century B.C. representations following the Persian Wars', in Cohen, pp. 443–80.

Cecchet, L. (2017), 'Re-shaping and re-founding citizen bodies: The case of Athens, Cyrene, and Camarina', in L. Cecchet and A. Busetto (eds) *Citizens in the Graeco-Roman World: Aspects of Citizenship from the Archaic Period to AD 212*, Leiden: Brill, pp. 50–77.

Chadwick, J. (1976), 'Who were the Dorians?', *PP*, 31: 103–17.

Challis, D. (2013), *The Archaeology of Race: The Eugenic Ideas of Francis Galton and Flinders Petrie*, New York: Bloomsbury.

Chamberlain, A. T. (2006), *Demography in Archaeology*, Cambridge: Cambridge University Press.

Chamberlain, A. T. and M. Parker Pearson (2001), *Earthly Remains: The History and Science of Preserved Human Bodies*, Oxford: Oxford University Press.

Champion, T. C. (ed.) (1989), *Centre and Periphery: Comparative Studies in Archaeology*, London: Unwin Hyman.

Charles, R. P. (1958), 'Étude anthropologique des nécropoles d'Argos: contribution à l'étude des populations de la Grèce antique', *Bulletin de correspondance hellénique*, 82: 268–313.

Charlier, P. (2008), 'The value of palaeoteratology and forensic pathology for the understanding of atypical burials: Two Mediterranean examples from the field', in Murphy, pp. 57–70.

Chenal-Velarde, I. (2006), 'Food, rituals? The exploitation of dogs from Eretria (Greece) during the Helladic and Hellenistic periods', in L. M. Snyder and E. A. Moore (eds) *Dogs and People in Social, Working, Economic or Symbolic Interaction*, Oxford: Oxbow Books, pp. 24–31.

Cheverud, J. M. (1988), 'A comparison of genetic and phenotypic correlations', *Evolution*, 42: 958–68.

Cheverud, J. M. et al. (1992), 'Effects of front-occipital artificial cranial vault modification on the cranial base and face', *Am J Phys Anthropol*, 88: 323–45.

Christensen, J. (2015), 'Diomedes' foot wound and Homeric reception of myth', in J. M. González (ed.) *Diachrony: Diachronic Studies of Ancient Greek Literature and Culture*, Berlin: De Gruyter, pp. 17–42.

Cifani, G. and S. Stoddart (eds) (2012), *Landscape, Ethnicity and Identity in the Archaic Mediterranean Area*, Oxford: Oxbow Books.

Clay, J. S. (2003), *Hesiod's Cosmos*, Cambridge: Cambridge University Press.

Clemente, F. et al. (2021), 'The genomic history of the Aegean palatial civilizations', *Cell*, DOI: https://doi.org/10.1016/j.cell.2021.03.039.

Clements, J. H. (2016), 'The terrain of autochthony: Shaping the Athenian landscape in the late fifth century BCE', in Kennedy and Jones-Lewis, pp. 315–40.

Cline, E. H. (2014), *1177 B.C.: The Year Civilization Collapsed*, Princeton: Princeton University Press.

Cohen, B. (2012), 'The non-Greek in Greek art', in Smith and Plantzos, pp. 456–79.

Cohen, B. (2001), 'Ethnic identity in democratic Athens and the visual vocabulary of male costume', in Malkin, pp. 235–74.

Cohen, B. (2000a), 'Introduction', in Cohen, pp. 1–20.

Cohen, B. (ed.) (2000b), *Not the Classical Ideal: Athens and the Construction of the Other in Greek Art*, Leiden: Brill.

Cohen, R. (1978), 'Ethnicity: Problem and focus in anthropology', *Annual Review of Anthropology*, 7: 379–403.

Coldstream, J. N. (1993), 'Mixed marriages at the frontiers of the early Greek world', *OJA*, 12: 89–107.

Cole, S. E. (2019), 'Cultural manoeuvering in the elite tombs of Ptolemaic Egypt', in Gondek and Sulosky Weaver, pp. 75–106.

Coleman, J. E. (1997), 'Ancient Greek ethnocentrism', in Coleman and Walz, pp. 175–220.

Coleman, J. E. and C. A. Walz (eds) (1997), *Greeks and Barbarians: Essays on the Interactions Between Greeks and Non-Greeks in Antiquity and the Consequences for Eurocentrism*, Bethesda, MD: CDL Press.

Connor, W. R. (1993), 'The Ionian era of Athenian civic identity', *PAPS*, 137: 194–206.

Constas, N. (2006), 'Death and dying in Byzantium', in D. Krueger (ed.) *Byzantine Christianity*, Minneapolis: Fortress Press, pp. 124–45.

Cox, M. (2000), 'Ageing adults from the skeleton', in Cox and Mays, pp. 61–81.

Cox, M. and S. Mays (eds) (2000), *Human Osteology in Archaeology and Forensic Science*, Cambridge: Cambridge University Press.

Crawford, S. (2000), 'Children, grave goods and social status in early Anglo-Saxon England', in Sofaer Derevenski, pp. 169–79.

Crenshaw, K. W. (2017), *On Intersectionality: Essential Writings*, New York: The New Press.

Crielaard, J. P. (2009), 'The Ionians in the Archaic period: Shifting identities in a changing world', in Derks and Roymans, pp. 37–84.

Cross, M. (1999), 'Accessing the inaccessible: Disability and archaeology', *Archaeological Review from Cambridge*, 15: 7–30.

Cummings, C. and E. Rega (2008), 'A case of dyschondrosteosis in an Anglo-Saxon skeleton', *IJO*, 18: 431–7.

Cunliffe, B. (1988), *Greeks, Romans, and Barbarians: Spheres of Interaction*, New York: Methuen.

D'Agostino, B. and A. M. D'Onofrio (1993), 'Morris, burial and ancient society', *Gnomon*, 65: 41–51.

Damyanov, M. (2005), 'Necropoleis and Ionian colonisation in the Black Sea', *AncWestEast*, 4: 77–97.

Dasen, V. (2017), 'The construction of physical Otherness in ancient iconography', *Journal of History of Medicine*, 29: 111–26.

Dasen, V. (2013), 'Becoming human: From the embryo to the newborn child', in Evans Grubbs et al., pp. 17–39.

Dasen, V. (2011), 'Childbirth and infancy in Greek and Roman antiquity', in B. Rawson (ed.) *A Companion to Families in the Greek and Roman Worlds*, Oxford: Blackwell, pp. 291–314.

Dasen, V. (2008), '"All children are dwarfs": Medical discourse and iconography of children's bodies', *OJA*, 27: 49–62.

Dasen, V. (1993), *Dwarfs in Ancient Egypt and Greece*, Oxford: Oxford University Press.

Dasen, V. (1990), 'Dwarfs in Athens', *OJA*, 9: 191–207.

Dasen, V. (1988), 'Dwarfism in Egypt and Classical antiquity: Iconography and medical history', *Med Hist*, 32: 253–76.

Davies, A. M. (2002), 'The Greek notion of dialect', in Harrison, pp. 153–71.

Davis, L. (2000), 'Dr. Johnson, Amelia, and the discourse of disability', in H. Deutsch and F. Nussbaum (eds) *'Defects': Engendering the Modern Body*, Ann Arbor: University of Michigan Press, pp. 54–74.

Dawson, W. R. (1986), 'Herodotus as a medical writer', *BICS*, 33: 87–96.

De Angelis, F. (2016), 'E pluribus unum: The multiplicity of models', in Donnellan et al., pp. 97–104.

de Mauriac, H. M. (1949), 'Alexander the Great and the politics of "homonoia"', *Journal of the History of Ideas*, 10: 104–14.

de Ste. Croix, G. E. M. (1981), *The Class Struggle in the Ancient Greek World from the Archaic Age to the Arab Conquests*, Ithaca, NY: Cornell University Press.

Dean O'Loughlin, V. (1996), 'Comparative endocranial vascular changes due to craniosynostosis and artificial cranial deformation', *Am J Phys Anthropol*, 101: 369–85.

Deene, M. (2011), 'Naturalized citizens and social mobility in Classical Athens: The case of Apollodorus', *GaR*, 58: 159–75.

Delcourt, M. (1961), *Hermaphrodite: Myths and Rites of the Bisexual Figure in Classical Antiquity*, London: Studio Books.

Delcourt, M. (1938), *Stérilités mystérieuses et naissances maléfiques dans l'antiquité*, Liège: Presses universitaires de Liège.

Delides, G. S. (2016), 'The royal tombs at Vergina Macedonia, Greece, revisited: A forensic review', *International Journal of Forensic Science and Pathology*, 4: 234–9.

Demand, N. (1998), 'Women and slaves as Hippocratic patients', in Murnaghan and Joshel, pp. 69–84.

DeMarrais, E., C. Gosden and C. Renfrew (eds) (2004), *Rethinking Materiality: The Engagement of Mind with the Material World*, Oxford: McDonald Institute for Archaeological Research.

Demetriou, D. (2012), *Negotiating Identity in the Ancient Mediterranean: The Archaic and Classical Greek Multiethnic Emporia*, Cambridge: Cambridge University Press.

Dench, M. (1995), *From Barbarians to New Men: Greek, Roman, and Modern Perceptions of Peoples of the Central Apennines*, Oxford: Clarendon Press.

Derks, T. and N. Roymans (eds) (2009a), *Ethnic Constructs in Antiquity: The Role of Power and Traditions*, Amsterdam: Amsterdam University Press.

Derks, T. and N. Roymans (2009b), 'Introduction', in Derks and Roymans, pp. 1–10.

Desnick, R. J. et al. (2019), 'The Himera dwarf: Bioarchaeological and genetic analyses of an ancient adult Greek skeleton with achondroplasia', *Archaeological Institute of America 121st Annual Meeting Abstracts*, 43: 153–4.

Dettwyler, K. A. (1991), 'Can paleopathology provide evidence for "compassion"?', *Am J Phys Anthropol*, 84: 375–84.

DeVries, K. (2000), 'The nearly Other: The Attic vision of Phrygians and Lydians', in Cohen, pp. 338–63.

Dewald, C. and J. Marincola (eds) (2006), *The Cambridge Companion to Herodotus*, Cambridge: Cambridge University Press.

Di Gaetano, C. et al. (2009), 'Differential Greek and northern African migrations to Sicily are supported by genetic evidence from the Y chromosome', *Eur J Hum Genet*, 17: 91–9.

Di Rocco, C. (2005), 'Craniosynostosis in old Greece: Political power and physical deformity', *Childs Nerv Syst*, 21: 859.

Di Rocco, C. et al. (1998), 'Posterior plagiocephaly: Craniosynostosis or skull molding?', *Critical Reviews in Neurosurgery*, 8: 122–30.

Dietler, M. (2005), 'The archaeology of colonization and the colonization of archaeology: Theoretical challenges from an ancient Mediterranean colonial encounter', in G. Stein (ed.) *The Archaeology of Colonial Encounters: Comparative Perspectives*, Santa Fe: SAR Press, pp. 33–68.

DiGangi, E. A. and J. D. Bethard (2021), 'Decloaking a lost cause: Decolonizing ancestry estimation in the United States', *Am J Phys Anthropol*, 2021: 1–15, DOI: https://doi.org/10.1002/ajpa.24212.

Dillon, M. (2017), 'Legal (and customary?) approaches to the disabled in ancient Greece', in Laes, pp. 167–81.

Dillon, M. (2002), *Girls and Women in Classical Greek Religion*, London: Routledge.

Dillon, M. (1995), 'Payments to the disabled at Athens: Social justice or fear of aristocratic patronage?', *AncSoc*, 26: 27–57.

Dimakis, N. (2016), *Social Identity and Status in the Classical and Hellenistic Northern Peloponnese*, Oxford: Archaeopress.

Dingwall, E. (1931), *Artificial Cranial Deformation: A Contribution to the Study of Ethnic Mutilations*, London: Bale and Danielsson.

Domínguez, A. J. (2002), 'Greeks in Iberia: Colonialism Without Colonization', in C. L. Lyons and J. K. Papadopoulos (eds) *The Archaeology of Colonization*, Los Angeles: Getty Research Institute, pp. 65–95.

Domurad, M. R. (1986), 'Populations of ancient Cyprus', PhD diss., University of Cincinnati.

Donnellan, L. (2016), '"Greek colonisation" and Mediterranean networks: Patterns of mobility and interaction at Pithekoussai', *Journal of Greek Archaeology*, 1: 109–48.

Donnellan, L. (2011), 'Funerary rites as a means of land appropriation', in L. Amundsen-Meyer, N. Engel and S. Pickering (eds) *Identity Crisis: Archaeological Perspectives on Social Identity*, Calgary: Chacmool Archaeological Association, pp. 62–74.

Donnellan, L., V. Nizzo and G.-J. Burgers (eds) (2016), *Conceptualising Early Colonisation: International Conference Contextualizing Early Colonization*, vol. 2, Rome: Brepols.

Dornan, J. L. (2002), 'Agency and archaeology: Past, present, and future directions', *Journal of Archaeological Method and Theory*, 9: 303–29.

Dotsika, E. et al. (2018), 'Isotopic composition of spring water in Greece: Spring water isoscapes', *Geosciences*, 8.

Doughtery, C. (2001), *The Raft of Odysseus: The Ethnographic Imagination of Homer's Odyssey*, Oxford: Oxford University Press.

Dougherty, C. and L. Kurke (eds) (2003), *The Cultures within Ancient Greek Culture: Contact, Conflict, Collaboration*, Cambridge: Cambridge University Press.

Draycott, J. (ed.) (2019), *Prostheses in Antiquity*, London: Routledge.

Draycott, J. and E-J. Graham (eds) (2017), *Bodies of Evidence: Ancient Anatomical Votives, Past, Present, and Future*, London: Routledge.

Drews, R. (1988), *The Coming of the Greeks: Indo-European Conquests in the Aegean and the Near East*, Princeton: Princeton University Press.

Driver, G. R. and J. C. Miles (eds) (1935), *The Assyrian Laws*, Oxford: Oxford University Press.

DuBois, P. (2009), *Slavery: Antiquity and its Legacy*, Oxford: Oxford University Press.

DuBois, P. (2008), *Slaves and Other Objects*, Chicago: University of Chicago Press.

DuBois, P. (1991), *Centaurs and Amazons: Women and the Prehistory of the Great Chain of Being*, Ann Arbor: University of Michigan Press.

Duday, H. (2009), *The Archaeology of the Dead: Lectures in Archaeothanatology*, Oxford: Oxford University Press.

Dunsworth, H. (2021), 'This view of wife. A reflection on Darwin's chapters 19 and 20: Secondary sexual characters of man', in J. M. DeSilva (ed.) *A Most Interesting Problem: What Darwin's* Descent of Man *got Right and Wrong about Human Evolution*, Princeton: Princeton University Press, pp. 183–203.

Durkheim, E. (1895), *Les règles de la méthode sociologique*, Paris: Librairie Félix Alcan.

Edgar, H. J. H. (2005), 'Prediction of race using characteristics of dental morphology', *J Forensic Sci*, 50: 269–73.

Edwards, M. [L.] (2012), 'Philoctetes in context', in D. A. Gerber (ed.) *Disabled Veterans in History*, Ann Arbor: University of Michigan, pp. 55–69.

Edwards, M. L. (1997a), 'Constructions of physical disability in the ancient Greek world: The community concept', in D. T. Mitchell and S. L. Snyder (eds) *The Body and Physical Difference: Discourses of Disability*, Ann Arbor: University of Michigan Press, pp. 35–51.

Edwards, M. L. (1997b), 'Deaf and dumb in ancient Greece', in L. J. Davis (ed.) *Disability Studies Reader*, London: Routledge, pp. 29–51.

Edwards, M. L. (1996), 'The cultural context of deformity in the ancient Greek world, "let there be a law that no deformed child shall be reared"', *AncHistB*, 10: 79–92.

Edwards, R. B. (1979), *Kadmos the Phoenician: A Study in Greek Legends and the Mycenaean Age*, Amsterdam: Adolf M. Hakkert.

Ekroth, G. (2015), 'Heroes – Living or Dead?', in E. Eidinow and J. Kindt (eds) *The Oxford Companion of Ancient Greek Religion*, Oxford: Oxford University Press, pp. 383–96.

Eliav-Feldon, M., B. Isaac and J. Ziegler (eds) (2009), *The Origins of Racism in the West*, Cambridge: Cambridge University Press.

Eliopoulos, C. et al. (2011), 'Greece', in N. Marquez-Grant and L. Fibiger (eds) *The Routledge Handbook of Archaeological Human Remains and Legislation. An International Guide to Laws and Practice in the Excavation and Treatment of Archaeological Human Remains*, London: Routledge, pp. 173–83.

Emery, M. V. et al. (2018), 'Mapping the origins of imperial Roman workers (1st–4th century CE) at Vagnari, Southern Italy, using $^{87}Sr/^{86}Sr$ and $\delta^{18}O$ variability', *Am J Phys Anthropol*, 166: 837–50.

Eng, J. T., Q. Zhang and H. Zhu (2010), 'Skeletal effects of castration on two eunuchs of Ming China', *Anthropological Science*, 118: 107–16.

Ensor, B. E. (2021), 'Making aDNA useful for kinship analysis', *Antiquity*, 95: 241–3.

Erlinger, C. M. (2016), 'How the eunuch works: Eunuchs as a narrative device in Greek and Roman literature', PhD diss., Ohio State University.

Erskine, A. (2005), 'Unity and identity: Shaping the past in the Greek Mediterranean', in Gruen, pp. 121–36.

Evans Grubbs, J. (2013), 'Infant exposure and infanticide', in Evans Grubbs et al., pp. 83–107.

Evans Grubbs, J., T. Parkin and R. Bell (eds) (2013), *The Oxford Handbook of Childhood and Education in the Classical World*, Oxford: Oxford University Press.

Evison, M. P. (2001), 'Ancient DNA in Greece: Problems and prospects', *Journal of Radioanalytical and Nuclear Chemistry*, 247: 673–8.

Fabbri, P. F. and F. Mallegni (1988), 'Dental anthropology of the Upper Palaeolithic remains from Romito cave at Papsidero (Cosenza, Italy)', *Bull Mem Soc Anthropol Paris*, 14: 163–78.

Fabre-Serris, J. and A. Keith (eds) (2015), *Women and War in Antiquity*, Baltimore: Johns Hopkins University Press.

Fahlander, F. (2012), 'Facing gender. Corporeality, materiality, intersectionality and resurrection', in I.-M. Back Danielsson and S. Thedéen (eds) *To Tender Gender: The Pasts and Futures of Gender Research in Archaeology*, Stockholm: Stockholm University, pp. 137–52.

Fahlander, F. and T. Oestigaard (eds) (2008a), *The Materiality of Death: Bodies, Burials, Beliefs, BAR International Series 1768*, Oxford: Archaeopress.

Fahlander, F. and T. Oestigaard (2008b), 'The materiality of death: Bodies, burials, beliefs', in Fahlander and Oestigaard, pp. 1–18.

Fehling, D. (1989), *Herodotus and his 'Sources': Citation, Invention, and Narrative Art*, Liverpool: Cairns.

Feldesman, M. R., J. G. Kleckner and J. K. Lundy (1990), 'Femur/stature ratio and estimates of stature in mid- and late-Pleistocene fossil hominids', *Am J Phys Anthropol*, 83: 359–72.

Felton, D. (2014), 'The motif of the "mutilated hero" in Herodotus', *Phoenix*, 68: 47–61.

Felton, D. (2010), 'The dead', in D. Ogden (ed.) *A Companion to Greek Religion*, reprint, Oxford: Blackwell Publishing, pp. 86–99.

Felton, D. (1999), *Haunted Greece and Rome: Ghost Stories from Classical Antiquity*, reprint. Austin: University of Texas Press.

Fernández, E. et al. (2006), 'MtDNA analysis of ancient samples from Castellón (Spain): Diachronic variation and genetic relationships', *International Congress Series*, 1288: 127–9.

Figueira, T. and C. Soares (eds) (2020), *Ethnicity and Identity in Herodotus*, London: Routledge.

Fine, J. V. A. (1983), *The Ancient Greeks: A Critical History*, Cambridge, MA: Harvard University Press.

Finley, M. I. (1981), 'The elderly in Classical antiquity', *GaR*, 28: 156–71.

Finley, M. I. (1976), 'Colonies: An attempt at typology', *Transactions of the Royal Historical Society*, 26: 167–88.

Finley, M. I. (1973), *The Ancient Economy*, Berkeley: University of California Press.

Finley, M. I. (1959), 'Was Greek civilization based on slave labour?', *Historia*, 8: 145–64.

Finnegan, M. (1978), 'Non-metric variation of the infracranial skeleton', *J Anat*, 125: 23–37.

Fitzjohn, M. (2007), 'Equality in the colonies: Concepts of equality in Sicily during the eighth to six centuries BC', *WorldArch*, 39: 215–28.

Fletcher, A., J. Pearson and J. Ambers (2008), 'The manipulation of social and physical identity in the pre-pottery Neolithic: Radiographic evidence for cranial modification at Jericho and its implication for the plastering of skulls', *CAJ*, 18: 309–25.

Flower, M. (2006), 'Herodotus and Persia', in Dewald and Marincola, pp. 274–89.

Fogel, R. W. et al. (1983), 'Secular changes in American and British stature and nutrition', *Journal of Interdisciplinary History*, 14: 445–81.

Formicola, V. (1993), 'Stature reconstruction from long bones in ancient population samples: An approach to the problem of its reliability', *Am J Phys Anthropol*, 90: 351–8.

Forsdyke, S. (2012), *Slaves Tell Tales and Other Episodes in the Politics of Popular Culture in Ancient Greece*, Princeton: Princeton University Press.

Forsdyke, S. (2008), 'Street theatre and popular justice in ancient Greece: Shaming, stoning and starving offenders inside and outside the courts', *Past and Present*, 201: 3–50.

Forsdyke, S. (2005), *Exile, Ostracism, and Democracy: The Politics of Expulsion in Ancient Greece*, Princeton: Princeton University Press.

Forsdyke, S. (2000), 'Exile, ostracism and the Athenian democracy', *CalifStClAnt*, 19: 232–63.

Forsén, B. (1996), *Griechische Gliederweihungen. Eine Untersuchung zu ihrer Typologie und ihrer religions- und sozialgeschichtlichen Bedeutung*, Helsinki: Papers and Monographs of the Finnish Institute at Athens.

Forsyth, C. J. and H. Copes (2014), 'Introduction', in C. J. Forsyth and H. Copes (eds) *Encyclopedia of Social Deviance*, Los Angeles: SAGE Publications, pp. xxv–xxvi.

Fortson, B. W. (2004), *Indo-European Language and Culture: An Introduction*, London: Blackwell.

Fowler, R. L. (2018), 'The *nostoi* and Archaic Greek ethnicity', in S. Hornblower and G. Biffis (eds) *The Returning Hero: Nostoi and Traditions of Mediterranean Settlement*, Oxford: Oxford University Press, pp. 43–63.

Fowler, R. L. (2003), 'Pelasgians', in E. Csapo and M. C. Miller (eds) *Poetry, Theory, Praxis: The Social Life of Myth, Word and Image in Ancient Greece*, Oxford: Oxbow Books, pp. 2–18.

Fox, S. (2012), 'The bioarchaeology of children in Graeco-Roman Greece', in M.-D. Nenna (ed.) *L'Enfant et la mort dans l'Antiquité II: Types de tombs et traitement du corps des enfants dans l'antiquité gréco-romaine*, Paris: De Boccard, pp. 409–28.

Fox Leonard, S. C. (1997), 'Comparative health from paleopathological analysis of the human skeletal remains dating to the Hellenistic and Roman periods, from Paphos, Cyprus, and Corinth, Greece', PhD diss., University of Arizona.

Foxhall, L. (1992), 'The control of the Attic landscape', in B. Wells (ed.) *Agriculture in Ancient Greece*, Stockholm: Svenska institutet I Athen, pp. 155–9.

Francalacci, P. et al. (2003), 'Peopling of three Mediterranean islands (Corsica, Sardinia, and Sicily) inferred by Y-chromosome biallelic variability', *Am J Phys Anthropol*, 121: 270–9.

Fraser, P. M. (2009), *Greek Ethnic Terminology*, Oxford: Oxford University Press.

Frederiksen, R. (1999), 'From death to life: The cemetery of Fusco and the reconstruction of early colonial society', in Tsetskhladze, pp. 229–52.

Fredicksonn, G. M. (2002), *Racism: A Short History*, Princeton: Princeton University Press.

Fuentes, A. (2021), '"On the races of man"': Race, racism, science, and hope', in J. M. DeSilva (ed.) *A Most Interesting Problem: What Darwin's Descent of Man got Right and Wrong about Human Evolution*, Princeton: Princeton University Press, pp. 144–61.

Fuentes, A. et al. (2019), 'AAPA statement on race and racism', *Am J Phys Anthropol*, 169: 400–2.

Fully, G. (1956), 'Une nouvelle méthode de determination de la taille', *Annales de Médecine Légales*, 36: 66–273.

Galanakis, Y. and M. Nowak-Kemp (2013), 'Ancient Greek skulls in the Oxford University Museum, Part II: The Rhousopoulos-Rolleston correspondence', *Journal of the History of Collections*, 25: 1–17.

Galton, D. J. (1998), 'Greek theories on eugenics', *Journal of Medical Ethics*, 24: 263–7.

Gantz, T. (1993), *Early Greek Myth: A Guide to Literary and Artistic Sources*, Baltimore: Johns Hopkins University Press.

García Alonso, J. L. (2017), '"Whoever is not Greek is a barbarian"', in A. P. Arnaut (ed.) *Identity(ies): A Multicultural and Multidisciplinary Approach*, Coimbra: Coimbra University Press, pp. 9–26.

Gardiner-Garden, J. (1989), 'Ateas and Theopompus', *JHS*, 109: 29–40.

Garland, R. (2017), 'Disabilities in tragedy and comedy', in Laes, pp. 154–66.

Garland, R. (2016), 'The invention and application of ethnic deformity', in Kennedy and Jones-Lewis, pp. 45–61.

Garland, R. (2014), *Wandering Greeks: The Ancient Greek Diaspora from the Age of Homer to the Death of Alexander the Great*, Princeton: Princeton University Press.

Garland, R. (2010), *The Eye of the Beholder: Deformity and Disability in the Graeco-Roman World*, second edition, Bristol: Bristol Classical Press.

Garland, R. (2001), *The Greek Way of Death*, second edition, Ithaca, NY: Cornell University Press.

Garland, R. (1994), 'The mockery of the deformed and the disabled in Graeco-Roman culture', in S. Jäkel and A. Timonen (eds), *Laughter Down the Centuries*, Turku: Turun Yliopisto, pp. 71–84.

Garland, R. (1989), 'Burial and the *polis*', *CR*, 39: 66–7.

Garmaise, M. (1996), 'Studies in the representation of dwarfs in Hellenistic and Roman art', PhD diss., McMaster University.

Geller, P. M. (2017), 'Brave old world: Ancient DNA testing and sex determination', in Agarwal and Wesp, pp. 71–98.

George, C. et al. (2008), *Greek and Latin from an Indo-European Perspective*, Cambridge: Cambridge Philological Society.

Georges, P. (1994), *Barbarian Asia and the Greek Experience from the Archaic Period to the Age of Xenophon*, Baltimore: Johns Hopkins University Press.

Gernaey, A. and D. Minnikin (2000), 'Chemical methods in palaeopathology', in Cox and Mays, pp. 239–53.

Geroulanos, S. (2014), 'Ancient Greek votives, vase and stelae depicting medical diseases', in D. Michaelides (ed.) *Medicine and Healing in the Ancient Mediterranean World*, Oxford: Oxbow Books, pp. 24–9.

Giannecchini, M. and J. Moggi-Cecchi (2008), 'Stature in archaeological samples from central Italy: Methodological issues and diachronic changes', *Am J Phys Anthropol*, 135: 284–92.

Giddens, A. (1979), *Central Problems in Social Theory: Action, Structure and Contradiction in Social Analysis*, Berkeley: University of California Press.

Gilchrist, R. (1999), *Gender and Archaeology: Contesting the Past*, London: Routledge.

Gill, D. W. J. (1988), 'Expressions of wealth: Greek art and society', *Antiquity*, 62: 735–43.

Gill, G. W. (1998), 'Craniofacial criteria in the skeletal attribution of race', in K. J. Reichs (ed.) *Forensic Osteology: Advances in the Identification of Human Remains*, second edition, Springfield: Charles C. Thomas Publisher, pp. 293–315.

Gill, G. W. and S. Rhine (eds) (1990), *Skeletal Attribution of Race: Methods of Forensic Anthropology*, Albuquerque: Maxwell Museum of Anthropology.

Gilleard, C. (2007), 'Old age in ancient Greece: Narratives of desire, narratives of disgust', *Journal of Aging Studies*, 21: 81–92.

Gilmore, H. F. and S. E. Halcrow (2014), 'Sense or sensationalism? Approaches to explaining high perinatal mortality in the past', in Thompson et al., pp. 123–38.

Gilmour, R. J. et al. (2019), 'Maintaining mobility after fracture: A biomechanical analysis of fracture consequences at the Roman sites of Ancaster (UK) and Vagnari (Italy)', *IJPP*, 24: 119–29.

Ginn, J. and S. Arber (1995), '"Only connect": Gender relations and ageing', in S. Arber and J. Ginn (eds) *Connecting Gender and Ageing: A Sociological Approach*, Buckingham: Open University Press, pp. 1–14.

Gist, N. P. (1967), 'Cultural versus social marginality: The Anglo-Indian case', *Phylon*, 28: 361–75.

Giuliani, L. (1987), 'Die seligen Krüppel. Zur Deutung von Mißgestalten in der hellenistischen Kleinkunst', *AA*, 102: 701–21.

Goldberg, D. T. (1993), *Racist Culture: Philosophy and the Politics of Meaning*, Oxford: Blackwell.

Golden, M. (2015), *Children and Childhood in Classical Athens*, second edition, Baltimore: Johns Hopkins University Press.

Golden, M. (2011), 'Slavery and the Greek family', in Bradley and Cartledge, pp. 134–52.

Golden, M. (1988), 'Did the ancients care when their children died?', *GaR*, 35: 152–63.

Golden, M. (1981), 'Demography and the exposure of girls at Athens', *Phoenix*, 35: 316–31.

Goldenberg, D. (2009), 'Racism, color symbolism, and color prejudice', in Eliav-Feldon et al., pp. 88–108.

Goldhill, S. (2002), 'Battle narrative and politics in Aeschylus' *Persae*', in Harrison, pp. 50–61.

Goldman, M. L. (2015), 'Associating the *aulétris*: Flute girls and prostitutes in the Classical Greek symposium', *Helios*, 42: 29–60.

Gondek, R. M. and C. L. Sulosky Weaver (eds) (2019), *The Ancient Art of Transformation: Case Studies from Mediterranean Contexts*, Oxford: Oxbow Books.

Goodenough, W. H. (1965), 'Rethinking "status" and "role": Toward a general model of the cultural organization of social relationships', in M. Banton (ed.) *The Relevance of Models for Social Anthropology*, London: Tavistock, pp. 1–24.

Goodey, C. F. (2005), 'Blockheads, roundheads, pointy heads: Intellectual disability and the brain before modern medicine', *Journal of the History of Behavioral Sciences*, 41: 165–83.

Goodey, C. F. (1999), 'Politics, nature, and necessity: Were Aristotle's slaves feeble minded?', *Political Theory*, 27: 203–24.

Goodey, C. F. and M. L. Rose (2013), 'Mental states, bodily dispositions, and table manners: A guide to reading "intellectual" disability from Homer to Late Antiquity', in Laes et al., pp. 17–44.

Gosbell, L. A. (2018), *The Poor, the Crippled, the Blind, and the Lame: Physical and Sensory Disability in the Gospels of the New Testament*, Tübingen: Mohr Siebeck.

Gosden, C. (2004), *Archaeology and Colonialism*, Cambridge: University of Cambridge.

Gourevitch, D. (1983), 'La psychiatrie de l'antiquité gréco-romaine', in J. Postel and C. Quétel (eds) *Nouvelle histoire de la psychiatrie*, Toulouse: Dunod, pp. 13–31.

Gowland, R. (2006), 'Ageing the past: Examining age identity from funerary evidence', in Gowland and Knüsel, pp. 143–54.

Gowland, R. L. and A. T. Chamberlain (2002), 'A Bayesian approach to ageing perinatal skeletal material from archaeological sites: Implications for the evidence of infanticide in Roman Britain', *JAS*, 29: 677–85.

Gowland, R. and C. Knüsel (eds) (2006), *Social Archaeology of Funerary Remains*, Oxford: Oxbow Books.

Gracia, J. J. E. (2017), 'Race and ethnicity', in Zack, pp. 180–90.

Graham, A. J. (1983), *Colony and Mother City in Ancient Greece*, second edition, Chicago: Ares.

Grassl, H. (2006), 'Marginalized groups', in H. Cancik and H. Schneider (eds) *Brill's New Pauly*, DOI: http://dx.doi.org/10.1163/1574-9347_bnp_e1018710.

Graumann, L. A. (2013), 'Monstrous births and retrospective diagnosis: The case of hermaphrodites in antiquity', in Laes et al., pp. 181–209.

Gravlee, C. C. (2009), 'How race becomes biology: Embodiment of social inequality', *Am J Phys Anthropol*, 139: 47–57.

Gray, C. L. (2011), 'Foreigners in the burial ground: The case of the Milesians in Athens', M. Carroll and J. Rempel (eds) *Living through the Dead: Burial and Commemoration in the Classical World*, Oxford: Oxbow Books, pp. 47–64.

Gray, V. (1995), 'Herodotus and the rhetoric of Otherness', *AJP*, 116: 185–211.

Green, M. J. (1997), 'Images in opposition: Polarity, ambivalence and liminality in cult representation', *Antiquity*, 71: 898–911.

Grinsell, L. V. (1961), 'The breaking of objects as a funerary rite', *Folklore*, 72: 475–91.

Grmek, M. D. (1991), *Disease in the Ancient Greek World*, reprint, Baltimore: Johns Hopkins University.

Groce, N. E. (1985), *Everyone Here Spoke Sign Language*, Cambridge, MA: Harvard University Press.

Gruen, E. S. (2013), 'Did ancient identity depend on ethnicity? A preliminary probe', *Phoenix*, 67: 1–22.

Gruen, E. S. (2011), *Rethinking the Other in Antiquity*, Princeton: Princeton University Press.

Gruen, E. S. (ed.) (2005), *Cultural Borrowings and Ethnic Appropriations in Antiquity*, Munich: Franz Steiner.

Gunnel, D., J. Rogers and P. Dieppe (2001), 'Height and health: Predicting longevity from bone length in archaeological remains', *J Epidemiol Community Health*, 55: 505–7.

Gurung, G. S. and M. Kollmair (2005), *Marginality: Concepts and their Limitations. IP6 Working Paper No. 4*, Zurich: Development Study Group.

Haines, M. R., L. A. Craig and T. Weiss (2003), 'The short and the dead: Nutrition, mortality, and the 'antebellum puzzle' in the United States', *Journal of Economic History*, 63: 382–413.

Hakenbeck, S. E. (2019), 'Genetics, archaeology and the far right: An unholy trinity', *WorldArch*, 54: 517–27.

Hakenbeck, S. E. (2007), 'Situational ethnicity and nested identities: New approaches to an old problem', *Anglo-Saxon Studies in Archaeology and History*, 14: 19–27.

Halcrow, S. E. and N. Tayles (2011), 'The bioarchaeological investigation of children and childhood', in Agarwal and Glencross, pp. 333–60.

Hales, S. (2002), 'Looking for eunuchs: The *galli* and Attis in Roman art', in Tougher, pp. 87–103.

Hales, S. and T. Hodos (eds) (2010), *Material Culture and Social Identities in the Ancient World*, Cambridge: Cambridge University Press.

Haley, S. P. (2009), 'Be not afraid of the dark: Critical race theory and classical studies', in L. Nasrallah and E. S. Fiorenza (eds) *Prejudice and Christian*

Beginnings: Investigating Race, Gender, and Ethnicity in Early Christian Studies, Minneapolis: Fortress Press, pp. 27–50.

Hall, E. (2018), 'Hephaestus the hobbling humorist: The club-footed god in the history of early Greek comedy', *IllinClSt*, 43: 366–87.

Hall, E. (2002), 'When is myth not a myth? Bernal's "Ancient Model"', in Harrison, pp. 133–54.

Hall, E. (1989), *Inventing the Barbarian: Greek Self-Definition through Tragedy*, Oxford: Clarendon Press.

Hall, J. M. (2003), '"Culture" or "cultures"? Hellenism in the late sixth century', in Dougherty and Kurke, pp. 23–34.

Hall, J. M. (2002), *Hellenicity: Between Ethnicity and Culture*, Chicago: University of Chicago Press.

Hall, J. M. (2001), 'Contested ethnicities: Perceptions of Macedonia within evolving definitions of Greek identity', in Malkin, pp. 159–86.

Hall, J. M. (1997), *Ethnic Identity in Greek Antiquity*, New York: Cambridge University Press.

Hall, J. M. (1995), 'The role of language in Greek ethnicities', *PCPS*, 41: 83–100.

Hall, T. D. (2014), 'Ethnicity and world-systems analysis', in J. McInerney (ed.) *A Companion to Ethnicity in the Ancient Mediterranean*, Oxford: Wiley-Blackwell, pp. 50–65.

Hansen, M. H. (2006), *Polis: An Introduction to the Ancient Greek City-State*, Oxford: Oxford University Press.

Hansen, M. H. (1991), *The Athenian Democracy in the Age of Demosthenes: Structure, Principles and Ideology*, Norman, OK: University of Oklahoma Press.

Hansen, M. H. and T. H. Nielsen (2004), *An Inventory of Archaic and Classical Poleis: An Investigation Conducted by the Copenhagen Polis Centre for Danish National Research Foundation*. Oxford: Oxford University Press.

Harari, M. (2004), 'A short history of pygmies in Greece and Italy', in Lomas, pp. 163–90.

Hardwick, L. (1990), 'Ancient Amazons – Heroes, outsiders or women?', *GaR*, 37: 14–36.

Härke, H. (1997), 'The nature of burial data', in C. K. Jensen and K. H. Nielsen (eds) *Burial and Society: The Chronological and Social Analysis of Archaeological Burial Data*, Aarhus: Aarhus University Press, pp. 19–27.

Harlow, M. and R. Laurence (2002), *Growing Up and Growing Old in Ancient Rome*, London: Routledge.

Harman, R. (2013), 'Looking at the Other: Visual mediation and Greek identity in Xenophon's *Anabasis*', in Almagor and Skinner, pp. 79–96.

Harokopos, N. A. (2019), 'On the threshold of old age: Perceptions of the elderly in Athenian red-figure vase-painting', in Gondek and Sulosky Weaver, pp. 7–32.

Harper, N. K. and S. C. Fox (2008), 'Recent research in Cypriot bioarchaeology', *Bioarchaeology of the Near East*, 2: 1–38.

Harris, E. M. (2004), 'Notes on a lead letter from the Athenian Agora', *HSCP*, 102: 157–70.

Harris, W. V. (ed.) (2013), *Mental Disorders in the Classical World*, Leiden: Brill.

Harris, W. V. (1982), 'The theoretical possibility of extensive infanticide in the Graeco-Roman world', *ClQ*, 32: 114–6.

Harrison, T. (2019), 'Classical Greek ethnography and the slave trade', *ClAnt*, 38: 36–57.

Harrison, T. (ed.) (2002), *Greeks and Barbarians*, London: Routledge.

Harrison, T. (1998), 'Herodotus' conception of foreign languages', *Histos*, 2: 1–45.

Hartog, F. (2009 [1988]), *The Mirror of Herodotus: The Representation of the Other in the Writing of History*, reprint, Berkeley: University of California Press.

Hartog, F. (2002), 'The Greeks as Egyptologists', in Harrison, pp. 211–28.

Hartog, F. (2001), *Memories of Odysseus: Frontier Tales from Ancient Greece*, Chicago: University of Chicago Press.

Harvati, K., E. Panagopoulou and C. Runnels (2009), 'The paleoanthropology of Greece', *Evolutionary Anthropology*, 18: 131–43.

Hawkey, D. E. and C. F. Merbs (1995), 'Activity-induced musculoskeletal stress markers (MSM) and subsistence energy changes among ancient Hudson Bay Eskimos', *IJO*, 5: 324–38.

Henneberg, M. and R. J. Henneberg (1998), 'Biological characteristics of the population based on analysis of skeletal remains', in J. C. Carter (ed.) *The Chora of Metaponto: The Necropoleis*, vol. 2, Austin: University of Texas Press, pp. 503–62.

Herda, A. (2013), 'Greek (and our) views of the Karians', in A. Mouton, I. Rutherford and I. Yakubovich (eds) *Luwian Identities: Culture, Language and Religion Between Anatolia and the Aegean*, Leiden: Brill, pp. 421–508.

Hermann, L. (1949), 'Une caricature de Phèdre', in *Mélanges d'archéologie et d'histoire offerts à Charles Picard à l'occasion de son 65e anniversaire*, vol. 1, Paris: Presses universitaires de France, pp. 435–7.

Herring, E. (2009), 'Ethnicity and culture', in A. Erskine (ed.) *A Companion to Ancient History*, Oxford: Wiley-Blackwell, pp. 123–33.

Hillson, S. (2009), 'The world's largest infant cemetery and its potential for studying growth and development', in Schepartz et al., pp. 137–154.

Himmelmann, N. (1998), *Reading Greek Art*, Princeton: Princeton University Press.

Hirsch, S. W. (1985), '1001 Iranian nights: History and fiction in Xenophon's *Cyropaedia*', in *The Greek Historians: Literature and History. Papers Presented to A. E. Raubitschek*, Saratoga, CA: ANMA Libri, pp. 65–85.

Hodder, I. (1982), 'The identification and interpretation of ranking in prehistory: A contextual approach', in C. Renfew and S. Shennan (eds) *Ranking, Resource and Exchange*, Cambridge: Cambridge University Press, pp. 150–4.

Hodder, I. (1980), 'Social structure and cemeteries: A critical appraisal', in P. Rahtz, T. Dickinson and L. Watts (eds) *Anglo-Saxon Cemeteries 1979: The Fourth Anglo-Saxon Symposium at Oxford*, British Archaeological Reports British Series 82, Oxford: BAR Publishing, pp. 161–9.

Hodos, T. (2010), 'Local and global perspectives in the study of social and cultural identities', in Hales and Hodos, pp. 3–31.

Hodos, T. (2009), 'Colonial engagements in the global Mediterranean Iron Age', *CAJ*, 19: 221–41.

Hodos, T. (2006), *Local Responses to Colonization in the Iron Age Mediterranean*, London: Routledge.

Hodos, T. (1999), 'Intermarriage in the western Greek colonies', *OJA*, 18: 61–78.

Hoffmann, H. and D. Metzler (1977), 'Zur theorie und methode der erforschung von rassimus in der antike', *Kritische Berichte*, 5: 5–20.

Holleran, C. and A. Pudsey (eds) (2011), *Demography and the Graeco-Roman World: New Insights and Approaches*, Cambridge: Cambridge University Press.

Hollimon, S. E. (2017), 'Bioarchaeological approaches to nonbinary genders: Case studies from native North America', in Agarwal and Wesp, pp. 51–70.

Hollimon, S. E. (2011), 'Sex and gender in bioarchaeological research: Theory, method, and interpretation', in Agarwal and Glencross, pp. 149–82.

Hooker, J. T. (1979), 'New reflexions on the Dorian invasion', *Klio*, 61: 353–60.

Horn, C. B. (2013), 'A nexus of disability in ancient Greek miracle stories: A comparison of accounts of blindness from the Asklepieion in Epidauros and the shrine of Thecla in Seleucia', in Laes et al., pp. 115–43.

Hornblower, S. (2008), 'Greek identity in the Archaic and Classical periods', in Zacharia, pp. 37–58.

Horstmanshoff, M. (2012), 'Disability and rehabilitation in the Graeco-Roman world', in R. Breitwieser (ed.) *Behinderungen und Beeinträchtigungen/Disability and Impairment in Antiquity*, British Archaeological Reports International Series 2359, Oxford: BAR Publishing, pp. 1–9.

Houby-Nielsen, S. H. (2000), 'Child burials in ancient Athens', in Sofaer Derevenski, pp. 151–66.

Houby-Nielsen, S. H. (1995), '"Burial language" in Archaic and Classical Kerameikos', *ProcDanInstAth*, 1: 129–92.

Huang, Y. (2010), 'Invention of barbarian and the emergence of Orientalism: Classical Greece', *Journal of Chinese Philosophy*, 37: 556–66.

Hubbard, A. R., D. Guatelli-Steinberg and J. D. Irish (2015), 'Do nuclear DNA and dental nonmetric data produce similar reconstructions of regional population history? An example from modern coastal Kenya', *Am J Phys Anthropol*, 157: 295–304.

Hubert, J. (ed.) (2000), *Madness, Disability and Social Exclusion: The Archaeology and Anthropology of 'Difference'*, London: Routledge.

Hughes, J. (2017), *Votive Body Parts in Greek and Roman Religion*, Cambridge: Cambridge University Press.

Humphreys, S. C. (1990), 'Review, *Burial and Ancient Society: The Rise of the Greek City-State* by I. Morris', *Helios*, 17: 263–8.

Hunt, P. (2018), *Ancient Greek and Roman Slavery*, Chichester: John Wiley & Sons.

Hunt, P. (2011), 'Slaves in Greek literary culture', in Bradley and Cartledge, pp. 22–47.

Hunt, P. (1998), *Slaves, Warfare and Ideology in the Greek Historians*, Cambridge: Cambridge University Press.

Hunter, V. (2000), 'Introduction: Status distinctions in Athenian law', in V. J. Hunter and J. C. Edmondson (eds) *Law and Social Status in Classical Athens*, Oxford: Oxford University Press, pp. 1–29.

Hurcombe, L. (2007), *Archaeological Artefacts as Material Culture*, London: Routledge.

Hurwit, J. M. (2007), 'The problem with Dexileos: Heroic and other nudities in Greek art', *AJA*, 111: 35–60.

Huys, M. (1996), 'The Spartan practice of selective infanticide and its parallels in ancient utopian tradition', *AncSoc*, 27: 47–74.

Iezzi, C. (2009), 'Regional differences in the health status of the Mycenaean women of East Lokris', in Schepartz et al., pp. 175–92.

Ingvarsson, A. and Y. Bäckström (2019), 'Bioarchaeological field analysis of human remains from the mass graves at Phaleron, Greece', *Opuscula*, 12: 7–158.

Ingold, T. (2007), 'Materials against materiality', *Archaeological Dialogues*, 14: 1–16.

Insoll, T. (2004), *Archaeology, Ritual, Religion*, London: Routledge.

Irwin, J. et al. (2008), 'Mitochondrial control region sequences from Northern Greece and Greek Cypriots', *Int J Legal Med*, 122: 87–9.

Isaac, B. (2009), 'Racism: A rationalization of prejudice in Greece and Rome', in Eliav-Feldon et al., pp. 32–56.

Isaac, B. (2006), 'Proto-racism in Graeco-Roman antiquity', *WorldArch*, 38: 32–47.

Isaac, B. (2004), *The Invention of Racism in Classical Antiquity*, Princeton: Princeton University Press.

Isler-Kerényi, C. (2015), 'Iconographical and iconological approaches', in C. Marconi (ed.) *The Oxford Handbook of Greek and Roman Art and Architecture*, Oxford: Oxford University Press, pp. 557–78.

Ivantchik, A. I. (2011), 'The funeral of Scythian kings: The historical reality and the description of Herodotus (4.71–2)', in Bonfante, pp. 71–106.

Jacobson, E. (1995), *The Art of the Scythians: The Interpenetration of Cultures at the Edge of the Hellenic World*, Leiden: Brill.

Jahn, O. (1843), *Archaeologische Beiträge*, Berlin: G. Reimer.

Jenkins, I. (2015), 'The human body in Greek art and thought', in I. Jenkins with C. Farge and V. Turner (eds) *Defining Beauty: The Body in Ancient Greek Art*, London: The British Museum, pp. 16–29.

Johnstone, S. (1998), 'Cracking the code of silence: Athenian legal oratory and the histories of slaves and women', in Murnaghan and Joshel, pp. 221–36.

Jonckheere, F. (1954), 'L'eunuque dans l'Égypte pharaonique', *Revue d'histoire des sciences et de leurs applications*, 7: 139–55.

Jones, C. P. (1999), *Kinship Diplomacy in the Ancient World*, Cambridge, MA: Harvard University Press.

Jones, O. A. (2018), 'Demography and burial exclusion in Mycenaean Achaia, Greece', *Journal of Greek Archaeology*, 3: 75–93.

Jones, S. (1997), *The Archaeology of Ethnicity: Constructing Identities in the Past and Present*, London: Routledge.

Jordan, D. R. (2000), 'A personal letter found in the Athenian Agora', *Hesperia*, 69: 91–103.

Joyce, R. A. (2017), 'Sex, gender, and anthropology: Moving bioarchaeology outside the subdiscipline', in Agarwal and Wesp, pp. 1–12.

Joyce, R. A. (2008), *Ancient Bodies, Ancient Lives: Sex, Gender, and Archaeology*, London: Thames and Hudson.

Junior, N. and J. Schipper (2013), 'Disability studies and the Bible', in S. L. McKenzie and J. Kaltner (eds) *New Meanings for Ancient Texts: Recent Approaches to Biblical Criticisms and Their Applications*, Westminster: John Knox Press, pp. 21–37.

Just, R. (1989), 'Triumph of the ethnos', in E. Tonkin, M. McDonald and M. Chapman (eds) *History and Ethnicity*, London: Routledge, pp. 71–88.

Kamen, D. (2013), *Status in Classical Athens*, Princeton: Princeton University Press.

Kamtekar, R. (2002), 'Distinction without a difference? Race and *genos* in Plato', in J. K. Ward and T. L. Lott (eds) *Philosophers on Race: Critical Essays*, Oxford: Blackwell, pp. 1–13.

Kaplan, P. (2016), 'Location and dislocation in early Greek geography and ethnography', in Kennedy and Jones-Lewis, pp. 299–314.

Karakostis, F. A. et al. (2017), 'Occupational manual activity is reflected on the patterns among hand entheses', *Am J Phys Anthropol*, 164: 30–40.

Kardulias, P. N. (1994), 'Towards an anthropological historical archaeology in Greece', *Historical Archaeology*, 28: 39–55.

Karttunen, K. (1984), 'Κυνοκέφαλοι and Κυναμολγοί in Classical ethnography', *Arctos*, 18: 31–6.

Kasimis, D. (2018), *The Perpetual Immigrant and the Limits of Athenian Democracy*, Cambridge: Cambridge University Press.

Katz, D. C., M. N. Grote and T. D. Weaver (2017), 'Changes in human skull morphology across the agricultural transition are consistent with softer diets in preindustrial farming groups', *PNAS*, 114: 9050–5.

Kazantsidis, G. and N. Tsoumpra (2018), 'Morbid laughter: Exploring the comic dimensions of disease in Classical antiquity', *IllinClSt*, 43: 273–97.

Keenleyside, A. (2015), 'Occipitalization of the atlas in two female skeletons from Apollonia Pontica, Bulgaria', *IJO*, 25: 74–8.

Keenleyside, A. (2011), 'Congenital aural atresia in an adult female from Apollonia Pontica, Bulgaria.' *IJPP*, 1: 63–7.

Keenleyside, A. and K. Panayotova (2006), 'Cribra orbitalia and porotic hyperostosis in a Greek colonial population (5th to 3rd centuries BC) from the Black Sea', *IJO*, 16: 373–84.

Keenleyside, A., H. P. Schwarcz and K. Panayotova (2011), 'Oxygen isotopic evidence of residence and migration in a Greek colonial population on the Black Sea', *JAS*, 38: 2658–66.

Kelley, N. (2007), 'Deformity and disability in Greece and Rome', in H. Avalos, S. J. Melcher and J. Schipper (eds) *This Abled Body: Rethinking Disabilities in Biblical Studies*, Atlanta: Society of Biblical Literature, pp. 31–46.

Kelley, O. (2012), 'Beyond intermarriage: The role of the indigenous Italic population at Pithekoussai', *OJA*, 31: 245–60.

Kellogg, D. L. (2013), *Marathon Fighters and Men of Maple: Ancient Acharnai*, Oxford: Oxford University Press.

Kemkes-Grottenthaler, A. (2002), 'Aging through the ages: Historical perspectives on age indicator methods', in R. D. Hoppa and J. W. Vaupel (eds) *Paleodemography: Age Distributions from Skeletal Samples*, Cambridge: Cambridge University Press, pp. 48–72.

Kennedy, K. A. R. (1998), 'Markers of occupational stress: Conspectus and prognosis of research', *IJO*, 8: 305–10.

Kennedy, R. F. (2019), 'Is there a "race" or "ethnicity" in Greco-Roman antiquity?', *Classics at the Intersections* <https://rfkclassics.blogspot.com/2019/04/is-there-race-or-ethnicity-in-greco.html> (last accessed 17 May 2020).

Kennedy, R. F. (2016), 'Airs, waters, metals, earth: People and land in Archaic and Classical Greek thought', in Kennedy and Jones-Lewis, pp. 9–28.

Kennedy, R. F. (2014), *Immigrant Women in Athens: Gender, Ethnicity, and Citizenship in the Classical City*, London: Routledge.

Kennedy, R. F. and M. Jones-Lewis (eds) (2016), *The Routledge Handbook of Identity and the Environment in the Classical and Medieval Worlds*, New York: Routledge.

Kennedy, R. F., C. S. Roy and M. L. Goldman (eds) (2013), *Race and Ethnicity in the Classical World: An Anthology of Primary Sources in Translation*, Indianapolis: Hackett Publishing Company.

Killgrove, K. (2010), 'Response to C. Bruun's "Water, oxygen isotopes, and immigration to Ostia-Portus"', *JRA*, 23: 133–6.

Kim, H. J. (2013), 'The invention of the "barbarian" in late sixth-century BC Ionia', in Almagor and Skinner, pp. 25–48.

Kim, H. J. (2010), 'Herodotus' Scythians viewed from a central Asian perspective: Its historicity and significance', *AncWestEast*, 9: 115–35.

King, H. (2015), 'Between male and female in ancient medicine', in Boschung et al., pp. 249–64.

Klanfer, J. (1965), *L'exclusion sociale: étude de la marginalité dans les sociétés occidentales*, Paris: Bureau de Recherches sociales.

Klaus, H. D., A. R. Harvey and M. N. Cohen (eds) (2017), *Bones of Complexity: Bioarchaeological Case Studies of Social Organization and Skeletal Biology*, Gainesville: University Press of Florida.

Klepinger, L. L. (2006), *Fundamentals of Forensic Anthropology*, Hoboken, NJ: Wiley-Liss.

Knüsel, C. (2015), 'Intersex', in P. Whelehan and A. Bolin (eds) *The International Encyclopedia of Human Sexuality*, Chichester: John Wiley & Sons.

Knüsel, C. (2000), 'Bone adaptation and its relationship to physical activity in the past', in Cox and Mays, pp. 381–401.

Knüsel, C. J. (1999), 'Orthopaedic disability: Some hard evidence', *Archaeological Review from Cambridge*, 15: 31–53.

Knüsel, C. and K. Ripley (2000), 'The *Berdache* of man-woman in Anglo-Saxon England and early medieval Europe', in W. O. Frazer and A. Tyrrell (eds) *Social Identity in Early Medieval Britain*, London: Leicester University Press, pp. 157–91.

Kömürcü, E. et al. (2014), 'Musculoskeletal injuries in Homer's *Iliad*: The war of Troy revisited', *Am J Phys Med Rehabil*, 93: 335–41.

Konigsberg, L. W., L. A. P. Kohn and J. M. Cheverud (1993), 'Cranial deformation and nonmetric trait variation', *Am J Phys Anthropol*, 90: 35–48.

Konstan, D. (2001), '*To Hellēnikon ethnos*: Ethnicity and the construction of ancient Greek identity', in Malkin, pp. 29–50.

Koukouli-Chrysanthaki, C. (2002), 'Excavating classical Amphipolis', in M. Stamatapoulou and M. Yeroulanou (eds) *Excavating Classical Culture: Recent Archaeological Discoveries in Greece*, British Archaeological Reports International Series 1031, Oxford: Beazley Archive and BAR Publishing, pp. 57–74.

Kozintsev, A. G. (2007), 'Scythians of the North Pontic region: Between-group variation, affinities, and origins', *Archaeology, Ethnology, and Anthropology of Eurasia*, 4: 143–57.

Kreuzer, B. (2009), 'An aristocrat in the Athenian Kerameikos: The Kleophrades Painter = Megakles', in J. H. Oakley and O. Palagia (eds) *Athenian Potters and Painters*, vol. 2, Oxford: Oxbow Books, pp. 116–24.

Kron, G. (2005), 'Anthropometry, physical anthropology, and the reconstruction of ancient health, nutrition, and living standards', *Historia*, 54: 68–83.

Kucharski, J. (2015), 'Capital punishment in Classical Athens', *Scripta Classica*, 12: 13–28.

Kunitz, S. J. (1987), 'Making a long story short: A note on men's height and mortality in England from the first through the nineteenth centuries', *Med Hist*, 31: 269–80.

Kurke, L. (2003), 'Aesop and the contestation of Delphic authority', in Dougherty and Kurke, pp. 77–100.

Kurth, G. and O. Röhrer-Ertel (1981), 'On the anthropology of the Mesolithic to Chalcolithic human remains from the Tell es-Sultan in Jericho, Jordan', in T. A. Holland (ed.) *Excavations at Jericho*, vol. 3, London: British School of Archaeology in Jerusalem, pp. 407–81.

Kurtz, D. C. and J. Boardman (1986), 'Booners', in J. Frel and M. True (eds) *Greek Vases at the J. Paul Getty Museum*, vol. 3, Malibu, CA: The J. Paul Getty Museum, pp. 35–70.

Kurtz, D. C. and J. Boardman (1971), *Greek Burial Customs*, London: Thames and Hudson.

Kwok, C. S. and A. Keenleyside (2015), 'Stable isotope evidence for infant feeding practices in the Greek colony of Apollonia Pontica', in Papathanasiou et al., pp. 147–70.

Kyle, B. et al. (2018), 'Examining the osteological paradox: Skeletal stress in mass graves versus civilians at the Greek colony of Himera (Sicily)', *Am J Phys Anthropol*, 167: 161–72.

Kyle, B., L. A. Schepartz and C. S. Larsen (2016), 'Mother city and colony: Bioarchaeological evidence of stress and impacts of Corinthian colonisation at Apollonia, Albania', *IJO*, 26: 1067–77.

Kyle, D. G. (2014), *Sport and Spectacle in the Ancient World*, Oxford: Wiley-Blackwell.

Kyrtatas, D. J. (2011), 'Slavery and economy in the Greek world', in Bradley and Cartledge, pp. 91–111.

Lacan, M. et al. (2013), 'Ancestry of modern Europeans: Contributions of ancient DNA', *Cellular and Molecular Life Sciences*, 70: 2473–87.

Laes, C. (ed.) (2017a), *Disability in Antiquity*, London: Routledge.

Laes, C. (2017b), 'Introduction: Disability studies in the ancient world – past, present and future', in Laes, pp. 1–21.

Laes, C. (2013), 'Raising a disabled child', in Evans Grubbs et al., pp. 125–44.

Laes, C. (2011a), 'How does one do the history of disability in antiquity? One thousand years of case studies', *Journal of History of Medicine*, 23: 915–46.

Laes, C. (2011b), 'Silent witnesses: Deaf-mutes in Graeco-Roman Antiquity', *CW*, 104: 451–73.

Laes, C. (2008), 'Learning from silence: Disabled children in Roman antiquity', *Arctos*, 42: 85–122.

Laes, C., C. Goodey and M. L. Rose (eds) (2013), *Disabilities in Roman Antiquity: Disparate Bodies a capite ad calcem*, Leiden: Brill.

Lagia, A. (2015a), 'Diet and the polis: An isotopic study of diet in Athens and Laurion during the Classical, Hellenistic, and Imperial Roman periods', in Papathanasiou et al., pp. 119–46.

Lagia, A. (2015b), 'The potential and limitations of bioarchaeological investigations in Classical contexts: An example from the polis in Athens', in D. C. Haggis and C. M. Antonaccio (eds) *Classical Archaeology in Context: Theory and Practice in Excavation in the Greek World*, Berlin: De Gruyter, pp. 149–76.

Lagia, A. (2014), 'Health inequalities in the Classical city: A biocultural approach to socioeconomic differentials in the polis of Athens during the Classical, Hellenistic, and imperial Roman periods', in A.-C. Gillis (ed.) *Corps, travail et statut social: l'apport de la paléoanthropologie funéraire aux sciences historiques*, Lille: PU Septentrion, pp. 95–115.

Lagia, A. (2007), 'Notions of childhood in the Classical polis: Evidence from the bioarchaeological record', in A. Cohen and J. B. Rutter (eds) *Constructions of Childhood in Ancient Greece and Italy*, *Hesperia* Supplement 41, Princeton: American School of Classical Studies at Athens, pp. 293–306.

Lagia, A. and W. Cavanagh (2010), 'Burials from Kouphovouno, Sparta, Lakonia', in A. Philippa-Touchais et al. (eds) *The Greek Mainland in the Middle Bronze Age*, Paris: École française d'Athènes, pp. 333–46.

Lagia, A., A. Papathanasiou and S. Triantaphyllou (2014), 'The state of approaches to archaeological human remains in Greece', in B. O'Donnabhain and M. C. Lozada (eds) *Archaeological Human Remains: Global Perspectives*, New York: Springer, pp. 105–26.

Laird, A. G. (1933), 'Herodotus on the Pelasgians in Attica', *AJP*, 54: 97–119.

Lampinen, A. (2019), 'Cultural artefacts in transit: Notes on the transmission and translation of ethnonyms in the Greco-Roman eastern Mediterranean', in J. Hämeen-Anttila and I. Lindstedt (eds) *Translation and Transmission: Collection of Articles*, Münster: Ugarit-Verlag, pp. 139–79.

Laneri, N. (2007), 'An archaeology of funerary rituals', in N. Laneri (ed.) *Performing Death: Social Analyses of Funerary Traditions in the Ancient Near East and Mediterranean*, Chicago: Oriental Institute of the University of Chicago, pp. 1–13.

Lape, S. (2010), *Race and Citizen Identity in the Classical Athenian Democracy*, Cambridge: Cambridge University Press.

Lape, S. (2003), 'Racializing democracy: The politics of sexual reproduction in Classical Athens', *Parallax*, 9: 52–63.

Larsen, C. S. (2015), *Bioarchaeology: Interpreting Behavior from the Human Skeleton*, second edition, Cambridge: Cambridge University Press.

Larson, S. L. (2007), *Tales of Epic Ancestry: Boiotian Collective Identity in the Late Archaic and Early Classical Periods*, Stuttgart: Franz Steiner.

Lattimore, R. (trans.) (1960), *Greek Lyrics*, Chicago: University of Chicago Press.

Lauffer, S. (1979), *Die Bergwerkssklaven von Laureion*, second edition, Wiesbaden: Franz Steiner.

Laurence, R. (2000), 'Metaphors, monuments and texts: The life course in Roman culture', *WorldArch*, 31: 442–55.

Lawton, C. L. (2007), 'Children in Classical Attic votive reliefs', in A. Cohen and J. B. Rutter (eds) *Constructions of Childhood in Ancient Greece and Italy*, *Hesperia* Supplement 41, Princeton: American School of Classical Studies at Athens, pp. 41–60.

Lazaridis, I. et al. (2017), 'Genetic origins of the Minoans and Mycenaeans', *Nature*, 548: 214–18.

Lazer, E. (2009), *Resurrecting Pompeii*, London: Routledge.

Lease, L. R. and P. W. Sciulli (2005), 'Discrimination between European-American and African-American children based on deciduous dental metrics and morphology', *Am J Phys Anthropol*, 126: 56–60.

Leclant, J. (2010), 'Egypt, land of Africa, in the Greco-Roman world', in Bindman and Gates, pp. 275–88.

Lee, M. M. (2015), *Body, Dress, and Identity in Ancient Greece*, Cambridge: Cambridge University Press.

Lefkowitz, M. R. and M. B. Fant (1992), *Women's Life in Greece and Rome: A Source Book in Translation*, second edition, Baltimore: Johns Hopkins University Press.

Lekovic, G. P. et al. (2007), 'New world cranial deformation practices: Historical implications for pathophysiology of cognitive impairment in deformational plagiocephaly', *Neurosurgery*, 60: 1137–47.

Lenfant, D. (2012), 'Ctesias and his eunuchs: A challenge for modern historians', *Histos*, 6: 257–97.

Lenfant, D. (1999), 'Monsters in Greek ethnography and society in the fifth and fourth centuries BCE', in R. Buxton (ed.) *From Myth to Reason? Studies in the Development of Greek Thought*, Oxford: Oxford University Press, pp. 197–214.

Lenoir, R. (1974), *Les exclus: un français sur dix*, Paris: Éditions du Seuil.

Levy-Coffman, E. (2005), 'We are not our ancestors: Evidence for discontinuity between prehistoric and modern Europeans', *Journal of Genetic Genealogy*, 1: 40–50.

Lewis, D. M. (2019), 'Piracy and slave trading in action in Classical and Hellenistic Greece', *Arquivos*, 10: 79–108.

Lewis, D. M. (2018a), *Greek Slave Systems in Their Eastern Mediterranean Context, c. 800–146 BC*, Oxford: Oxford University Press.

Lewis, D. M. (2018b), 'Notes on slave names, ethnicity, and identity in Classical and Hellenistic Greece', *Studia Źródłoznawcze, U Schyłku Starożytności*, 16: 169–99.

Lewis, D. M. (2015), 'The market for slaves in the fifth- and fourth-century Aegean', in E. M. Harris, D. M. Lewis and M. Woolmer (eds) *The Ancient Greek Economy: Markets, Households, and City-States*, Cambridge: Cambridge University Press, pp. 316–36.

Lewis, D. M. (2011), 'Near Eastern slaves in Classical Attica and the slave trade with Persian territories', *ClQ*, 61: 91–113.

Lewis, M. E. (2007), *The Bioarchaeology of Children: Perspectives from Biological and Forensic Anthropology*, Cambridge: Cambridge University Press.

Lewis, S. (1998/9), 'Slaves as viewers and users of Athenian pottery', *Hephaistos*, 16/17: 71–90.

Lightfoot, J. L. (2002), 'Sacred eunuchism in the cult of the Syrian goddess', in Tougher, pp. 71–86.

Lindenlauf, A. (2001), 'Thrown away like rubbish: Disposal of the dead in ancient Greece', *Papers from the Institute of Archaeology*, 12: 86–99.

Link, B. G. and J. Phelan (1995), 'Social conditions as fundamental causes of disease', *J Health Soc Behav*, 35: 80–94.

Lissarrague, F. (2002), 'The Athenian image of the foreigner', in Harrison, pp. 101–24.

Lissarrague, F. (2000), 'Aesop, between man and beast: Ancient portraits and illustrations', in Cohen, pp. 132–49.

Lissarrague, F. (1995), 'Identity and otherness: The case of Attic head vases and plastic vases', *Source: Notes in the History of Art*, 15: 4–9.

Liston, M. A. (2017), 'Human skeletal remains', in J. K. Papadopoulos and E. L. Smithson (eds) *The Athenian Agora, Volume XXXVI: The Early Iron Age Cemeteries*, Princeton: American School of Classical Studies at Athens, pp. 503–60.

Liston, M. A. (2012), 'Reading the bones: Interpreting the skeletal evidence for women's lives in ancient Greece', in S. L. James and S. Dillon (eds) *A Companion to Women in the Ancient World*, London: Blackwell Publishing, pp. 125–40.

Liston, M. A. (1993), 'The human skeletal remains from Kavousi, Crete: A bioarchaeological analysis', PhD diss., University of Tennessee.

Liston, M. A. and S. I. Rotroff (2013), 'Babies in the well: Archaeological evidence for newborn disposal in Hellenistic Greece', in Evans Grubbs et al., pp. 62–82.

Liston, M. A., S. I. Rotroff and L. M. Snyder (2018), *The Agora Bone Well*, Princeton: American School of Classical Studies at Athens.

Little, L. M. and J. K. Papadopoulos (1998), 'A social outcast in Early Iron Age Athens', *Hesperia*, 67: 375–404.

Littman, R. J. (2009), 'The plague of Athens: Epidemiology and paleopathology', *The Mount Sinai Journal of Medicine*, 76: 456–67.

Llewellyn-Jones, L. (2002), 'Eunuchs and the royal harem in Achaemenid Persia (559–331 BC)', in Tougher, pp. 19–49.

Lo Presti, R. (2012), 'Shaping the difference: The medical inquiry into the nature of places and the early birth of anthropology in the Hippocratic treatise *Airs Waters Places*', in P. A. Baker, H. Nijdam and K. van't Land (eds) *Medicine and Space: Body, Surroundings and Borders in Antiquity and the Middle Ages*, Leiden: Brill, pp. 169–96.

Lohmann, H. (2012), 'Ionians and Carians in the Mycale: The discovery of Carian Melia and the Archaic Panionion', in Cifani and Stoddart, pp. 32–50.

Lomas, K. (ed.) (2004), *Greek Identity in the Western Mediterranean: Papers in Honour of Brian Shefton*, Leiden: Brill.

Lomas, K. (2000), 'The polis in Italy: Ethnicity, colonization, and citizenship in the western Mediterranean', in Brock and Hodkinson, pp. 167–85.

Lombardo, S. (trans.) (1997), *Homer. Iliad*, Indianapolis: Hackett Publishing.

Lonoce, H. et al. (2018), 'The Western (Buonfornello) necropolis (7th to 4th BC) of the Greek colony of Himera (Sicily, Italy): Site-specific discriminant functions for sex determination in the common burials resulting from the battle of Himera (ca. 480 BC)', *IJO*, 28: 766–74.

Loogväli, E.-L. et al. (2004), 'Disuniting uniformity: A pied cladistic canvas of mtDNA haplogroup H in Eurasia', *Mol Biol Evol*, 21: 2012–21.

Loraux, N. (2000), *Born of the Earth: Myth and Politics in Athens*, Ithaca, NY: Cornell University Press.

Loraux, N. (1986), *The Invention of Athens: The Funeral Oration in the Classical City*, Cambridge, MA: Harvard University Press.

Lorentz, K. O. (2009), 'The malleable body: Headshaping in Greece and the surrounding regions', in Schepartz et al., pp. 75–98.

Lorentz, K. O. (2005), 'Late Bronze Age burial practices: Age as a form of social difference', in V. Karageorghis, H. Matthaus and S. Rogge (eds) *Cyprus: Religion and Society from the Late Bronze Age to the End of the Archaic Period. Proceedings of an International Symposium on Cypriote Archaeology, Erlangen, 23–24 July 2004*, Mohnesee-Wamel: Bibliopolis, pp. 41–55.

Lorentz, K. O. (2004), 'Age and gender in eastern Mediterranean prehistory: Depictions, burials, and skeletal evidence', *Ethnographisch-Archäologische Zeitschrift*, 45: 297–315.

Lorentz, K. O. (2003), 'Minding the body: The growing body in Cyprus from the Aceramic Neolithic to the Late Bronze Age', PhD diss., University of Cambridge.

Low, P. (2012), 'Monuments to the war dead in Classical Athens: Form, contexts, meanings', in P. Low, G. Oliver and P. J. Rhodes (eds) *Cultures of*

Commemoration: War Memorials, Ancient and Modern, Oxford: Oxford University Press, pp. 13–39.

Lozada, M. C. (2011), 'Cultural determinants of ancestry: A lesson for studies of biological relatedness and ethnicity in the past', in A. Baadsgaard, A. T. Boutin and J. E. Buikstra (eds) *Breathing New Life into the Evidence of Death: Contemporary Approaches to Bioarchaeology*, Santa Fe: SAR Press, pp. 135–49.

Lucy, S. J. (2000), *The Anglo-Saxon Way of Death: Burial Rites in Early England*, Stroud: Sutton Publishing.

Lull, V. (2000), 'Death and society: A Marxist approach', *Antiquity*, 74: 576–80.

Luraghi, N. (2008), *The Ancient Messenians: Constructions of Ethnicity and Memory*, Cambridge, MA: Harvard University Press.

Macaulay, V. et al. (2005), 'Single, rapid coastal settlement of Asia revealed by analysis of complete mitochondrial genomes', *Science*, 308: 1034–6.

McCall, D. F. (1999), 'Herodotus on the Garamantes: A problem in protohistory', *History in Africa*, 26: 197–217.

McCoskey, D. E. (2019), *Race: Antiquity and Its Legacy*, reprint, New York: Bloomsbury.

Macfarlane, P. and R. Polansky (2004), 'Physical disability in earlier Greek philosophy', *Skepsis: A Journal for Philosophy and Interdisciplinary Research*, 15: 25–41.

McIlvaine, B. K. (2015), 'Implications of reappraising the iron-deficiency anemia hypothesis', *IJO*, 25: 997–1000.

McIlvaine, B. K. and L. A. Schepartz (2015), 'Femoral subtrochanteric shape variation in Albania: Implications for use in forensic applications', *HOMO: Journal of Comparative Human Biology*, 66: 79–89.

McIlvaine, B. K. et al. (2014), 'Evidence for long-term migration on the Balkan peninsula using dental and cranial nonmetric data: Early interaction between Corinth (Greece) and its colony at Apollonia (Albania)', *Am J Phys Anthropol*, 153: 236–48.

McInerney, J. (2018), 'Greek colonization', *Oxford Bibliographies*, DOI: https://doi.org/10.1093/OBO/9780195389661-0307.

McInerney, J. (2014), 'Pelasgians and Leleges: Using the past to understand the present', in C. Pieper and J. Ker (eds) *Valuing the Past in the Greco-Roman World*, Leiden: Brill, pp. 25–55.

McInerney, J. (2001), 'Ethnos and ethnicity in early Greece', in Malkin, pp. 51–73.

McInerney, J. (1999), *The Folds of Parnassos: Land and Ethnicity in Ancient Phokis*, Austin: University of Texas Press.

McKeown, N. (2011), 'Resistance among chattel slaves in the Classical world', in Bradley and Cartledge, pp. 153–75.

MacKinnon, M. (2007), 'State of the discipline: Osteological research in classical archaeology', *AJA*, 11: 473–504.

MacLachlan, B. (2012), *Women in Ancient Greece: A Sourcebook*, New York: Bloomsbury.

McNally, S. (1978), 'The maenad in early Greek art', *Arethusa*, 11: 101–35.

MacSweeney, N. (2009), 'Beyond ethnicity: The overlooked diversity of group identities', *JMA*, 22: 101–26.

Malama, P. and S. Triantaphyllou (2001), 'Anthropologikes plirofories apo to anatoliko nekrotafeio tis Amfipolis', *To Archaeologiko Ergo sti Makedonia kai Thraki*, 15: 127–36.

Malkin, I. (2016), 'Migration and colonization: Turbulence, continuity, and the practice of Mediterranean space (11th–5th centuries BCE)', in M. Dabag et al. (eds) *New Horizons: Mediterranean Research in the 21st Century*, Paderborn: Ferdinand Schöningh, pp. 285–308.

Malkin, I. (2015), 'Foreign founders: Greeks and Hebrews', in N. MacSweeney (ed.) *Foundation Myths in Ancient Societies: Dialogues and Discourses*, Philadelphia: University of Pennsylvania Press, pp. 20–40.

Malkin, I. (2011), *A Small Greek World: Networks in the Ancient Mediterranean*, Oxford: Oxford University Press.

Malkin, I. (2005), 'Networks and the emergence of Greek identity', in I. Malkin (ed.) *Mediterranean Paradigms and Classical Antiquity*, London: Routledge, pp. 56–74.

Malkin, I. (2004), 'Postcolonial concepts and ancient Greek colonization', *Modern Language Quarterly*, 65: 341–64.

Malkin, I. (2002), 'A colonial middle ground: Greek, Etruscan, and local elites in the Bay of Naples', in C. L. Lyons and J. K. Papadopoulos (eds) *The Archaeology of Colonization*, Los Angeles: Getty Research Institute, pp. 151–81.

Malkin, I. (ed.) (2001a), *Ancient Perceptions of Greek Ethnicity*, Washington, DC: Center for Hellenic Studies.

Malkin, I. (2001b), 'Greek ambiguities: "Ancient Hellas" and "barbarian Epirus"', in Malkin, pp. 187–212.

Malkin, I. (1998), *The Returns of Odysseus: Colonization and Ethnicity*, Berkeley: University of California Press.

Malkin, I. (1994), 'Inside and outside: Colonization and the formation of the mother city', *Archeologia e Storia*, 16: 1–9.

Malkin, I. (1987), *Religion and Colonization in Ancient Greece*, Leiden: Brill.

Manolis, S. K. (2001), 'The ancient Minoans of Crete: A biodistance study', *Human Evolution*, 16: 125–36.

Mant, M., C. de la Cova and M. B. Brickley (2021), 'Intersectionality and trauma research in bioarchaeology', *Am J Phys Anthropol*, 2021: 1–12.

Marconi, C. (2007), *Temple Decoration and Cultural Identity in the Archaic Greek World: The Metopes of Selinus*, Cambridge: Cambridge University Press.

Martin, S. R. (2017), *The Art of Contact: Comparative Approaches to Greek and Phoenician Art*, Philadelphia: University of Pennsylvania Press.

Matheson, S. B. (2009), 'Old age in Athenian vase-painting', in J. H. Oakley and O. Palagia (eds) *Athenian Potters and Painters*, vol. 2, Oxford: Oxbow Books, pp. 191–9.

Mattingly, D. (2010), 'Cultural crossovers: Global and local identities in the Classical world', in Hales and Hodos, pp. 283–95.

Mayor, A. (2014), *The Amazons: Lives and Legends of Warrior Women Across the Ancient World*, Princeton: Princeton University Press.

Mayor, A. (2008), *Greek Fire, Poison Arrows and Scorpion Bombs: Biological and Chemical Warfare in the Ancient World*, New York: Overlook Press.

Mays, S. (2012a), 'The impact of case reports relative to other types of publication in palaeopathology', *IJO*, 22: 81–5.

Mays, S. (2012b), 'The relationship between paleopathology and the clinical sciences', in A. L. Grauer (ed.) *A Companion to Paleopathology*, Oxford: Blackwell, pp. 285–309.

Mays, S. (2010), *The Archaeology of Human Bone*, second edition, London: Routledge.

Mays, S. (2003), 'Comment on "A Bayesian approach to ageing perinatal skeletal material from archaeological sites: Implications for the evidence for infanticide in Roman Britain", by R. L. Gowland and A. T. Chamberlain', *JAS*, 30: 1695–700.

Mays, S. (2000a), 'Biodistance studies using craniometrics variation in British archaeological skeletal material', in Cox and Mays, pp. 277–88.

Mays, S. (2000b), 'New directions in the analysis of stable isotopes in excavated bones and teeth', in Cox and Mays, pp. 425–38.

Mays, S. (1993), 'Infanticide in Roman Britain', *Antiquity*, 82: 883–8.

Mays, S. and M. Cox (2000), 'Sex determination in human skeletal remains', in Cox and Mays, pp. 117–30.

Mays, S. and M. Faerman (2001), 'Sex identification in some putative infanticide victims from Roman Britain using ancient DNA', *JAS*, 28: 555–9.

Meeusen, M. (2017), 'Plutarch's "philosophy" of disability: Human after all', in Laes, pp. 197–209.

Mehretu, A., B. W. Pigozzi and L. M. Sommers (2000), 'Concepts in social and spatial marginality', *Geografiska Annaler, Series B: Human Geography*, 82: 89–101.

Mellars, P. (2006), 'Going East: New genetic and archaeological perspectives on the modern human colonization of Eurasia', *Science*, 313: 786–800.

Meskell, L. (ed.) (2005), *Archaeologies of Materiality*, Malden, MA: Blackwell.

Metcalf, P. and R. Huntington (2005), *Celebrations of Death: The Anthropology of Mortuary Ritual*, second edition, Cambridge: Cambridge University Press.

Metcalfe, N. H. (2007), 'In what ways can human skeletal remains be used to understand health and disease from the past?', *Postgrad Medical Journal*, 83: 281–4.

Meyer, E. A. (2009), *Metics and the Athenian Phialai-Inscriptions: A Study in Athenian Epigraphy and Law*, Wiesbaden: Franz Steiner.

Meyer, E. A. (1993), 'Epitaphs and citizenship in Classical Athens', *JHS*, 113: 99–121.

Meyer, M. (1989), 'Alte männer auf attischen grabdenkmälern', *AM*, 104: 49–82.

Michael, D.-E. and S. K. Manolis (2014), 'Using dental caries as a nutritional indicator, in order to explore potential dietary differences between sexes in an ancient Greek population', *Mediterranean Archaeology and Archaeometry*, 14: 237–48.

Miles, M. (2003), 'Segregated we stand? The mutilated Greeks' debate at Persepolis, 330 BC', *Disability and Society*, 18: 865–79.

Millar, J. (2007), 'Social exclusion and social policy research: Defining exclusion', in D. Abrams, J. Christian and D. Gordon (eds) *Multidisciplinary Handbook of Social Exclusion Research*, Chichester: John Wiley & Sons, pp. 1–16.

Miller, D. (ed.) (2005), *Materiality*, Durham, NC: Duke University Press.

Miller, M. C. (2005), 'Barbarian lineage in Classical Greek mythology and art: Pelops, Danaos and Kadmos', in Gruen, pp. 68–89.

Miller, M. C. (2000), 'The myth of Bousiris: Ethnicity and art', in Cohen, pp. 413–42.

Miller, M. C. (1999), 'Reexamining transvestism in Archaic and Classical Athens: The Zewadski Stamnos', *AJA*, 103: 223–53.

Miller, M. C. (1997), *Athens and Persia in the Fifth Century BC: A Study in Cultural Receptivity*, Cambridge: Cambridge University Press.

Milner, G. R., J. W. Wood and J. L. Boldsen (2008), 'Advances in paleodemography', in M. A. Katzenberg and S. R. Saunders (eds) *Biological Anthropology of the Human Skeleton*, second edition, New York: Wiley-Liss, pp. 561–600.

Mirto, M. S. (2012), *Death in the Greek World: From Homer to the Classical Age*, Oklahoma City: University of Oklahoma Press.

Mitchell, A. (2017), 'The Hellenistic turn in bodily representations: Venting anxiety in terracotta figurines', in Laes, pp. 182–96.

Mitchell, A. G. (2009), *Greek Vase-Paintings and the Origins of Visual Humour*, Cambridge: Cambridge University Press.

Mitchell, D. T. and S. L. Snyder (1997), 'Introduction: Disability studies and the double bind representation', in D. T. Mitchell and S. L. Snyder (eds) *The Body and Physical Difference: Discourses of Disability*, Ann Arbor: University of Michigan Press, pp. 1–31.

Mitchell, L. (2007), *Panhellenism and the Barbarian in Archaic and Classical Greece*, Swansea: Classical Press of Wales.

Mitchell, R. J., L. Earl and B. Fricke (1997), 'Y-chromosome specific alleles and haplotypes in European and Asian populations: Linkage disequilibrium and geographic diversity', *Am J Phys Anthropol*, 104: 167–76.

Moffat, T. and T. Prowse (2018), 'Biocultural and bioarchaeology approaches to infant and young child feeding in the past', in Beauchesne and Agarwal, pp. 98–126.

Molleson, T. (1999), 'Archaeological evidence for attitudes to disability in the past', *Archaeological Review from Cambridge*, 15: 69–77.

Molleson, T. and S. Campbell (1995), 'Deformed skulls at Tell Arpachiyah: The social context', in S. Campbell and A. Green (eds) *The Archaeology of Death in the Ancient Near East*, Oxford: Oxbow Books, pp. 44–55.

Monoson, S. S. (2011), 'Navigating race, class, polis, and empire: The place of empirical analysis in Aristotle's account of natural slavery', in Alston, Hall and Proffitt, pp. 133–51.

Montgomery, J. et al. (2010), '"Gleaming, white and deadly": Using lead to track human exposure and geographic origins in the Roman period in Britain', in H. Eckardt (ed.) *Roman Diasporas: Archaeological Approaches to Mobility and Diversity in the Roman Empire*, Portsmouth, RI: Journal of Roman Archaeology, pp. 199–226.

Morgan, C. (2001), 'Ethne, ethnicity, and early Greek states, ca. 1200–480 B.C.: An archaeological perspective', in Malkin, pp. 75–112.

Morgan, C. (2000), 'Politics without the polis: Cities and the Achaean ethnos, *c*. 800–500 BC', in Brock and Hodkinson, pp. 189–211.

Morgan, C. (1999), 'Cultural subzones in Early Iron Age and Archaic Arkadia?', in Nielsen and Roy, pp. 382–456.

Morgan, C. (1991), 'Ethnicity and early Greek states: Historical and material perspectives', *PCPS*, 37: 131–63.

Morgan, K. A. (2015), 'Autochthony and identity in Greek myth', in D. Hammer (ed.) *A Companion to Greek Democracy and the Roman Republic*, Chichester: John Wiley & Sons, pp. 67–82.

Morin, D., R. Herbach and P. Rosenthal (2012), 'The Laurion shafts, Greece: Ventilation systems and mining technology in antiquity', *Historical Metallurgy*, 46: 9–18.

Morris, I. (2011), 'Archaeology and Greek slavery', in Bradley and Cartledge, pp. 176–93.

Morris, I. (2007), 'Early Iron Age Greece', in W. Scheidel, I. Morris and R. P. Saller (eds) *Cambridge Histories Online: The Cambridge Economic History of the Greco-Roman World*, Cambridge: Cambridge University Press, pp. 211–41.

Morris, I. (2001), *Death-Ritual and Social Structure in Classical Antiquity*, reprint, Cambridge: Cambridge University Press.

Morris, I. (2000), *Archaeology as Cultural History: Words and Things in Iron Age Greece*, Oxford: Blackwell.

Morris, I. (1998), 'Remaining invisible: The archaeology of the excluded in Classical Athens', in Murnaghan and Joshel, pp. 193–220.

Morris, I. (1994), 'Everyman's grave', in Boegehold and Scafuro, pp. 67–101.

Morris, I. (1987), *Burial and Ancient Society: The Rise of the Greek City-State*, Cambridge: Cambridge University Press.

Morris, M. (2018), *Slave-Wives, Single Women and 'Bastards' in the Ancient Greek World: Law and Economics Perspectives*, Oxford: Oxbow Books.

Morris, S. P. (2018), 'Material evidence: Looking for slaves? The archaeological record: Greece', in S. Hodkinson, M. Kleijwegt and K. Vlassopoulos (eds) *The Oxford Handbook of Greek and Roman Slaveries*, Oxford: Oxford University Press, DOI: https://doi.org/10.1093/oxfordhb/9780199575251.013.8.

Morris, S. P. (1992), *Daidalos and the Origins of Greek Art*, Princeton: Princeton University Press.

Morris, S. P. and J. K. Papadopoulos (2005), 'Greek towers and slaves: An archaeology of exploitation', *AJA*, 109: 155–225.

Morriss-Kay, G. M. and A. O. M. Wilkie (2005), 'Growth of the normal skull vault and its alteration in craniosynostosis: Insights from human genetics and experimental studies', *J Anat*, 207: 637–53.

Movsesian, A. A. and V. Y. Bakholdina (2017), 'Nonmetric cranial trait variation and the origins of the Scythians', *Am J Phys Anthropol*, 162: 589–99.

Mukhopadhyay, C. C., R. Henze and Y. T. Moses (2014), *How Real Is Race? A Sourcebook on Race, Culture, and Biology*, second edition, New York: AltaMira Press.

Muller, Y. (2018), 'Infirmité et mutilation corporelle en Grèce ancienne: le cas de la famille étymologique de ϖηρός', *Pallas*, 106: 289–308.

Munson, M. V. (2006), 'An alternate world: Herodotus and Italy', in Dewald and Marincola, pp. 257–73.

Munson, M. V. (2005), *Black Doves Speak: Herodotus and the Languages of Barbarians*, Cambridge, MA: Harvard University Press.

Murnaghan, S. and S. R. Joshel (eds) (1998), *Women and Slaves in Greco-Roman Culture: Differential Equations*, London: Routledge.

Murphy, E. M. (ed.) (2008), *Deviant Burial in the Archaeological Record*, Oxford: Oxbow Books.

Murphy, M. S. and H. D. Klaus (eds) (2017), *Colonized Bodies, Worlds Transformed: Toward a Global Bioarchaeology of Contact and Colonialism*, Gainesville: University Press of Florida.

Murray, O. (1996), 'Herodotus and oral history', in H. Sancisi-Weerdenburg and A. Kúhrt (eds) *Achaemenid History II: The Greek Sources*, reprint, Leiden: Netherlands Institute, pp. 93–115.

Murray, O. (1993), *Early Greece*, second edition, Cambridge, MA: Harvard University Press.

Musgrave, J. H. (1990), 'The cremated remains from Tombs II and III at Nea Mihaniona and Tomb Beta at Derveni', *BSA*, 85: 301–25.

Musgrave, J. H. (1985), 'The skull of Philip II of Macedon', in S. J. W. Lisney and B. Matthews (eds) *Current Topics in Oral Biology*, Bristol: University of Bristol Press, pp. 1–16.

Musgrave, J. H. and M. R. Popham (1991), 'The Late Helladic IIIC intramural burials at Lefkandi, Euboea', *BSA*, 86: 273–96.

Musgrave, J. H., R. A. Neave and A. J. N. W. Prag (1984), 'The skull from tomb II at Vergina: King Philip II of Macedon', *JHS*, 104: 60–78.

Musgrave, J. et al. (2010), 'The occupants of Tomb II at Vergina: Why Arrhidaios and Eurydice must be excluded', *International Journal of Medical Sciences*, 7: s1–s15.

Nafplioti, A. (2011), 'Tracing population mobility in the Aegean using isotope geochemistry: A first map of biologically available ^{87}Sr/^{86}Sr signatures', *JAS*, 38: 1560–70.

Nafplioti, A. (2009), 'Mycenae revisited part 2. Exploring the local versus non-local geographical origin of the individuals from Grave Circle A: Evidence from strontium isotope ratio (^{87}Sr/^{86}Sr) analysis', *BSA*, 104: 279–91.

Nafplioti, A. (2008), '"Mycenaean" political domination of Knossos following the Late Minoan IB destructions on Crete: Negative evidence from strontium isotope ratio analysis (^{87}Sr/^{86}Sr)', *JAS*, 35: 2307–17.

Nakassis, D., M. L. Galaty and W. A. Parkinson (2010), 'State and society', in E. H. Cline (ed.) *The Oxford Handbook of the Bronze Age Aegean*, Oxford: Oxford University Press, pp. 240–50.

Námerová, A. (2010), 'Relations between Greeks and Scythians in the Black Sea area', *Anodos*, 10: 207–11.

Nawrocki, S. P. (2010), 'The nature and sources of error in the estimation of age at death from the skeleton', in K. E. Latham and M. Finnegan (eds) *Age Estimation of the Human Skeleton*, Springfield, IL: Charles C. Thomas, pp. 79–101.

Neils, J. (2012), 'Age, gender, and social identity', in Smith and Plantzos, pp. 498–509.

Neils, J. (2007), 'The Group of the Negro Alabastra reconsidered', in F. Giudice and R. Panvini (eds) *Il greco, il barbaro e la ceramica Attica: Immaginario del diverso, processi di scambio e autorappresentazione degli indigeni*, vol. 4, Rome: L'Erma di Bretschneider, pp. 67–74.

Neils, J. (2000), 'Others within the Other: An intimate look at hetairai and maenads', in Cohen, pp. 203–26.

Neils, J. (1980), 'The Group of the Negro Alabastra: A study in motif transferal', *AntK*, 23: 13–23, pls. 3–7.

Neils, J. and J. H. Oakley (eds) (2003), *Coming of Age in Ancient Greece: Images of Childhood from the Classical Past*, New Haven: Yale University Press.

Nelson, A. (2016), *The Social Life of DNA: Race, Reparations, and Reconciliation after the Genome*, Boston: Beacon Press.

Nicholson, N. J. (2005), *Aristocracy and Athletics in Archaic and Classical Greece*, Cambridge: Cambridge University Press.

Nielsen, T. H. (1999), 'The concept of Arkadia: The people, their land, and their organisation', in Nielsen and Roy, pp. 16–79.

Nielsen, T. H. and J. Roy (eds) (1999), *Defining Ancient Arkadia*, Copenhagen: Royal Danish Academy of Sciences and Letters.

Nielsen, T. H. et al. (1989), 'Athenian grave monuments and social class', *GRBS*, 30: 411–20.

Nikita, E. et al. (2019), 'A three-dimensional digital microscopic investigation of entheseal changes as skeletal activity markers', *Am J Phys Anthropol*, 169: 704–13.

Nikita, E., A. Lagia and S. Triantaphyllou (2016), 'Epidemiology and pathology', in G. L. Irby (ed.) *A Companion to Science, Technology, and Medicine in Ancient Greece and Rome*, Oxford: Wiley-Blackwell, pp. 465–82.

Nilsson, L. (1998), 'Dynamic cadavers: A "field-anthropological" analysis of the Skateholm II burials', *LundAR*, 4: 5–17.

Nippel, W. (2002), 'The construction of the "Other"', in Harrison, pp. 278–310.

Nippel, W. (1996), 'Facts and fiction: Greek ethnography and its legacy', *History and Anthropology*, 9: 125–38.

Norbeck, E., D. E. Walker and M. Cohen (1962), 'The interpretation of data: Puberty rites', *American Anthropologist*, 64: 463–85.

Nordbladh, J. and T. Yates (1990), 'This perfect body, this virgin text: Between sex and gender in archaeology', in I. Bapty and T. Yates (eds) *Archaeology after Structuralism*, London: Routledge, pp. 222–37.

Nowak-Kemp, M. and Y. Galanakis (2012), 'Ancient Greek skulls in the Oxford University Museum. Part I: George Rolleston, Oxford and the formation of the human skulls collection', *Journal of the History of Collections*, 24: 89–104.

N'Shea, O. (2016), 'Royal eunuchs and elite masculinity in the Neo-Assyrian empire', *NEA*, 79: 214–21.

Oakley, J. H. (2003), 'Death and the child', in Neils and Oakley, pp. 163–94.

Oakley, J. H. (2000), 'Some "other" members of the Athenian household: Maids and their mistresses in fifth-century Athenian art', in Cohen, pp. 227–47.

Ober, J. (2018), 'Institutions, growth, and inequality in ancient Greece', in G. Anagnostopoulos and G. Santas (eds) *Democracy, Justice, and Equality in Ancient Greece: Historical and Philosophical Perspectives*, New York: Springer, pp. 15–38.

Ober, J. (2010), 'The instrumental value of others and institutional change: An Athenian case study', in Rosen and Sluiter, pp. 155–78.

Ober, J. (1989), *Mass and Elite in Democratic Athens: Rhetoric, Ideology, and the Power of the People*, Princeton: Princeton University Press.

Oestigaard, T. (2004), 'The world as artefact: Material culture studies and archaeology', in F. Fahlander and T. Oestigaard (eds) *Material Culture and Other Things: Post-Disciplinary Studies in the 21st Century*, Vällingby: Elanders Gotab, pp. 21–55.

Ogden, D. (1997), *Crooked Kings of Ancient Greece*, London: Bloomsbury.

Ogden, D. (1996), *Greek Bastardy in the Classical and Hellenistic Periods*, Oxford: Clarendon Press.

Ogden, D. (1994), 'Crooked speech: The genesis of the Spartan rhetra', *JHS*, 114: 85–102.

Oldenziel, R. (1987), 'The historiography of infanticide in antiquity: A literature stillborn', in J. Blok and P. Mason (eds) *Sexual Asymmetry: Studies in Ancient Society*, Amsterdam: J. C. Gieben, pp. 87–107.

Oliver, G. (2000), 'Athenian funerary monuments: Style, grandeur, and cost', in G. J. Oliver (ed.) *The Epigraphy of Death: Studies in the History and Society of Greece and Rome*, Liverpool: Liverpool University Press, pp. 59–80.

Orsi, P. (1906), 'Gela: Scavi del 1900–1905', *MonAnt*, 17: 5–758.

Ortner, D. J. (2003), *Identification of Pathological Conditions in Human Skeletal Remains*, second edition, San Diego: Academic Press.

Osborne, R. (2012), 'Landscape, ethnicity and the *polis*', in Cifani and Stoddart, pp. 24–31.

Osborne, R. (2011), *The History Written on the Classical Greek Body*, Cambridge: Cambridge University Press.

Osborne, R. (2009), *Greece in the Making, 1200–479 BCE*, second edition, London: Routledge.

Osborne, R. (2000), 'An Other view: An essay in political history', in Cohen, pp. 21–42.

Osborne, R. (1997), 'Men without clothes: Heroic nakedness and Greek art', *Gender and History*, 9: 504–28.

Osborne, R. (1992), '"Is it a farm?" The definition of agricultural sites and settlements in ancient Greece', in B. Wells (ed.) *Agriculture in Ancient Greece*, Stockholm: Svenska institutet i Athen, pp. 21–7.

Osborne, R. (1991), 'Pride and prejudice, sense and subsistence', in J. Rich and A. Wallace-Hadrill (eds) *City and Country in the Ancient World*, London: Routledge, pp. 119–46.

Osborne, R. (1987), *Classical Landscape with Figures: The Ancient Greek City and Its Countryside*, London: George Philip.

Ovadiah, A. and S. Mucznik (2017), 'Myth and reality in the battle between the pygmies and the cranes in the Greek and Roman worlds', *Gerión*, 35: 151–66.

Owen, S. (2005), 'Analogy, archaeology and Archaic Greek colonization', in H. Hurst and S. Owen (eds) *Ancient Colonizations: Analogy, Similarity and Difference*, London: Duckworth, pp. 5–22.

Oxenham, M. F. and I. Cavill (2010), 'Porotic hyperostosis and cribra orbitalia: The erythropoietic response to iron-deficiency anaemia', *Anthropological Science*, 118: 199–200.

Pader, E. J. (1982), *Symbolism, Social Relations and the Interpretation of Mortuary Remains*, British Archaeological Reports International Series 130, Oxford: BAR Publishing.

Pader, E. J. (1980), 'Material symbolism and social relations in mortuary studies', in P. Rahtz, T. Dickinson and L. Watts (eds) *Anglo-Saxon Cemeteries 1979: The Fourth Anglo-Saxon Symposium at Oxford*, British Archaeological Reports British Series 82, Oxford: BAR Publishing, pp. 143–59.

Padgett, J. M. (2003), *The Centaur's Smile: The Human Animal in Early Greek Art*, New Haven: Yale University Press.

Padgett, J. M. (2000), 'The stable hands of Dionysos: Satyrs and donkeys as symbols of social marginalization in Attic vase painting', in Cohen, pp. 43–70.

Panagiotopoulou, E. et al. (2018), 'Detecting mobility in Early Iron Age Thessaly by strontium isotope analysis', *EJA*, 21: 590–611.

Papadopoulos, J. K. (2017), 'Burial customs and funerary rites', in J. K. Papadopoulos and E. L. Smithson (eds) *The Athenian Agora, Volume XXXVI: The Early Iron Age Cemeteries*, Princeton: American School of Classical Studies at Athens, pp. 576–688.

Papadopoulos, J. K. (2000), 'Skeletons in wells: Towards an archaeology of social exclusion in the ancient Greek world', in Hubert, pp. 96–118.

Papadopoulos, J. K. (1993), 'To kill a cemetery: The Athenian Kerameikos and the Early Iron Age in the Aegean', *JMA*, 6: 175–206.

Papageorgopoulou, E. M.-C. (2004), 'Anthropological study of the population of Nea Philadelfeia', in D. Grammenos and S. Triantafyllou (eds) *Anthropological Research in North Greece*, vol. 2, Thessaloniki: Publications of the Archaeological Institute of Northern Greece, pp. 272–505, 566.

Papathanasiou, A. (2005), 'Health status of the Neolithic population of Alepotrypa Cave, Greece', *Am J Phys Anthropol*, 126: 377–90.

Papathanasiou, A. et al. (2013), 'Inferences from the human skeletal material of the Early Iron Age cemetery at Agios Dimitrios, Fthiotis, Central Greece', *JAS*, 40: 2924–33.

Papathanasiou, A., M. P. Richards and S. C. Fox (eds) (2015), *Archaeodiet in the Greek World: Dietary Reconstruction from Stable Isotope Analysis*, Hesperia Supplement 49, Princeton: American School of Classical Studies at Athens.

Papathanassiou, M., M. Hoskin and H. Papadopoulou (1992), 'Orientations of tombs in the late-Minoan cemetery at Armenoi, Crete', *Journal of History of Astronomy, Archaeoastronomy Supplement*, 23: S43–55A.

Park, R. E. (1928), 'Human migration and the marginal man', *American Journal of Sociology*, 33: 881–93.

Parker Pearson, M. (2005), *The Archaeology of Death and Burial*, reprint, Phoenix Mill: Sutton Publishing.

Parker Pearson, M. (1982), 'Mortuary practices, society and ideology: An ethnoarchaeological study', in I. Hodder (ed.) *Symbolic and Structural Archaeology*, Cambridge: Cambridge University Press, pp. 99–113.

Parlama, L. and N. C. Stampolidis (2001), *Athens: The City Beneath the City. Antiquities from the Metropolitan Railway Excavations*, Athens: Kapon Editions.

Patterson, C. (2006), '"Citizen cemeteries" in Classical Athens?', *ClQ*, 56: 48–56.

Patterson, C. (1994), 'The case against Neaira and the public ideology of the Athenian family', in Boegehold and Scafuro, pp. 199–216.

Patterson, C. (1985), '"Not worth rearing": The causes of infant exposure in ancient Greece', *TAPA (1974–2014)*, 115: 103–23.

Patterson, C. (1981), *Pericles' Citizenship Law of 451–50 B.C.*, Salem, NH: The Ayer Company.

Patterson, L. E. (2010), *Kinship Myth in Ancient Greece*, Austin: University of Texas Press.

Patterson, O. (1982), *Slavery and Social Death: A Comparative Study*, Cambridge, MA: Harvard University Press.

Pavel, C. (2017), 'Hephaistos and knowledge from below: Crooked feet on Mount Olympus', in M. Mazoyer and V. Faranton (eds) *Homère et l'Anatolie III*, Paris: L'Harmattan, pp. 77–114.

Pearson, J. (2018), 'Biocultural influences of total versus exclusive breastfeeding: Stable isotope evidence of European and Asian trends for the last 10,000 years', in Beauchesne and Agarwal, pp. 61–97.

Pedley, J. G. (2012), *Greek Art and Archaeology*, fifth edition, Boston: Prentice Hall.

Pelekidis, S. (1916), 'Anaskafi Falirou', *Archaeologiko Deltio*, 2: 13–64.

Pelling, C. (2009), 'Bringing autochthony up-to-date: Herodotus and Thucydides', *CW*, 102: 471–83.

Penrose, W. D. (2015), 'The discourse of disability in ancient Greece', *CW*, 108: 499–523.

Perdrizet, P. (1911), *Bronzes Grecs d'Égypte de la Collection Fouquet*, Paris: Berger-Levrault.

Perego, E. et al. (2015), 'Practices of ritual marginalisation in Late Prehistoric Veneto: Evidence from the field', in Z. Devlin and E.-J. Graham (eds) *Death Embodied: Archaeological Approaches to the Treatment of the Corpse*, Oxford: Oxbow Books, pp. 129–59.

Perrin, C. and K. Anderson (2013), 'Reframing craniometry: Human exceptionalism and the production of racial knowledge', *Social Identities*, 19: 90–103.

Perry, B. E. (1952), *Aesopica: A Series of Texts Relating to Aesop or Ascribed to Him or Closely Connected with the Literary Tradition That Bears His Name I. Greek and Latin Texts*, Urbana: University of Illinois Press.

Peschel, E. R. and R. Peschel (1986), 'Medicine and music: The castrati in opera', *The Opera Quarterly*, 4: 21–38.

Petersen, J. H. (2010), *Cultural Interactions and Social Strategies on the Pontic Shores: Burial Customs in the Northern Black Sea Area c. 550–270 BC*, Aarhus: Aarhus University Press.

Petsalis-Diomidis, A. (2016), 'Between the body and the divine: Healing votives from Classical and Hellenistic Greece', in I. Weinryb (ed.) *Ex Voto: Votive Giving Across Cultures*, New York: Bard Graduate Center, pp. 49–75.

Pietrusewsky, M. (2014), 'Biological distance in bioarchaeology and human osteology', in C. Smith (ed.) *Encyclopedia of Global Archaeology*, New York: Springer.

Pinto, M. (2013), 'Ancient Greek warrior took one to the chin – and in the arm', *The New Standard*, 2: 13, 87.

Pinto-Cisternas, J., J. Moggi-Cecchi and E. Pacciani (1995), 'A morphological variant of the permanent upper lateral incisor in two Tuscan samples from different periods', in J. Moggi-Cecchi (ed.) *Aspects of Dental Biology: Palaeontology, Anthropology and Evolution*, Florence: International Institute for the Study of Man, pp. 333–9.

Pipili, M. (2000), 'Wearing an Other hat: Workmen in town and country', in Cohen, pp. 153–79.

Pojman, P. (2012), *Food Ethics*, Boston: Wadsworth.

Pollitt, J. J. (1986), *Art in the Hellenistic Age*, Cambridge: Cambridge University Press.

Pomeroy, S. (1983), 'Infanticide in Hellenistic Greece', in A. Cameron and A. Kuhrt (eds) *Images of Women in Antiquity*, London: Routledge, pp. 207–22.

Powell, L., W. Southwell-Wright and R. Gowland (eds) (2016), *Care in the Past: Archaeological and Interdisciplinary Perspectives*, Oxford: Oxbow Books.

Pretzler, M. (1999), 'Myth and history at Tegea: Local tradition and community identity', in Nielsen and Roy, pp. 89–129.

Prevedorou, E.-A. and J. E. Buikstra (2019), 'Bioarchaeological practice and the curation of human skeletal remains in a Greek context: The Phaleron cemetery', *Advances in Archaeological Practice*, 7: 60–7.

Pritchett, W. K. (1961), 'Five new fragments of the Attic stelai', *Hesperia*, 30: 23–9.

Pritchett, W. K. (1956), 'The Attic stelai: Part II', *Hesperia*, 25: 178–328.

Prohászka, M. (1995), *Reflections from the Dead: The Metal Finds from the Pantanello Necropolis at Metaponto. A Comprehensive Study of Grave Goods from the 5th to 3rd Centuries BC*, Jonsered: Paul Åströms.

Prowse, T. L. (2016), 'Isotopes and mobility in the ancient Roman world', in L. de Ligt and L. E. Tacoma (eds) *Approaches to Migration in the Early Roman Empire*, Leiden: Brill, pp. 205–33.

Prowse, T. L. et al. (2010), 'Stable isotope and mitochondrial DNA evidence for geographic origins on a Roman estate at Vagnari (Italy)', in H. Eckardt (ed.) *Roman Diasporas: Archaeological Approaches to Mobility and Diversity in the Roman Empire*, Portsmouth, RI: Journal of Roman Archaeology, pp. 175–97.

Prowse, T. L. et al. (2007), 'Isotopic evidence for age-related immigration to imperial Rome', *Am J Phys Anthropol*, 132: 510–19.

Pudsey, A. (2017), 'Disability and *infirmitas* in the ancient world: Demographic and biological facts in the longue durée', in Laes, pp. 22–34.

Pütz, B. (2007), *The Symposium and Komos in Aristophanes*, second edition, Warminster: Aris & Phillips.

Quercia, A. and M. Cazzulo (2016), 'Fear of the dead? "Deviant" burials in Roman northern Italy', in M. J. Mandich et al. (eds) *TRAC 2015: Proceedings of the Twenty-Fifth Annual Theoretical Roman Archaeology Conference*, Oxford: Oxbow Books, pp. 28–42.

Quintana-Murci, L. et al. (2003), 'Genetic structure of Mediterranean populations revealed by Y-chromosome haplotype analysis', *Am J Phys Anthropol*, 121: 157–71.

Raeck, W. (1981), *Zum Barbarenbild in der Kunst Athens im 6. und 5. Jahrhundert v. Chr.*, Bonn: Habelts Dissertationsdrucke.

Rathmann, H. et al. (2019), 'Population history of southern Italy during Greek colonization inferred from dental remains', *Am J Phys Anthropol*, 170: 519–34.

Rathmann, H., G. Saltini Semerari and K. Harvati (2017), 'Evidence for migration influx into the ancient Greek colony of Metaponto: A population genetics approach using dental nonmetric traits', *IJO*, 27: 453–64.

Redfield, J. (1985), 'Herodotus the tourist', *CP*, 80: 97–118.

Reilly, J. (1989), 'Many brides: "Mistress and maid" on Athenian lekythoi', *Hesperia*, 58: 411–44.

Reinberger, K. L. et al. (2021), 'Isotopic evidence for geographic heterogeneity in ancient Greek military forces', *PLoS ONE*, 16: e0248803.

Reitsema, L. J. and B. K. McIlvaine (2014), 'Reconciling "stress" and "health" in physical anthropology: What can bioarchaeologists learn from other subdisciplines?', *Am J Phys Anthropol*, 155: 181–5.

Reitsema, L. J., B. Kyle and S. Vassallo (2020), 'Food traditions and colonial interactions in the ancient Mediterranean: Stable isotope evidence from the Greek Sicilian colony Himera', *JAnthArch*, 57: 101144.

Relethford, J. H. (2017), 'Biological anthropology, population genetics, and race', in Zack, pp. 160–9.

Rempel, J. (2011), 'Burial in the Bosporan Kingdom: Local traditions in regional context(s)', in M. Carroll and J. Rempel (eds) *Living Through the Dead: Burial and Commemoration in the Classical World*, Oxford: Oxbow Books, pp. 21–46.

Reusch, K. (2020), 'Dependent deviance: Castration and deviant burial', in T. K. Betsinger, A. B. Scott and A. Tsaliki (eds) *The Odd, the Unusual, and the Strange: Bioarchaeological Explorations of Atypical Burials*, Gainesville: University of Florida Press, pp. 376–96.

Reusch, K. (2013), 'Raised voices: The archaeology of castration', in L. Tracy (ed.) *Castration and Culture in the Middle Ages*, Rochester, NY: D. S. Brewer, pp. 29–47.

Richards, J. D. (1987), *The Significance of Form and Decoration of Anglo-Saxon Cremation Urns*, British Archaeological Reports British Series 166, Oxford: BAR Publishing.

Richter, G. M. A. (1913), 'Grotesques and the mime', *AJA*, 17: 149–56.

Riddle, C. A. (2013), 'The ontology of impairment: Rethinking how we define disability', in M. Wappett and K. Arndt (eds) *Emerging Perspectives on Disability Studies*, New York: Palgrave Macmillan, pp. 23–40.

Riginos, A. S. (1994), 'The wounding of Philip II of Macedon: Fact and fabrication', *JHS*, 114: 103–19.

Rihll, T. E. (2011), 'Classical Athens', in Bradley and Cartledge, pp. 48–73.

Riley, J. C. (1994), 'Height, nutrition, and mortality risk reconsidered', *Journal of Interdisciplinary History*, 24: 465–92.

Riva, C. (2010), 'Ingenious inventions: Welding ethnicities east and west', in Hales and Hodos, pp. 79–113.

Robb, J. (2007), 'Burial treatment as transformations of bodily ideology', in N. Laneri (ed.) *Performing Death: Social Analyses of Funerary Traditions in the Ancient Near East and Mediterranean*, Chicago: Oriental Institute of the University of Chicago, pp. 287–98.

Robb, J. et al. (2001), 'Social "status" and biological "status": A comparison of grave goods and skeletal indicators from Pontecagnano', *Am J Phys Anthropol*, 115: 213–22.

Roberto, U. and P. A. Tuci (eds) (2015), *Tra marginalità e integrazione: Aspetti dell'assistenza sociale nel mondo greco e romano*, Milan: LED.

Roberts, C. A. (2009), *Human Remains in Archaeology: A Handbook*, York: Council for British Archaeology.

Roberts, C. A. (2000), 'Did they take sugar? The use of skeletal evidence in the study of disability in past populations', in Hubert, pp. 46–59.

Roberts, C. A. (1999), 'Disability in the skeletal record: assumptions, problems and some examples', *Archaeological Review from Cambridge*, 15: 79–97.

Roberts, C. [A.] and K. Manchester (2007), *The Archaeology of Disease*, third edition, Ithaca, NY: Cornell University Press.

Roberts, C. [A.] et al. (2005), 'Health and disease in Greece: Past, present and future', in H. King (ed.) *Health in Antiquity*, London: Routledge, pp. 32–57.

Robinson, M. (1999), 'Salmacis and Hermaphroditus: When two become one (Ovid, *Met.* 4.285–388)', *ClQ*, 49: 212–23.

Roebuck, C. (1951), *Corinth XIV: The Asklepieion and Lerna*, Princeton: American School of Classical Studies at Athens.

Rolle, R. (1980), *The World of the Scythians*, Berkeley: University of California Press.

Roller, D. W. (2006), *Through the Pillars of Herakles: Greco-Roman Exploration of the Atlantic*, London: Routledge.

Roller, M. B. (2006), *Dining Posture in Ancient Rome: Bodies, Values, and Status*, Princeton: Princeton University Press.

Romano, A. J. (2009), 'The invention of marriage: Hermaphroditus and Salmacis at Halicarnassus and in Ovid', *ClQ*, 59: 543–61.

Romero, M. (2017), *Introducing Intersectionality*, Cambridge: Polity Press.

Romm, J. (1996), 'Dog heads and noble savages: Cynicism before the Cynics?', in R. Bracht Branham and M.-O. Goulet-Cazé (eds) *The Cynics: The Cynic Movement in Antiquity and Its Legacy*, Berkeley: University of California Press, pp. 121–35.

Rood, T. (2006), 'Herodotus and foreign lands', in Dewald and Marincola, pp. 290–305.

Roostalu, U. et al. (2007), 'Origin and expansion of haplogroup H, the dominant human mitochondrial DNA lineage in West Eurasia: The Near Eastern and Caucasian perspective', *Mol Biol Evol*, 24: 436–48.

Rose, M. L. (2017), 'Ability and disability in Classical Athenian oratory', in Laes, pp. 139–53.

Rose, M. L. (2003), *The Staff of Oedipus: Transforming Disability in Ancient Greece*, Ann Arbor: University of Michigan Press.

Rose, P. W. (2012), *Class in Archaic Greece*, Cambridge: Cambridge University Press.

Rosen, R. M. and I. Sluiter (eds) (2010), *Valuing Others in Classical Antiquity*, Leiden: Brill.

Rosivach, V. J. (1987), 'Autochthony and the Athenians', *ClQ*, 37: 294–306.

Ross, S. A. (2005), '*Barbarophonos*: Language and Panhellenism in the *Iliad*', *CP*, 100: 299–316.

Rothschild, B. (2012), 'Extirpation of the mythology that porotic hyperostosis is caused by iron deficiency secondary to dietary shift to maize', *Advances in Anthropology*, 2: 157–60.

Rotroff, S. I. (1997), 'The Greeks and the Other in the age of Alexander', in Coleman and Walz, pp. 221–36.

Roush, S. E. (2017), 'Consideration of disability from the perspective of the medical model', in Byrnes and Muller, pp. 39–55.

Rousselle, R. (2001), '"If it is a girl, cast it out": Infanticide/exposure in ancient Greece', *Journal of Psychohistory*, 28: 303–33.

Rowlands, M., M. Larsen and K. Kristiansen (eds) (1987), *Centre and Periphery in the Ancient World*, Cambridge: Cambridge University Press.

Rubini, M. (1996), 'Biological homogeneity and familial segregation in the Iron Age population of Alfedena (Abruzzo, Italy), based on cranial discrete traits analysis', *IJO*, 6: 454–62.

Rubinsohn, Z. (1975), 'The Dorian invasion again', *PP*, 30: 105–31.

Rudhardt, J. (2002), 'The Greek attitude to foreign religions', in Harrison, pp. 172–85.

Ruff, C. B. and C. S. Larsen (2001), 'Reconstructing behavior in Spanish Florida: The biomechanical evidence', in C. S. Larsen (ed.) *Bioarchaeology of Spanish Florida: The Impact of Colonialism*, Gainesville: University Press of Florida, pp. 113–45.

Rzepka, J. (2013), 'Monstrous Aetolians and Aetolian monsters: A politics of ethnography?' in Almagor and Skinner, pp. 117–129.

Saïd, S. (2002), 'Greeks and barbarians in Euripides' tragedies: The end of differences?', in Harrison, pp. 62–100.

Saïd, S. (2001), 'The discourse of identity in Greek rhetoric from Isocrates to Aristides', in Malkin, pp. 275–99.

Saiki, R. K. et al. (1988), 'Primer-directed enzymatic amplification of DNA with a thermostable polymerase', *Science*, 239: 487–91.

Salamone, F. A. (1982), 'Persona, identity, and ethnicity', *Anthropos*, 77: 475–90.

Salibra, R. (2003), 'La necropoli di Passo Marinaro a Camarina: Nuove acquisizioni dalla di scavo 1972–73', *Kokalos* (1999) 45: 41–110.

Saltini Semerari, G. (2016), 'Greek-indigenous intermarriage: A gendered perspective', in Donnellan et al., pp. 77–88.

Samama, E. (2017), 'The Greek vocabulary of disabilities', in Laes, pp. 121–38.

Samama, E. (2013), 'A king walking with pain? On the textual and iconographical images of Philip II and other wounded kings', in Laes et al., pp. 231–48.

Samson, R. (1987), 'Social structures from Reihengräber: Mirror or mirage?', *Scottish Archaeological Review*, 4: 116–26.

Samuels, T. (2015), 'Herodotus and the black body: A critical race theory analysis', *Journal of Black Studies*, 46: 723–41.

Samuels, T. (2013), 'Misreading black Others in Greco-Roman antiquity. Rezension zu: Erich S. Gruen, *Rethinking the Other in Antiquity* (Princeton 2011)', *Frankfurter elektronische Rundschau zur Altertumskunde*, 22: 39–42.

Sanchez-Lara, P. A. et al. (2007), 'The morphogenesis of wormian bones: A study of craniosynostosis and purposeful cranial deformation', *Am J Med Genet A*, 143A: 3243–51.

Saracino, M. et al. (2017), 'Funerary deviancy and social inequality in protohistoric Italy: What the dead can tell', *PreistAlp*, 49: 73–83.

Sassi, M. M. (2001), *The Science of Man in Ancient Greece*, Chicago: University of Chicago Press.

Sauer, N. J. and J. C. Wankmiller (2009), 'The assessment of ancestry and the concept of race', in S. Blau and D. H. Ubelaker (eds) *Handbook of Forensic Anthropology and Archaeology*, Walnut Creek, CA: Left Coast Press, pp. 187–200.

Sazzini, M., S. Sarno and D. Luiselli (2014), 'The Mediterranean human population: An anthropological genetics perspective', in S. Goffredo and Z. Dubinsky (eds) *The Mediterranean Sea: Its History and Present Challenges*, New York: Springer Science, pp. 529–51.

Scafuro, A. C. (1994), 'Witnessing and false witnessing: Proving citizenship and kin identity in fourth-century Athens', in Boegehold and Scafuro, pp. 156–98.

Scham, S. A. (2001), 'The archaeology of the disenfranchised', *Journal of Archaeological Method and Theory*, 8: 183–213.

Scheer, T. S. (2011), 'Ways of becoming Arcadian: Arcadian foundation myths in the Mediterranean', in E. S. Gruen (ed.) *Cultural Identity in the Ancient Mediterranean*, Los Angeles: Getty Research Institute, pp. 11–25.

Schepartz, L. A. et al. (2017), 'Mycenaean hierarchy and gender roles: Diet and health inequalities in Late Bronze Age Pylos, Greece', in Klaus et al., pp. 141–72.

Schepartz, L. A., S. C. Fox and C. Bourbou (eds) (2009a), *New Directions in the Skeletal Biology of Greece. Hesperia Supplement 43*, Princeton: American School of Classical Studies at Athens.

Schepartz, L. A., S. Miller-Antonio and J. M. A. Murphy (2009b), 'Differential health among the Mycenaeans of Messenia: Status, sex, and dental health at Pylos', in Schepartz et al., pp. 155–74.

Scheuer, L. and S. Black (2000), *Developmental Juvenile Osteology*, New York: Academic Press.

Schulte-Campbell, C. (1986), 'Human skeletal remains', in I. Todd (ed.) *Vasilikos Valley Project I: The Bronze Age Cemetery in Kalavasos Village*, Uppsala: P. Åströms, pp. 168–78.

Schulte-Campbell, C. (1983a), 'A Late Bronze Age Cypriot from Hala Sultan Tekke and another discussion of artificial cranial deformation: Appendix V', in *Hala Sultan Tekke 8: Excavations 1971–79*, Göteborg: P. Åströms, pp. 249–52.

Schulte-Campbell, C. (1983b), 'The human skeletal remains from Palaepaphos-Skales: Appendix XII', in V. Karageorghis and F. G. Maier (eds) *Palaepaphos-Skales: An Iron Age Cemetery in Cyprus*, Konstanz: Universitätsverlag Konstanz, pp. 439–51.

Schulte-Campbell, C. (1979), 'Preliminary report on the human skeletal remains from Kalavasos-Tenta', in I. A. Todd, 'Vasilikos Valley Project: Third Preliminary Report, 1978', *Journal of Field Archaeology*, 6: 298–9.

Schwartz, J. H. and I. Tattersall (2002), *The Human Fossil Record, Volume I: Terminology and Craniodental Morphology of Genus Homo (Europe)*, New York: Wiley-Liss.

Scott, A. B., T. K. Betsinger and A. Tsaliki (2020), 'Deconstructing "deviant": An introduction to the history of atypical burials and the importance of context in the archaeological record', in T. K. Betsinger, A. B. Scott and A. Tsaliki (eds) *The Odd, the Unusual, and the Strange: Bioarchaeological*

Explorations of Atypical Burials, Gainesville: University of Florida Press, pp. 1–17.

Scott, E. (2001a), 'Killing the female? Archaeological narratives of infanticide', in B. Arnold and N. L. Wicker (eds) *Gender and the Archaeology of Death*, Walnut Creek, CA: Alta Mira Press, pp. 3–21.

Scott, E. (2001b), 'Unpicking a myth: The infanticide of female and disabled infants in antiquity', in G. Davies, A. Gardner and L. Lockyear (eds) *TRAC 2000: Proceedings of the Tenth Annual Theoretical Roman Archaeology Conference, London 2000*, Oxford: Oxbow Books, pp. 143–51.

Scott, E. (1999), *The Archaeology of Infancy and Infant Death*, British Archaeological Reports International Series 819, Oxford: BAR Publishing.

Scott, G. R. and C. G. Turner II (1997), *The Anthropology of Modern Human Teeth*, Cambridge: Cambridge University Press.

Sen, A. (2000), *Social Exclusion: Concept, Application, and Scrutiny*, Manila: Asian Development Bank.

Shakespeare, T. (1999), 'Commentary: Observations on disability and archaeology', *Archaeological Review from Cambridge*, 15: 99–101.

Shapiro, [H.] A. (2015), 'Alkibiades' effeminacy and the androgyny of Dionysos', in Boschung et al., pp. 287–312.

Shapiro, H. A. (2000), 'Modest athletes and liberated women: Etruscans on Attic black-figure vases', in Cohen, pp. 313–37.

Shapiro, H. A. (1998), 'Autochthony and the visual arts in fifth-century Athens', in D. Boedecker and K. A. Raaflaub (eds) *Democracy, Empire, and the Arts in Fifth-Century Athens*, Cambridge, MA: Harvard University Press, pp. 127–51.

Shapiro, H. A. (1984), 'Notes on Greek dwarfs', *AJA*, 88: 391.

Shaw, B. D. (1982/3), '"Eaters of flesh, drinkers of milk": The ancient Mediterranean ideology of the pastoral nomad', *AncSoc*, 13/14: 5–32.

Shaw, H. et al. (2016), 'Identifying migrants in Roman London using lead and strontium stable isotopes', *JAS*, 66: 57–68.

Shay, T. (1985), 'Differentiated treatment of deviancy at death as revealed in anthropological and archaeological material', *JAnthArch*, 4: 221–41.

Shea, T. D. (2018), 'Mapping immigrant communities through their tombstones in Archaic and Classical Athens', PhD diss., Duke University.

Shepherd, G. (2018), 'Where are the children? Locating children in funerary space in the ancient Greek world', in S. Crawford, D. M. Hadley and G. Shepherd (eds) *The Oxford Handbook of the Archaeology of Childhood*, Oxford: Oxford University Press, pp. 521–38.

Shepherd, G. (2013), 'Ancient identities: Age, gender, and ethnicity', in S. Tarlow and L. Nilsson Stutz (eds) *Oxford Handbook of the Archaeology of Death and Burial*, Oxford: Oxford University Press, pp. 543–57.

Shepherd, G. (2007), 'Poor little rich kids? Status and selection in Archaic western Greece', in S. Crawford and G. Shepherd (eds) *Children, Childhood and Society*, British Archaeological Reports International Series 1696, Oxford: BAR Publishing, pp. 93–106.

Shepherd, G. (2005), 'Dead men tell no tales: Ethnic diversity in Sicilian colonies and the evidence of the cemeteries', *OJA*, 24: 115–36.

Shepherd, G. (1999), 'Fibulae and females: Intermarriage in the western Greek colonies and the evidence from the cemeteries', in Tsetskhladze, pp. 267–300.

Shepherd, G. (1995), 'The pride of most colonials: Burial and religion in the Sicilian colonies', *ActaHyp*, 6: 51–82.

Shuttleworth, R. and H. Meekosha (2017), 'Accommodating critical disability studies in bioarchaeology', in Byrnes and Muller, pp. 19–38.

Sidoti Jr, E. J. et al. (1996), 'Long-term studies of metopic synostosis: Frequency of cognitive impairment and behavioral disturbances', *Plast Reconstr Surg*, 97: 276–81.

Silverman, F. N. (1965), 'Re: Why did Hephaestus Limp?', *American Journal of Diseases of Children*, 109: 392.

Simmel, G. (1908), *Soziologie: Untersuchungen über die Formen der Vergesellschaftung*, Leipzig: Duncker & Humblot.

Simms, R. C. (2005), 'The missing bones of Thersites: A note on "Iliad" 2.212–19', *AJP*, 126: 33–40.

Skinner, J. E. (2012), *The Invention of Greek Ethnography: From Homer to Herodotus*, Oxford: Oxford University Press.

Skomal, S. N. and E. C. Polomé (eds) (1987), *Proto-Indo-European: The Archaeology of a Linguistic Problem. Studies in Honor of Marija Gimbutas*, Washington, DC: Institute for the Study of Man.

Slater, B. J. et al. (2008), 'Cranial sutures: A brief review', *Plast Reconstr Surg*, 121: 170e–8e.

Smedley, A. and B. H. Smedley (2005), 'Race as biology is fiction, racism as a social problem is real: Anthropological and historical perspectives on the social construction of race', *Am Psychol*, 60: 16–26.

Smith, P. and G. Kahila (1992), 'Identification of infanticide in archaeological sites: A case study from late Roman–early Byzantine periods at Ashkelon, Israel', *JAS*, 19: 667–75.

Smith, R. R. R. (1991), *Hellenistic Sculpture*, London: Thames and Hudson.

Smith, S. K. (2000), 'Skeletal and dental evidence for social status in Late Bronze Age Athens', in S. J. Vaughan and W. D. E. Coulson (eds) *Palaeodiet in the Aegean*, Oxford: Oxbow Books, pp. 105–13.

Smith, T. J. (2010), *Komast Dancers in Archaic Greek Art*, Oxford: Oxford University Press.

Smith, T. J. (2009), 'Komastai or "Hephaistoi"? Visions of comic parody in Archaic Greece', *BICS*, 52: 69–92.

Smith, T. J. (2002), 'Transvestism or travesty? Dance, dress and gender in Greek vase-painting', in L. Llewellyn-Jones (ed.) *Women's Dress in the Ancient Greek World*, London: Duckworth, pp. 33–54.

Smith, T. J. and D. Plantzos (eds) (2012), *A Companion to Greek Art*, 2 vols, Oxford: Wiley-Blackwell.

Sneed, D. (2020), 'The architecture of access: Ramps at ancient Greek healing sanctuaries', *Antiquity*, 94: 1015–29.

Snell, D. C. (2011), 'Slavery in the ancient Near East', in Bradley and Cartledge, pp. 4–21.

Snodgrass, A. M. (2001), *The Dark Age of Greece*, reprint, London: Routledge.

Snowden Jr, F. M. (2010), 'Iconographic evidence on the black populations in Greco-Roman antiquity', in Bindman and Gates, pp. 142–250.

Snowden Jr, F. M. (1997), 'Greeks and Ethiopians', in Coleman and Walz, pp. 71–102.

Snowden Jr, F. M. (1983), *Before Color Prejudice: The Ancient View of Blacks*, Cambridge, MA: Harvard University Press.

Snowden Jr, F. M. (1970), *Blacks in Antiquity: Ethiopians in the Greco-Roman Experience*, Cambridge, MA: Harvard University Press.

Snyder, S. L. and D. T. Mitchell (2006), *Cultural Locations of Disability*, Chicago: University of Chicago Press.

Soares, P. et al. (2012), 'The expansion of mtDNA haplogroup L3 within and out of Africa', *Mol Biol Evol*, 29: 915–27.

Sodini, S. M. et al. (2018), 'Comparison of genotypic and phenotypic correlations: Cheverud's conjecture in humans', *Genetics*, 209: 941–8.

Sofaer, J. R. (2011), 'Towards a social bioarchaeology of age', in Agarwal and Glencross, pp. 285–311.

Sofaer Derevenski, J. (ed.) (2000), *Children and Material Culture*, London: Routledge.

Sørensen, L. W. (2002), 'The Archaic settlement at Vroulia on Rhodes and Ian Morris', in A. Rathje, M. Nielsen and B. B. Rasmussen (eds) *Pots for the Living, Pots for the Dead, ActaHyp*, 9: 243–53.

Sourvinou-Inwood, C. (2003), 'Herodotus (and others) on Pelasgians: Some perceptions of ethnicity', in P. Derow and R. Parker (eds) *Herodotus and His World: Essays from a Conference in Memory of George Forrest*, Oxford: Oxford University Press, pp. 103–44.

Sourvinou-Inwood, C. (1995), *'Reading' Greek Death to the End of the Classical Period*, Oxford: Clarendon Publishing.

Sourvinou-Inwood, C. (1988), *Studies in Girls' Transitions: Aspects of the Arkteia and Age Representation in Attic Iconography*, Athens: Kardamitsa.

Southwell-Wright, W. (2013), 'Past perspectives: What can archaeology offer disability studies', in M. Wappett and K. Arndt (eds) *Emerging Perspectives on Disability Studies*, New York: Palgrave Macmillan, pp. 67–95.

Sperduti, A. et al. (2018), 'Bones, teeth, and history', in W. Scheidel (ed.) *The Science of Roman History: Biology, Climate, and the Future of the Past*, Princeton: Princeton University Press, pp. 123–73.

Sprague, R. (1968), 'A suggested terminology and classification for burial description', *AmerAnt*, 33: 479–85.

St. Hoyme, L. E. and M. Y. İşcan (1989), 'Determination of sex and race: Accuracy and assumptions', in M. Y. İşcan and A. R. Kennedy (eds) *The Reconstruction of Life from the Skeleton*, New York: Wiley-Liss, pp. 11–21.

Stampolidis, N. C. and Y. Tassoulas (eds) (2014), *Hygieia: Health, Illness, and Treatment from Homer to Galen*, Athens: Hellenic Ministry of Culture and Sports.

Steele, D. G. (1970), 'Estimation of stature from fragments of long limb bones', in T. D. Stewart (ed.) *Personal Identification in Mass Disasters*, Washington, DC: Smithsonian Institute, pp. 85–97.

Steiner, D. T. (2001), *Images in Mind: Statues in Archaic and Classical Greek Literature and Thought*, Princeton: Princeton University Press.

Sternberg, R. H. (1999), 'The transport of sick and wounded soldiers in classical Greece', *Phoenix*, 53: 191–205.

Stevenson, W. (1995), 'The rise of eunuchs in Greco-Roman antiquity', *Journal of the History of Sexuality*, 5: 495–511.

Stewart, A. (2014), *Art in the Hellenistic World*, Cambridge: Cambridge University Press.

Stewart, A. (1995), 'Imag(in)ing the Other: Amazons and ethnicity in fifth-century Athens', *Poetics Today*, 16: 571–97.

Stiker, H. (1999), *A History of Disability*, translated by W. Sayers, Ann Arbor: University of Michigan Press.

Stodder, A. L. W. (2017), 'Quantifying impairment and disability in bioarchaeological assemblages', in Byrnes and Muller, pp. 183–200.

Stojanowski, C. M. and J. E. Buikstra (2004), 'Biodistance analysis, a biocultural enterprise: A rejoinder to Armelagos and Van Gerven (2003)', *American Anthropologist*, 106: 430–1.

Stone, A. C. (2008), 'DNA analysis of archaeological remains', in M. A. Katzenberg and S. R. Saunders (eds) *Biological Anthropology of the Human Skeleton*, second edition, Hoboken, NJ: Wiley-Liss, pp. 461–83.

Stonequist, E. V. (1937), *The Marginal Man: A Study in Personality and Culture Conflict*, New York: Charles Scribner's Sons.

Stratton, S. (2016), '"Seek and you shall find". How the analysis of gendered patterns in archaeology can create false binaries: A case study from Durankulak', *J Archaeol Method Theory*, 23: 854–69.

Strouhal, E. (1973), 'Five plastered skulls from pre-pottery Neolithic B Jericho: Anthropological study', *Paléorient*, 1: 231–47.

Sulosky Weaver, C. L. (2019a), 'Greater in death: The transformative effect of convivial iconography on Roman cineraria', in Gondek and Sulosky Weaver, pp. 153–80.

Sulosky Weaver, C. L. (2019b), 'To include or exclude? Marginalization of the deformed in the Classical Greek world', *Journal of Greek Archaeology*, 4: 163–79.

Sulosky Weaver, C. L. (2015), *The Bioarchaeology of Classical Kamarina: Life and Death in Greek Sicily*, Gainesville: University Press of Florida.

Sulosky Weaver, C. L. and B. Kyle (forthcoming), 'At the intersection of biology and identity: Nonmetric traits as indicators of ethnicity in Greek colonial contexts', in A. Lagia and S. Voutsaki (eds) *Bioarchaeological Perspectives on Inequality and Social Differentiation from the Ancient Greek World*, Gainesville: University Press of Florida.

TallBear, K. (2013), *Native American DNA: Tribal Belonging and the False Promise of Genetic Science*, Minneapolis: University of Minnesota Press.

Tanner, J. (2010), 'Introduction to the new edition. Race and representation in ancient art: *Black Athena* and after', in Bindman and Gates, pp. 1–39.

Tartaron, T. F. (2014), 'Cross-cultural interaction in the Greek world: Culture contact issues and theories', C. Smith (ed.) *Encyclopedia of Global Archaeology*, New York: Springer, pp. 1804–21.

Tattersall, I. and R. DeSalle (2011), *Race? Debunking a Scientific Myth*, College Station: Texas A&M University Press.

Taylor, C. (2017), *Poverty, Wealth, and Well-Being: Experiencing Penia in Democratic Athens*, Oxford: Oxford University Press.

Taylor, C. (2011), 'Migration and the demes of Attica', in Holleran and Pudsey, pp. 117–34.

Thalmann, W. G. (2011), 'Some ancient Greek images of slavery', in Alston, Hall and Proffitt, pp. 72–96.

Themelis, P. G. (1982), 'Kaïadas', *Archaeologiká Análekta ex Athenón*, 15: 183–201.

Thomas, R. (2002), *Herodotus in Context: Ethnography, Science and the Art of Persuasion*, Cambridge: Cambridge University Press.

Thomas, R. (2001), 'Ethnicity, genealogy, and Hellenism in Herodotus', in Malkin, pp. 213–33.

Thompson, D. J. (2011), 'Slavery in the Hellenistic world', in Bradley and Cartledge, pp. 194–213.

Thompson, F. H. (2003), *The Archaeology of Greek and Roman Slavery*, London: Duckworth.

Thompson, J. L., M. P. Alfonso-Durruty and J. J. Crandall (eds) (2014), *Tracing Childhood: Bioarchaeological Investigations of Early Lives in Antiquity*, Gainesville: University Press of Florida.

Tilley, C. (1989), 'Interpreting material culture', in I. Hodder (ed.) *The Meaning of Things*, London: Harper Collins Academic, pp. 185–94.

Tilley, L. (2015), *Theory and Practice in the Bioarchaeology of Care*, New York: Springer International.

Tilley, L. and Oxenham, M. F. (2011), 'Survival against the odds: Modeling the social implications of care provision to the seriously disabled', *IJPP*, 1: 35–42.

Tilly, C. (1978), 'Migration in modern European history', in W. McNeill and R. Adams (eds) *Human Migration: Patterns and Policies*, Bloomington: University of Indiana Press, pp. 48–74.

Tofanelli, S. et al. (2015), 'The Greeks in the West: Genetic signatures of the Hellenic colonisation in southern Italy and Sicily', *Eur J Hum Genet*, 8: 429–36.

Torroni, A. et al. (2006), 'Harvesting the fruit of the human mtDNA tree', *Trends Genet*, 22: 339–45.

Torroni, A. et al. (1996), 'Classification of European mtDNAs from an analysis of three European populations', *Genetics*, 144: 1835–50.

Tougher, S. (ed.) (2002), *Eunuchs in Antiquity and Beyond*, London: Duckworth and the Classical Press of Wales.

Trakosopoulou-Selekidou, E. (1993), 'Apo tis anaskafes tis anat. Chalkidikis', *To Archaeologiko Ergo sti Makedonia kai Thraki*, 7: 413–28.

Trentin, L. (2015), *The Hunchback in Hellenistic and Roman Art*, New York: Bloomsbury.

Trentin, L. (2009), 'What's in a hump? Re-examining the hunchback in the Villa Albani-Torlonia', *The Cambridge Classical Journal*, 55: 130–56.

Triantaphyllou, S. (2012), 'Kephala Petras: The human remains and burial practices in the rock shelter', in M. Tsipopoulou (ed.) *Petras-Siteia: 25 Years of Excavations and Studies. Acts of a Two-Day Conference Held at the Danish Institute at Athens, 9–10 October 2010*, Athens: Monographs of the Danish Institute at Athens, pp. 161–6.

Triantaphyllou, S. (2004), 'The Archaic cemetery of Agia Paraskevi: The human remains', in D. Grammenos and S. Triantafyllou (eds) *Anthropological Research in North Greece*, vol. 2, Thessaloniki: Publications of the Archaeological Institute of Northern Greece, pp. 89–264, 564.

Triantaphyllou, S. (1998), 'An Early Iron Age cemetery in ancient Pydna, Pieria: What do the bones tell us?', *BSA*, 93: 353–64.

Triantaphyllou, S. and M. Bessios (2005), 'A mass burial at fourth century BC Pydna, Macedonia, Greece: Evidence for slavery?', *Antiquity*, 79(305).

Triantaphyllou, S. et al. (2008), 'Isotopic dietary reconstruction of humans from Middle Bronze Age Lerna, Argolid, Greece', *JAS*, 35: 3028–34.

Trigger, B. G. (1977), 'Comments on archaeological classification and ethnic groups', *Norwegian Archaeological Review*, 10: 20–3.

Tritsaroli, P. (2017), 'The Pigi Athinas tumuli cemetery of Macedonian Olympus: Burial customs and the bioarchaeology of social structure at the dawn of the Late Bronze age, central Macedonia, Greece', in Klaus et al., pp. 224–62.

Tritsaroli, P. and S. Koulidou (2018), 'Human remains from the Pigi Artemidos LBA tumulus, region of Macedonian Olympus, Pieria', *Athens University Review of Archaeology*, 1: 9–24.

Tronchetti, C. and P. van Dommelen (2005), 'Entangled objects and hybrid practices: Colonial contacts and elite connections at Monte Prama, Sardinia', *JMA*, 18: 183–209.

Trotter, M. (1970), 'Estimation of stature from intact long limb bones', in T. D. Stewart (ed.) *Personal Identification in Mass Disasters*, Washington, DC: Smithsonian Institute, pp. 71–83.

Tsakirgis, B. (1995), 'Morgantina: A Greek town in central Sicily', *ActaHyp*, 6: 123–47.

Tsaliki, A. (2008), 'Unusual burials and necrophobia: An insight into the burial archaeology of fear', in Murphy, pp. 1–16.

Tsaliki, A. (2004), 'Spine pathology and disability at Lesbos, Greece', *Paleopathology Newsletter*, 125: 13–17.

Tsetskhladze, G. R. (ed.) (1999), *Ancient Greeks West and East*, Leiden: Brill.

Tsiafakis, D. (2015), 'Thracian tattoos', in Boschung et al., pp. 89–117.

Tsiafakis, D. (2000), 'The allure and repulsion of Thracians in the art of Classical Athens', in Cohen, pp. 364–89.

Tubbs, R. S., E. G. Salter and W. J. Oakes (2006), 'Artificial deformation of the human skull: A review', *Clin Anat*, 19: 372–7.

Tuplin, C. (1999), 'Greek Racism? Observations on the character and limits of Greek prejudice', in Tsetskhladze, pp. 47–75.

Turfa, J. M. (2018), 'Archaeology's *Tir Na N-óg* ("The Land of the Young"): Understanding burials of children in ancient Italy', in J. Tabolli (ed.) *From Invisible to Visible: New Methods and Data for the Archaeology of Infant and Child Burials in Pre-Roman Italy and Beyond*, Nicosia: Astrom Editions, pp. 3–19.

Turner, C. G. II, C. R. Nichols and G. R. Scott (1991), 'Scoring procedures for key morphological traits of the permanent dentition: The Arizona State University dental anthropology system', in M. A. Kelley and C. S. Larsen (eds) *Advances in Dental Anthropology*, New York: Wiley-Liss, pp. 13–31.

Turner, S. and R. Young (2007), 'Concealed communities: The people at the margins', *International Journal of Historical Archaeology*, 11: 297–303.

Tyrrell, A. (2000), 'Skeleton non-metric traits and the assessment of inter- and intra-population diversity: Past problems and future potential', in Cox and Mays, pp. 289–306.

Tyrrell, W. B. (1984), *Amazons: A Study in Athenian Mythmaking*, Baltimore: Johns Hopkins University Press.

Ustinova, Y. (1998), *The Supreme Gods of the Bosporan Kingdom: Celestial Aphrodite and the Most High God*, Leiden: Brill.

Vaiglova, P. et al. (2018), 'Of cattle and feasts: Multi-isotope investigation of animal husbandry and communal feasting at Neolithic Makriyalos, northern Greece', *PLoS ONE*, 13: e0194474.

Van Dommelen, P. (2006), 'The Orientalizing phenomenon: Hybridity and material culture in the Western Mediterranean', in C. Riva and N. Vella (eds) *Debating Orientalization: Multidisciplinary Approaches to Change in the Ancient Mediterranean*, London: Equinox, pp. 135–52.

Van Dommelen, P. and A. B. Knapp (eds) (2010), *Material Connections in the Ancient Mediterranean: Mobility, Materiality and Identity*, London: Routledge.

Van Noorden, H. (2015), *Playing Hesiod: The 'Myth of the Races' in Classical Antiquity*, Cambridge: Cambridge University Press.

Van Nortwick, T. (2008), *Imagining Men: Ideals of Masculinity in Ancient Greek Culture*, London: Praeger.

Van Straten, F. T. (1981), 'Gifts for the gods', in H. S. Versnel (ed.) *Faith, Hope and Worship: Aspects of Religious Mentality in the Ancient World*, Leiden: Brill, pp. 65–151.

Vasiliadis, E. S., T. B. Grivas and A. Kaspiris (2009), 'Historical overview of spinal deformities in ancient Greece', *Scoliosis*, 4: 6.

Vickers, M. (1990), 'Golden Greece: Relative values, minae, and temple inventories', *AJA*, 94: 613–25.

Vika, E. (2011), 'Diachronic dietary reconstructions in ancient Thebes, Greece: Results from stable isotope analyses', *JAS*, 38: 1157–63.

Vika, E. (2009), 'Strangers in the grave? Investigating local provenance in a Greek Bronze Age mass burial using $\delta^{34}S$ analysis', *JAS*, 36: 2024–8.

Virchow, R. (1893), 'Über griechische Schädel aus alter und neuer Zeit, und über einen Schädel von Menidi der für den des Sophokles gehalten wird', *Sitzungsberichte der Königlich Preussischen Akademie der Wissenschaften zu Berlin*, pp. 677–700.

Vlachou, V. (2007), 'Oropos: The infant and child inhumations from the settlement (late 8th–early 7th centuries BC', in A. Mazarakis Ainian (ed.) *Oropos and Euboea in the Early Iron Age*, Volos: University of Thessaly Press, pp. 213–40.

Vlahogiannis, N. (2005), '"Curing" disability', in H. King (ed.) *Health in Antiquity*, London: Routledge, pp. 180–91.

Vlahogiannis, N. (1998), 'Disabling bodies', in D. Monserrat (ed.) *Changing Bodies, Changing Meanings: Studies on the Human Body in Antiquity*, London: Routledge, pp. 13–36.

Vlassopoulos, K. (2016), 'Finley's slavery', in D. Jew, R. Osborne and M. Scott (eds) *M. I. Finley: An Ancient Historian and His Impact*, Cambridge: Cambridge University Press, pp. 76–99.

Vlassopoulos, K. (2015), 'Ethnicity and Greek history: Re-examining our assumptions', *BICS*, 58: 1–13.

Vlassopoulos, K. (2013a), *Greeks and Barbarians*, Cambridge: Cambridge University Press.

Vlassopoulos, K. (2013b), 'The stories of the Others: Storytelling and intercultural communication in the Herodotean Mediterranean', in Almagor and Skinner, pp. 49–75.

Vlassopoulos, K. (2010), 'Athenian slave names and Athenian social history', *ZPE*, 175: 113–44.

Vlassopoulos, K. (2009), 'Slavery, freedom and citizenship in Classical Athens: Beyond a legalistic approach', *EurRHist*, 16: 347–63.

Vlassopoulos, K. (2008), 'The regional identity of the Peloponnese', in *Being Peloponnesian* <https://www.nottingham.ac.uk/csps/documents/beingpeloponnesian/kostas.pdf> (last accessed 11 May 2020).

Vlassopoulos, K. (2007a), 'Between east and west: The Greek *poleis* as part of a world-system', *AncWestEast*, 6: 91–111.

Vlassopoulos, K. (2007b), 'Beyond and below the polis: Networks, associations, and the writing of Greek history', *MedHistR*, 22: 11–22.

Von Staden, H. (1990), 'Incurability and hopelessness: The *Hippocratic Corpus*', in P. Potter, G. Maloney and J. Desautels (eds) *La maladie et les maladies dans la Collection Hippocratique*, Quebec: Éditions du Sphinx, pp. 75–112.

Wace, A. J. B. (1903–4), 'Grotesques and the evil eye', *BSA*, 10: 103–14.

Wagner, J. K. et al. (2017), 'Anthropologists' views on race, ancestry, and genetics', *Am J Phys Anthropol*, 162: 318–27.

Waldron, T. (2009), *Paleopathology*, Cambridge: Cambridge University Press.

Waldron, T. (2000), 'Hidden or overlooked? Where are the disadvantaged in the skeletal record?', in Hubert, pp. 29–45.

Waldschmidt, A. (2017), 'Does public disability history need a cultural model of disability?', *Public Disability History*, 2: 7.

Walker, P. L. et al. (2009), 'The causes of porotic hyperostosis and cribra orbitalia: A reappraisal of the iron-deficiency-anemia hypothesis', *Am J Phys Anthropol*, 139: 109–25.

Wallace, R. W. (2010), 'Tecmessa's legacy: Valuing outsiders in Athens' democracy', in Rosen and Sluiter, pp. 137–54.

Walsh, D. (2009), *Distorted Ideals in Greek Vase-Painting: The World of Mythological Burlesque*, Cambridge: Cambridge University Press.

Walsh, J. St. P. (2011/12), 'Urbanism and identity at Classical Morgantina', *MAAR*, 56/7: 115–36.

Ward, J. K. (2002), '*Ethnos* in the *Politics*: Aristotle and race', in J. K. Ward and T. L. Lott (eds) *Philosophers on Race: Critical Essays*, Oxford: Blackwell, pp. 14–37.

Waters-Rist, A. L. and M. L. P. Hoogland (2013), 'Osteological evidence of short-limbed dwarfism in a nineteenth century Dutch family: Achondroplasia or hypochondroplasia', *IJPP*, 3: 243–56.

Watson, J. (2010), 'The origin of metic status in Athens', *The Cambridge Classical Journal*, 56: 259–78.

Waxenbaum, E. B. and M. E. Feiler (2020), 'Influence of climatic stress on nonmetric sexually dimorphic features of the skull and pelvis', *Am J Hum Biol*, e23559.

Weaver, D. S. (1998), 'Osteoporosis in the bioarchaeology of women', in A. L. Grauer and P. Stuart-Macadam (eds) *Sex and Gender in Paleopathological Perspective*, Cambridge: Cambridge University Press, pp. 27–44.

Weber, M. (1978 [1921]), *Economy and Society: An Outline of Interpretive Sociology*, Berkeley: University of California Press.

Weiler, I. (2012), 'Zur physiognomie und ikonographie behinderter menschen in der antike', in R. Breitwieser (ed.) *Behinderungen und Beeinträchtigungen/ Disability and Impairment in Antiquity*, British Archaeological Reports International Series 2359, Oxford: BAR Publishing, pp. 11–24.

Weisberger, A. (1992), 'Marginality and its directions', *Sociological Forum*, 7: 425–46.

Weiss-Krejci, E. (2013), 'The unburied dead', in S. Tarlow and L. Nilsson Stutz (eds) *Oxford Handbook of the Archaeology of Death and Burial*, Oxford: Oxford University Press, pp. 281–301.

Wells, S. (2006), *Deep Ancestry: Inside the Genographic Project, the Landmark DNA Quest to Decipher Our Distant Past*, Washington, DC: National Geographic.

Wesp, J. K. (2017), 'Embodying sex/gender systems in bioarchaeological research', in Agarwal and Wesp, pp. 99–128.

West, M. L. (1997), *The East Face of Helicon*, Oxford: Oxford University Press.

West, M. L. (1983), *The Orphic Poems*, Oxford: Clarendon Press.

West, M. L. (1971), *Early Greek Philosophy and the Orient*, Oxford: Clarendon Press.

Whelton, H. L. et al. (2018), 'Strontium isotope evidence for human mobility in the Neolithic of northern Greece', *JAS: Reports*, 20: 768–74.

White, R. (1991), *The Middle Ground: Indians, Empires, and Republics in the Great Lakes Region, 1650–1815*, Cambridge: Cambridge University Press.

Whitehead, D. (1977), *The Ideology of the Athenian Metic*, Cambridge: Cambridge Philological Society.

Whitley, J. (2012), 'Agency in Greek art', in Smith and Plantzos, pp. 579–96.

Whitley, J. (1994), 'The monuments that stood before Marathon: Tomb cult and hero cult in Archaic Attica', *AJA*, 98: 213–30.

Wiedemann, T. (1988), *Greek and Roman Slavery*, London: Routledge.

Wilgaux, J. (2018), 'Infirmités et prêtrise en Méditerranée antique', *Pallas*, 106: 275–87.

Wille, R. and K. M. Beier (1989), 'Castration in Germany', *Annals of Sex Research*, 2: 103–33.

Winkler, J. J. (1990), *Constraints of Desire: The Anthropology of Sex and Gender in Ancient Greece*, London: Routledge.

Wolfe, M. (2013), *Cut These Words into My Stone: Ancient Greek Epitaphs*, Baltimore: Johns Hopkins University Press.

Wood, J. W. et al. (1992), 'The osteological paradox: Problems of inferring prehistoric health from skeletal samples', *CurrAnthr*, 33: 343–70.

Wood, M. M. (1934), *The Stranger: A Study in Social Relationships*, New York: Columbia University Press.

Wrede, H. (1988), 'Die tanzenden Musikanten von Mahdia und der alexandrinische Götter- und Herrscherkult', *Römische Mitteilungen*, 95: 97–114.

Wrenhaven, K. L. (2013), 'Barbarians at the gate: Foreign slaves in Greek city-states', *Electryone*, 1: 1–17.

Wrenhaven, K. L. (2012), *Reconstructing the Slave: The Image of the Slave in Ancient Greece*, London: Bloomsbury.

Wrenhaven, K. L. (2011), 'Greek representations of the slave body: A conflict of ideas?', in Alston, Hall and Proffitt, pp. 97–120.

Wright, L. E. and C. J. Yoder (2003), 'Recent progress in bioarchaeology: Approaches to the osteological paradox', *Journal of Archaeological Research*, 11: 43–70.

Wright, M. R. (1981), *Empedocles: The Extant Fragments*, New Haven: Yale University Press.

Wünsche, R. (2007), *The Munich Glypothek: Masterpieces of Greek and Roman Sculpture*, Munich: C. H. Beck.

Xydas, F. (2003), 'Representations of Persians in Greek Attic vase paintings: The frontal face of a foreigner', *Penn History Review*, 61–86.

Yang, D. Y. and K. Watt (2005), 'Contamination controls when preparing archaeological remains for ancient DNA analysis', *JAS*, 32: 331–6.

Yannopoulos, S. et al. (2017), 'History of sanitation and hygiene technologies in the Hellenic world', *Journal of Water, Sanitation and Hygiene for Development*, 7: 163–80.

Zacharia, K. (ed.) (2008a), *Hellenisms: Culture, Identity, and Ethnicity from Antiquity to Modernity*, Burlington: Ashgate.

Zacharia, K. (2008b), 'Herodotus' four markers of Greek identity', in Zacharia, pp. 21–36.

Zack, N. (ed.) (2017), *The Oxford Handbook of Philosophy and Race*, Oxford: Oxford University Press.

Zakrzewski, S. (2011), 'Population migration, variation, and identity: An Islamic population in Iberia', in Agarwal and Glencross, pp. 183–211.

Zanatta, A. et al. (2016), 'Occupational markers and pathology of the castrato singer Gaspare Pacchierotti (1740–1821)', *Scientific Reports*, 6: 28463.

Zelnick-Abramovitz, R. (2005), *Not Wholly Free: The Concept of Manumission and the Status of Manumitted Slaves in the Ancient Greek World*, Leiden: Brill.

Ziskowski, A. (2012), 'Clubfeet and Kypselids: Contextualising Corinthian padded dancers in the Archaic period', *BSA*, 107: 211–32.

Zuchtriegel, C. (2018), *Colonization and Subalternity in Classical Greece: Experience of the Nonelite Population*, Cambridge: Cambridge University Press.

Index

Page numbers in *italics* are illustrations and those followed by n are notes

Chicago School of sociology, 30n
children
  abuse, 108, 157n
  age, 31–2n
  congenital conditions, 108–9
  exposure of disabled infants, 106–8,
    157n, 158n
  growth rate and health, 169–70
  illegitimate, 175, 186
  not full members of society, 8, 31n
  under-representation of burials, 174–8
  weaning of, 176–7
  see also infant
Chios, 100n
Chloe cemetery, Pherae, 204–5
Chryse, Lemnos, 121
circumcision, 83
'citizen cemeteries', 174
citizenship, 52–3, 56–8, 89, 95n, 189n,
  199–200
Citizenship Law, 47–8, 56–7, 58, 185, 187
city state (polis), 39, 40, 41
Clazomenaeans, 122
Cleisthenes, 56
Cleobis, 153
Cleomenes, 42
club foot, 112–14
Codrus Painter from Tarquinia, Italy,
  58, *59*
Colchians, 88, 94n
colonialisation, 74–6, *75*, 97–9n,
  193–6, 223
  non-metric traits, 209–11
comedy, 49, 50, 52, 153
congenital adrenal hyperplasia, 143
congenital conditions, 14, 71, 102–3,
  107–15, 126, 143, 159
congenital hip dislocation, 114–15, 158n
Corcyraeans, 148
Corinth, 22, 98n, 100n, 148, 154,
  158n, 210
Corinthian alabastron, by the La Trobe
  Painter depicting two komast
  dancers, 112, *113*
Cos, 141

craftsmen, 52–4, 61
  Attic red-figure kylix, *54*, 54–5
cranial trauma, 225
craniometrics, 207–8, 220n
craniosynostosis, 132–40, *133*, 136,
  137, *138*
Crenshaw, Kimberlé, 27
Crete, 100n, 206, 208, 212–13, 217
criminals, 21–2, 224
Croesus, 107
Cronus, 144
Croton, 129
Crypteia, 66
Ctesias of Cnidus, *Persica*, 148
cultural theories of human difference,
  72–3
Cunaxa, 81–2
'Cup of Nestor', 194, 219n
curved spines, 124–32, *130*, *131*
Cycladic Islands, 213
Cylonian Coup, 22
Cyprus, 18, 139, 160n
Cypselus, 158n
Cyrene, Libya, 76
Cyrus the Great, 81, 146, 148, 161n
Cytenion, Doris, 44

Danaus, 80
Darius, 120, 148
Dasen, Véronique, 126–7
de Ste Croix, Geoffrey, 37–8
De vitae Sophoclis poetae, 136
'Deadman's Pit', Athens, 21
deafness, 102, 107
Deceleia, 136
degenerative joint disease, 153–4, 162n,
  172–3, 181
Delian League, 77, 191
Delos, 22
Delphi, 77, 129, 151, 225
Demetriou, Denise, 95n
Demosthenes, 60, 65, 81, 122, 159n, 192
  Against Neaera, 185–6
dental variants, 8, 208–9, 220n
  'Etruscan upper lateral incisor', 209

Printed and bound by CPI Group (UK) Ltd, Croydon, CR0 4YY

21/03/2025

01835371-0003